# EARLY TWENTIETH-CENTURY
# CONTINENTAL PHILOSOPHY

# Early Twentieth-Century Continental Philosophy

*Leonard Lawlor*

Indiana University Press

*Bloomington & Indianapolis*

*This book is a publication of*

Indiana University Press
601 North Morton Street
Bloomington, IN 47404-3797 USA

www.iupress.indiana.edu

*Telephone orders*   800-842-6796
*Fax orders*   812-855-7931

Manufactured in the United States of
America

Library of Congress Cataloging-in-
Publication Data

Lawlor, Leonard, [date]
  Early twentieth-century Continental
philosophy / Leonard Lawlor.
    p. cm. — (Studies in Continental
thought)
  Includes bibliographical references
(p.     ) and index.
  ISBN 978-0-253-35702-1 (cloth : alk.
paper) — ISBN 978-0-253-22372-2 (pbk.
: alk. paper) — ISBN 978-0-253-00516-8
(electronic book) 1. Continental philosophy—History—20th century. I. Title.
  B804.L35 2012
  190.9'04—dc23
                              2011027334

1 2 3 4 5  17 16 15 14 13 12

# CONTENTS

PREFACE

# The Four Conceptual Features

The book you are about to read concerns early twentieth-century continental philosophy, that is, French and German philosophy from 1903, the original publication date of Bergson's "Introduction to Metaphysics," to 1966, the original publication date of Foucault's "The Thought of the Outside." This book aims to be a general introduction to "continental philosophy." It should enable one to study, with insight, not only the figures covered here (Bergson, Freud, Husserl, early Heidegger, later Heidegger, later Merleau-Ponty, and early Foucault), but also most of the central texts written after the 1950s by Derrida, Deleuze, Deleuze and Guattari, Foucault, Lacan, Levinas, Lyotard, Gadamer, and the so-called "French feminists" such as Irigaray and Kristeva. Although one strain of European thought has usually defined "continental philosophy," that is, phenomenology (both its German and French versions)—and we shall spend a significant amount of time discussing phenomenology—we shall consider three other strains: Bergsonism, psychoanalysis, and then finally what is commonly called "structuralism" (although we shall not use the word "structuralism" below).

In a survey of early twentieth-century continental philosophy, more could be said here; we could have included a discussion of "the Frankfurt school" (Adorno, for example), Levinas, or Sartre. These exclusions indicate that there is an idiosyncratic reason for the selection of the figures examined here. It seems to me that the specific figures selected set up what I have called "the great French philosophy of the Sixties."[1]

---

1. Leonard Lawlor, *Thinking through French Philosophy: The Being of the Question* (Bloomington: Indiana University Press, 2003).

vii

Therefore the book is laid out in a series of readings of specific texts (ar-
ranged chronologically by the original publication date of the texts). Each
chapter provides first what I am calling a "Summary-Commentary," that
is, a relatively traditional and linear exposition of the text under consideration. But then second, each chapter provides an "Interpretation."
While influenced by the readings Derrida, Deleuze, and Foucault (and
others) have provided of these figures, each "Interpretation" pushes to
the side their well-known criticisms: Derrida's criticism of Husserl and
Heidegger, Deleuze's criticism of phenomenology, Deleuze and Guattari's
criticism of Freud, Foucault's distancing himself from Bergson, Freud, and
Merleau-Ponty. Each "Interpretation" aims to take up a creative relation
to the text being considered and thereby produce a positive history of this
period. More precisely, by suppressing some ideas and exaggerating others, each chapter's "Interpretation" attempts to assemble and systematize
the four conceptual features that animate "the great French philosophy
of the Sixties." The four features are: (1) the starting point in immanence
(where immanence is understood first as internal, subjective experience,
but then, due to the universality of the epoché, immanence is understood
as ungrounded experience); (2) difference (where difference gives way to
multiplicity, itself emancipated from an absolute origin and an absolute
purpose; being so emancipated, multiplicity itself becomes the absolute);
(3) thought (where thought is understood as language liberated from the
constraints of logic, and language is understood solely in terms of its
own being, as indefinite continuous variation); and (4) the overcoming
of metaphysics (where metaphysics is understood as a mode of thinking
based in presence, and overcoming is understood as the passage to a new
mode of thought, a new people, and a new land). Through the phrase "the
overcoming of metaphysics," the fourth feature in particular indicates the
central role that Heidegger plays in this book. It is Heidegger who shows,
in 1929, that we can understand thought only when we suspend its object,
when it is the thought of the nothing. It is Heidegger, in 1950, who shows
that "language is language"; he shows that, grounded in nothing but itself,
language opens out over an abyss, a void, an outside. It is Heidegger who
inspires Foucault's title "The Thought of the Outside." Therefore, this book
aims at demonstrating a movement from Bergson, through Freud, Husserl, Heidegger, and Merleau-Ponty, toward what Foucault, Derrida, and
Deleuze have called "the outside." For "the great French philosophers of
the Sixties," Derrida, Deleuze, and Foucault, the outside is conceived in

two ways, which overlap and intersect. On the one hand, the outside is the external as opposed to the internal; for example, the unconscious as opposed to consciousness. On the other, the outside is the difference between oppositions such as the conscious and the unconscious, psychological consciousness and transcendental consciousness, being and beings, the visible and the invisible. In this sense, the "between" is a fold, a gap, a minuscule hiatus, *"un écart infime"* (MC: 351/OT: 340). The minuscule hiatus joins as it disjoins events and repetitions; below the difference therefore a multiplicity of traits swarms. We must not underestimate the importance of this comment from Deleuze's 1968 *Difference and Repetition*:

> There is a crucial experience of difference and a corresponding experiment: every time we find ourselves confronted or bound by a limitation or an opposition, we should ask what such a situation presupposes. It presupposes a swarm of differences, a pluralism of free, wild or untamed differences, a properly differential and original space and time, all of which persist across the simplification of limitation and opposition.[2]

Or this one, ten years later, from Foucault's 1978 course "Security, Territory, Population":

> Must intelligibility arise in no other way than through the search for the one that splits into two or produces the two? Could we not, for example, start not from the unity, and not even from [the] nature-state duality, but from the multiplicity of extraordinarily diverse processes?[3]

Or finally, this one, more than twenty years later, from Derrida's 2001 course "The Beast and the Sovereign":

> Every time one puts an oppositional limit in question, far from concluding that there is identity, we must on the contrary multiply attention to differences, refine the analysis in a restructured field.[4]

---

2. Gilles Deleuze, *Différence et répétition* (Paris: Presses Universitaires de France, 1968), p. 71, English translation by Paul Patton as *Difference and Repetition* (New York: Columbia University Press, 1994), p. 50.

3. Michel Foucault, *Sécurité, Territoire, Population. Cours au Collège de France, 1977–1978* (Paris: Hautes Études Gallimard Seuil, 2004), p. 244, English translation by Graham Burchell as *Security, Territory, Population: Lectures at the Collège de France, 1977–1978* (New York: Palgrave MacMillan, 2007), p. 238.

4. Jacques Derrida, *Séminaire. La bête et le souverain. Volume I (2001–2002)* (Paris: Galilée, 2008), p. 36, English translation by Geoff Bennington as *The Beast and the Sovereign, Volume I* (Chicago: University of Chicago Press, 2009), p. 16.

Derrida and Foucault would call these untamed differences "a murmur"; Deleuze says "clamor." Thought—or philosophy—therefore consists in listening to this clamoring murmur. Late in his career, in his 1984 "What Is Enlightenment?" essay, Foucault laid out a project for philosophizing: "to separate out, from the contingency that has made us what we are, the possibility of no longer being, doing, or thinking what we are, do, or think." He called this transformative project "the indefinite work of freedom." That the work of freedom is indefinite means that it is always incomplete, that freedom is always still to come, that the work always raises further questions. It is these further questions that define and drive, that must drive, still today, what we call continental philosophy.

The fact that Derrida, Deleuze, and Foucault are no longer with us should make us consider the condition of what we call "continental philosophy." The immense popularity of the term cannot be denied, and yet, as so many recent attempts have demonstrated, it seems virtually undefinable. Or at best it is defined as a catchall phrase for all the kinds of philosophy that analytic philosophy does not welcome, from mystical discourse to race theory. At worst, it refers to the exposition of the ideas of French and German philosophers, most of whom, like Derrida, Deleuze, and Foucault, are now dead. What future can there be for continental philosophy when it is nothing more than exposition? What future can a hodgepodge of ideas have? Is it possible to determine something like a project for continental philosophy? *Early Twentieth-Century Continental Philosophy* attempts to answer this question. Indeed, the selection of the figures discussed in this book arose from the attempt, my attempt, to conceive continental philosophy as a philosophical project (or a philosophical research agenda). In other words, if it is true that the great diversity of texts and authors usually associated with continental philosophy seems not to constitute anything remotely like a tradition, then by selecting certain philosophers (and not others) I am attempting to show that a tradition can be constituted. *Early Twentieth-Century Continental Philosophy* argues that a continuous working out of an impulse unifies, at the least, these philosophers. The impulse is an attempt to open up an experience that makes us think, that transforms who we are. In this regard, *Early Twentieth-Century Continental Philosophy* functions as a kind of "prequel" for my earlier *Thinking through French Philosophy*. Or, while *Thinking through French Philosophy* attempts to determine a "diffraction" of philosophical positions, *Early Twentieth-Century Continental Philosophy* attempts to determine the "light" that is being diffracted. *Early Twentieth-Century Continental Philosophy* therefore is the reverse of *Thinking through French Philosophy*. Yet whether we are concerned with the reverse or obverse, the aim remains the same. This work aims at the renewal of the impulse of twentieth-century continental philosophy for the future. More modestly, however, in light of the feeling that the times, just since the death of Derrida, have already changed—the recent past seeing at once the re-emergence of naturalism and a call for a "return to Plato"—it aims at preserving the memory (the potentiality) of this way of thinking, a way of thinking that is paradoxical. We know we have come across continental philosophy when we find a mode of thinking that always "repudiates easiness" (CENT: 1328/CM: 87).

# ACKNOWLEDGMENTS

This book evolved out of a course called Recent Continental Philosophy, which I taught several times at the University of Memphis from 1999 until 2008; then, under the title Twentieth-Century Philosophy, I taught the same course, its final version, at Penn State University in the fall of 2009. I owe a debt of gratitude to all the students who participated in these courses. Sabrina Aggleton helped with revisions of the content and with the proofreading; she also composed the index. Finally, I must thank Dee Mortensen and John Sallis for their support and encouragement. As always, my family showed remarkable patience as I wrote this book over 2010.

# ABBREVIATIONS

Reference is always made first to the original French or German, then to the English translation. I have frequently modified the English translations.

CENT/CM
Henri Bergson. *La pensée et le mouvant,* in *Œuvres,* Édition du Centenaire. Paris: Presses Universitaires de France, 1959. English translation by Mabelle L. Andison as *The Creative Mind.* New York: The Citadel Press, 1992 (1946). *The Creative Mind* contains "Introduction to Metaphysics" (its chapter VI), which is the focus of the first chapter. There is also an updated version of Andison's translation of "Introduction to Metaphysics" revised by John Mullarkey as *Introduction to Metaphysics.* New York: Palgrave Macmillan, 2007.

GW X /SE XIV
Sigmund Freud. "Das Unbewusste," in *Gesammelte Werke, Zehnter Band, Werke aus den Jahren 1913–1917.* London: Imago Publishing Company, 1949, pp. 263–303. English translation by James Strachey, in collaboration with Anna Freud, and assisted by Alex Strachey and Alan Tyson as "The Unconscious," in *The Standard Edition of the Complete Psychological Works of Sigmund Freud, Volume XIV (1914–1916).* London: The Hogarth Press, 1957, pp. 159–204.

French translation by Jean Laplanche and J.-B. Pontalis as "L'inconscient," in *Métapsychologie*. Paris: Gallimard, 1968, pp. 65–123. There is an additional English translation by Cecil M. Baines as "The Unconscious," in *General Psychological Theory*, ed. Philip Rieff. New York: Simon & Schuster, 1997, pp. 116–50.

HUA IX/CH — Edmund Husserl. "A. Abhandlungen. Der Encyclopaedia Britannica Artikel," in *Phänomenologische Psychologie*. The Hague: Martinus Nijhoff, 1968, pp. 277–301. English translation by Richard E. Palmer as "Phenomenology," *Encyclopedia Britannica* article. Draft D, in *Psychological and Transcendental Phenomenology and the Confrontation with Heidegger (1927–1931)*, translated and edited by Thomas Sheehan and Richard E. Palmer. Dordrecht: Kluwer Academic Publishers, 1997, pp. 159–79.

GA 9/PM — Martin Heidegger. *Gesamtausgabe. 1. Abteilung: Veröffentlich Schriften 1910–1976. Band 9. Wegmarken*. Frankfurt am Main: Klostermann, 2004. English translation edited by William McNeil as *Pathmarks*. New York: Cambridge University Press, 1998. This volume contains "What Is Metaphysics?" pp. 82–96; "Postscript to 'What Is Metaphysics?'" pp. 231–38; and "Introduction to 'What Is Metaphysics?'" pp. 277–90.

GA 12/OWL or PLT — Martin Heidegger. In *Gesamtausgabe, Band 12, Unterwegs zur Sprache*. Frankfurt am Main: Klostermann, 1976. Partial English translation by Peter D. Hertz as *On the Way to Language*. New York: Harper and Row, 1971. The abbreviation OWL refers to *On the Way to Language*. The essay "Die Sprache" has been translated into English by Albert Hofstader as "Language," in

*Poetry, Language, Thought.* New York: Harper Collins, 2001, pp. 185–208. The abbreviation PLT refers to *Poetry, Language, Thought.*

OE/MPR     Maurice Merleau-Ponty. *L'Œil et l'esprit.* Paris: Gallimard, 1964. English translation by Michael B. Smith as "Eye and Mind," in *The Merleau-Ponty Reader,* ed. Ted Toadvine and Leonard Lawlor. Evanston, Ill.: Northwestern University Press, 2007, pp. 351–78.

DE I/EWF 2     Michel Foucault. "La pensée du dehors," in *Dits et écrits I, 1954–1975.* Paris: Quarto Gallimard, 2001, pp. 546–67. English translation by Brian Massumi as "The Thought of the Outside," in *Essential Works of Foucault 1954–1984, volume 2: Aesthetics, Method, and Epistemology,* Paul Rabinow, series editor. New York: The New Press, 1998, pp. 147–69.

## ABBREVIATIONS FOR OTHER TEXTS DISCUSSED

CENT/DI     Henri Bergson. *Les données immediate de la conscience,* in *Œuvres,* Édition du Centenaire, pp. 1–157; English translation by F. L. Pogson as *Time and Free Will.* Mineola, N.Y.: Dover Publishing Company, 2001.

CENT/EC     Henri Bergson. *L'Évolution créatrice,* in *Œuvres,* Édition du Centenaire, pp. 487–809. English translation by Arthur Mitchell as *Creative Evolution.* Mineola, N.Y.: Dover Publications, Inc., 1998 (1911).

HUA VI/CR     Edmund Husserl. *Die Krisis der Europäischen Wissenschaft und die Transzendentale Phänomenologie, Husserliana VI.* The Hague: Martinus Nijhoff, 1976. English translation by David Carr as *The Crisis of European Sciences*

|          | *and Transcendental Phenomenology*. Evanston, Ill.: Northwestern University Press, 1970. |
|----------|---|
| SZ/BT    | Martin Heidegger, *Sein und Zeit*. Tübingen: Niemeyer, 1979. English translation by Joan Stambaugh (revised and with a foreword by Dennis J. Schmidt) as *Being and Time* (Albany: The State University of New York Press, 2010). |
| NC 59–61 | Maurice Merleau-Ponty, *Notes de cours 1959–1961*. Paris: NRF Gallimard, 1996. There is no English translation of this volume. All translations are my own. |
| VIF/VIE  | Maurice Merleau-Ponty, *Le visible et l'invisible*. Paris: Tel Gallimard, 1964. English translation by Alphonso Lingis as *The Visible and the Invisible*. Evanston, Ill.: Northwestern University Press, 1968. |
| MC/OT    | Michel Foucault, *Les mots et les choses*. Paris: Tel Gallimard, 1966. Anonymous English translation as *The Order of Things*. New York: Vintage Books, 1994. |
| AS/AK    | Michel Foucault, *l'archéologie du savoir*. Paris: NRF Gallimard, 1969. English translation by A. M. Sheridan Smith as *The Archeology of Knowledge*. New York: Pantheon Books, 1972. |

# EARLY TWENTIETH-CENTURY
# CONTINENTAL PHILOSOPHY

# Structure and Genesis of
# Early Twentieth-Century Continental Philosophy

In order to define "continental philosophy" (and perhaps philosophy in general), we must say, without any equivocation, that there is one and only one driving question. The question is given to us by Heidegger, and, in his book on Foucault, Deleuze calls this question "the arrow shot by Heidegger, the arrow par excellence."[1] The driving question of continental philosophy is the question of thinking: what is called or what calls for thinking. Continental philosophy amounts to a kind of project, which remains incomplete today, and perhaps like all great philosophical questions remains essentially incomplete. It is possible, however, to construct four formulas that define continental philosophy, four formulas for the structure that defines the kind of thinking that the phrase "continental philosophy" designates. Here are the four formulas.[2]

1. What continental philosophy wants is a renewal of thinking.
2. Thinking happens in the moment.
3. The moment is the experience of the conditions of experience.
4. Continental philosophy constantly moves back and forth across a small step between metaphysical and abstract issues and ethical or political and concrete issues.

## Structure in Four Formulas

Continental philosophy is paradoxical, because the very matter of think-ing is paradox. The matter of thinking brings us to the first formula. The first formula concerns what we might call the "project" of continen-tal philosophy, what continental philosophy wants (as in desire, love, or friendship, as in *philo-sophia*). What continental philosophy wants is a renewal of thinking. In other words, it wants to think otherwise and in new ways, and produce new ways of being. The renewal of thought implies that continental philosophy does not consist in a justification of common opinions. Instead, it concerns the transgression of common opinions. And in this regard, while continental philosophy has deep affinities with the tradition of transcendental philosophy, it breaks with it over the idea that conditions of possibility are supposed to justify beliefs. This break can be seen in all the philosophers associated with continental philosophy: the anti-Platonism of Bergson, Heidegger, Merleau-Ponty, Derrida, Deleuze, and Foucault, for instance. It is important to recognize that thinking, in these philosophers, is not an abstract endeavor. It always concerns concrete situations; thinking occurs in action. Thinking happens to you, and thus insofar as it happens to you, thinking, according to continental philosophy, originates, as Freud showed, in the unconscious.[3] The idea that thinking happens to you implies that thinking is not a natural ability. It occurs under the pressure of extreme experiences and experimentation. Because thinking happens in an experience, continental philosophy is always interested in the experience of death, madness, and blindness. All of these experiences concern disorientation in time. Here continental philosophy recalls Aristotle's claim that all thinking begins with wonder. A general way of defining thinking in continental philosophy is the fol-lowing: Under the pressure of a concrete and extreme experience such as blindness, a concrete experience that disorients time, thinking happens as an event, an event in which something new, a work, a concept, a way of life, is invented.

No one has gone farther than Deleuze in his 1968 *Difference and Rep-etition* to define what thinking is. Following Heidegger, Deleuze criticizes Kant's critical project. He criticizes Kant's critical project because, accord-ing to Deleuze, Kant "copied" (*décalqué*: copied like a decal) the categories of possible experience off common experiences, so that the categories are

no more than the expression of common sense.[4] The copying off of experience, for Deleuze, is especially evident in the second critique, *The Critique
of Practical Reason*, where the foundation or groundwork of morality is
copied off commonsense moral values. The problem with copying concepts off common sense, as Kant seems to do, is that it changes nothing; it
merely justifies common sense. Copying concepts off common sense turns
philosophy into an image with an original, a repetition of the identical,
with the result that philosophy creates no new differences or new concepts. We know we are dealing with common sense when someone says,
"everybody knows" or "they say." For Deleuze, what "everybody knows"
refers to the belief that there is in everyone a natural capacity for thinking.
Here we need think only of Descartes, for whom what properly defines
us is thinking. Common sense means that what everyone has in common is thinking. To say that thinking is a natural faculty distributed to
everyone equally rests on an old saying: People are prepared to complain
of not having a good memory or of not being very imaginative, or not being able to hear well, but they always believe that they are smart and are
able to think. Everybody naturally thinks that everybody is supposed to
know implicitly what it means to think. The natural capacity for thinking
means not only that everyone has a talent for truth, but also that everyone
wants the truth. Deleuze calls these two aspects of the natural faculty of
thinking the rightness of thinking and the goodwill of the thinker, or,
more precisely, the natural faculty consists in common sense and good
sense.[5] The natural capacity to think, to want the truth (good sense) and
to be able to get it (common sense), provides us with what Deleuze calls
"a natural image of thought": an affinity with the truth and a desire for
the truth. With Kant again, philosophy starts with this natural image, as
if philosophical thinking were nothing more than a more sophisticated
version, a conceptualized version of this image.

When we speak of this natural thought, the model is, according to
Deleuze, recognition. Recognition is the harmony between a mental representation and the way things are. It is a relation of copying. So we should
note immediately how this word "re-cognition" resembles "re-petition":
with recognition there is always the same and no difference. The model
of recognition implies that the only questions we ever ask are questions
like the following: Is this Frank or Richard? Is this a bird or a fish? If I
say "Frank" and it turns out to be Richard, then I have made a mistake,

an error. But this error can be corrected, since there is a correct answer: "It's Richard." If the model for all questions is one of recognition, then the most difficult questions we can encounter are those that have an answer. The model of recognition means that the actual model for questioning and thinking is the schoolteacher, who asks students only questions to which the teacher already knows the answer. We can wonder then if thinking ever takes place in the classroom, if anything new is ever invented there. According to Deleuze in *Difference and Repetition*, this mode of questioning maintains a hierarchy of parent-child; the student is treated like a child and therefore controlled or, better, disciplined.[6] Foucault showed in his 1975 *Discipline and Punish* that the technique of discipline practiced in the classroom in the early nineteenth century will be imported into the prisons by the end of the century.[7] The prison then becomes more humane, but also the prison becomes more efficient, more efficiently controlling the behavior and thinking of the prisoners in the same way that children are controlled in the classroom. In other words, and more generally, this model of questioning based in re-cognition results in no liberation: the answer the student gives must correspond to the answer that the teacher already knows.

Now, in order to understand common sense, we started with the well-known fact that people never complain about their ability to think, but they do complain about having bad memories or of being unimaginative. Deleuze asks, why should thinking be any different from these other faculties? Is it not the case that, in fact, humans think rarely, and more often only under the impulse of shock? Do humans really possess a taste for thinking from the start? Thinking, as I already indicated (but this claim is true for all continental philosophy), begins only under a constraint, under force, which breaks up the habits we have formed. So thinking, instead of involving a "goodwill," is based in ill will, even violence.[8] The person asking the question is not a teacher, but someone who is unpleasant and angry; this person does not already know the answer to the question. This person does not want a common opinion, an opinion that "everybody knows." This person says, "I don't know what everybody knows." But if we take the model of recognition at the heart of the natural image of thought as the model for philosophical thinking, then this model can only be the model of right or correct belief. The Greek word for "belief" is "*doxa,*" which also means opinion. Can such a model of common sense, belief, and opinion be the model for philosophy, for philosophical thinking? According to the ancient Greeks, and here continental philosophy remains faithful to the Greek inspiration for philosophy, philosophy is supposed to be knowledge—*episteme*—not belief, not *doxa*. In fact, it is supposed to break with all common opinion. When thinking begins with "para-doxa" (this word literally means "against opinion"), we have a form of thinking that is not based in the natural image of thought; it is not based in common sense and good sense. According to Deleuze, philosophical thinking does not take place in the attempt to harmonize with the natural image, to develop concepts of the natural image. Instead, philosophical thinking amounts to a rigorous struggle against the natural image, a radical critique or deconstruction of the image. With Deleuze, but also with all continental philosophy, thinking has to be imageless, imageless thought. And we must be aware that to say imageless means that it does not duplicate anything natural.

Even with this digression into Deleuze's idea of an image of thought, we have not, however, come to the heart of thinking, which is time. The second formula, in order to define continental philosophy, concerns the experience of time. Continental philosophy wants a renewal of thinking because all thinking so far has thought on the basis of the present, or it is a thinking that is non-temporal, like an eternal present. As Derrida would say, also following Heidegger, thinking so far has been bound up with "the metaphysics of presence." So far, all thinking has been on the basis of the same, a mere repetition of the present. In other words, thinking has not yet taken into account the past and the future; it has not taken the non-present or invisibility into account. But to think from the non-present does not place thinking in the beyond, in transcendence; in contrast, to root thinking within time is to place thinking within what Deleuze calls "immanence." Thinking within immanence is why continental philosophy is always historical; it explains as well continental philosophy's reliance on proper names (historical figures) and textual exegesis. Thinking is temporal, and, insofar as it is temporal, it is based on the past. There is a sentence that characterizes continental philosophy, a sentence from a book that is hardly read today, Jean Hyppolite's 1952 *Logic and Existence*. In it, characterizing Hegel's thought (to which we shall briefly return below when we speak of the genesis), Hyppolite says that "immanence is complete," which means that there is no second world behind the world of appearance.[9] There is no transcendent world, no Platonic world of ideas. Thus, with the expression "immanence is complete," we can also say that all continental philosophy is defined as the "reversal of Platonism." Continental philosophy concerns the overcoming of metaphysics where the "meta" refers us to something transcendent, like the second realm of ideas, permanently present.

The phrase "reversal of Platonism" comes from Nietzsche, and there is a second thought from Nietzsche that is basic to continental philosophy: time has no beginning and no end. This is the idea of the doctrine of the eternal return.[10] The doctrine of the eternal return means that the present is always contextualized between two unknowns, the past and the future. Nietzsche introduces the doctrine of eternal return in *Thus Spoke Zarathustra* (in Book III, in the section called "The Vision and the Riddle"). He points to a gateway over a road that extends infinitely in either direction, and there is a word printed on the arch; it says "the moment." Continental philosophy always concerns the experience of the moment, of the *Augenblick*. Heidegger in *Being and Time* speaks of the anticipation of one's own death as the *Augenblick*.[11] With the experience of the moment, Heidegger implies that, in the moment, there is a different kind of seeing, a seeing that does not consist in the vision of things that are present. This seeing, in other words, would be a blindness to the present. The German word "Augenblick" literally means "the blink of the eye." If the eye blinks, it closes and there is a kind of blindness. Now the experience of the moment is either an experience in which the present is split indefinitely between the past and the future or in which the past and the future indefinitely contaminate one another (Deleuze versus Derrida).[12] In any case, because continental philosophy concerns itself with the experience of the moment, continental philosophy is always defined as an empiricism, in fact, as a "superior empiricism." Superior empiricism brings us to the third formula.

The experience of the moment, which is indeed the experience of thinking, is fundamental in continental philosophy. Because the experience of the moment is fundamental, continental philosophy (despite its hostility to Kantian critical philosophy) is nevertheless a kind of transcendental philosophy (quasi- or ultra-transcendental). It is transcendental, however, not, as we already noted, in the sense of justifying beliefs, but in the sense of determining *within* experience the conditions *for* experience.

These conditions would be those that generate thinking itself. Notice, on the one hand, that we are still speaking of immanence, since the conditions of experience are *within* experience. On the other, notice that we are now speaking of conditions of experience that are themselves experienced, which means that these conditions are a kind of experience, a strange experience, *the* experience. But the idea of transcendental philosophy means that continental philosophy is inseparable from the phenomenological method of the reduction or the epoché. In recent analytic philosophy, there is a lot of talk about phenomenology. In this regard, it is important to recall what Eugen Fink, Husserl's assistant at the end of his life in the 1930s, said. Fink said that there is no phenomenology without the reduction.[13] Therefore continental philosophy always starts with the epoché, the universal suspension of what Husserl called "the natural attitude."[14] The natural attitude is Husserl's phrase for common sense. The method of the reduction is necessary because, in the Western tradition, the natural view of thinking is the present, what is going on consciously for me right now. As well, the natural view of all reality, of everything that exists, of "being" to use Heidegger's terminology, would be present to me right here and now, available: presence. Thus this view of being or thinking must be suspended, put out of play, canceled, even deconstructed, so that we can find the conditions that themselves are not present. Or, the epoché means "to the things themselves" (both in Bergson and in Husserl) in the sense that we cannot rely on ready-made concepts and symbols for thinking. The reduction means that continental philosophy always starts as a relativism—it makes reality, external objective reality, relative to my experience—and it always starts out being a subjectivism (a Cartesianism) since it takes my subjective experience as fundamental. But again, just as Fink said about phenomenology, there can be no continental philosophy without the epoché.

But how is the epoché possible? How is it possible to change the natural way we think about thinking and being, that is, the natural way of conceiving everything in terms of the present? The epoché must happen to you; it must be an experience. This is why, to say this again, Derrida, Deleuze, and Foucault are all interested in the experience of madness. It is mad to think that thinking could be defined as unconscious; it is mad to think that the world comes about on the basis of subjective experience. Yet this mad experience must happen to you, even do violence to you. And when it does, the experience of the moment is a conversion experience; it changes you. We shall return to the idea of a conversion in a moment when we speak about the step from the abstract to the concrete. But now let us return to the question of time.

In light of the eternal return doctrine—time having no beginning and no end—the moment is experienced as indefinitely divided between past and future or it is experienced as indefinitely contaminated with the past and the future. The description of the moment brings to light immediately that the moment is defined by difference; the difference between past and future is indefinitely divided or indefinitely contaminated. The experience of the moment is always an experience of difference. The entire 1960s discourse of the philosophy of difference arises out of this experience. And the entire discourse of the double or the twin is due to this experience. But what continental philosophy is most interested in is not the doubles (the companions) as such, but what lies between them. So in his important 1966 *The Order of Things*, the French title of which is *Les mots et les choses* ("Words and Things"), in the chapter called "Man and his Doubles," Foucault says that between the words and the things—words and things reflect one another, forming a double, a kind of mirror image—there is *"un écart infime"* ("a minuscule hiatus") (MC: 351/OT: 340). For Foucault, thinking is possible only in the space of this miniscule hiatus. Yet we can say something else about this experience. Because the past and the future are not present, thus unknown, we experience the moment as a sort of question. I do not know—in the most literal sense of visual or perceptual presence, and thus we are speaking of blindness with this "I do not know"—the past and the future. Thus the moment comes to me as questions: What happened? What is going to happen? These two questions link forgetfulness and awaiting, and indicate the specific kind of messianism that arises in continental philosophy late in the twentieth century. This kind of messianism without a messiah indicates a promise, always made but never kept.

If I experience the moment as a question or even as a promise, then the experience I am having is an experience of language. We can see the parallel between time and language. Language comes to me out of the past; I do not know its origin. I speak a "natural" language but this language preceded me. But equally, I do not know the destination of my speaking; it can always exceed its destination, and this excess of destination is a necessary possibility of any letter. Thus, lacking knowledge of the origin and the end of language, I experience the past and the future of language as questions: Where did my speaking come from; where is it going? The answer to these questions is somewhere else and someone other (the companion who does not accompany me). The speaking comes from and goes to what is not me (Is it a friend or enemy? An animal, a beast?), comes from and goes to what is not my present. The speaking comes from outside of my present, from the outside. Because the past and the future are not mine, are not present, are outside of me, we must define the temporal question as the question of death. Continental philosophy, as I already indicated, is always concerned with the experience of death. The concern with death starts with Heidegger's 1927 *Being and Time*. The experience of thinking is the experience of the moment, and the experience of the moment is always the experience of what is outside of me, and what is outside of me, at the limit of life, is death. The experience of the moment being the experience of death implies that although all continental philosophy starts out being a relativism and a subjectivism, all continental philosophy ends up being an "absolutism" and an "objectivism." Death is what is outside of subjective experience; therefore, being non-subjective, death is "objective." Death is what I cannot relate to, since relating to it destroys my life; therefore being non-relative, death is "absolute." These terms, "absolutism" and "objectivism," appear in quotation marks because what we are now referring to really has no name: the outside.

There is one more thing about the experience of the moment. The experience of the moment is not our normal experience of time. Normally or according to common sense, we conceive time as the present. Perhaps we also think that there was a fall from full presence and perhaps there will be a return to full presence (as in Christian theology, for example, but also in Platonism). But continental philosophy does not conceive time in this way. Because time is not experienced as the succession of present moments, continental philosophy frequently describes the experience of the moment in spatial terms. Here we should note that the French philosophy of the 1960s used to be called "structuralism." The idea of a structure itself is spatial. So when I am in the experience of the moment, I have managed to insert myself into a structure. And to speak of a structure is to speak of the spatialization of time; we have entered into a strange kind of place. Derrida, Deleuze, and Foucault have all three called this place the "non-place" and they have provided images of it: the desert, islands, and the beach. This non-place is a place in which it is possible once more to think.

We have returned to the question of thinking. As we saw at the beginning, thinking in continental philosophy is never merely abstract. It always involves, as both Heidegger and Foucault say, action. If I say that I have a new idea, I cannot really say that this idea is worth anything unless it is tested out in the concrete, and it is in the testing out in the concrete that the real thinking occurs. Again all three—Derrida, Deleuze, and Foucault—describe thinking as a test or an ordeal. Foucault, in particular, was interested in how different forms of truth were produced in the different forms of interrogation. But, without thinking of the historical forms of interrogation, we know that a police interrogation is an ordeal in which one is tested. In this idea of testing out, which may be an ordeal for me and which may involve me risking my life, we can see—here is the last and fourth formula—that all continental philosophy is ethical or political. For continental philosophy, the step is small from the most profound, say, transcendental issues to ethical and political issues, from abstract issues to concrete issues. You need only think of the problem of difference. On the one hand, the problem of difference requires that one go back to very abstract texts, at least to Hegel's *Greater Logic*, if not to *Plato's Sophist*. But on the other hand, the problem requires that one think of sexual difference, racial difference, or the difference between humans and animals. Continental philosophers are always able to move quickly from transcendental discourse to political discourse. The move from transcendental discourse to ethical discourse, however, in no way implies that continental philosophers provide norms. In fact, it is precisely norms, that is, normative ethics, that continental philosophers oppose. Continental philosophers are opposed to norms because norms stop thinking. Norms allow us to deduce actions, and then we do not really struggle with the decision. Norms stop thinking because they close off the new. As Deleuze might have said in the 1960s (or Merleau-Ponty in the 1950s), being opposed to all norms, continental philosophy is engaged in "perpetual revolution."

But how might this move from metaphysics to ethics work? In the experience of the moment, the difference between past and future is really "out of joint" (as in Hamlet), which means that things are not right, which means that things are not just. All of a sudden, from this very abstract idea of the moment, we are at the ethical or political idea of justice. Starting in the 1940s with Heidegger, there is a constant reflection on an ancient fragment from Anaximander who described the passing of time as *dike*, as justice. Yet all of a sudden we see that thinking consists now in rectifying an injustice or at least in attempting to rectify the injustice of time. Thinking consists in responding to the imperative to render justice. Or we can see the movement to ethics in a different way. If the experience of the moment is the experience of the question, then what is thinking? In this way of describing the experience, thinking consists in trying to find an answer to the question. Or, to convert this discourse to ethics, it consists in responding and responsibility. So, to conclude, we must define continental philosophy as a philosophy of responsibility. As Deleuze says (with Guattari), "[w]e are not responsible for the victims but responsible before them."[15] This kind of responsibility consists in the constant pressure of guilty conscience out of the past, but it is also a responsibility to keep trying to render justice into the future. The last formula for continental philosophy—continental philosophy consists in the movement from time to justice and politics, the movement from the question to responsibility and ethics—I think that this formula most distinguishes continental philosophy from any other sort of philosophy. The connection, the small step, between transcendental issues and ethical or political issues, between abstract concepts and the concrete, is the distinguishing mark of continental philosophy.

## Genesis in the Nineteenth Century

What we call twentieth-century continental philosophy emerged out of developments in nineteenth-century philosophy. Nineteenth-century philosophy begins with Hegel. It is Hegel who first attempted to complete the philosophical project that began with Plato. If the Platonic project had consisted in constructing a transcendent system of concepts that could explain all experience—the ideas—then Hegelianism must consist in constructing a system of concepts with the same function, but a system of concepts that are immanent to experience. We have just discussed this turn to immanence; it is characteristic of continental philosophy and consists in the reversal of Platonism that Nietzsche made famous. Hegel indicates the idea of immanence already in the preface to *The Phenomenology of Spirit* when he speaks of experience as the movement of becoming an other to itself and of overcoming this otherness.[16] As Hyppolite says, by conceiving otherness as within experience (and not transcendent to it), Hegel makes immanence be complete. Nevertheless, making otherness immanent to experience would not, Hegel believed, make them relative; for Hegel, it was possible, by passing through stages of experience, to arrive at absolute knowledge. Knowledge has to be science.[17]

But Hegel's call for knowledge to be experiential and scientific led to the nineteenth century's being known as the "age of science." Hegel's attempt to systematize knowledge, including knowledge of nature, gave way to the experimental method of the natural science. The progress of natural science in particular led to the demise of any sort of metaphysical thinking, as a thinking that is not naturalistic (or physical). This reduction of metaphysical or speculative thinking to positive facts of the natural science would give rise to the call for a renewal of metaphysics in Bergson, Husserl, and the early Heidegger. In a way, Freud's project of a meta-psychology must be included in this renewal of metaphysics. But, as we shall see, the renewal of metaphysics that they conceive does not amount to a return to pre-Kantian metaphysics. Heidegger, in particular, recognizes that the call for a renewal of metaphysics in fact calls for a new kind of thinking, one that breaks with all prior metaphysical forms of thought, one that breaks precisely with the implicit metaphysics of the natural sciences. Indeed, the later Heidegger and Merleau-Ponty will abandon the word "metaphysics." While Heidegger will speak simply of "thinking," Merleau-Ponty will speak of an "a-philosophy."[18]

Over the course of the nineteenth century we see the collapse of idealism (Hegel) and traditional metaphysics under the pressure of scientific positivism. Instead of speculation, science must be based in positive, measurable facts. Positivism even spread to the newly emerging science of psychology.[19] As a science, psychology looked to provide knowledge about the mind, knowledge that philosophers could not ignore. The expansion of psychology results in the philosophical movement called "psychologism," in which Husserl participated early in his career. But obviously, Freud is involved in the development of psychology as a science, and so is Bergson, who published his early essays in psychology journals. Psychologism claimed that all knowledge, including mathematics, could be derived from psychical processes. As Husserl would show in his first major work, the 1900 *Logical Investigations*, psychologism's belief that mathematics and logic are dependent on the psychological laws of the human mind is a form of skepticism and relativism.[20] In order to emerge from psychologism, Husserl in his 1913 *Ideas I* will transform "phenomenology" from "descriptive psychology" to transcendental philosophy.[21] But the development of psychology as a science also involved an attempt to reduce psychological phenomena down to natural processes. Freud begins his career in the 1895 "Project for a Scientific Psychology" by borrowing from the constancy principle of physics.[22] As we shall see, however, Freud will move away from any type of organic explanation of neurosis, and when he develops his psychical topography he will not explain it by reference to brain anatomy. Bergson, however, is the great critic of what is called "psychophysics." Psychophysics conceived the psyche in terms of quantitatively determinable distinct parts, as if the soul were a multiplicity of juxtaposed and homogeneous parts.[23] In *Time and Free Will*, his first book, Bergson will argue that the psyche consists in a different kind of *multiplicity*. Therefore we are starting with Bergson. In fact, we must start with Bergson because the idea of a qualitatively heterogeneous and temporal multiplicity is the guiding idea of all twentieth-century continental philosophy.

# 1

# Thinking beyond Platonism:
# Bergson's "Introduction to Metaphysics" (1903)

Near the end of "Introduction to Metaphysics," Bergson says, "The partial eclipse of metaphysics since the last half century has been caused more than anything else by the extraordinary difficulty the philosopher experiences today in making contact with a science already much too scattered" (CENT: 1432/CM: 200). Science has become scattered "today" because it is based on acquiring knowledge by analysis, that is, by taking up separate and particular viewpoints on things, from the exterior. Analysis is the work done by one faculty, the understanding (in French, *l'entendement* or, in German, *der Verstand:* the intellect). The understanding breaks things up and for each separate perspective, it assigns a symbol—so that knowledge looks to be based on symbols, relative to them, and metaphysics, based on relative knowledge, becomes impossible. For Bergson, analysis must be *overcome*. It is overcome by means of a different faculty, the faculty of intuition. Based in intuition, and not in symbolization, knowledge is immediate and absolute. Through intuition, then, metaphysics is possible once again. According to Bergson there is a second reason why metaphysics went into eclipse in the nineteenth century. In "Introduction to Metaphysics," again near its end, Bergson speaks of modern philosophy as the reversal of Platonism, reversing the relation of idea (or form) and the soul (or experience). No doubt, Bergson is thinking of Descartes. Yet in the prioritization of the soul, Platonism persists insofar as the understanding—here too in modern metaphysics—defines cognitive activity. Here Bergson is thinking of Kant. No one more than Kant (the Kant of *The Critique of Pure Reason,* where the faculty of the understanding or the intellect, *der Verstand,* plays such an important role[1]), for Bergson has misunderstood the soul. Therefore, insofar as Bergson wants to overcome analysis, we can also say that he wants to overcome modern metaphysics. And if we can say that, then we can say that Bergson's project bears strong similarities to Heidegger's project of overcoming metaphysics.[2]

Nevertheless, as Heidegger and Husserl and perhaps Freud recognized, it is possible to overcome modern metaphysics only by adopting the discovery made by Descartes: *immanence*. For Bergson, as we shall see shortly, intuition is self-sympathy, even introspection. But the specific kind of introspection that Bergson thinks leads to absolute knowledge is not the slender experience of my current state of mind. Intuition for Bergson requires the effort to expand or dilate one's present. Self-dilation puts us in contact with what Bergson famously calls the duration, the temporal flow of experience. This flow includes a kind of unity and a kind of multiplicity, a kind of continuity and a kind of heterogeneity, which means that through self-dilation I come into contact with something other than myself. Intuition does not enclose me, but opens me to the *outside*. In Bergsonian intuition therefore we find the basic impulse of all continental philosophy. Starting from a certain inside, it is driven by an impulse to exit. The impulse to the outside requires the reconception of *thinking*. Like Heidegger, Bergson too calls for such a reconception when he tries to reconceive the very concept of concept. He calls for this reconception because the duration is in itself inexpressible and yet knowledge of it given in intuition requires expression, even conceptual expression. In our "Interpretation," we shall be particularly interested in Bergson's new concept of concept. Just as the qualitative *multiplicity* of the duration sets the stage for all investigations of difference,[3] the idea of a "fluid concept" sets the stage for all the investigations of *language*. It shows that thinking is capable of more than Platonizing. But first in our commentary, let us see what Bergson does with immanent subjective experience.

## Summary-Commentary: Intuition and Duration

### ANALYSIS AND INTUITION[4]

The context for Bergson's revival of metaphysics and intuition is the development of modern philosophy since Kant (CENT: 1427–28/CM: 195).[5] Kant had made metaphysics impossible because he showed that human knowledge is always and merely relative. For Bergson, however, our knowledge can be absolute (CENT: 1424/CM: 192). If our knowledge is absolute, then metaphysics is possible. For Bergson, the mistake Kant had made was that he relied on the "habitual work of the intelligence" (CENT: 1409/CM: 177). The habitual work of intelligence serves a practical interest; it consists in going from the general concepts that we have already acquired to the things. The general concepts classify things, separating them and juxtaposing them; when classified, the things are then labeled, and by means of these labels, the general concepts allow the things to be manipulated for our own benefit. Yet for Bergson, metaphysics is possible only if we go from the things—we might say here that "we must go from the things themselves"—to the concepts (CENT: 1410/CM: 177). Only through this "reversal" of the habitual work of intelligence—Husserl would speak of the reversal of the natural attitude—is it possible to intuit. But what is intuition in Bergson?

In the opening pages of "Introduction to Metaphysics," Bergson differentiates between analysis and intuition, which are mixed together within knowing (connaître) (CENT: 1392–93/CM: 159). Bergson makes the distinction between analysis and intuition along the line of inside and outside.[6] Analysis remains outside the thing; it consists in turning about the thing and adopting viewpoints on the thing. The turning about aims at taking the thing apart, at division and complexity; it is "analysis" in the literal sense. The result of analysis is "elements" or what Bergson will call "partial expressions" of the thing (CENT: 1405/CM: 171).[7] Then one reconstructs the thing out of the partial expressions or one "translates" the thing, as Bergson says, into symbols. Analysis always results in symbolization. In analysis our access to the thing is mediated by these partial viewpoints and these symbols; thus it is relative and abstract. It is important to realize immediately that the distinction Bergson is making between analysis and intuition does not imply that intuition, being opposed to analysis, is a kind of synthesis (CENT: 1362/CM: 125). For Bergson, synthesis is the process of reconstruction of partial expressions broken apart by the analysis, a process that results in mixtures (CENT: 1409/CM: 176). So, in contrast to both analysis *and* synthesis, intuition in Bergson involves no viewpoints and supports itself on no symbols used in a reconstruction.[8] Intuition is concrete; "one enters into" (*en*) the thing. One coincides with it immediately in its simplicity and indivisibility. Therefore, intuitive knowledge in Bergson is absolute and, we must say, even a-perspectival.

Bergson illuminates the distinction between intuition and analysis with two examples, the first of which is "the movement of an object in space," in particular, the simple movement of me lifting my arm (CENT: 1395/CM: 161). This example is important since Bergson defines intuition as "sympathy" (CENT: 1393/CM: 159[9]), and first of all as *self*-sympathy (CENT: 1396/CM: 163): *me* lifting *my* arm (CENT: 1396/CM: 162–63). If I look at my arm lifting from the outside, I perceive the moving and the changes according to viewpoints. Being points, the viewpoints look to be points on a line, which can then be coordinated on a grid. The points on the grid, which are unrelated to one another and all homogeneously the same, can be expressed by one symbol. Now, translated into a spatial grid of points, into a symbol, the movement no longer moves.[10] With the translation I have lost the original. So, in contrast, when I perceive my arm lifting from the inside, I sense change and changes immediately. But the sensing changes not according to the different viewpoints adopted; rather as my arm moves, my feelings change. Then I am "sympathizing" with the object, which in this case is my own arm. But any example of bodily movement will illuminate the distinction. When I am running, I experience or sense change all the time, but I do not take the movement apart and coordinate it with spatial axes; I do not symbolize the movement on a grid. To do this coordination, I would have to be *standing still,* not running. I would have to be perceiving the running from the outside.

The second example is a literary example. This example too is important since it concerns creativity in language; we shall return to language below in the "Interpretation." The example works this way. A novelist, Bergson says, will be able to multiply the features of the character about whom he is writing (CENT: 1394/CM: 160). The novel would recount thousands of incidents, but these thousands of incidents would be only viewpoints taken on the character. The features described would be symbols, according to Bergson, by means of which the reader would come to know the character only by "comparing" him to other things he or she already knows. This description of what the novelist does means that the reader remains outside the character, in the divided, multiple elements. But, as Bergson says, "if I were to identify for a single moment with the character himself," if, in other words, I could intuit the character, the character would be "given with one blow in its entirety and the thousand incidents that manifest the character . . . do not exhaust or impoverish" the simple and indivisible feeling I would be having (CENT: 1394/CM: 160). In contrast, what the novel gives us (instead of me entering into the character's life) is the *analysis* of the character into "the thousand incidents." If we again think of any bodily movement, we see that any bodily movement can be potentially or virtually analyzed into an infinite number of points that would fill every interval of the movement. So, as Bergson says, "Now what lends itself at the same time to an indivisible apprehension and to an inexhaustible enumeration is, by the very definition of the word, an infinite [*infini*]" (CENT: 1395/CM: 161).

### DURATION AND CONSCIOUSNESS

Of course, the infinite that is given in intuition—after the reversal of the normal work of intelligence—and that with which metaphysics concerns itself is the flow (or movement) of experience *within* the self. If intuition is first of all "entering in," then our starting point is immanent subjective experience, which Bergson calls "the duration." The duration is a succession of states, each one of which announces what follows and contains what precedes. The duration does *not* consist in multiple *separate* states. And if we think it does consist of states, this belief is based in retrospection, when we "observe the track" of what has flowed (CENT: 1397/CM: 163). As Bergson says, "while I was experiencing them they were so solidly organized, so profoundly animated with a common life, that I could never have said where any one of them finished or the next one began" (CENT: 1397/CM: 163). Instead of separation and juxtaposition, the "states" "prolong themselves" into one another. One finds therefore in the depth of the self, according to Bergson, "a continuous flux [*écoulement*] which is not comparable to any other flux I have ever seen" (CENT: 1397/CM: 163). For Bergson, the duration is primarily defined by continuity, more precisely continuity without contiguity or juxtaposition, or continuity with heterogeneity.[11] But also for Bergson the flow of the duration is unique. Being unique, the duration cannot be conceived by means of resemblances and comparisons. It is even inexpressible (CENT: 1395/CM: 161). Nevertheless, we are able to get closer to what duration is by means of images (CENT: 1355–56/CM: 118). For Bergson, images are intermediary between intuition and the elaboration of the intuition in words and concepts (CENT: 1347/ CM: 109). Here, in "Introduction to Metaphysics," Bergson provides three images. Each of the images is necessarily inadequate to the flow of the duration. All the images can do is lead us to the place where we might be able to have the intuition (CENT: 1399/CM: 166).

The first image of the duration is two spools, with a tape running between them, one spool unwinding the tape, the other winding it up.[12] The duration resembles this image, according to Bergson, because, as we grow older, our future grows smaller and our past grows larger. The benefit of this image is that it presents a continuity of experiences without juxtaposition. Yet there is a drawback to it: Because a tape moves between the two spools, the image presents the duration as being homogeneous, as if one could fold the tape back over other parts of it, as if the tape were superposable, implying that two moments in consciousness might be identical and homogeneous. Yet, as Bergson says, "There are no two identical moments in the life of the same conscious being" (CENT: 1398/CM: 164). The duration, for Bergson, is continuity of progress *and* heterogeneity. Continuity, Bergson realizes, never makes difference vanish; difference becomes internal.[13] There is difference, because, as this image shows, the duration conserves the past. Indeed, for Bergson, and this is the center of his truly novel idea of memory, memory conserves the past and this conservation does not imply that one experiences the same (re-cognition), but difference. One moment is added onto the old ones, and thus, when the next moment occurs, it is added onto all the other old ones plus the one that came immediately before. The current moment cannot be the same as the one immediately before, because the past is "larger" for the current moment than it was for the last moment. Although Bergson does not say this, one might say that Tuesday is different from Monday because Monday only includes itself and Sunday, while Tuesday includes itself, Monday, and Sunday.[14] This first image, therefore, implies that the duration is memory; it the prolongation of the past into the present. The second image is the color spectrum. Since a color spectrum has a multiplicity of different shades or nuances, the second image helps us see that the duration is constant difference or heterogeneity, precisely the characteristic of the duration that was lacking in the spool image. But there is a drawback to the color spectrum image as well. With the color spectrum, we lose the characteristic of continuity or unity since the spectrum has colors juxtaposed. The color spectrum is a spatial image, while the duration is time.

So, as Bergson says, "pure duration excludes all idea of juxtaposition, reciprocal externality, and extension" (CENT: 1398/CM: 164). We come then to the third image, which is an elastic being stretched. Bergson tells us first to contract the elastic to a mathematical point, which represents the now of our experience, then draw it out to make a line growing progressively longer. But he warns us not to focus on the line but on the action that traces it. If we can focus on the action of tracing, then we can see that the movement—which is duration—is not only continuous and differentiating or heterogeneous, but also indivisible. We can always insert breaks into the spatial line that *represents* the motion, but the motion itself is indivisible. In Bergson, there is always a priority of movement over the thing that moves; the thing that moves is an abstraction from the movement. Now, the elastic being stretched is a more exact image of duration. But the image of the elastic is still, according to Bergson, incomplete. With this image, we forget the wealth of coloring (as we saw in the color spectrum) characteristic of the duration as it is lived. Instead, with the elastic we see only the simple movement of consciousness as it goes from one shade to another. Importantly, we must recall that the color spectrum image does not represent the duration since the color spectrum is "a thing already made, while the duration is in the process of making itself continually" (CENT: 1399/CM: 166). Although never presenting the duration itself— such a presentation takes place only in intuition—these three images are supposed to bring us into the disposition or attitude in which we are able to have an intuition of the duration (CENT: 1399–1400/CM: 165–66). We can see a progression here: from intuition to image to concept. Conceptual representations, however, never enclose the duration, especially "if we give to the word concept its *proper* meaning" (CENT: 1402/CM: 168; my emphasis). Literally, a concept (based on the Latin root "*capere*," to take or to grasp) immobilizes, while the duration is pure mobility (it is always in the process of being made). Below, in the "Interpretation," we shall return to the problem of conceptual representation. But we can say now that Bergson needs some sort of conceptual representation in order to communicate the knowledge that intuition provides. This improper conceptual representation is what we shall call a "fluid concept," a concept enlarged, as we see already, with images.

Despite the inadequacy of all three images, Bergson brings them together: "the unrolling of our duration [the tape between the spools] on one side resembles the unity of a movement which progresses [the elastic being stretched], on the other side, a multiplicity of states spreading out [the color spectrum]" (CENT: 1399/CM: 165). On the basis of playing the images off one another, we are able to see that the duration seems to consist in two "sides": unity and multiplicity. So, Bergson says, "Let us try for an instant to consider our duration as a multiplicity" (CENT: 1402/CM: 168). According to Bergson, the "endpoints" (*termes*) of *this* multiplicity are not "distinguished" like those of any multiplicities whatsoever, but "encroach" (*empiètent*) on one another (CENT: 1402/CM: 168). As it progresses, the duration is a multiplicity (remember the color spectrum image), but the multiplicity of the duration "bears no resemblance," according to Bergson, to "*any other multiplicity we know*" (CENT: 1402/CM: 168; my emphasis). This multiplicity—as we shall see, it is a *qualitative* multiplicity—does not mean that we have no unity. There is always a *continuity* of elements being prolonged into one another. As well then, we have a unity like no other. As Bergson says, "this moving, changing, colored, living unity has hardly anything in common with the abstract, motionless and empty unity which the concept of pure unity circumscribes" (CENT: 1402/CM: 169). No matter how I arrange the two *concepts* (frozen representations or symbols) of unity and multiplicity, according to Bergson, I shall never obtain anything that resembles the simple intuition of duration. These concepts—in the literal sense—are merely external viewpoints on duration and do not make us penetrate the duration, as images do (CENT: 1402–3/CM: 169). Where have the concepts come from? They have come from the analysis of the mind, not an intuition of it. As Bergson says, "It is because of a confusion between the roles of analysis and intuition that the dissensions between schools of thought and conflicts between systems will arise" (CENT: 1403/CM: 169). Throughout "Introduction to Metaphysics," Bergson will denounce this confusion. In order to enter into metaphysics (in Bergson's sense, which, we might say, hardly counts as metaphysics), one must not start from the results of analysis; one must start from an intuition.

## COMPONENT PART AND PARTIAL EXPRESSION[15]

Psychology, like all the sciences, starts from the results of analysis. Psychology "resolves" the self into "elements," sensations, feelings, images, etc., which it studies separately as psychological states.[16] Bergson compares the psychological analysis to "sketching" or "note taking," and the notes taken he calls "schema." These schemas are abstractions. Even if the psychologist finds some change in the state, he or she says there is not a simple sensation but several successive sensations. The psychologist then transfers the characteristic of being immutable to each successive sensation, like the translation of movement into immobile points on a grid. The immobility or immutability of the partial expressions allows psychology to have a solid foundation, but psychological analysis (not Freudian psychoanalysis, about which Bergson seems not to have known much) never penetrates the self.

Component parts of the duration, however, are different from partial expressions (CENT: 1404–5/CM: 171). Bergson explains the distinction between component parts and partial expressions by means of two images. First, Bergson compares the work of the psychologist to the artist. An artist who is visiting Paris would make a sketch of a tower of Notre Dame. The tower is inseparably connected to the edifice, which is inseparably connected to the soil, to the surrounding city of Paris, etc. The artist must begin by detaching the tower, making note of an aspect of the whole, which is this specific tower. While the tower is in fact composed of stones, the artist is not interested in the stones; he takes note only of the tower's silhouette. So, as Bergson says, "He substitutes for the real and internal organization of the thing an external and schematic reconstitution" (CENT: 1404/CM: 170). The result is a certain viewpoint based in a certain mode of representation. Likewise, the psychologist starts by extracting a psychological state from the whole person. This isolated state is nothing more than a sketch, from which an artificial recomposition begins. The sketch is the whole under a certain elementary aspect in which the psychologist is interested. As Bergson says, the psychological state "is not a part, but an element." So, while the artist, having been within Paris and therefore having had an intuition of it, is able to arrange his sketches in relation to one another, the psychologist, lacking an intuition, is not able to put his "sketches" back into relation to one another. The second image is that of a poem. Bergson says, suppose someone puts before me all the letters of a poem but they are jumbled or mixed together: "If the letters were *parts* of the poem, I could attempt to reconstruct it with them by trying various possible arrangements, as a child does with the pieces of a jigsaw puzzle. But I should never for a moment think of attempting such a thing, because the letters are not *component parts,* but only *partial expressions*" (CENT: 1404/CM: 171; Bergson's emphasis). This is an important quotation. Like the image of the artist sketching a tower of Notre Dame, this image of the scrambled poem indicates the impossibility of going from the partial expression—the letters and the sketches, and in psychology the notes taken on a psychological state—to the whole. Here too, just as the artist has been within Paris and therefore knows the city and can reunite the sketches, "I put each one of the letters in its proper place and link them together by means of *a continuous trait,* if I know the poem" (CENT: 1405/CM: 171; my emphasis). Or, if I do not know the poem, "I must give myself *an intuition* of a plausible signification, and from the intuition I try to descend to elementary symbols which reconstitutes its expression" (CENT: 1405/CM: 171; my emphasis). It is from this intuition of a continuous trait (or feature) that I must descend back to the disassembled parts in order to reconstitute the whole poem. Likewise, in psychology, I must give myself an intuition of a continuous trait (an experience of sympathy, for example) and then I can reunite all the fragments of the whole of my psychic life, of "the whole of my personality [*l'ensemble d'une personnalité*] (CENT: 1403/CM: 169). Notice that Bergson says "*un trait continu*" and "*une intuition.*" The *singularity* of the trait given in *one* intuition implies a relation to a *whole* (*l'ensemble* or *le tout*). It is from a part of the duration that I can follow a "continuous trait" to find the whole of the duration. The terminology of parts and whole (partial expressions and composite parts), or singularity and multiplicity really indicates what intuition is for Bergson. While not being an external viewpoint, and thus while not being perspectival, intuition is an internal finite opening onto an infinite mobility.[17] The finitude of an intuition is why one must use the definite article in English for "*la durée,*" because *the* duration—not *my* duration alone—is the whole. We shall return to the finitude of expression below in the "Interpretation."

## EMPIRICISM AND RATIONALISM

According to Bergson, when philosophers want to recompose what the person is, they undertake to recompose it by means of psychological states, by means of partial notions (instead of entering into the real parts). As Bergson says, "Empiricists and rationalists are both dupes of the same illusion" (CENT: 1405/CM: 172). The illusion is that one takes the negation of self-intuition, analysis, as the proper method for understanding the self. Through analysis—and what else could it give us?—psychology uncovers nothing more than psychological states. On the psychological states, the psychologist will place the word "self," thinking that by remaining within this symbol one will be able to find something behind the word. But the psychological states are not the self. Even placing the states side by side, that is, by placing the notes taken, the schematic representations side by side, does not give us the self: "One might just as well deny that the *Iliad* has a sense, on the plea that one has looked in vain for the sense in the intervals between the letters in which it is composed" (CENT: 1406/CM: 173). Philosophical empiricism, building on psychological analysis, suffers from the same illusion of taking the translation for the original; it says that the original does not exist since it cannot be found in the translation. For Bergson, rationalism is no better than empiricism. Bergson says, "Like empiricism, [rationalism] takes the psychological states to be so many fragments *detached* from a self who unifies them" (CENT: 1406/CM: 173; Bergson's emphasis). Even though for rationalism, the self too disappears behind the translation, it persists in affirming—unlike empiricism, which denies—the unity of the person. Since rationalism too looks for the unity of the self in the psychological states, it recognizes that the determinations provided by those states cannot define the self. So it affirms something still more unreal: a form without matter, the absolute indeterminate, the absolute void (CENT: 1407/CM: 174). Bergson finally reduces the two positions to this sole difference. On the one hand, since empiricism looks for the unity of the self in the interstices of psychological states, in these empty spaces that are never completely filled in, the self tends toward Zero. On the other hand, since rationalism seeks the unity of the self in the place where the states are lodged, in an "empty space" that one has no reason to limit, then the self tends in this case not toward Zero, but toward the Infinite (CENT: 1407-8/CM: 174-75). According to Bergson, no mixing of these two positions—a thesis and an antithesis—no mixing of this abstract multiple and this abstract one will give us the moving life of the person, the person that endures. However if one places oneself above, superior to these two viewpoints, in "a unique intuition," Bergson says, then I would be able to come down to the various concepts and to the divisions of the schools (CENT: 1408/CM: 176).

## THE REAL DURATION

We just saw that psychological analysis results in the "illusion" of what the self is: immobile elements and their expressions. The illusion also results in an unreal duration insofar as objective time (clock time) represents change as spatial and homogeneous: the thing moves through time means that the same thing occupies different points (CENT: 1411–12/CM: 179). For Bergson, however, there is no psychical state that does not change at every instant, since there is no consciousness without memory, since there is "no continuation of a state without the addition, to the present feeling, of the memory of past moments" (CENT: 1411/CM: 179). This is Bergson's definition of the real duration: "the continuous life of a memory [*une mémoire*] which prolongs the past into the present, the present either contains the ever-growing image of the past, or rather, by its continual changing of quality, it attests rather the increasingly heavy burden dragged along behind one the older one grows. Without this survival of the past in the present, there would be no duration, but merely instantaneity" (CENT: 1411/CM: 179). In other words, what defines the "real duration" for Bergson is "variability" (CENT: 1412/CM: 180). Variability for Bergson is not the variation of a thing; the thing that varies is an abstraction from variability just as the thing that moves is an abstraction from mobility. Variability without an original form and without an ultimate purpose is becoming (CENT: 1412/CM: 179).[18] If the duration in Bergson is variability, then the duration cannot be mere psychological duration, which would itself be only one potential variation of *the* duration. If the duration is not solely psychological duration, then intuition cannot consist solely in "self-sympathy" or in "self-contemplation"; when I intuit, it cannot be the case that I merely "watch myself merely live, 'as a sleepy shepherd watches the water flow'" (CENT: 1416/CM: 184). Instead of a passive feeling, intuition in Bergson then is an activity; intuition always requires effort. Through the "dilation of the mind" (CENT: 1415/CM: 183), Bergson says, we are able "to affirm the existence of objects that are inferior and superior to us, though however in a certain sense within us [*intérieurs à nous*]" (CENT: 1416/CM: 184).[19] In other words, if I place myself in the duration by an effort of intuition, "we have the feeling," Bergson says, "of a certain very determinate *tension,* in which the determination itself appears as a choice between an infinity of possible durations. This being so one catches sight of as numerous durations as we wish, all very different from each other" (CENT: 1417/CM: 185; Bergson's emphasis). To explain this idea, Bergson refers us back to the image of the color spectrum.[20] It may be that there is no other duration than my own, just as there may be no other color in the world than orange. But if I place myself in orange, that is, if I make the effort to sympathize with orange and not perceive orange from the outside, my consciousness of color "would feel itself caught" (*se sentirait prise*), Bergson says, between red and yellow; it would "have a sense" (*pressentirait*) of a whole spectrum in which the continuity of red to yellow prolongs itself naturally (CENT: 1419/CM: 187). The case is the same with the intuition of my duration: we place ourselves in a continuity of durations that "we must try to follow either upward or downward" (CENT: 1419/CM: 187). Although we shall return to this comparison below in the "Interpretation," we can say now that the comparison means that there is an infinity of other possible durations *in* my self. Or, more precisely, I would say, the inferior and superior objects are in a certain sense *in* me because our or my psychological duration is a component part of *the* duration; my psychological duration is *in* the whole duration. Following the component parts that are different from one another and yet connected to one another, we "indefinitely," Bergson says, "dilate ourselves by a more and more vigorous effort and in both cases [both upward and downward] we transcend [*transcendons*] ourselves" (CENT: 1419/CM: 187). Descending, we have a duration, more scattered, whose palpitations are more rapid than ours, dividing our simple sensation, diluting its quality into quantity; "by advancing into the other direction, we go towards a duration which stretches, tightens, and becomes more and more intensified" (CENT: 1419/CM: 187). At the two limits, we would find on the one hand all matter and repetition, and on the other all memory and difference. Bergson concludes, "Between the two extreme limits [of the duration] moves intuition" (CENT: 1419/CM: 188).

## Interpretation: Thinking beyond Platonism

Writing at the end of the nineteenth century, Bergson sees himself in the tradition of "modern philosophy." According to Bergson, "the masters of modern philosophy, who were renovators of science in addition to being metaphysicians," reversed Platonism. He says, "Modern philosophy tends to lift the Soul above the Idea. In this, as in modern science and even more so, it tends to move in the *reverse* direction from ancient thought" (CENT: 1426/CM: 194; my emphasis). In other words, as a reversal of Platonism, modern philosophy and modern science is Cartesian.[21] With the elevation of the soul over the idea, however, modern philosophy and modern science, as in Descartes, prioritized the faculty of the understanding, with its work of stabilizing, dividing, and reconstructing; in a word, it prioritized analysis. Indeed, the understanding believes that it is independent from experience, so independent that "it is exposed to what is only seen in all its work, to an artificial arrangement of symbols" (CENT: 1427/CM: 195). This independence makes modern science be a universal mathematics and modern metaphysics a barely reworked Platonism (CENT: 1289/CM: 47). The ideas have come down from the heavens to earth as the understanding's ready-made conceptual arrangements that set up the conditions for the possibility of science. Experience serves as nothing more than the verification of "clear ideas" (CENT: 1426/CM: 196). Here Bergson is no longer thinking of Descartes; he is now thinking of Kant. Bergson concludes, "The whole *Critique of Pure Reason rests upon the postulate that our thought is incapable of anything but Platonizing,* that is, of pouring the whole of possible experience into pre-existing molds" (CENT: 1429/CM: 196; Bergson's emphasis). He adds importantly, "That [whether our thought is capable of anything but Platonizing] is the whole question" (CENT: 1429/CM: 196). The modern elevation of the soul over the idea therefore has not completed the reversal of Platonism. To complete the reversal for Bergson, we must "break" with analysis (CENT: 1425/CM: 194). No philosophical thinking is possible, for Bergson, through analysis (CENT: 1410/CM: 178). It must be *overcome,* and being based in analysis (as a kind of barely reworked Platonism), modern metaphysics and modern science must be overcome. As we shall see in chapter 4, Heidegger will make a similar criticism of the faculty of the understanding or the intellect (*der Verstand*). To overcome analysis and its determinative role in modern metaphysics and science, we must place the faculty of understanding back within the faculty of intuition, making the understanding once more *dependent* on experience. But here, experience is *immanent* subjective experience reconceived as the duration. The duration completes the reversal of Platonism and shows the true meaning of the modern elevation of the soul. The Bergsonian duration transforms the concept of immanence. We have moved beyond Cartesianism.

Let us again examine the Bergsonian duration. As we saw in the "Summary-Commentary" in "Introduction to Metaphysics," Bergson says that the duration consists in *"a multiplicity like no other"* (CENT: 1402/CM: 168; my emphasis). For Bergson, the duration is a qualitative multiplicity—as opposed to a quantitative multiplicity. In *Time and Free Will* (where Bergson first developed his concept of multiplicity), we find several examples of a quantitative multiplicity; the example of a flock of sheep is perhaps the easiest to grasp (CENT: 52–53/DI: 76–77). When we look at a flock of sheep, what we notice is that they all look alike. Thus a quantitative multiplicity is always homogeneous. But we also notice that we can enumerate the sheep, despite their homogeneity. We are able to enumerate them because each sheep is spatially separated from or juxtaposed to the others; in other words, each occupies a discernible spatial location. Therefore, quantitative multiplicities are homogeneous and spatial. Moreover, because a quantitative multiplicity is homogeneous, we can represent it with a symbol, for instance, a sum: "25." In contrast, *qualitative multiplicities* are heterogeneous and temporal; this is a difficult idea since we would normally think that if there is heterogeneity, there is juxtaposition. But in a qualitative multiplicity, heterogeneity does not imply juxtaposition; it implies continuity.

As with quantitative multiplicity, Bergson in *Time and Free Will* gives us many examples of qualitative multiplicity. Perhaps the easiest example to grasp is the feeling of sympathy (CENT: 16–17/DI: 18–19). Here Bergson calls sympathy a "moral feeling," but we know it also comes to define intuition. So the *Time and Free Will* description of sympathy shows us how closely together Bergson conceives intuition and duration; one and the same description counts for both. According to Bergson, our experience of sympathy begins with our putting ourselves in the place of others, in feeling their pain. But if sympathy consisted only in feeling the pain of others, sympathy would inspire in us abhorrence of others, and we would want to avoid them, not help them. Bergson concedes that the feeling of horror may be at the root of sympathy. But then, one realizes that if one does not help this "poor wretch," it is going to turn out that no one will come to one's own aid when one needs help. There is a "need" to help the suffering. For Bergson, these two phases are "inferior forms of pity." In contrast, true pity is not so much fearing pain as desiring it. It is as if "nature" has committed a great injustice and what we want is not to be seen as complicitous with it. As Bergson says, "The essence of pity is thus a need for self-abasement, an aspiration downward [into pain]." But this painful aspiration develops upward into a sense of being superior. One realizes that one can do without certain sensuous goods; one is superior over them since one has managed to dissociate oneself from them. In the end, one feels humility, humble since one is now stripped of these sensuous goods. Bergson calls this feeling "a qualitative progress." It consists in a "transition from repugnance to fear, from fear to sympathy, and from sympathy itself to humility." The genius of Bergson's description is that there is a heterogeneity of feelings here, and yet no one would be able to juxtapose them. The feelings are continuous with one another; they interpenetrate one another, and importantly there is an opposition between inferior needs and superior needs, between abasement and aspiration. A qualitative multiplicity is therefore heterogeneous (or virtually singularized), continuous (or interpenetrating), oppositional (or dualistic) at the extremes, and progressive (or temporal, an irreversible flow, which is not given all at once). Because a qualitative multiplicity is heterogeneous, it cannot be represented by a symbol (which would classify items homogeneously); indeed, a qualitative multiplicity is "indefinable" (CENT: 15/DI: 17), or, as Bergson says in "Introduction to Metaphysics, "inexpressible" (CENT: 1395/CM: 161).

The inexpressibility of the duration brings us to what is probably the central problem in Bergson's thought: conceptualization. The problem is this: In order for intuitive knowledge to be communicated, it requires a linguistic form, yet concepts in the proper or literal sense cannot capture the duration. Simply, concepts in the proper sense are frozen, while the duration is fluid.[22] In "Introduction to Metaphysics," Bergson suggests that there might be improper concepts, "flexible, mobile, almost *fluid* representations, always ready to mold themselves on the fleeting forms of intuition" (CENT: 1402/CM: 168; my emphasis). In order to understand this possible reconception of the concept (which means a reconception of thinking), let us examine what Bergson thinks concepts in the proper sense are (CENT: 1401/CM: 168).

A concept in the proper or literal sense of the term is a concept formed by analysis. As we know, in analysis the perceiver occupies a viewpoint outside the object. From what is perceived at that viewpoint, a property is abstracted. The abstracted property then is compared to other viewpoints and other objects. The result of the comparison (based on resemblance) is a commonality that is represented by a symbol or a word (CENT: 1400/ CM: 166). The commonality is a simple concept. Since the property looks as though it were a part of the object, we are persuaded to think that by juxtaposing the concepts of the properties we shall be able to recompose the "whole" of the object and obtain from the juxtaposition of the "parts" an intellectual equivalent. But this belief about recomposition is an illusion because the simple concept is a partial expression and not a component part (CENT: 1400/CM: 166). But besides the illusion of recomposition, there is "the danger," Bergson says, that frozen concepts are generalities (CENT: 1400/CM: 167). Through the comparison, the property acquires a larger and larger extension. As Bergson says, "The concept can symbolize a particular property only by making it common to an infinity of things" (CENT: 1401/CM: 167). The concept can even acquire an extension to all possible worlds (CENT: 1287/CM: 44). General concepts therefore are modes of classification or recognition (CENT: 1299/CM: 57). Once these classificatory genera are formed, they look to be prior to experience, the result being that we always start from these frozen concepts (from the faculty of the understanding) and then we go to experience. Experience becomes nothing more than content to be molded by concepts. A proper concept is a mold into which experience is poured. With frozen concepts, it looks as though our thought is able to do nothing but Platonize.

In contrast, fluid concepts show that our thinking is capable of more than Platonizing.[23] Genuine philosophical thinking for Bergson—the true metaphysics, he would say, or the true empiricism (CENT: 1408/CM: 175)—starts from experience (the faculty of intuition) and then goes to concepts (CENT: 1415/CM: 183). As Bergson says in the second introduction to The Creative Mind, "[The true metaphysics] must begin by eliminating ready-made concepts . . . and rely upon experience. But that inner experience of which we speak will nowhere find a strictly appropriate language. It will of course be compelled to return to the concept, by adding to it at the most an image; but then it will be necessary that the image enlarge [élargisse] the concept, making it more flexible, and it will be necessary that the image indicate, by the colored shading with which it will surround the concept, that the concept does not contain the complete experience [ne contient pas l'expérience tout entière]" (CENT: 1288/CM: 45; my emphasis; also CENT: 1285/CM: 42–43). This is a crucial comment for understanding Bergsonian fluid concepts. In it, Bergson provides a negative definition: a fluid concept does not contain the entire experience. So, while concepts in the proper sense are general ideas whose extension applies to many different things (a property common to all of them)—proper concepts attempt to take, grasp, or capture, conceive in the literal sense the entire experience—a fluid concept (an improper concept) would not be a general idea, not a common property; it would not extend to many things. Having a more limited extension, a fluid concept would fit only the thing to which it is referring (CENT: 1272/CM: 31).[24] Fitting only one thing, the fluid concept would be distinguishable from other concepts. The attempt to make the concept fit solely one thing is why Bergson distinguishes, for instance, between two senses of knowledge—intuition versus analysis. We might think that an improper concept would be imprecise. But because it does not contain the entire experience, an improper or metaphorical concept is more precise than general concepts. Despite having a limited extension, an improper concept must be, as Bergson says, "enlarged." It must be enlarged by the addition of images. The images surrounding the concept indicate that the concept does not contain the entire experience, that there is more to the experience than what is expressed in the concept's formal definition.

We are able to recapitulate the distinction between frozen concepts and fluid concepts in the following way. *First,* a concept in the proper sense molds experience, while a concept in the improper sense is molded by experience. This first distinction implies a reversal between frozen and fluid concepts. For frozen concepts, one goes from the concept to the experience; for a fluid concept, one goes from the experience to the concept. *Second,* a concept in the proper sense extends to many things. At the limit, it extends to everything that exists, as do traditional philosophical terms like "Ego," "Soul," "Will," or "Idea" (CENT: 1290–91/CM: 48–49). In contrast, an improper concept extends to only one thing. Extending only to one thing explains why these "concepts" are not proper or literal. Proper concepts are generalities, while improper concepts are antigeneralities or singularities. But there is another reason for their impropriety. *Third,* a concept is proper when it is subtracted from anything figurative or imagistic. In contrast, a concept is improper when an image is added to it. The addition of the images, however, does not extend the scope of the concept. In fact, the additional images do the reverse of extension. The images indicate what is not contained in the concept. *Fourth,* while concepts in the proper sense seem to contain the entire experience, fluid concepts do not contain the entire experience.

In order to understand the enlargement of a concept with images, let us return to the concept of intuition. The concept of intuition must be distinguished from analysis (or the understanding). Analysis is the indirect view of something. In contrast—and this is the precise definition Bergson provides in the second introduction to *The Creative Mind*—intuition is "the direct vision of the mind by the mind" (CENT: 1285/CM: 42). Yet, as we have seen, Bergson in "Introduction to Metaphysics" has also added onto this definition the image of dilation (CENT: 1419/CM: 187).

The reversal of the habitual work of intelligence, the reversal with which intuition starts, is supposed to make us, so to speak, "open" our vision wider than the present experience we have of ourselves. In his 1911 essay "The Perception of Change" (also collected into *The Creative Mind*), Bergson describes this process of opening up and making wider (CENT: 1385–87/CM: 151–52). Bergson starts by asking us to "reflect for a moment on this 'present' which alone is considered to have existence." We might think that the present instant is like a geometrical point in space. If we say that it is something like a mathematical point, we are confronted with a problem: If each instant is a point, then how are we to get a line out of the points? We cannot say that what lies between the instants are intervals of time since we have already hypothetically reduced time to the juxtaposition of instants. Therefore the two points or instants seem to be separated by nothing. And if nothing separates the points, one has no choice but to let them collapse into one another: "two mathematical points which touch merge into one another" (CENT: 1386/CM: 151). We must conclude by saying they are really only one *thick* point.

With the image of a thickening spot, we must digress to another essay from 1911, "Philosophical Intuition." Here Bergson focuses on the images in Berkeley's thought, in particular, the images in what Berkeley says about matter. According to Bergson, for Berkeley, matter is a thin, transparent film between humans and God. But metaphysicians make the thin, transparent film thick and opaque when they place words such "Substance," "Force," and "Extension" behind the film; these words, Bergson says, paraphrasing Berkeley, "settle there like a layer of dust, and hinder us from seeing God through the transparency" (CENT: 1356/CM: 119; also CENT: 1417/CM: 185 for "a dust of moments"). To this first Berkeleyan image Bergson adds another, an "auditory transposition of the visual image" of the transparent film: "matter is a language which God speaks to us." Like the transparent film, God's language is clear. But "the metaphysicians of matter" "thicken up" each syllable of the speech, propagate that syllable or small word, and set it up as an independent entity. The word is like the mathematical point of the present, which being thickened takes on an immense extension, as if it captures all existence, as if it were a cloud of dust. The thickening, Bergson says, makes us turn "our attention away from the sense to the sound and hinders us from following the divine word" (CENT: 1356/CM: 119). We must take note of some of the French words in this quotation. The French word rendered as "word" is "*parole*," which also means speech; the image of matter as God's language is an auditory image. And connected to the word "*parole*" is the French word "*sens*" here rendered as "sense," which (like the German "*Sinn*") means not only meaning but also direction. As a direction, the sense of a speech is something fluid, mobile, which we follow as we listen.

Now let us return from Berkeley's dust to the dilation description. If my present is not a "thickened-up" point-like instant, then what is it? Bergson answers that it is "a certain interval of duration" (CENT: 1386/CM: 151). At this moment, the present is the sentence with which I am concerned to pronounce. (Bergson's "The Perception of Change" was first an oral lecture, a speech.) My present is the sentence I am uttering right now. My attention is turned toward the present sentence; the field of my attention is limited to the current sentence. Then Bergson says, "This attention is something that can be made longer or shorter, like the interval between two points [*pointes*] of a compass" (CENT: 1386/CM: 151). The French word "*pointe*" refers back to the image of the instant as a *point* on a line, but here the "*pointe*" while referring to the sharp points of the device for making circles, a compass, is not restricted to mathematics. The sharp points of the compass mark the distance spanned by the attention of speaking (or hearing) the span from the beginning of a sentence to the end of that sentence. The sharp points are also punctuation points; punctuation marks connect words together and do not allow a word or syllable to be set up as independent. But the punctuation marks are also sharp points; the sharp points do not allow syllables to merge themselves into one syllable or words to merge themselves into one word. Here with the image of the compass there is no cloud of dust. Yet the two sharp points of the compass can be enlarged. So if I wanted, I could with effort make the distance greater than the current sentence. I would then include the sentence that went ahead of the one with which I am concerned to pronounce now. But we could go further. We could indefinitely embrace with the preceding sentence all the prior sentences of the lecture: "All I should have had to do is to adopt another punctuation" (CENT: 1386/CM: 151). With effort, the dilation could include the events that preceded the lecture, and as large a part of our past as we desire. According to Bergson, the conclusion must be that the distinction we usually make between our present and the past is relative if not arbitrary: "The 'present' occupies exactly as much space as this effort" (CENT: 1386/CM: 152).

We recall that the precise and formal definition of intuition is "the direct vision of the mind by the mind." At the end of the "Summary-Commentary," we suggested that self-sympathy or self-contemplation does not solely define Bergsonian intuition. And in the "Interpretation" we have seen that sympathy is a complex experience, not restricted to the self. But now with the images added onto the concept of intuition, we see that the formal definition of intuition does not contain the entire experience. We should not forget that the definition fits the experience since the experience is not one of analysis. But the image of dilation and its associated images of the mathematical point, the thick cloud of dust, the voice or speech, and the sharp points of the compass tell us more about intuition than does the definition. The image of God's speech that overlaps with the speech of the address called "The Perception of Change" indicates that intuition is not solely vision; it is also listening. Indeed, in "Introduction to Metaphysics," Bergson calls intuition "spiritual auscultation," the attentive and sympathetic listening of a doctor to the patient's heart (CENT: 1408/CM: 175). The image of dilation does not suggest the indirect access to something by means of symbolic recomposition; it does not suggest analysis. Yet it suggests some sort of indirectness because there is no dilation without effort. Finally, the image of the sharp points of the compass suggests that intuition is not limited to self-intuition. The articulations it makes indicate that the duration always exceeds what is given to me in intuition, that the duration is always other than me, that the duration is always larger, that it is still outside, that it is the outside. Overall, the images indicate that the concept of intuition does not contain the entire experience of the duration. In fact, the colored fringe of the images indicates that the concept is unfinished. The concept is not a frozen mold. Once again, we can say that thought is capable of more than Platonizing. It can follow the sense, or better, as Bergson says, it can follow "a continuous trait," which is never given completely.[25]

The conclusion that thought is capable of following a trait that is never given completely brings us to the most basic principle of Bergsonism. The principle is found in his 1907 *Creative Evolution*. We had already seen that the duration is a whole within which there are component parts, the plurality of component parts being the duration's multiplicity. But for the duration to be a true heterogeneous multiplicity, it must be the case that "the whole is never given" (CENT: 526/EC: 37, CENT: 527/EC: 39, and CENT: 699/EC: 240).[26] This simple sentence allows us to understand that intuition in Bergson is always finite (even if it is not perspectival).[27] It is finite, because intuition—even though it places itself within the outside— never grasps all of the duration. In order to lead us to the idea that the whole is not given, Bergson distinguishes between two senses of possibility. On the one hand, there is the sense of possibility in which something is possible because there is no obstacle to its being realized. So, in this sense of possibility, we can say that a music composer's symphony—this is Bergson's example—was possible before it was written because "there was no insurmountable barrier to its realization." But mixed in with this negative sense of possibility is another positive sense. We also think that if the symphony was possible, it was pre-existent as an idea in the composer's mind prior to its realization (CENT: 1339/CM: 99). Bergson says, however (in the first introduction to *The Creative Mind*),

> This [second positive sense of possibility] is an absurd conception in the case of a work of art, for from the moment that the musician has the precise and complete idea of the symphony he means to compose, his symphony is done. Neither in the artist's thought nor, what is more, in any other thought comparable to ours, whether impersonal or even simply virtual, did the symphony exist in its quality of being possible before being real (CENT: 1262–63/CM: 21; also CENT: 1341–42/CM: 102).

More than anything else, musical and linguistic composition forms the basis for Bergson's conception of the duration.[28] Added onto the concept of duration with its formal definition of multiplicity, the image of artistic creation, like that of the novelist, tells us that the duration is never a mere copying of a pre-existent mold. The duration is always creative. The image implies that because the idea was not given at the beginning, prior to its realization, the movement of the duration has no absolute origin or first aim. Lacking an initial absolute determination, the duration therefore has no absolute end or final purpose. In other words, prior to the sense or direction of the duration, there is no one absolute sense. The lack of absolute determination frees the duration to create not only reality, but also possibilities. In other words, lacking a determinate aim and purpose, the duration never comes to an end; more duration is always possible.

## Transition

Bergson's thought is radical. Even though in 1903 Bergson attempts to renew metaphysics in light of its decline in the nineteenth century, the attempt at renewal in fact aims to overcome the modern metaphysics of subjectivity; and insofar as the modern metaphysics of subjectivity continues Platonism, Bergsonism attempts to overcome Platonism.[29] Indeed, by raising the soul over the form, Bergson radicalizes subjective immanent experience by conceiving it as the duration. The duration is a multiplicity like no other: a continuous heterogeneity. But the experience of the duration, intuition, is inexpressible. The inexpressibility of intuitive knowledge leads to Bergson's idea of a fluid concept. As we have just seen, a fluid concept is fundamentally incomplete, just as the duration itself is. The fluid concept, while fitting the duration, while being enlarged with images, always calls for more thinking. Indeed, intuition and duration are virtually identical. If that is so and if intuition is able to mold a fluid concept and, more than a fluid concept, a kind of discourse, if it is able to call forth thought, then we have to say that the duration is not alien to language or that language is not alien to the duration. Sense, Bergson says, "is less a thing thought than a movement of thought, less a movement than a direction" (CENT: 1358/CM: 121). This direction for Bergson is larger than my conscious present. Therefore, like Freud, the duration emerges from the unconscious (CENT: 1273/CM: 32).

# 2

# Schizophrenic Thought:
## Freud's "The Unconscious" (1915)

If the outside is the outside of the conscious present, then we must investigate Freud's thought. In particular, we must investigate the place where he most thoroughly defines the unconscious, his 1915 essay "The Unconscious." Written well after the discoveries of his *Interpretation of Dreams* (1900) and after many years of clinical work, the "Papers on Meta-Psychology," of which "The Unconscious" is one, attempt to present the systems of the human mind.[1] These systems, which are topographical, dynamic, and energetic or economical, reduce consciousness to the status of being a symptom of unconscious processes. Freud says, "In proportion as we try to win our way to a meta-psychological view of mental life, we must learn to emancipate ourselves from our sense of the importance of that symptom which consists in 'being conscious'" (GW X: 291/SE XIV: 193). The reduction of consciousness to being a symptom of the unconscious provides a sense to this word "meta-psychology," a word clearly similar to "meta-physics." "Meta-psychology," for Freud, means going beyond the psychic insofar as the psychic is defined by consciousness. Like Bergson's introduction to metaphysics, Freud's meta-psychology attempts to overcome the then current psychology. The overcoming of the psychology of consciousness opens the two problems that animate "The Unconscious."

On the one hand, "The Unconscious" concerns the question of how we are able to *recognize* the unconscious when we have access to it only mediately, that is, through what Freud calls its "derivatives." In a way, Freud's response to this first question amounts to a kind of "apology" for the belief in the unconscious. Appropriating Kantian critique, Freud argues here that the concept of the unconscious (and psychoanalysis) corrects inner perception. On the other hand, since we have access to the unconscious only through the derivatives, the question becomes how we can conceive the relation between the unconscious and the conscious. In other words, how does the unconscious become conscious? As we are going to see, the relation between consciousness and the unconscious is defined by translation and therefore by language.[2] Famously, "The Unconscious" distinguishes between neurosis and schizophrenia by means of the fact that the schizophrenic speaks. Freudian psychoanalysis therefore anticipates the great reflections on language that we find in the later Heidegger, in the later Merleau-Ponty, and Foucault.[3] Indeed, Deleuze and Guattari say that in "The Unconscious" Freud "discovers the greatest art of the unconscious."[4] This art is the liberation of language—of what Freud calls derivatives—from its object. Freud discovers schizophrenic thought.

## Summary-Commentary: The "Recognition" of the Unconscious[5]

### THE PROCESS OF REPRESSION[6]

The opening paragraph of "The Unconscious" sets up the problems we just mentioned: "On the basis of psychoanalysis we have experienced that the essence of the process of repression lies not in sublating [*aufzuheben*] a representational idea of the drive [*eine den Trieb repräsentierende Vorstellung*], or in annihilating it, but rather in withholding it from consciousness" (GW X: 264/SE XIV: 166).[7] This opening sentence means that there is a drive (libido) that seeks satisfaction of a need (its aim: pleasure) by investing itself in a representational idea (of an object); the "*Vorstellung*" is a "representative" of the unconscious drive. Repression does not annihilate the drive's representative; repression withholds it from consciousness, and that withholding stops the sublation (*Aufhebung*) of it. If repression has led to some sort of mental illness such as neurosis, the cure consists in allowing the sublation to happen. When the sublation occurs, then we are able to gain knowledge of (recognize) the unconscious. But is it possible to know the unconscious?

### THE JUSTIFICATION OF THE UNCONSCIOUS[8]

Freud argues that certain kinds of "proofs" (*Beweise*) can be presented that show the necessity of "presuming"—the German verb "*annehmen*" and the noun "*Annahme*" are two of the most common words in the essay and other writings of this period such as *Beyond the Pleasure Principle*—the existence of the unconscious. To be able to explain phenomena such as slips of the tongue and dreams, phenomena that remain inexplicable for consciousness, we must presuppose the unconscious.[9] Freud argues, however, not only that the presumption of the existence of the unconscious is necessary but also that it is legitimate. The legitimacy of the existence of the unconscious in fact "corrects" our customary way of thinking. Although in primitive time, we identified our consciousness with all living things—Freud calls this extension of consciousness to all living things "primitive animism" (GW X: 270/SE XIV: 171)—our current "critique" (*Kritik*) has corrected this identification; we are not even sure we should attribute consciousness to animals. The identification of my consciousness with that of other humans has however withstood the critique. But, as Freud notes, this identification must be done by means of inference and analogy (GW X: 268/SE XIV: 169). So psychoanalysis asks us to make the same inference and analogy with ourselves (GW X: 268/SE XIV: 169). If we do this, we must say that all the acts and manifestations that I notice and which do not "link up"[10] with anything else in my psychical life must be judged as if they belong to another person. But when applied to oneself, this inference does not lead to the disclosure of an unconscious. Rather, it leads in "a correct way" to the presumption of another or second consciousness, which is appropriated into my person with my familiar consciousness (GW X: 269/SE XIV: 170). But here, according to Freud, a "just" (*berechtigen*) occasion for "critique" appears.

Freud lays out three aspects of this legitimate critique. *First,* a consciousness of which the bearer knows nothing is something other than a foreign consciousness; moreover, lacking its most important characteristic, immediate knowledge, this consciousness is not worthy of discussion. Instead of an unconscious psychical process, we seem to have the inconsistent idea of an unconscious consciousness. *Second,* analysis shows that individual latent psychical processes have a high degree of mutual independence, "as though each had no connection with another, and knew nothing about any other" (GW X: 269/SE XIV: 170). We would then have to assume a third or fourth or an unlimited number of states of consciousness all unknown to us and to one another, which is another inconsistent idea. *Third,* "and this is the most serious argument of all," analytic investigation shows, according to Freud, that some of these latent processes have characteristics which seem "alien to us, or even incredible, and which run directly counter to the well-known attributes of consciousness" (GW X: 269/SE XIV: 170). So Freud concludes that we have grounds for modifying our inference about ourselves. What is proved is that there is no second consciousness in us; rather, there is the existence of certain psychical acts deprived of consciousness. According to Freud, this critique, which is psychoanalysis, is the "continuation" (*Fortsetzung*) of Kant's critique of external perception. Freud says, "Just as Kant warned us not to overlook the fact that our perceptions are subjectively conditioned and must not be regarded as identical with what is perceived though unknowable, so psychoanalysis warns us not to put [*setzen*] perceptions of consciousness in place of unconscious psychical processes which are the object of that perception. Like the physical, the psychical is not necessarily in reality what it seems to us to be" (GW X: 270/SE XIV: 171). Freud therefore aims to correct inner perception. We shall return to this correction in the "Interpretation" below since through inner perception the unconscious can be recognized but not known. The contribution of Kantian critique to psychoanalysis lies in the fact that the appearance of the object of external perception is not identical to what it is in reality. This difference between appearance and reality implies that the objects of inner perception are more alien to me than an alien consciousness. Nevertheless, the objects of inner perception are less unknowable than the external world because, unlike the external world, the unconscious produces derivatives of itself.

### THE VARIOUS MEANINGS OF THE UNCONSCIOUS AND THE TOPOLOGICAL VIEWPOINT

The analogy of the unconscious to an alien consciousness indicates that a terminological clarification of the unconscious is required. On the one hand, the term "unconscious" refers to the status of psychical acts that are merely latent and have the capacity to become conscious. On the other hand, the term refers to processes entirely foreign to consciousness; it then refers to the system unconscious (abbreviated as Ucs, while the system conscious is abbreviated as Cs). According to Freud, usually a psychical act goes through two phases. First, the psychical act is unconscious and belongs to the system Ucs. If the psychical act is rejected by the

censorship, it is not allowed to pass into the second phase. It is then said
to be "repressed" and must remain unconscious. If however the psychical
act passes the censorship, it enters the second phase and then belongs to
the second system, the Cs (GW X: 272/SE XIV: 173). But the fact that the
psychical act belongs to consciousness does not determine, according
to Freud, its relation to consciousness univocally (GW X: 272/SE XIV:
173). It is not yet conscious, but it is "capable," Freud says, under certain
conditions, of entering consciousness (GW X: 272/SE XIV: 173). Because
of the psychical act's capacity to become conscious, Freud also calls the
system Cs the "preconscious" (and uses the abbreviation Pcs). The system
Pcs shares the characteristics of the Cs. And the censorship exercises its
office at the "passage" (*Übergang*) from the Ucs to the Pcs (or Cs). It is this
passage and its barrier—the testing-censorship—that suggests that the
psyche is a topography.

On the one hand, the topography (and the dynamic description of
psychical processes such as repression) makes us see that psychoanalysis
differs from the descriptive psychology of consciousness. Freud therefore
notes that psychoanalysis has already been called "depth-psychology." But
the relation of the "localities" raises an unresolved question:

> When a psychical act (we restrict ourselves to those that have the nature
> of an idea [*Vorstellung*] [this parenthetical comment anticipates the next
> section on emotions]) undergoes the transposition [*Umsetzung*] from the
> system Ucs into the system Cs or Pcs, are we to presume that this trans-
> position involves a new registration comparable to a second record of the
> idea in question, situated, moreover, in a new psychical locality and with
> which the original unconscious record continues to exist side by side? Or
> are we to believe instead that the transposition consists in an alteration
> of the state, which is fulfilled in the so-called material and in the same
> locality? (GW X: 272–73/SE XIV: 174)

This is the crucial question that organizes the rest of the essay. Freud does
not provide an answer to it until the seventh and last section of the essay.
Here in section two, however, he says that although the question may
appear "abstruse," it must be raised since it gives a better sense of what
psychical topography means, a better sense of the depth in the soul. The
depth shows us that psychoanalysis differs from psychology of consciousness, but the depth does not mean that psychoanalysis is anatomy (GW X:
273/SE XIV: 174). Freud takes note of the then current brain physiology,

and, sounding quite contemporary, he speaks of a "hiatus" between brain physiology and psychology which at present cannot be filled (GW X: 273/ SE XIV: 174). So Freud concludes, and this comment shows how distant psychoanalytical speculation is from science, "Our psychical topography has for the present nothing to do with anatomy. . . . In this respect, then, our work is untrammeled and may proceed according to its own requirements" (GW X: 273–74/SE XIV: 175).

To ensure that "our work" is untrammeled, Freud reminds us not to take the two "hypotheses" (*Annahmen*) to refer to literal anatomical locations; the spatial images they suggest are merely illustrative of the relation between the systems. Then he considers the value of the two hypotheses. The first hypothesis of the two registrations, Freud says, is "cruder but more convenient," while "the functional change of state" hypothesis is "from the outset, more probable but it is less plastic, less easy to handle" (GW X: 274/SE XIV: 174). The two-registrations hypothesis is bound up with the additional hypothesis of a "separation" (*Trennung*) between the systems Ucs and Cs; it implies that the idea may exist simultaneously in two parts of the psychical apparatus. That is, if the idea is not inhibited by the censorship, it regularly advances from one position to another. It is possible however that, advancing to the conscious position, the idea's first location or record is not abandoned. Freud reports that if a patient is told about one of his or her repressed ideas, this information does not change the repression. The patient now has in actual fact the *same* idea in two forms in two separate localities in his or her psychical apparatus. But, this "identity of communication" to the repressed memory is only apparent. As Freud points out, "To have listened to something and to have experienced something are psychologically two different things, even though the content of each be the same" (GW X: 275/SE XIV: 176). So for the moment, according to Freud, we cannot decide between the two possible hypotheses of how to define the difference between a conscious and an unconscious idea. But we can see that the unconscious idea must be *experienced,* which leads us to the question of emotions.

### UNCONSCIOUS FEELINGS

In the two hypotheses, Freud had restricted the discussion to unconscious ideas, but now with the recognition that the idea must be experienced or lived, he raises the question of unconscious "drive-impulses" (*Triebregungen*), "feelings" (*Gefühle*), and "sensations" (*Empfindungen*). In reference to drive-impulses, Freud makes several important claims, claims to which we shall return in the "Interpretation." A drive as such can never become conscious: "A drive can never be an object [*Objekt*] of consciousness—only the idea that represents it [*nur die Vorstellung, die ihn repräsentiert*]" (GW X: 275/SE XIV: 177). Even in the unconscious, the drive can be represented only by the idea. If the drive did not attach itself to an idea or manifest itself in an affective state, Freud says, we could know nothing about it (GW X: 276/SE XIV: 177). The drives are always mediated by representations or representatives, by what Freud here calls "derivatives."[11] Therefore, if we speak of an unconscious drive-impulse, we actually mean the representative idea of the drive-impulse.

This conclusion would seem to imply that we should never be able to speak of an unconscious feeling. Although the drive-impulse is never present as such, never felt as such, although it is mediated by its representative idea, feelings are *felt,* that is, they are always conscious. However, as Freud points out, it is possible to perceive a feeling and yet "fail to recognize" it (GW X: 276/SE XIV: 177). An affect or a feeling-impulse is always connected to a representative. But when that representative is repressed, the affect is forced into being "knotted" with another idea. After the affect is knotted to the other idea, consciousness interprets the affect as the "externalization" of this other idea. If we restore the "true connection," that is, the connection to the first representative, we call the so-connected affect unconscious. In other words, although the affect was never unconscious, its representational idea had undergone repression. Unconscious affects and feelings refer to the "destiny," brought about by repression, of the quantitative factor in the drive-impulse. This quantitative factor refers us to an energetics or economic description. According to Freud here, an affect may be subjected to three different destinies: either it remains, wholly or in part, as it is; or it is transformed into a qualitatively different charge of affect, above all into anxiety (*Angst*); or its development is hindered altogether. Indeed, the true aim of repression lies in the suppression of the affect. When repression has succeeded in driving out the affect, that affect is, according to Freud, unconscious.[12]

Freud admits that this difference between unconscious affect and unconscious idea is difficult. This is an important quote for understanding the energetics: "The whole difference arises from the fact that ideas are investments [*Besetzungen,* "cathexes" or "occupations"]—ultimately of memory traces—whilst affects and emotions correspond with processes of discharge, the final externalization of which is perceived as sensations (GW X: 277/SE XIV: 178). In other words, the difference is that the unconscious idea as idea is repressed, that is, the idea of the object that can satisfy the drive's aim; this idea is charged with affective energy, but the repression prevents the dis-charge (*Abfuhr*) from developing. The discharge then remains a potential. Repression aims at inhibiting the transformation of a drive-impulse into affective externalization (the discharge as the satisfaction of pleasure). As Freud says, there is a "constant struggle," operating through the agency of the censorship, between the Cs system and Ucs system for control of affectivity (GW X: 278/SE XIV: 179). The struggle between the two systems at first involves the affect appearing directly in the system Cs. When it does, it always has the character of anxiety; "repressed" affects are always exchanged for anxiety (GW X: 278/SE XIV: 179).[13] But when anxiety is driven back, it waits until it has found a "substitutive idea" (*Ersatzvorstellung*) in the Cs system, through which it will assert itself again. In fact, the nature of the substitutive idea determines the qualitative character of the affect; it changes the content of the idea. Freud now provides a clear example of how the substitutive idea determines the affect.

## TOPOGRAPHY AND DYNAMICS OF REPRESSION

Repression must involve, Freud thinks, a "withdrawal of investment," the withdrawal of the charge of the quantity of affective excitation. In other words, repression is not just two records but a change in the state of the affect, in the content of the idea; the two-registrations hypothesis is clearly inadequate (GW X: 279/SE XIV: 180). But for Freud, the question is: In what system does the withdrawal take place and to which system does the investment withdrawn belong (GW X: 1279/SE XIV: 180)? In the Ucs, the repressed idea remains capable of action, its potential for discharge remains; it must therefore have retained its charge of investment. So something else must have been withdrawn.[14] Freud says, "Repression can consist here only in the withdrawal, from the idea, of the (pre)conscious charge which belongs to the system Pcs" (GW X: 279/SE XIV: 180). Repression withdraws the affect the Cs system put into the idea. In other words, it withdraws the reaction to the appearance of the idea, the reaction of anxiety. But this withdrawal leaves the unconscious drive and its investment in place. Since drives are incessant, the same process of withdrawal would have to happen interminably. In short, the result would not be repression. We must presume therefore, according to Freud, an "anti-charge [Gegenbesetzung] by means of which the system Pcs guards itself against the pressure of the unconscious idea" (GW X: 280/SE XIV: 181). The anti-charge is the sole mechanism of primal repression, that is, the repression of the drives and their objects that occurs in childhood. When the drives' ideas reappear later in life, there is again the anti-charge and, in addition, the withdrawal of the preconscious charge (GW X: 280/SE XIV: 181). It is very possible, Freud thinks, that the preconscious charge withdrawn from the idea is the very one used for anti-charge. The withdrawal of investment brings us to the economic view of the psychical apparatus. The economic view means that we try to follow out the destiny of a given quantity of excitation or energy (GW X: 280/SE XIV: 181); in other words, we try to follow the investment and determine its payoff. To be able to describe a psychical process economically, dynamically, and topologically, Freud says, is "the consummation of psychoanalytic research." He gives a special name to this three-way description, a name we have already seen: "meta-psychological" (GW X: 281/SE XIV: 181).

We come now to the illuminating example of substitute formation that we mentioned above, the meta-psychological description of the process of repression in transference neuroses, in particular, in anxiety hysteria (GW X: 281–82/SE XIV: 182–83). It is important to keep this example in mind since, later in "The Unconscious," Freud will go beyond transference neuroses by considering narcissistic neuroses, in particular, schizophrenia. In regard to transference neurosis, however, Freud lays out three phases. The first phase occurs when anxiety occurs without the person (a child) knowing what has caused the anxiety. What has happened is that in the Ucs there was present some sexual impulse (libido), which demanded to be transferred into the system Pcs. The preconscious charge amounts to a recoil from the impulse represented in the idea; the unconscious libidinal charge of the rejected idea is then discharged as anxiety. In other words, a charged idea representing a sexual impulse makes itself present to the child; rather than discharging the quantity of excitation in the idea as pleasurable actions, the child undergoes anxiety. The affect of anxiety makes it seem as though the charged sexual idea were a perceived threat from the outside from which the child could flee. The repression therefore is not yet successful. The affect of anxiety nevertheless has set up the second phase.

The *second* phase occurs when the idea presents itself again (and again and again). The child again feels anxiety, but now an attempt is made at "conquering" the anxiety. The conquering of anxiety occurs through transference, that is, the charge attaches itself to a substitute idea. Because the substitute idea is distant enough from the rejected idea, it allows the child to rationalize his or her uncontrollable outbreak of anxiety (GW X: 281/SE XIV: 182). The two ideas—the rejected idea and the substitute idea—must be tied together by means of association. Here Freud is describing animal phobia. So the association means that anxiety about the idea of getting pleasure from, for instance, the father (whose idea has been invested with a sexual drive and whose idea has now been rejected) gets knotted to the idea of a dog, for instance, since the dog's barking and growling also makes the child anxious. The idea of the dog becomes the substitute idea. On the one hand, the substitute idea acts as a "conductor" from the system Ucs to the system Cs, since the anxiety has its "place of emergence" in the Ucs. On the other, the substitutive idea acts as an "independent source for the release of anxiety"; it occasions the discharge of anxiety (GW X: 282/SE XIV: 182). In other words, the idea of the dog secures the Cs system against the emergence into consciousness of the repressed idea; it has become the anti-charge since it is now invested with anxiety (a quantity of energy or excitation). The idea of the dog, the external perception of the dog, has become the point at which anxiety breaks out (GW X: 282/SE XIV: 182). By making the substitute idea of the dog the source of anxiety, the child no longer has the idea of the father as a source of anxiety (GW X: 281/SE XIV: 183). The child has become free of the father, but now has anxiety in the face of the dog from which the child is able to flee.

The *third* phase of anxiety hysteria expands the substitutive idea into a substitute formation. The substitute formation is a protective structure, a defensive enclave, a first line of defense, a defense mechanism. The defense mechanism begins to operate only when the substitute idea (the idea of the dog) has successfully taken over the representation of what has been repressed (the idea of the father). The defense mechanism attempts to isolate the substitutive idea (the idea of a particular dog) so that it does not produce a new excitation. What happens is that all the associations to the substitute idea are endowed with a peculiar intensity so that they exhibit a high degree of sensibility to excitation (GW X: 282/SE XIV: 183). Excitation at any point of the protective structure gives rise to a slight degree of the development of anxiety. The slight degree of anxiety is used as a signal to inhibit; it results in a new flight from any further development of anxiety. The further the sensitive and vigilant anti-charge becomes extended around the anxiety-producing substitute idea, the more exactly is the mechanism able to function. It is the protective "rampart" (*Wall*) of a phobia, in this case, an animal phobia. Perhaps at first, it was a particularly vicious dog in the neighborhood that occasioned the anxiety. Then the anxiety is generalized to all dogs, and then perhaps to the houses where the dogs reside even when the dogs are away, and then to the street where the houses are, etc. Where before there was only one point (a particular dog) where the repressed idea could break through and produce anxiety, now it is able to break through with the whole protective structure of the phobia: any street where any dogs live produces a slight feeling of anxiety. The outbreak of anxiety now seems to come not from the drive, but from the perception, which allows the child to react with flight (GW X: 283/SE XIV: 184). Repression succeeds in inhibiting the discharge of anxiety by keeping the child within the ramparts of the substitute formation. The defense mechanism, however, never operates with complete security because one of the peculiar characteristics of the unconscious is its persistence.

## THE SPECIAL CHARACTERISTICS OF THE SYSTEM UCS

Freud's discussion of the characteristics of the Ucs system in "The Unconscious" is famous. First, Freud defines the Ucs: "The kernel of the system Ucs consists of drive-representations [*Triebrepräsentanzen*] whose aim is to discharge their charge, that is, the kernel consists of wish impulses [*Wunschregungen,* movements or stirrings of a wish or a desire]" (GW X:

285/SE XIV: 186). The drive "movements" are coordinate with one another, exist independently side by side, and are exempt from mutual contradiction. When we have two impulses or wishes whose aims seem to be incompatible, when they become simultaneously active, the two impulses do not "cancel" (*aufheben*) each other out. They combine to form an intermediate aim, they form a "compromise." Therefore, in the Ucs, there is no negation, no dubiety, no varying degree of certainty; all negation, dubiety, varying degrees of certainty, come from the censorship that exists between the two systems. Negation, as Freud says, is at a higher level, a substitute for repression. This "higher level" refers, above repression, to judgments of condemnation in which a firm "no" is expressed. In the Ucs, however, there are only contents more or less strongly charged; everything is a "yes."

Intensity of charge is more mobile in the Ucs than other systems. By means of displacement (*Verschiebung*), one idea may gain the whole charge of another. Or by condensation (*Verdichtung*), one idea may gain the charges of many ideas. These two processes of *condensation* and *displacement* are characteristics of what Freud calls "the primary psychical processes." They are primary because they are the processes of the unconscious as in dreams; secondary processes such as repression are those of the Pcs and are found in wakeful life.[15] The mobility of the energy and the topography allows us to see that the processes of condensation and displacement (as they function, for instance, in dream production) resemble literary tropes, in particular the tropes of metaphor and metonymy.[16] Freud also tells us that the Ucs processes are "timeless" (*zeitlos*), that is, they are not ordered temporally and are not altered by the passage of time. In fact, they bear no relation to time at all; the time relation is bound up with the work of the system Cs. In *Beyond the Pleasure Principle*, Freud clarifies the claim about timelessness by calling the concept of time with which we usually work (including the one found in philosophy; Freud here mentions Kant) "abstract," meaning a qualitatively undifferentiated, homogenizing time.[17] Calling the concept "abstract" implies that there could be a qualitatively differentiated time that would not contradict the idea that drives have destinies. In the "Interpretation," we shall return to this word "abstract" and to the fact that the primary processes resemble literary tropes. In any case, like their relations to time, "the processes of the Ucs are just as little related to reality. They are subject to the pleasure-principle; their destiny depends only upon the degree of their strength and upon their conformity to regulation by pleasure and pain" (GW X:

286/SE XIV: 187). Unconscious processes, finally, "are knowable" only in dreams and in neurosis. Independently, "in and for themselves," the primary processes are "unrecognizable, indeed are not capable of existing" (even though we must *presume* the existence of the unconscious) (GW X: 286/SE XIV: 187). Here is a summary of the characteristics of the unconscious: exemption from mutual contradiction (there is no "no" in the Ucs); primary process of condensation and displacement (the mobility of charge); timelessness; the substitution of psychic reality (pleasure and pain) for external reality; and knowable only indirectly.

Freud turns to the characteristics of the system Pcs. In general, the system Pcs is the "inhibition" of the discharge of charged ideas. In the Pcs, displacement and condensation are excluded or very much restricted. The exclusion and restriction of the processes of condensation and displacement leads Freud to assume two different stages of charged energy in psychical life. On the one hand, energy is "tonically bound," that is, inhibited from discharge, making it "tonic" or tense; and on the other hand, it moves freely and presses toward discharge (GW X: 287/SE XIV: 188). There is one more characteristic of the system Pcs. The Pcs consists in "communicatability" between the different "ideational contents," which means that the Pcs allows the different ideas to influence one another. As we have seen, as the seat of the censorship, the Pcs establishes the "reality principle" (GW X: 287/SE XIV: 188). In other words, the system Pcs is the location where ideas are tested against what reality permits. Conscious memory seems to depend entirely on the Pcs. It must be distinguished from memory traces, in which experiences of the Ucs become registered. The difference between conscious memories and memory traces suggests again the two-registrations hypothesis, but this hypothesis has already been shown to be inadequate. So here is the list of the characteristics of the system Pcs: inhibition of charge; restriction and exclusion of condensation and displacement; and communication between the systems Ucs and Cs, conscious memory. This word, "*Verkehr*"—here rendered as "communication"; the French translation of the essay renders it as "*relation*"[18]—really means trafficking or circulation. Therefore, Freud concludes this section by saying that we must recognize pathological conditions under which the two systems alter or even exchange both their content and their characteristics (GW X: 288/SE XIV: 189). While we just saw Freud differentiate the systems, now he will show us the intersystemic circulation.

## COMMUNICATION (*VERKEHR*) BETWEEN THE TWO SYSTEMS

On the basis of the meta-psychological description of transference neurosis (anxiety hysteria), we know already that the Ucs is persistent and
relentless. Freud reasserts this observation: the Ucs does not remain at
rest while the Pcs does all the psychical work. The Ucs is not something
left over and undone by childhood development. Also, the communication
between the two systems is not restricted to the act of repression, which
throws all that disturbs it back into the "abyss" of the Ucs. On the contrary,
the Ucs is living; it is capable of development and maintains a number
of other relations to the Pcs. The Ucs is continued into its "derivatives."

Here, in the question of the intersystemic relations, the derivatives
play the most important role since they occupy the middle area between
the Ucs and the Cs. Freud immediately states that the study of the derivatives implies that there is no "schematically pure division" between the
two systems (GW X: 289/SE XIV: 190). Some of the derivatives are hardly
distinguishable from the Cs insofar as they are not contradictory; and yet,
even though we would expect them to be able to enter consciousness, the
same derivatives are unconscious and cannot become conscious. So qualitatively they belong to the system Pcs, but in fact they descend from Ucs;
the descent is decisive for their destiny. Freud mentions fantasy formations
in normal people and in neurotics as examples of qualitatively organized
derivatives that cannot become conscious. But other derivatives, as we
saw with the animal phobia, go through distortion and are able to become
conscious. These "exceptions" to inhibition lead Freud to think that the
most important difference in the psychical apparatus lies between the Ucs
and the Pcs. On this "border," the censorship thrusts back the Ucs, but
its derivatives can "circumvent" this censorship, achieve a high degree of
organization, and reach a certain intensity of charge in the Pcs (GW X:
291–92/SE XIV: 193). When, however, this intensity becomes excessive and
the derivatives try to force themselves into consciousness, they are "recognized" as derivatives of the Ucs and are repressed once more by another
censorship operating at the border between the Cs and the Pcs. Thus the
former censorship is exercised against the Ucs itself, while the latter works
against the preconscious derivatives. We must presume, Freud concludes,
that there are multiple censorships (GW X: 290/SE XIV: 192).

The presumption of multiple censorships leads Freud to consider consciousness. Consciousness for Freud is the only part of the psychical apparatus "directly available" to us. It is the part of the psychical apparatus—the surface—related to the external world. Its relation to the internal is not simple (GW X: 291/SE XIV: 192). There is material that belongs to consciousness but that can be temporarily latent. According to Freud, observation shows that the material sharing the attributes of the system Pcs does not become conscious. Moreover, the entry into consciousness is circumscribed by certain dispositions of attention; as we saw already, if the child must pay attention to dogs, it stops the entry into consciousness of the idea of the father. The formation of the dog idea substitute, according to Freud, does not happen in consciousness. Therefore he says, "What is repressed is alien to consciousness and some of the impulses that dominate our ego [Ich]—impulses such as the formation of substitutes and symptoms—and which therefore form the strongest functional antithesis to what is repressed are alien to consciousness" (GW X: 291/SE XIV: 192). When Freud speaks of the ego here in 1915 in "The Unconscious," he is referring to the agency that unifies the drives (unifies the libido) by forming "substitutes and symptoms," that is, objects toward which they move. But as we see here, being alien to consciousness, the ego's impulses are the strongest antithesis to the repressed. The ego therefore is the agency of the censorships.[19]

The "proof" of there being multiple censorships, according to Freud, comes from psychoanalytic treatment. It seems that all the paths from external perception to the Ucs normally remain open; only the paths from the Ucs to the Cs are subject to repression. Although these paths from the external to the internal normally remain open, it is not clear, according to Freud, how much influence the Cs system can have on the Ucs. Nevertheless, psychoanalytic treatment aims to have the Cs influence the Ucs. Treatment consists in the patient being required to form derivatives of the Ucs freely; the patient is directed to overcome the objections of the censorship against the preconscious formation becoming conscious. By overthrowing this censorship, the way is open for the "sublation" of the repression accomplished by the censorship operating at the border between the Ucs and the Pcs. Importantly, Freud adds, "The existence of the censorship between the Pcs and the Cs teaches us that becoming conscious is no mere act of perception, but is probably also a *super-charge*

[*Überbesetzung,* hyper-cathexis], a further advance in the psychical organization" (GW X: 292/SE XIV:194). A super-charge occurs when the two
forces, so to speak, meet up and join forces, making a charge greater than
either charge alone, as for instance in the animal phobia example, when
the charge of the idea of the father joins forces with the anxiety about the
idea of dogs. But here, by speaking of psychoanalytic treatment, Freud is
implying that the most important derivatives involve speech. Since the
psychoanalytic treatment obligates the patient to speak, we are led to the
problem of schizophrenia.

## RECOGNITION (*AGNOSZIERUNG*) OF THE UNCONSCIOUS

Freud turns to schizophrenia because this neurosis—narcissistic psycho-
neurosis—may be able to tell us more about the unconscious, more than
what we have learned so far from transference neuroses such as childhood animal phobia. In schizophrenic autism, there is a split between the
external world and the internal world; in dementia praecox—precocious,
adolescent madness—there is withdrawal, with delusions and halluci-
nations. Freud tries to understand this kind of illness by means of the
relation, or more precisely the "antithesis," between the "ego" (or "I") and
its object (*Objekt*) (GW X: 294/SE XIV: 196). As we saw above, the ego in
Freud unifies the libido and directs it toward an object, a substitute. In
transference neurosis, although the charge seemed to shift from one object
to another, the charge being placed in some object was retained even in
repression. Indeed, because the charge can be transferred, transference
is useful in psychoanalytic therapy. In schizophrenia, however, after the
process of repression, the withdrawn libido does *not* seek a new object,
but retreats into the "ego." Here the object charges "are given up and a
primitive *objectless* condition of narcissism is re-established" (GW X: 295/
SE XIV: 196–97). Schizophrenics exhibit many characteristics that support
the conclusion that the object charges have been given up: their incapac-
ity for transference; their inaccessibility to therapeutic efforts (since there
can be no transference); their repudiation of the external world; signs that
they have given a super-charge to their own "ego"; and the final outcome
of complete apathy (GW X: 295/SE XIV: 197). Yet besides the abandonment of object charges in schizophrenia, there is one more characteristic
that distinguishes the schizophrenic from the neurotic: the schizophrenic

"consciously expresses a great deal." At first, according to Freud, it was impossible to establish an intelligible link between the abandonment of the object charges and these conscious expressions.

Yet the conscious expressions of schizophrenics, according to Freud, are striking: "In schizophrenics we observe—especially in the initial stages, which are so instructive—a number of changes in *speech,* some of which deserve to be regarded from a particular point of view" (GW X: 295/ SE XIV: 197; Freud's emphasis). In order to elaborate on these verbal changes, Freud appropriates observations based on three patients. The first is a female patient in the initial stages of schizophrenia (GW X: 296/SE XIV: 197).[20] The girl was brought to the clinic after a quarrel with her lover; she complained that her eyes were not right, they were twisted. She then proceeded to explain the symptom in coherent language by saying that her lover was a hypocrite, an "eye-twister" or a deceiver; he had twisted her eyes and now she saw the world with different eyes (GW X: 297/SE XIV: 198). The second patient is male. He has withdrawn from all interest in life because he has bad skin; he has blackheads and deep holes in his face that everyone notices. Working on the blackheads remorselessly, he received satisfaction in squeezing them out, because, as he said, something spurted out when he did so. Then he started to think that a deep cavity appeared whenever he got rid of a blackhead; then he reproached himself for having ruined his skin forever by "constantly fiddling about with his hand." The third patient is also male. He took hours to wash and dress; in particular, putting on his socks presented difficulties. Like the first patient, he explained himself. Freud says, "He was disturbed by the idea that he must pull apart the stitches in the knitting, i.e., holes, and to him every hole was a symbol of the female genital aperture" (GW X: 299/SE XIV: 201).

From the observations of these three patients, Freud draws four conclusions. *First,* he notices that the whole train of thought is dominated by the element that has for its content the sensation of some nerve stimulus, for instance, as in the first patient, a feeling that one's eyes are twisted. *Second,* there is a difference between the way the feeling occurs in the schizophrenic and in the hysteric. A hysteric would not only feel the sensation that her eyes are twisted, but also she would have in fact moved: "she would have convulsively twisted her eyes." But also, according to Freud, the hysteric would have had neither any conscious thoughts accompanying the sensation nor any expression of the sensations. It is the words, the conscious expression or explanation of the feelings and impulses, that distinguishes the schizophrenic from the hysteric. Yet, the *third* conclusion makes the schizophrenic look like the hysteric. In the schizophrenic, the words are the words of the body; the explanation of the schizophrenic patients is "organ-speech" (GW X: 297/SE XIV: 198–99). In schizophrenia, Freud notes, words are subject to the same processes as those that form dream images, the primary processes of condensation and displacement. So, by means of such processes, the charge of the object has been transferred to the words. Indeed, as Freud says, "The process may go so far that a single word, if it is especially suitable on account of its numerous connections, takes over the representation of a whole train of thought" (GW X: 298/SE XIV: 199). But the processes of condensation and displacement make the schizophrenic symptoms and formations resemble those of the transference neurotic, the hysteric. In the case of the second patient—Freud says that the second patient is "playing out his castration complex" (GW X: 298/SE XIV: 199)—it is clear from the words "spurting something out, fiddling about with the hand" that the squeezing of the blackheads resembles masturbation, and the cavities left behind symbolize the vagina. Yet, as Freud says, "we have a feeling that something different must be going on here" (GW X: 299/SE XIV: 200). This strange feeling brings us to the *fourth* conclusion. The similarity between the hysteric and the schizophrenic is only *apparent* since "a tiny cavity such as a pore of the skin would hardly be used by a hysteric as a symbol of a vagina, which he is otherwise ready to compare with every imaginable object that encloses a hollow space. Besides, we should expect the *multiplicity* [*Vielheit*] of these cavities to prevent him from using them as a substitute for the female genital" (GW X: 299/SE XIV: 200; I have emphasized "multiplicity" since I shall return to it in the "Interpretation"). As Freud stresses, there is only a "slight similarity between squeezing out a blackhead and an emission from the penis, and still less similarity between the innumerable shallow pores of the skin and the vagina" (GW X: 299/SE XIV: 200–201). However, it is verbally true that something squirts out in both the squeezing of the blackhead and in the emission from the penis and, after all, "a hole is a hole." Freud concludes, "What has dictated the substitution is not the resemblance between the things indicated, but the sameness of the words used to express them. Where the two—word and thing—do not coincide,

the formation of substitutes in schizophrenia deviates from that in transference neurosis" (GW X: 299–300/SE XIV: 201).

The schizophrenic lack of coincidence between the idea of the thing
and the idea of the word leads Freud to define the conscious idea of the
object in this way:

> What we could permissibly call the conscious idea of the object can now
> be carved up into the idea of the word (verbal idea) and the idea of the
> thing (concrete idea); the latter consists in the charge, if not of the direct
> memory-images of the things, at least of remoter memory-traces derived
> from these. (GW X: 300/SE XIV: 201)

The divided definition of the conscious idea of the object (idea of the
thing plus idea of the word) implies that the answer to the question that
has driven the entire essay must lie in unification. First, let us recall the
question as it appeared earlier in the essay:

> When a psychical act (we restrict ourselves to those that have the nature
> of an idea) undergoes the transposition from the system Ucs into the
> system Cs or Pcs, are we to presume that this transposition involves a
> new registration comparable to a second record of the idea in question,
> situated, moreover, in a new psychical locality and side by side with which
> the original unconscious record continues to exist? Or are we to believe
> instead that the transposition consists in an alteration of the state, which
> is fulfilled in the so-called material and in the same locality? (GW X:
> 272–73/SE XIV: 174)

Here is the answer Freud provides near the end of the essay:

> It strikes us all at once that now we know what the difference is between a
> conscious and an unconscious idea. The two are not, as we supposed, dif-
> ferent records of the same content situated in different psychical localities,
> nor yet different functional states of charge in the same locality; but the
> conscious idea comprises the concrete idea [*Sachvorstellung:* representa-
> tion or idea of the thing understood as a subject matter] plus the idea of
> the word corresponding to it, while the unconscious idea is that of the
> thing alone [*Sachvorstellung*]. The system Ucs contains the thing-charges
> [*Sachbesetzung*] of the objects, the first and true object-charges; the sys-
> tem Pcs comes about by the idea of the thing [*Sachvorstellung*] being
> super-charged [*überbesetzt,* hyper-cathected] through the knotting up
> of it with the ideas of the words [*Wortvorstellungen*] corresponding to it.
> It is such super-charges [*Uberbesetzungen*], we may suppose, that bring

about higher psychical organization and make it possible for the primary process to be succeeded by the secondary process which dominates Pcs." (GW X: 300/SE XIV: 201–2)[21]

In order to understand this complicated answer, we must recall the three-way description that defines meta-psychology. First, there is the topographical view; there are regions of the psyche, which means that the psyche is spatial but not in a normal sense and not in a sense correlated with anatomy. But then, second, there is the energetic view of the psychic apparatus. Freud speculates that the drives are quantities of psychic energy, charges seeking discharge. Then, third, there is the dynamic view; the drives are mobile and, being mobile, they can be invested in or placed in, they can occupy and charge different ideas. The important phrase in the second quote is: "The two [conscious idea versus unconscious idea] are *not,* as we supposed, *different* records of the *same* content situated in different psychical localities, *nor* yet *different* functional states of charge in the *same* locality" (my emphasis of the negations and "same" and "different"). This is a negative definition, telling us that the answer to the question is neither of the two hypotheses first considered: neither two *different* records of the *same* content in *different* places nor *different* states of charge in the *same* place. Specifically, the neither-nor definition means that the answer consists in the same state of charge in different places and different content in the same place. In other words, the charge must have the *same* intensity in *different* localities, that is, in both the Ucs and the Cs systems, and what is charged must be *different,* that is, both the idea of the thing and the idea of the word must be charged in the *same* system, in the Cs system. In other words, the "no" of the censorship has been "relieved" or "lifted" (*aufgehoben*), when the idea of the thing has been "knotted" to the idea of the word. The limit of the censorship is transgressed when the unconscious act is able to operate with the activity of the "ego" (GW X: 293/SE XIV: 195). Operating in the "same sense" (*gleichsinnig*) as the activity of the "ego"—"co-operation"—implies translation. The transposition of an unconscious idea of the thing occurs when it is translated into the idea of words that bear the sense. But in fact, the sameness of sense between the idea of the thing and the idea of the word is not all that happens. When co-operation occurs, when there is a coincidence, the anti-charge has been converted to being the same charge as the unconscious one. The "anti" or

"no" of anxiety has been converted into a "yes" of the drive, or, more precisely, into a "no" to the "no," a more than one "no." Putting this claim into
the language of charge, we can say that the unconscious charge has been
added to the charge coming from the preconscious "ego," reinforcing it,
strengthening it, and increasing it (*Verstärkung* [GW X: 293/SE XIV: 195]),
making it a super-charge. As Freud says above, "It is such super-charges,
we may suppose, that bring about higher psychical organization" such as
a cure. In contrast, neurotics, in particular, lack the super-charge of the
word. This is Freud's precise definition of repression: repression denies
"the translation into words, which are to remain knotted to the object.
The idea which is not put into words or the psychical act which has not
received super-charging then remains in the unconscious in a state of
repression" (GW X: 300/SE XIV: 202).[22]

While this definition applies to transference neurosis, it is not clear,
according to Freud, that it applies to schizophrenia. What is common to
both neurosis and schizophrenia is the "ego's" attempt at flight. Insofar
as the schizophrenic does not transfer the charge to another object, his
or her attempt at flight seems more radical and profound than that of the
neurotic (GW X: 302/SE XIV: 203). As we have seen, the specific characteristic of the schizophrenic is verbalization, the words. Repression in the
schizophrenic has withdrawn the charge from the places that represent
the unconscious idea of the object. But it allows the ideas of the word
corresponding to it to receive a more intense charge. According to Freud,
the reason the schizophrenic can speak about his or her symptoms is that
this speaking is the first part of the cure; through the words the making
conscious of the idea of the object is at least potential. With the words,
however, what the schizophrenic is seeking is the lost object, the idea of
the object into which the drive had placed a charge of affect demanding
discharge. To find the object that has been lost, the schizophrenic must
be on the "path" (*Weg*) of these words. Being on the path of the words,
the schizophrenic moves in one of the possible directions of our psychical
activity. Either psychical activity starts from the drives, passes through
the system Ucs, ending up at conscious activity of thought; or beginning with an external stimulus, it passes through the systems Cs and
Pcs, ending in the Ucs with its charges of objects. Despite repression, this
second path must have remained open, and for some distance there is
nothing blocking the efforts the neurosis makes to regain its object. But

the schizophrenic seems to be content with the words. At the end Freud makes a final comparison. "Our philosophizing" looks like—Freud calls this "an undesirable resemblance"—the schizophrenic's way of thinking: it treats concrete things as though they are abstract (GW X: 303/SE XIV: 204). It is not surprising that the essay should end with philosophy, since, as we have seen, Freud explicitly mentions Kant and alludes to Hegel through the word "*Aufhebung.*" The title of section 7 reinforces the connection of Freud's work to philosophy. The entire essay has aimed at the knowledge, the "recognition" (*Agnoszierung*) of the unconscious, and at a correct determination of the "difference" between an unconscious idea and a preconscious one.

## Interpretation: Schizophrenic Thought[23]

The word "*Agnoszierung*" is a strange word. Based on its Greek roots, "*a*" = "not" and "*gignōskein*" = "to know," the word "*Agnoszierung*" means the impossibility of knowledge, as in the word "agnostic." As we have seen, "in and for themselves," the unconscious primary processes are "unrecognizable." To use the terminology of Kant, which is not alien to Freud, "the thing in itself" ("the real," as Lacan would say) is never given. Yet, as the French translation by Laplanche and Pontalis shows, rendering "*Agnoszierung*" as "*reconnaissance,*"[24] the word "*Agnoszierung*" in fact means "recognition." The kind of recognition that is possible is mediated. Unconscious processes "are knowable" only in dreams and in neurosis (GW X: 286/SE XIV: 187); or, "A drive can *never* be an object [*Objekt*] of consciousness—*only* the idea that represents it [*nur die Vorstellung, die ihn repräsentiert*]" (GW X: 275/SE XIV: 177; my emphasis). Meta-psychology entirely concerns the derivatives, the substitutes, and the representatives. But there is another sense to the word "*Agnoszierung.*" It is recognition, but in the specific sense of recognizing a dead body. As we saw in animal phobia, the hysteric constructs an enclave, sets up walls, as if under attack. The Freudian topography—the difference between the Ucs and the Cs—is a *battlefield.* The violent struggle at the borderline between the Cs and the Ucs (the borderline of the Pcs with its multiple censorships) is a struggle to the death. The image of a struggle between the Ucs and the Pcs anticipates Freud's discovery of the death drive in *Beyond the Pleasure Principle.* As is well known, the death drive appears in the compulsion to repeat. Freud interprets the compulsion as the drive "to restore an earlier state."[25] The death drive therefore implies loss, the loss of the original state.[26] The loss, however, always seems already to have happened. The death drive refers to the fact that the drives never had an absolute starting point or aim, an absolute determination: groundlessness. Just as Bergson showed that the whole is not given, Freud shows that the original object is lacking. If the death drive consists in a compulsion to repeat, this repetition is not the repetition of an original model. Indeed, given that the drives are persistent and constant, all drives—both the libido or *Eros* and the death drive—are defined by repetition: "a universal characteristic of drives."[27] But since we have no direct or immediate knowledge of the drives, we are in fact speaking of the re-presentatives. The re-presentatives of the drives (both the re-presentations of the thing, memory traces, and the re-presentatives of the words, acoustic images) are nothing more than minimally repeatable traits. The re-presentatives are charged with energy, have directions and senses, but that energy is anarchic. Indeed, the withdrawal and reuse of energy, as well as all of the terms based in the verb "*setzen*," indicates a "freely mobile" energy.[28] The energies are liberated. Below Freud's dualism, a genuine multiplicity swarms: "we should expect the *multiplicity* [*Vielheit*] of these cavities to prevent [the schizophrenic] from using them as a substitute for the female genital" (GW X: 299/SE XIV: 200; my emphasis). This genuine multiplicity is the outside.

The liberation of energy liberates thought. At the end of "The Unconscious," Freud tells us that thought processes, that is, those acts of charging that are more distant from perception, are in themselves without quality and are unconscious. But then Freud speculates: "Probably however thought proceeds in systems so far remote from original perceptual residues that they have no longer retained anything of the qualities of those residues, and, in order to become conscious, need to be reinforced by new qualities," that is, by the qualities of the words. This comment reinforces the importance of the substitutes, the derivatives, and the re-presentatives. It means that the multiplicity of the unconscious is nothing but the residues of auditory images somehow charged with energy. To speak like Lacan again, the multiplicity is a multiplicity of signifiers. The knot between the signifier and the signified has been untied. All is affirmed; no sublation takes place. If the sublation of repression occurs through translation, then the original text to be translated has been lost. What does translation with Freud become, what does "placing over" (*Über-setzung*) become? Through his insight into the most striking characteristic of schizophrenia, Freud has raised the question that Foucault will ask in "The Thought of the Outside": the question of the being of language. Or by showing that the unconscious is the reservoir from which the schizophrenic draws his or her speech, Freud anticipates Heidegger's claim in "Language" that "language speaks, not man." In the "Summary-Commentary," we noted that the primary processes of condensation and displacement resemble the literary tropes of metaphor and metonymy. But in the schizophrenic—recall that Freud says that "we have a feeling that *something different* must be going on here" (GW X: 299/SE XIV: 200; my emphasis)—the association that leads one idea to have the charge of many (condensation: metaphor) and the association that leads one idea to have the charge of another (displacement: metonymy) is based on "a slight similarity." Schizophrenic thought is indeed "abstract," as Freud says, but not in the sense of a qualitatively undifferentiated, homogenizing association. The abstractness of schizophrenic thought is qualitatively differentiated and heterogeneous, since the slight similarity is not restricted to logical form and mutual contradiction. If we take seriously the absence of the determining object, the absence of the one absolute aim, then the association is necessarily heterogeneous. Schizophrenic thought is timeless in the sense that it is not ordered chronologically, insofar as it is not ordered by a prior form. Schizophrenic thought is "time-ful" insofar as it is open to indefinite destinies.[29] Like Bergson's fluid concept, schizophrenic thought does not consist in molds into which experience is poured. The image of the pore (a protrusion that erupts) and the image of the sock (a container that is porous) indicate that the sense of the word "hole" in the schizophrenic speech is not limited to the idea of cavity; the images indicate that the sense does not contain the whole of the experience of holes. The sense of the word "hole" is open to indefinite variation. It indicates neither a progression to higher organization nor flight; rather, as Deleuze and Guattari would say, schizophrenic thought "becomes" and moves on "a line of flight." Schizophrenic language is, as Foucault would say, "the absence of a work."[30]

## Transition

Meta-psychology is a critique and correction of inner perception. It appears that my consciousness is the foundation of the self, but in reality it is not. Meta-psychology begins with immanent, subjective experience, but goes beyond it. We must presume, according to Freud—it is necessary and legitimate—the existence of the unconscious. Yet meta-psychology is speculative because the knowledge we have of the unconscious is always indirect; it is mediated by the substitutes, the derivatives, and the re-presentatives of the drives. In fact, when Freud discovers the great art of the schizophrenic (in contrast to what happens in transference neurosis), he implies that no one absolute object or aim has ever determined the re-presentatives of the drives. Freud goes beyond immanent subjective experience therefore to *multiplicity*. This is a genuine multiplicity (continuous heterogeneity) because it is a repetition not bound to a prior form. The re-presentatives are nothing more than the slight similarity of a repeatable trait. The multiplicity is displayed in the indefinite variation of schizophrenic speech: "a hole is a hole." Schizophrenic thought therefore could not have been discovered by a psychology of consciousness. Finding a foundation deeper than consciousness, meta-psychology overcomes the psychology of consciousness. It is for this reason that Freudian psychoanalysis has been called an "anti-phenomenology."[31]

# 3

## Consciousness as Distance:
## Husserl's "Phenomenology"
## (the 1929 *Encyclopedia Britannica* Entry)

Freudian psychoanalysis makes a twofold contribution to the project of continental philosophy. On the one hand, like Bergsonism, it places consciousness within a larger system, that of the unconscious. It truly opens the way for the outside. On the other, by means of the priority of the derivatives, it raises the question of the being of language. On the surface, we find neither of these contributions in Husserl. Nevertheless, phenomenology is the dominant movement of continental philosophy in the twentieth century.[1] Like psychoanalysis and Bergsonism, phenomenology develops from the nineteenth-century decline of metaphysics and the ascent of psychology. In the first edition of his first major work, the 1900–1901 *Logical Investigations*, Husserl defines phenomenology as "descriptive psychology."[2] Here, however, phenomenology looks not to be "depth psychology," but a psychology of consciousness. In 1907, in *The Idea of Phenomenology*, Husserl establishes a firm and lasting link between phenomenology and Descartes' philosophy. There is no question that phenomenology elaborates on Descartes' discovery of the "ego cogito." The discovery is made possible by methodical doubt. Husserl adopts this method.[3] Husserlian phenomenology is made possible by the suspension of belief in transcendent reality (the epoché) and then by a reduction to subjective experience, to immanence (the phenomenological reduction). The epoché places immanent, subjective experience on a level that is no longer merely psychological. So in 1913, in the first book of his *Ideas*, Husserl redefines phenomenology as "transcendental." Kant first defines transcendental philosophy as a philosophy concerned with determining the conditions for the possibility of experience. These conditions are not transcendent or otherworldly. Although they are immanent to experience, the conditions cannot, for Kant, be experienced; insofar as they are conditions, they must be different from experience. For Husserl, however, the conditions of experience must be able to be experienced; there must be intuitive evidence for them. So Husserl speaks of transcendental experience. Yet Husserl recognizes the need for the conditions to be different from experience. We see here with phenomenology that difference is the central issue: a difference within experience, a difference that produces a paradoxical ambiguity. It is this paradoxical ambiguity that allows us to understand phenomenology as the "destruction" of the "immediate givenness of consciousness." This destruction makes phenomenology a thought of the outside.

The Husserl text we are going to investigate appears much later than *Ideas I*. It is the final version of his 1929 *Encyclopedia Britannica* entry for "phenomenology."[4] We have chosen this text not only because it is a compact presentation of Husserl's mature thought, but also because, at the beginning, the text was to be written by both Husserl and Heidegger. At the time of the writing, Heidegger had just published *Being and Time*. For the *Encyclopedia Britannica* entry, Heidegger wrote the first half of the second version. He introduces phenomenology historically and in terms of the question of the meaning of being; he defines phenomenology as the return to the being of pure subjectivity, consciousness.[5] Heidegger also made marginal notes on the parts and versions that Husserl himself wrote; Heidegger's marginal notes stress repeatedly the need to conceive transcendental subjectivity within human existence and not as a separation of transcendental subjectivity from human existence. The collaboration fails. Evidence of the failed collaboration can be seen in a letter from Heidegger to Husserl on October 22, 1927; here Heidegger criticizes the second draft Husserl had completed. The appendices to this letter are particularly important (HUA IX: 603/CH: 138–39). Heidegger stresses that beings (or entities) with the sense of mundane being (in the world) cannot be explained by going back to entities with the same mode of being. But then he stresses that this difference does not mean that the transcendental is not an entity or being at all. For Heidegger, in order to understand this difference, we must determine the nature of the being called human existence (*Dasein*). Moreover, Heidegger asks, "what is the mode of being of this absolute ego—in what sense is it the *same* as the ever factical 'I'; in what sense is it *not* the same?" Because Heidegger insists on the centrality of human existence, Husserl thinks that Heidegger has misunderstood the nature of the transcendental, falling into a kind of anthropologism. But Heidegger's criticisms force Husserl to try to understand how one can disentangle the transcendental from the psychological.

## Summary-Commentary: Disentangling the Transcendental from the Psychological and Its Consequences

### PURE PSYCHOLOGY: ITS FIELD OF EXPERIENCE, ITS METHOD, AND ITS FUNCTION[6]

In the introductory opening paragraph, Husserl says that the term "phenomenology" refers to two things. On the one hand, it refers to a new kind of descriptive method, and on the other it refers to an a priori science derived from the method. The science is to be an "instrument" (an "organon," that is, a body of methodological rules for acquiring knowledge, a propaedeutic) for the development of philosophy, and thereby a reform of all the sciences. Insofar as phenomenology will achieve what philosophy seems to have always sought, a rigorous grounding of the sciences, Husserl speaks of a "philosophical phenomenology." But here at the beginning, Husserl also speaks of psychological phenomenology. The phenomenological reforms apply first of all to empirical psychology. And once applied, we can then speak of phenomenological psychology. But more importantly, psychological phenomenology stands "nearer to our natural thinking," so it is able to serve as a preliminary step leading to an understanding of philosophical phenomenology (HUA IX: 278/CH: 159).[7] We start from the natural way of thinking, but this starting point does not define phenomenology. Phenomenology must be transcendental, not psychological. Always, in Husserl, one must pay attention to the word "nature." That psychological phenomenology is closer to our natural way of thinking means that transcendental phenomenology is not natural. It is a strange and unfamiliar kind of thinking.

According to Husserl, modern psychology looks to be the science of the psychical taken within the "concrete context" of nature. Human reality and animal reality seem to belong to nature. So psychology looks to be a branch of anthropology or zoology. However, nature is the universal theme of a pure natural science. A *pure* natural science would exclude all extraphysical predications of reality. Likewise, a *pure* psychology would take nothing physical into account. Is a pure psychology possible? As Husserl says, "It is by no means clear from the very outset, however, how far the idea of a pure psychology—as a psychological discipline sharply separate in itself and as a parallel to the pure physical science of nature—has a meaning that is legitimate and necessary of realization" (HUA IX: 279/ CH: 160). So what we are trying to do here in this first part is *disentangle* psychology from physical science, the psyche (or the egoical) from nature. We are engaged in a project of purification.

According to Husserl, in order to establish the idea of a pure psychology, we must first clarify what is peculiar to experience, and especially what is peculiar to the pure experience of the psychical (HUA IX: 279/CH: 160–61). For Husserl, no phenomenology is possible without a "turning back" or reversal of the gaze. This refocusing, Husserl says, "necessarily takes place as reflection, as a turning back of a gaze [*Blick*] which had previously been directed elsewhere" (HUA IX: 279/CH: 160–61). When we are engaged in a thing, even an ideal object such as a number, we are focused on the thing and not on the psychical experience as such. Through reflection, however, instead of grasping simply the matter as such, we grasp the subjective lived experiences (*Erlebnisse*), in which we become conscious of the things; we grasp the lived experiences in which they *appear* (where "appearance" is taken in the broadest sense). This reflection loses nothing of the world; instead, the things on which our gaze would be focused naturally are included *in* the psychical lived experiences; they have become *phenomena*. Husserl says, "If this realm of what we call 'phenomena' proves to be the possible field for a pure psychological discipline related exclusively to phenomena, we can understand the designation of it as *phenomenological psychology*" (HUA IX: 279–80/CH: 161; Husserl's emphasis). The most general essential characteristic of phenomena is to be as "consciousness of" or "'appearance of' the specific things, thoughts (judged states of affair, grounds, conclusions), plans, decisions, hopes, and so forth" (HUA IX 279/CH: 161). Here (as elsewhere), Husserl introduces the Scholastic term "intentionality" to designate "the basic character of being as consciousness, as consciousness of something" (HUA IX: 280/CH:

161). Neo-Kantianism (such as we find it, for example, in Hans Rickert) had conceived intentionality as a characteristic of *only* the lived experiences that are directed toward *real* things. The Neo-Kantian conception implies that there are lived experiences (such as those of fantasy, memory, or even of mathematics) that are non-intentional. Instead, for Husserl, intentionality is no longer dependent on reality; for Husserl and for phenomenology in general, *every* lived experience is a directedness-toward.[8] Lived experience, in other words, as Husserl says in the *Britannica* essay, consists in a "relativity" (*Relativität*) (HUA IX: 279/CH: 161).[9] As in *Ideas I* (in 1913),[10] here in the *Britannica* essay Husserl describes this relativity in terms of *noesis* and *noema*. The psychic field consists in a correlation between *noesis* (thought) and *noema* (the object thought about), the *intentio* and the *intentum*. The general concept of intentionality includes many cases. Consciousness of something is not an empty holding of something. Every phenomenon has its whole intentional form, but at the same time it has a structure, which, through intentional analysis, can be broken into components, which themselves are intentional. Husserl provides the example of the perception of a die (HUA IX: 280/CH: 161). This is a particularly significant example since a die, that is, a cube, would seem to be the most objective of objects. Yet the description shows how it comes to be through a process in which the varying modes of its appearing (produced by changes in orientation and perspective, which then disclose sides seen and unseen) are subjectively synthesized: "one finds that every phase and portion of the flux is already in itself 'consciousness of'—but in such a manner that there is formed within the constant emerging of new phases the synthetically unified awareness that this is one and the same object" (HUA IX: 280/CH: 162). According to Husserl, the intentional structure of any process of perception has its fixed essential type, which must be realized in all its complexity in order for a simple physical body to be perceived. This applies to every category of psychical process; there is a fixed essential type for each process. Thus, "[f]or psychology, the universal task presents itself: to investigate systematically the elementary intentionalities, and from out of these unfold the typical shapes of intentional lived-experiences, their possible variants, their syntheses to new shapes, their structural composition, and from this advance towards a descriptive knowledge of the totality of lived experiences, towards a comprehensive type of a life of the psyche" (HUA IX: 281/CH: 162). Husserl adds that the descriptive knowledge mentioned here will have validity beyond the experiences of the psychologist's own particular psychic existence. This addition is not insignificant. It implies that for phenomenology knowledge is defined as being "for everyone." In order for knowledge to reach this "universal" level—in other words, to be genuine knowledge—it must be intersubjective. Phenomenology is always and necessarily the phenomenology of intersubjectivity.

Although we can see a whole range of tasks arising with the idea of phenomenological psychology, we do not yet know if we have a field for a science, a field of being free from everything psycho-physical so that we have a *pure* psychology. Here we encounter difficulties that have remained hidden from psychologists. Husserl says, "Ultimately, the great difficulty rests on the way that already the self-experience of the psychologist is everywhere *intertwined* [*verflochten*] with external experience, with that of extra-psychical real things" (HUA IX: 282/CH: 163; my emphasis). The difficulty that Husserl is confronting is the *disentangling* of the purely psychical from the physical or natural, and it anticipates the difficulty of disentangling the transcendental from the psychical to which Husserl will turn in a moment in the *Britannica* entry. Moreover, Husserl's characterization of the experience of extrapsychic real things as "external experience" means that psychic experience is *internal:* "genuine inner experience." What is at issue here is the possibility of a really pure self-experience and a really pure psychic datum. The question of access to this purity brings us to the method of the phenomenological reduction (HUA IX: 281–82/CH: 163). This method is the foundation of pure psychology. With the reduction, we must not think that we are retreating inside away from the world; the world itself is *included* in inner experience; it will no longer be external. As Husserl says, "The experienced 'exterior' does not belong to one's intentional interiority, although certainly the experience itself belongs to it as experience—*of* the exterior. Exactly this same thing is true of every kind of awareness directed at something out there in the world" (HUA IX: 282/CH: 163). If the phenomenologist wants to break through to his own consciousness as pure phenomenon, a consistent epoché is required.[11] That is, in what is accomplished within phenomenological reflection, one is required to suspend all the unreflective accomplishments (which are accompanying the reflection) that posit objective being; this suspension includes inhibiting every way in which, through a judgment, the world is pulled in as "existing" straightforwardly for the psychologist. With the epoché, I am no longer in the world, but rather the world is in me as a phenomenon, related to me; it no longer exists over and against me. The specific experience of the object (this house, for example, but also the world) is and remains according to its essential content, inseparably experience of. ... One cannot describe an intentional lived experience without at the same time describing the object of that consciousness as an object. The *universal* epoché—the putting between parentheses—"shuts out, from the phenomenological field, the world as it exists for the subject in *simple absoluteness*" (HUA IX: 282/CH: 163; my emphasis). The world is now relative: the world as world but also as given *in* consciousness. Anything that we took as absolute is now replaced by the respective sense (*Sinn*) of each in consciousness in its various modes of perceiving, believing, etc. As Husserl says, "In going back [*Rückgang*] from the unities posited in the natural attitude to the multiple modes of consciousness in which they appear, the unities as inseparable from these multiplicities—but as 'bracketed'—are also to be reckoned among what is purely psychical, and always specifically in the appearance-character in which they present themselves" (HUA IX: 282–83/CH: 164). Husserl then outlines the two components of the phenomenological reduction, the reduction to the purely psychical: (1) the methodical and consistent epoché of every objective positing in the psychic sphere, both of individual phenomena and of the whole psychic field in general; (2) the methodically practiced seizing and describing of the multiple "appearances" as appearances of their objective units as units of sense. Now we should note that the phenomenological reduction so far only gives us phenomenon as purely psychic; *it is not yet transcendental.* So far, we have only *disentangled* the psychical from the physical. The purely psychical directs us to a twofold description, that of thought (the *noesis*) and that of the object of thought (the *noema* or sense).[12] Only the phenomenological reduction provides "genuine [*echte*] 'inner experience' [*Erfahrung*]." Husserl has placed scare quotes around "inner experience," because what is at stake is our understanding of the inside and the outside.

Husserl raises another question: Does the unity of the field of phenomenological experience assure the possibility of a psychology exclusively based on it? In other words, is a pure phenomenological psychology assured by this field? According to Husserl, more is needed. An empirically

pure science of facts does not assure that everything psycho-physical has
been abstracted. Psychology must be an a priori science, which means that
the fact that the experience is mine, is located in me, becomes irrelevant,
or, more precisely, it becomes an example. As an example, it serves as a
foundation for a free but intuitive variation of the factual individual and
communal psyche. If the theoretical gaze now directs itself to the invariant in the variation, the eidetically necessary typical form, the *eidos* of the
psyche, arises. If it is to be intuitively presentable or intuitively thinkable,
the *eidos,* Husserl says, must manifest itself throughout all the potential
forms of psychic being in particular cases.[13] Phenomenological psychology
must be established as "eidetic phenomenology." The eidetic reduction,
in addition to the phenomenological reduction, gives us access to the
invariant essential shapes of the total pure, a priori psychic sphere (HUA
IX: 284/CH: 165).

That phenomenological psychology will be an eidetics allows Husserl
to claim that it is now possible to construct an "exact" empirical science
of psychology. Since "modern times," however, the exactitude of empirical psychology has been sought on the model of the exact pure sciences
of nature. Yet since we have just disentangled the psychological from the
physical, it must be the case that the sense of exactitude is different in the
two sciences. So, on the one hand, Husserl stresses that the principal sense
of exactitude in the natural sciences lies in its being founded on an a priori
form-system; specific disciplines such as pure geometry, pure theory of
time and motion, allow us to have a thinkable nature. This formal system
is then applied to factual nature, thereby giving the inductive sciences a
degree of exactitude. This application gives a new methodical sense to
empirical natural science: "that of working out for all vague concepts and
rules their indispensable basis of rational concepts and laws" (HUA IX:
285/CH: 166).[14] Psychology, however, remains different from the natural
sciences even though there is a resemblance between the two; both sciences must draw their rigor from "the rationality of essences." So, in psychology, we have an a priori set of types without which psychic being as
such would be inconceivable. This set of types "produces a prodigious field
of exactness that can be carried over into research on the psyche," and here
Husserl adds an important qualification, "without the intervening link
of Limes-Idealization" (HUA IX: 285/CH: 166). This qualification means
that in psychology, we have rigor without the idealization of limit-forms

as in geometry, that is, without the forms toward which a variation would approximate; here in the realm of the psychic we do not have such forms and therefore do not have approximation. The kind of rigor that defines the psychic opens up a different kind of variation, to which we shall return below in the "Interpretation." It is a kind of variation that maintains a similarity of structure but also opens itself to becoming otherwise.

Husserl admits that phenomenological psychology will not be able to account for everything in psychology, in particular the psycho-physical relation. Although the psycho-physical relation would require the a priori forms of the physical, it would also require the a priori of phenomenological psychology. Thus, according to Husserl, the systematic construction of a phenomenologically pure psychology demands the following tasks: (1) the description of peculiarities universally belonging to the essence of intentional lived experiences, which includes the most general rules of synthesis; (2) the exploration of single forms of intentional lived experiences which in essential necessity must or can present themselves to the psyche. The movement here is from universal or general structure (general rules of synthesis) to more specific structures (single forms). Then we have (3) the demonstration and eidetic description of the total structure of psychic life in general, and the essential kind of a universal stream of consciousness (of what Bergson would call the duration). Here we are talking about movement or flow or dynamic, not structures. Finally, we have (4) the term "I" designates a new direction for research, in reference to the essential forms of habituality. The fourth task indicates that the "I" or "ego" is historical; it relies in its "convictions" on past acquisitions. Husserl calls these four kinds of investigations "static" investigations, the static descriptions of essences. But such static investigations lead to an all-pervasive genesis (which itself is eidetic) that governs the whole life and development of the personal "I." As Husserl says, "So on top of the first 'static phenomenology' will be constructed in higher levels a dynamic or genetic phenomenology. As the first and founding genesis, it will deal with that of passivity—genesis in which the 'I' does not actively participate" (HUA IX: 286/CH: 167). As we shall see, the idea of genesis will be central to Heidegger's and Merleau-Ponty's thinking. In fact, Heidegger's thought (after the so-called "turn") revolves around an event called "*Ereignis*" (event of propriation), while Merleau-Ponty's final thought revolves around the idea of a "muffled historicity"; both ideas refer to a fundamental experience that opens the possibility of history. Anticipating Part II, Husserl makes a historical reference (to "David Hume's great discovery" of association) in order to explicate the genetic investigation. In genetic investigations, we are interested in the a priori genesis out of which a real spatial world constitutes itself for the psyche in habitual validity. The idea of an a priori genesis leads to the problem Husserl develops in *The Crisis* and in the texts associated with *The Crisis* such as "The Origin of Geometry" and the text known as "The Earth Does not Move": "the static and then the genetic phenomenology of reason" (HUA IX: 287/CH: 167). As we shall see in the "Interpretation," this kind of genetic phenomenology of reason is why one can speak of an *unconscious* in Husserl.

## Phenomenological Psychology and Transcendental Phenomenology

We come now to the heart of the *Britannica* essay. As the Hume reference indicated, we are now going to adopt a historical outlook.[15] A purely phenomenological psychology does not *just* have the function of reforming empirical psychology. For deeply rooted reasons—this reason would be the "semblance" (the *Schein*) of which Husserl will speak later here—phenomenological psychology can also serve as "a preliminary step for laying open the essence of a transcendental phenomenology" (HUA IX: 287/CH: 167). As we know, the idea of transcendental philosophy did not historically originate from the needs of psychology. Originally in the modern tradition, psychology had been placed in the service of philosophy because Descartes had awakened the transcendental problem. As Husserl says, "In Descartes' Meditations, the thought that had become the guiding one for 'first philosophy' was that, all of 'reality,' and finally the whole world of what exists and is so *for us,* is only as the representational content of our own representations" (HUA IX: 287/CH: 167; my emphasis). "Descartes' transcendental reversal [*Wendung*]" is expressed in this "for us";[16] "for us" defines all phenomenology. The idea of *reality being for us* motivates, according to Husserl, all transcendental problems, whether they are genuine or false. Descartes' method of doubt brought "transcendental subjectivity" to light for the first time; but also, the "ego cogito" led to the first conceptual formulation of transcendental subjectivity. Yet, although Locke was engaged, according to Husserl, in a transcendental-philosophical interest, he transformed Descartes' transcendentally pure *mens* into the *human soul.* So, as Husserl says, "[Locke] is the founder of psychologism as a transcendental philosophy on the basis of a psychology of inner experience" (HUA IX: 287/CH: 168). Psychologism, as noted in the introduction to this chapter, is the philosophical position that claims that all knowledge and all sense of reality is based on the human, where "human" means a soul that is itself something that exists as other things in nature or as the world exist; thus psychologism is a form of relativism and therefore a form of skepticism. Already in the *Logical Investigations,* Husserl had presented criticisms of psychologism. But here late in his life, he still demands (speaking like Heidegger) the *overcoming (Überwindung)* of psychologism. The overcoming of psychologism, according to Husserl, must "expose the fundamental absurdity of psychologism, but also [it must do] justice to its transcendentally significant kernel of truth" (HUA IX: 287/ CH: 168). Its kernel of truth and its attractiveness throughout modern philosophy lies in the "doubleness" *(Zweideutigkeit)* of all the concepts of the subjective. The uncovering of this "ambiguity" *(Doppeldeutigkeit)* must involve a "sharp separation" and at the same time the "parallelization" of pure phenomenological psychology (genuine inner experience) and transcendental phenomenology as genuine transcendental philosophy. The ambiguity justifies, Husserl says, our starting point in psychology. Because the sense of the transcendental problem (even in Descartes) is obscure and unstable, we must determine the "genuine" or "true" *(echte)* transcendental problem.

The essential sense of the transcendental problem includes its "universality" *(Universalität).*[17] Thus it places in question the world and all the sciences investigating the world. The transcendental problem arises from a "general reversal" *(allgemeinen Umwendung)* of the "natural attitude." This is the attitude in which everyday life as a whole as well as the positive sciences operate; it is the "general field" of our practical and theoretical activities. Husserl defines the natural attitude in this way: "the world is for us the self-evidently existing [*seiende*] universe of realities which are continuously pre-given [*beständig vorgegeben*] in question-less givenness [*fragloser Vorhandenheit*]" (HUA IX: 288/CH: 168). Here the word translated as "givenness" is "*Vorhandenheit*": "presence." The quote therefore means that the world looks to be "pre-given," that is, ahead of time, in unquestioned presence. When the theoretical interest, however, abandons the natural attitude and *reverses* its gaze to the life of consciousness—"in which the 'world' is for us precisely that, the world which is present [*vorhandene*] *to us*" (Husserl's emphasis)—we find ourselves in a new epistemic "situation" (*Lage*). The word "situation" renders the German term "*Lage*," which has a geological sense of layer or bed (as in bedrock); this goes along with the image of the soil (*Boden*). The "new layer" is this: *every* (that is, universally) sense that the world has for us is now seen as a conscious sense, a sense that is formed in subjective genesis. And every ontological validity, that is, everything that counts as existing (again universally), is fulfilled *within ourselves*. This placing of every sense and validity within ourselves even concerns the world in its self-evident determination; in particular, it concerns the sense that the world exists in and for itself, whether anyone experiences it or not. Once the world in this "full universality" has been related to the subjectivity of consciousness, in whose living consciousness it makes its appearance precisely as "the" world in its varying sense, then its whole mode of being acquires a dimension of unintelligibility or questionableness (HUA IX: 289/CH: 169). Having become a problem, the subjective genesis of the world requires clarification. This is the question: How could consciousness in its immanence bring forth such accomplishments of sense and validity? In other words, the question is: "How it [consciousness], so to speak, manages in its immanence that something which manifests itself can present itself *as* something existent in itself [*als an sich seiend*], and not only as something meant but as something authenticated in coherent experience?" (HUA IX: 289/CH: 169; Husserl's emphasis). We should note the word "immanence." On the one hand, the word implies that the question is: How does the world acquire a transcendent sense from the immanence of our consciousness? On the other, "immanence" implies that the subjective genesis of the world's transcendent sense lies deeper (the new layer that was previously hidden) than what is immediately given to consciousness. As we saw above in relation to phenomenological psychology, genetic phenomenology suggests something like the unconscious. The genesis must be deeper since the question implies that this genesis is taking place "in us," that in the "us" the world gains sense and validity; yet "as humans, we ourselves are supposed to belong to the world." This "in us" implies that the world belongs to us, to us who are nevertheless a part of the world. We are mundane or worldly, yet the mundane sense is generated in us. This relativity "to us," according to Husserl, does not, however, apply only to this factual world and this factual subjectivity. In its universality, "the relativity" applies to every conceivable world and subjectivity (HUA IX: 289/CH: 169). The recognition that the investigation in which we are engaged is eidetic raises the transcendental problem to its final level.

By determining the investigation as eidetic, it looks as though phenomenological psychology is the place to carry out all transcendental elucidation (HUA IX: 290/CH: 170). Yet, Husserl stresses, we must not overlook the fact that psychology is a positive science; it is a science operating within the natural attitude, the natural attitude being that in which the simply present world is the thematic soil (*Boden*). What it wants to explore are the psyches and communities of psyches that are actually to be found "*in* the world" (*in der Welt*). Thus, Husserl says, even in the eidetic investigations of phenomenological psychology, the psyche retains the "*ontological sense* [*Seinsinn*] of *mundane presence* [*weltlich Vorhandenen*]; it is merely related to possible real [*reale*] worlds" (HUA IX: 290/CH: 170; my emphasis). This comment implies that the phenomenological psychologist has not reopened the question of the sense of being. In other words, he has not put the conviction that the real is presence, the world as *Vorhandenheit,* into question. Even as an eidetic phenomenologist, the psychologist is transcendentally naive: he takes the possible "minds" (*Seelen*) completely according to the relative sense of the word as those of humans and animals considered purely and simply as present in a possible spatial world (HUA IX: 290–91/CH: 170). So, Husserl says, "If, however, we let the transcendental interest be decisive, instead of the natural-worldly interest, then psychology as a whole receives the stamp of what is transcendentally problematic, and thus it can by no means supply the premises for transcendental philosophy" (HUA IX: 291/CH: 170). By no means can psychology be the premise for transcendental philosophy since it does *not* transcend the world determined ontologically as presence. Likewise, the subjectivity of consciousness to which it goes back cannot be the one to which we return in our questioning into the transcendental. We must keep the sense of the transcendental problem sharply in view. We must be able to "cut apart" (*scheiden*) what is problematic and what is not problematic. The theme of transcendental philosophy is the intentional correlation that belongs essentially to any possible world, and not just possible worlds of *this* world, but the ontological sense of any possible world *whatsoever.*

So the ontological sense of all possible worlds must be clarified. How? Here is Husserl's answer: "Like every meaningful question, this transcendental question presupposes a soil [ground, *Boden*] of unquestioned being, in which all means of solution must be contained. This soil is here the subjectivity of that kind of conscious life in which a possible world, of whatever kind, is constituted as presence [*vorhandene*]" (HUA IX: 291/CH: 171). What is in question here is the sense of being as *Vorhandenheit*. The movement in which Husserl has been engaged consists in moving from questionless presence to making presence questionable (through the "to us," which is mundane and yet must be extra-mundane), and then to an unquestioned ground or soil (*Boden*), which is transcendental subjectivity (HUA IX: 291/CH: 171). We have also seen an image develop. Speaking of soil and layer, the image Husserl is suggesting is that of a tree where the natural attitude is the trunk, the branches are the sciences, and the roots are transcendental subjectivity. What guides the movement from questionless presence to the unquestioned soil into the roots is the universality of the transcendental question. We must not confuse this unquestioned *Boden* with what the transcendental question, "in its universality," puts into question. The entire realm of the transcendentally naive and therefore every possible world simply claimed in the natural attitude have been put into question. Finally, as well, all positive sciences are to be subjected to the epoché, *including psychology itself.* If we do not follow the universality of the question, then we find ourselves in a *circle* since we would be basing an answer to the question on what has been put into question, that is, on psychology (HUA IX: 292/CH: 171). In other words, we would be using as our ground one of the things that we are trying to ground; we would be using a mundane region (even though it is eidetic) to ground all mundane regions. But now, according to Husserl, by recognizing the circle, we face the "paradoxical ambiguity" (*paradoxen Zweideutigkeit*); the subjectivity and the consciousness to which the transcendental question recurs can thus really *not* be the subjectivity and consciousness with which psychology deals (HUA IX: 292/CH: 171). This negative claim—the subjectivity to which we are returning in the transcendental question is *not* the psychological subjectivity—is truly paradoxical since the negation does not imply a real difference; we shall return to the difference below in the "Interpretation."

Thanks to this astonishing claim, we have a new question: "Are 'we' then supposed to be dual beings, psychological, as human subjectivities in the world, and at the same time transcendental, as the subjects of a transcendental, world-constituting life?" (HUA 292/CH: 171; Husserl's scare quotes). Husserl puts the "we" (the "*wir*") in scare quotes because it is precisely this "we" that is at issue. We must now clarify the duality. The phenomenological-psychological reduction gives us access to the "I" and the "we" of ordinary discourse, and, as we know, this psychic subjectivity can be modified into eidetic form. Then Husserl says,

> Transcendental subjectivity, which is inquired into in the transcendental problem, and which subjectivity is presupposed in its ontological ground [*Seinsboden*], is nothing other than this "I myself" and "we ourselves"; but not as found in the natural attitude of everyday or of positive science, that is, as apperceived as little pieces of existence [*Bestandstücke*] of the objectively present world before us, but rather as subjects of conscious life, *in* which this world and all that is present—for "us"—"makes" itself through certain apperceptions (HUA IX: 292/CH: 172; Husserl's italics; note the italicized "in").

The term "apperception" comes from Leibniz, but it makes its most famous appearance in Kant: "the transcendental unity of apperception." It means a background perception or a background awareness of consciousness. It means self-awareness. Husserl continues, "As humans with souls and flesh [*leiblich*] present in the world, we are *for* 'ourselves,' we are *appearances* [*Erscheinendes*] standing within a multiple intentional life, 'our' life, *in which* this presence [*vorhandene*] makes itself [*sich macht*] for us apperceptively, with its entire sense-content" (HUA IX: 292/172; Husserl's emphasis of "in which," mine of "for" and "appearances"). Here we have a variant of the word "*Erscheinung*" (appearance); it is connected to a word to which Husserl will turn in a moment: the word "*Schein*," which means both deceptive semblance and shining through. "However," Husserl says, and this is an important "however," "The (apperceived) present [*vorhandene*] I and we *presuppose* an (apperceiving) I and we, for which they [that is, the first apperceived I and we] are present, which, however, is *not* itself present again in the same sense" (HUA IX: 292/CH: 172; my emphasis). This is the most difficult discussion of the entire essay. Husserl is arguing the following: If the present I and we are present, as appearances (in which the sense of the present I and we is made), then insofar as they are appearances, the present I and we must be present *to* or *for* another I and we; then, this second I and we *cannot* be present in the same sense as the first I and we. Husserl is making an ontological difference between one sense of presence and another.[18]

The second sense of the I and we, the transcendental sense, is indeed given to us, Husserl claims, directly in a transcendental experience. The "transcendental inner experience" results from the *universal epoché* that the sense of the transcendental question requires. We must bracket the pure psyches and the pure phenomenological psychology related to them, thereby transforming them into transcendental phenomena. We reduce the pure psychological element to transcendental pure subjectivity, that is, to that which performs and posits *within itself* the apperception of the world and *therein* the objectivating apperception of a "psyche [belonging to] animal reality." I must posit the world, including my own human existence, as mere phenomena, and then investigate the entire apperception "of" the world, and, in particular, the apperception of my soul. This too is an astonishing idea: transcendental phenomenology investigates the apperception of *my own soul,* how my soul is present. As Husserl says, it takes practice to achieve this universal epoché: "For the transcendental philosopher, who through a previous universal resolve of his will has instituted in himself the firm habituality of the transcendental 'bracketing,' even this 'mundanization' of consciousness which is omnipresent in the natural attitude is inhibited once and for all" (HUA IX: 293/CH: 173). This experience opens up an endless ontological field, which is "parallel" to the purely psychological one. The parallelism brings us to the paradox, "My transcendental ego is thus evidently 'different' [*verschieden*] from the natural ego, but by no means as a second, as one separated [*getrenntes*] from it in the usual [*natürlichen*] sense of the word, just as on the contrary it is by no means bound up with it or intertwined [*verflochtenes*] with it, in the usual [*natürlichen*] sense of these words" (HUA IX: 294/CH: 173). This is the paradox: different and yet not separate, intertwined and bound together, but not in the usual, habitual, or natural (that is, in the natural attitude) way of using these words. We have here an identity and a difference of the I and the we, but Husserl is using neither "identity" nor "difference" in the natural or habitual sense. Instead of the natural sense, there is a "complex interpenetration of ontological senses [*Ineinander des Seinsinnes*]" (HUA IX: 294/CH: 173). As we have seen, all the claims that hold for transcendental subjectivity hold for intersubjectivity. So, after the transcendental reduction, the psychic intersubjectivity leads to transcendental intersubjectivity. The "ontological soil" (*Seinsboden*) is transcendental intersubjectivity from which everything transcendent (that is, "all real, mundane beings": "*alles real weltlich Seiende*") receives its "existential sense" or "ontological sense" (*Seinsinn*): "transcendental sense-bestowal."

Now, according to Husserl, we see that psychologism rests on deep grounds: "Its power lies in an essential transcendental *semblance* [*Schein*] which, since undisclosed, had to remain effective" (HUA IX: 295/CH: 174). We shall return to this word "*Schein*" in the "Interpretation" below since the word suggests distance. The word "*Schein*," however, is ambiguous; it means both a deceptive appearance—Husserl had already anticipated this term when he spoke of the I and the we as "appearances," as *Erscheinungen*—and a shining through. Psychologism remains compelling because of the duplication of consciousness between psychological and transcendental. The two *seem* to be the same, seem to be one, the human mind (the psychological), but they are two, with the transcendental *shining through* the psychological. Because we have clarified the "*Schein*," we can see not only the "independence" (*Unabhängigkeit*) of transcendental phenomenology from phenomenological pure psychology, but also the propaedeutic usefulness of phenomenological psychology as a means of ascent to transcendental phenomenology (HUA IX: 295/CH: 174). As we saw at the beginning of this part, historically, as with Descartes, the ascent to transcendental phenomenology through phenomenological psychology was not the path taken; pure phenomenological psychology was not available. The direct path to transcendental phenomenology lies in connecting immediately the phenomenological and eidetic reduction to the disclosure, in an intuition, of the transcendental relativity. The path taken here, which is indirect, was through the establishment of phenomenological psychology. Like all positive sciences, phenomenological psychology, despite its novelty, has the advantage of being accessible. Only once phenomenologically pure psychology has become clear are we then able to clarify the true sense of the transcendental field of problems and of the transcendental reduction. Then we see that the "doctrinal content" of phenomenological psychology must be converted into transcendental terms. Although Husserl calls this conversion "a mere reversal," he also says—as he does often late in his career—that we must remember that "the transcendental attitude involves such a change of focus from one's entire form of life-style, one which goes so completely beyond all previous experiencing of life, that it will, in virtue of its absolute *strangeness*, necessarily be difficult to understand" (HUA IX: 295/CH: 174; my emphasis). In particular, there are two basic difficulties: (1) understanding the true method of "inner experience," which belongs to the possibility of an "exact" psychology as a rational science of facts, and (2) understanding what properly defines the transcendental way of posing questions and its methods. Overcoming these difficulties, we see that the transcendental interest is, according to Husserl, the highest and ultimate scientific interest, which means that transcendental theories should be formed into an autonomous, absolute system of transcendental philosophy. As well, within the absolute system of transcendental philosophy itself, by means of showing us the characteristic features of the natural attitude in contrast to the transcendental, the possibility should be exhibited of "reinterpreting" all transcendental, phenomenological doctrine into those of natural positivity (HUA IX: 296/CH: 175). We have gone from the ascent of a "reversal" (*Wendung*) to a descent of "reinterpretation" (*Umdeutung*). In other words, remarkable consequences follow from the significance of transcendental phenomenology.

## TRANSCENDENTAL PHENOMENOLOGY AND PHILOSOPHY AS UNIVERSAL SCIENCE WITH ABSOLUTE FOUNDATIONS

Transcendental phenomenology realizes the idea of a universal ontology as the systematic unity of all conceivable a priori sciences; it "overcomes" dogmatism (HUA IX: 296/CH: 175). The ontology, however, would not be based on a dogmatic foundation, but on a foundation given to us by the phenomenological reduction. Phenomenology as the science of all conceivable transcendental phenomena is *eo ipso* the a priori science (ontology) of all conceivable beings (*Seienden*). And this ontology is not limited to objective being, objectively existing beings, but rather it concerns the full concretion of being in general including subjectivity and even transcendental subjectivity itself. Thus a phenomenology properly carried through is the truly universal ontology, as opposed to the "illusory" (*scheinbar*) universal ontology of positivity. This universal ontology means that every a priori is ultimately prescribed in its ontological validity precisely as a transcendental "achievement." The subjective method of this achievement is itself made transparent. Thus, for Husserl, there are no paradoxes; no crisis of the foundations can exist. As will become apparent in the *Crisis* texts, the Husserlian concept of crisis is a lack of elucidation of the subjective achievements; in other words, it is objectivism, a mere ontology of the object. As Husserl says, "The consequence that arises with reference to the a priori sciences that have come into being historically and in transcendental naivety is that only a radical, phenomenological grounding [*Begründung*] can transform them into true, methodical, fully self-justifying sciences. But precisely by this, they will cease to be positive (dogmatic) sciences and become dependent branches [*Zweigen*] of the one phenomenology as universal eidetic ontology" (HUA IX: 297/CH: 176). We see here again the image of the tree and its roots. Even a "branch" like mathematics, which is an exact science, still requires a subjective grounding. But also the factual sciences (like biology) require phenomenological grounding. In order to have a universal and fully grounded science of empirical facts, it is necessary, according to Husserl, that the "complete universe of the a priori" be presented in its relativity to the transcendental subjectivity. Even a universal science of facticity (contingencies, in other words, such as our bodies, history, and community) must have a phenomenological form; Husserl calls this phenomenology of facticity an empirical (rather than transcendental) phenomenology, which would be based on the "foundation of eidetic phenomenology as the science of any possible transcendental subjectivity whatsoever" (HUA IX: 298/CH: 176).

Therefore, according to Husserl, through phenomenology we restore the most originary concept of philosophy, as universal science based on radical self-justification, which is alone truly science in the Platonic and Cartesian sense. Phenomenology is identical with the philosophy that encompasses all genuine knowledge. It consists in both eidetic phenomenology (universal ontology) as first philosophy, and in second philosophy, the science of the universe of "facta" (HUA IX: 299/CH: 177). All the traditional problems of reason, all the traditional philosophical problems, have their place in phenomenology. On the basis of the absolute sources of transcendental experience (eidetic intuition), these problems obtain their genuine foundation for the first time and their possible solution. Phenomenology then recognizes its particular function within a possible life of humanity at the transcendental level. For Husserl, "the ultimate and highest" problem is that of a humanity that lives and moves in truth and genuineness. Phenomenology brings about the relative resolution of this problem by recognizing intuitively the absolute norms. Phenomenology is directed teleologically toward the disclosure of these norms and their conscious practical operation (HUA IX: 299/CH: 177). Phenomenology, in other words, is "in the service of a universal praxis of reason" (HUA IX: 299/CH: 177). It strives toward the teleological idea of reason in humanity. Even more, phenomenology is the disclosure of the idea, and it helps humanity itself consciously and purposively to direct itself toward the idea (HUA IX: 299/CH: 178). But besides resolving the practical problem, phenomenology resolves all the old philosophical antitheses. There are half-truths in these oppositions and the positions themselves are one-sided. So, as Husserl says, "subjectivism can only be overcome by the most universal and consistent subjectivism (the transcendental)" (HUA IX: 300/CH: 178). Similarly, relativism can be overcome only through a universal relativism, that of transcendental phenomenology. This relativity proves itself to be the only possible sense of absolute being. We find the same solution with empiricism. There must be the most universal and consistent empiricism, which makes use of a broadened sense of experience, intuition, eidetic intuition. And yet phenomenology is rationalistic by overcoming dogmatic rationalism by means of eidetic investigations. Finally, the tracing back of all being to transcendental subjectivity and its constitutive intentional functions leaves open no other way of contemplating the world than as teleological. And yet there is a kernel of truth in naturalism since constitutive intentional functions originate in what is given passively. Phenomenology therefore, according to Husserl, is the pure "working out" of the methodical intentions that already animated Greek philosophy from its beginnings. And it continues the great movements of modern philosophy. But the way of true science is infinite. So Husserl concludes the *Britannica* essay with the teleological infinite idea of philosophy; he says, "Accordingly, phenomenology demands that the phenomenologist foreswear the ideal of a philosophic system and yet as a humble worker in community with others, the phenomenologist lives for a *philosophia perennis*" (HUA IX: 301/CH: 179).

## Interpretation: Consciousness as Distance

We selected this Husserl text because it is written under the pressure of Heidegger's influence. Its proximity to the late *Crisis* texts indicates that it contains a different conception of phenomenology than the one we find in early works like *The Idea of Phenomenology* and *Ideas I*. Is phenomenology defined as a philosophy of consciousness, of present consciousness, in a word, of the phenomenon, a word that necessarily means presence?

Or does it question beyond presence and somehow contain something like the unconscious, does it somehow "converge" with Freudian psychoanalysis?[19] In order to answer this question, we are going to examine a short text from 1936 written by Husserl's assistant, Eugen Fink, on "the problem of the unconscious."[20] It is important to recognize that Fink's writings on phenomenology had a profound impact on the French reception of Husserlian phenomenology. Fink's writings at once led to the French criticisms of phenomenology such as those of Derrida, and to the French innovations of phenomenology such as those of Merleau-Ponty.[21]

In the fragment on the "Unconscious," Fink considers the objection that any attempt to understand the unconscious by means of consciousness is a prejudice: "Has one not thus made a prior decision that the unconscious is somehow obscured consciousness . . . , something that can be traced back to consciousness?" (HUA VI: 473/CR: 386). As we saw, Freud in "The Unconscious" criticized this prejudice. The prejudice consists in thinking that life and consciousness are the same. Alluding to Freudian psychoanalysis, Fink says that "depth psychology" has tried to show that consciousness is a mere stratum of the concrete human person, that it must be opposed to other dimensions of life not traceable to consciousness, "that ultimately [consciousness] represents a derivative dimension of 'life'" (HUA VI: 474/CR: 386). Fink, however, argues that this objection is based on a fundamental philosophical naiveté. The naiveté consists in an "omission" (HUA VI: 474/CR 386). According to Fink, remaining within this naiveté, one fails to investigate the subject matter of what the conscious is, the very subject matter from which depth psychology must demarcate itself. In short, one thinks that one is already acquainted with consciousness. Fink says,

> Naturally, when we are awake, we always know and are acquainted with what is commonly meant by "consciousness." It is in a certain sense *what is closest to us* [*das Nächste*]: we see things, think about something, desire something, judge, etc. Just this typical familiarity and pregivenness of "consciousness" in its rough articulation . . . gives rise to the *illusion* [*Schein*] that consciousness is immediately given. . . . Phenomenology, however, *destroys* the illusion [*Schein*] of the "immediate givenness of consciousness" (HUA VI 474/CR 386, my emphasis).[22]

Here Fink provides a different definition of phenomenology from that of a "consciousness-idealism" (HUA VI: 474/CR: 386). As we saw above in the "Summary-Commentary," there is a "*Schein*" that gives us the illusion that consciousness consists merely in psychological or anthropological consciousness. That is, as Fink says here, the illusion consists in thinking that the being of the conscious is what is nearest. However, the *"Schein"* implies—what shines through the phenomenon—that consciousness involves a latency; consciousness involves a *distance*. With the recognition of this distance, we are therefore not very far away from the Freudian topology. It is possible to say that phenomenology, like Freudian psychoanalysis, "corrects inner perception." Indeed, we saw in the "Summary-Commentary" that phenomenology is pursuing genuine inner experience. Now with the distance, we can see that Husserl is in fact transforming the idea of lived experience (*Erlebnis*).[23] The move to the inner is a move to the outside. We could even say that genetic phenomenology "destroys" what is immediately given to consciousness by showing that it is generated through habitualities and passivity. In *The Crisis* (and in texts associated with *The Crisis* such as "The Origin of Geometry" and the text known as "The Earth Does not Move"), Husserl methodically parenthesizes the accomplishments of science in order to show that the present-day experience of geometrical space leads back to a nongeometrical experience that remains hidden in the past. It is this thick past that Merleau-Ponty will pursue in his final writings under the title of "institution," which itself is a Husserlian word. And, like Husserl, Merleau-Ponty will never renounce the epoché in all its universality. In its universality, the epoché is the only means of access to institution.

As we move forward, we shall return repeatedly to the following point. Indeed, it cannot be stressed enough: the universality of the epoché transforms the very concept of immanence. Through the epoché, immanence is no longer immanent to consciousness; consciousness is immanent to immanence: a "strange" transcendental experience.[24] We must say that no investigation placed under the category of continental philosophy can take place without undergoing the epoché. In this regard, we must also say that all continental philosophy is Cartesian, even though, as Husserl points out in *The Crisis*, Descartes himself did not understand the radicality of his discovery (HUA VI: 80/CR: 79). The radicalism of the epoché, in its universality, is supposed to put all previous opinions and ideas in question. It results in a presuppositionless level of experience. Insofar as it is presuppositionless, this level of experience—immanence—is based on nothing but itself; it is abyssal. Being based in nothing, the level of experience is ontological. Not only does the epoché put all presuppositions in question, its radicalism also "destroys" the hierarchy of the senses of being. It equalizes all the senses of being. Even as it disentangles the presuppositions and the senses of being, the epoché points us in the direction of the question of difference, the intertwining, even the ontological difference. Therefore, as we saw above in the "Summary-Commentary," Husserl claims to overcome the sense of being called positivity; phenomenology overcomes all dogmatic ontology, all relativism, all subjectivism. Prior to Heidegger's famous claim, Husserl, thanks to the discovery of the epoché, can also claim to overcome metaphysics.[25] And when Husserl speaks of "the transcendental attitude [involving] a change of focus from one's entire form of life-style," he is anticipating the full meaning of the overcoming of metaphysics: the transformation of who we are.

We must, however, add two qualifications to the points we are making about the irreducible importance of the epoché. On the one hand, as Deleuze has indicated, the concept of multiplicity is different in Husserl than in Bergson.[26] For instance, in Husserl's 1929 *Formal and Transcendental Logic,* sounding much like Bergson, Husserl speaks of multiplicities in "the pregnant sense." But he also says, "Multiplicity meant properly the formal idea of an infinite province of objects for which there exists the *unity* of a theoretical explanation."[27] For Husserl, the unity of a theoretical explanation means a complete explanation. Being complete, the explanation would not allow for any consequence that is not deductively true or is not an analytic contradiction: "tertium non datur."[28] The pregnant sense of multiplicity is a multiplicity that is completely determinate, and for Husserl, any other way of speaking of multiplicities (other than determinate) is "unclear." Husserl therefore eliminates the very idea of Bergson's multiplicity: with Husserl, multiplicity could never be understood as a continuous heterogeneity. On the other hand, although the epoché opens up the "paradoxical ambiguity," Husserl aims at resolving the paradox. Even in this late version, Husserlian phenomenology seems to aim at disentanglement, even though the difference between the transcendental and psychological, the extramundane and the mundane, is not a real difference. It is a difference of sense in which the senses interpenetrate one another. Moreover, Husserl never, as Derrida points out, develops the idea of a transcendental language that would disambiguate the doubleness of the "we."[29] In fact, Husserl never considers the essence of language in general. As Husserl says, again in *Formal and Transcendental Logic*, "The fundamental treatment of the great problems that concern clarification of the sense and constitution of objectivities belonging to the cultural world . . . , including language, makes up a realm by itself. . . . This whole group of problems will be left out of consideration in our further investigations."[30] And even when Husserl seems to take the "great problems" of language seriously, as in the late "The Origin of Geometry," language is still considered under the *telos* of univocity.[31] Although we have been referring to Derrida here, it is Foucault to whom we shall turn for the being of language; it is Foucault who wants to "destroy" the "ambiguity" of the "anthropological quadrilateral."

Yet what Derrida and Foucault (and Deleuze) say about phenomenology perhaps does not exhaust the possibilities of phenomenology. As we noted above, when Husserl considers the kind of rigor that is specific to psychology he points to a kind of essential variation that is not determined by limit-forms. Here, Husserl is referring to what he calls, in *Ideas I*, "morphological essences" or "an-exact essences."[32] "An-exact" is not the opposite of exactitude; it is not the inexact. Rather the "an-exact" indicates its own kind of rigor. In *The Crisis*, when he is describing the origin of Galilean science, Husserl stresses that the secondary qualities, which he calls "the material that fills in the shape," are *no way* analogous to the shapes. The material cannot be idealized as the shapes can be idealized. While the shapes can be made approximate to a geometrical form (as round things can approximate a circle), the material possesses no such ideal form and therefore approximation makes no sense here (HUA VI: 33/CR: 35). As Husserl says, "there is no exact measurement [with the material that fills in the shapes], no growth of exactness or of methods of measurement" (HUA VI: 32/CR: 34). Husserl implies therefore in *The Crisis* that it is absurd to speak of an ideal form of blue that could be applied to real blue things, as circularity is applied to real round things. With the material that fills in the shapes, Husserl speaks of generalized color types that allow for recognition.[33] But never does the generalized blue type eliminate the equivocity of the color, never does it eliminate the continuity of one color into another, as shades of blue pass into shades of red. The essential equivocity to the colors means that the variation of them *cannot* be equivalent to a determinate progression. Instead, there is an essential indetermination to all colors, which grants them an indefinite continuous variation.[34] Here perhaps, with the an-exact, we have variation freed from univocity and teleology. Here perhaps Husserl reaches something like Bergsonian multiplicity and Freudian schizophrenic thought.

## Transition

Phenomenology has turned out to be one of the most resilient philosophies of the twentieth and twenty-first centuries. It is resilient precisely because its investigations are *not* limited to the immediate data of consciousness. This expansion of its investigations explains why we must not define phenomenology as a "philosophy of consciousness." It explains why we are able to speak of a convergence between psychoanalysis and phenomenology. Just as Freud's meta-psychology goes beyond both science and the evidence of consciousness, Husserl's phenomenology, thanks to the universal epoché, goes beyond the sense of being of objects and subjects, beyond presence—to consciousness as distance, or, as Heidegger would say, as being held out into the nothing. Indeed, by 1929, by discovering the paradoxical ambiguity between the psychological and the transcendental, Husserl is meditating on the ontological difference. The phrase "ontological difference," the difference between beings (*Seiende*), that is, things whose existence is defined by ready availability, and Being (*Sein*), the sense of all beings but not a conceptual generality, is a phrase that belongs to Heidegger. As we saw with Bergson, to think beyond things already formed raises the problem of language, a problem to which Bergsonism responds with fluid concepts. At least in his lifetime, Husserl does not raise this problem, the problem of a transcendental language. Strictly, the reflections on language still lie ahead of us. They truly begin only with Heidegger.

# 4

# The Thought of the Nothing:
# Heidegger's "What Is Metaphysics?" (1929)

Before we turn to the transition that Heidegger represents, let us recapitulate the structure of thinking we have seen up to this point. *First,* the
starting point is Cartesian. This kind of thinking starts from immanence.
Freud is not an exception to this claim since he too speaks of inner perception. Yet, and *second,* we have seen a transformation of immanence into
difference. All the philosophers we have considered discover within immanence a relation: the battlefield topology of the Ucs and the Cs; the un-
common parallelism between the transcendental and the psychological.
Yet it is Bergson who discovers, within immanence, multiplicity. The Bergsonian concept of multiplicity is an incomplete multiplicity since there is
no unitary theoretical explanation; the whole is not given. Multiplicity in
Bergson is no longer an adjective, modifying multiple things like multiple
objects or multiple subjects. Being incomplete, this multiplicity makes
immanence immanent to nothing but itself. Husserl recognized that this
idea of immanence (continuous heterogeneity) is paradoxical. Therefore,
*third,* immanence requires a thinking beyond logic, beyond "*tertium non
datur.*" In contrast to his definition of multiplicity as determinate, Husserl
also, as we saw, argues for a kind of an-exact rigor for phenomenological psychology and for phenomenological philosophy. Similarly, Bergson
speaks of improper or fluid concepts. These contestations of traditional or
formal logic lead to a new understanding of language: language is more
than logic. As Heidegger says (in the 1943 "Postscript" to "What Is Metaphysics?"), "It now becomes necessary to ask the question . . . of whether

thinking already stands within the law of its truth when it merely follows the thinking whose forms and rules are conceived by 'logic.' . . . 'Logic' is only one interpretation of the essence of thinking" (GA 9: 308/PM: 235). But then, *fourth*, and following from this transformation of the concept of language and thinking, Bergson, Freud, and Husserl call for a reform of psychology. For Husserl, in particular, we saw that the epoché must be universal, the universal suspension of all positing of existence whether in everyday life or in science. The universality of the epoché means the overcoming of psychologism, but also, and more importantly, going beyond the reform of psychology, it means the overcoming of dogmatic-positivistic metaphysics. The universal method of the epoché leads at first to what looks like a renewal of metaphysics, but then to an overcoming of metaphysics *as such*. Therefore the four components of the structure of this thinking, of the research agenda called continental philosophy, are: (1) the starting point in immanence; (2) the transformation of immanence into multiplicity; (3) the liberation of language (and thinking) from logic; and (4) the overcoming of metaphysics. Overcoming metaphysics means the creation of concepts oriented by the idea that the whole is not given, that is, the creation of concepts not oriented by the idea that all things are defined by the ready availability of what is present before our eyes, that is, by static forms and teleological genesis. But it is Heidegger who shows us that the overcoming of metaphysics includes a transformation of humanity. Heidegger represents the transition from the renewal of metaphysics to the overcoming of metaphysics. But to overcome metaphysics, we must ask, "What is metaphysics?"

We have selected the 1929 essay "What Is Metaphysics?" because, like the *Encyclopedia Britannica* essay, it is a compact presentation of Heidegger's early thought (the period around *Being and Time* up to the middle of the 1930s). But there is an additional reason for selecting it. Heidegger himself in effect singles out "What Is Metaphysics?" for its importance, since he writes a "Postscript" for it in 1943 (which we just mentioned) and an "Introduction" to it in 1949. These elaborations provide the thread to Heidegger's later writings, after the so-called "turn." To anticipate, we can say that Heidegger's thought as a whole, both earlier and later, is driven by the attempt to make us—this is the transformation of humanity that truly defines the overcoming of metaphysics—understand our place in the difference between Being (*Sein*) and beings (*Seiende*),[1] to make us learn how to dwell in the ontological difference, which Heidegger will eventually call "the event of propriation" (*Ereignis*). As we shall see, the learning to dwell within the event of propriation occurs only through the experience of language. Therefore, in the next chapter, we shall examine Heidegger's 1950 essay called "Language." Here, however, with "What Is Metaphysics?" we come to understand our place in the ontological difference by asking the question of how it is with the nothing. By asking the question of how is it with the nothing, "What Is Metaphysics?" aims to make us experience Being from the perspective of the beings (GA 9: 123/ PM: 97). From the perspective of beings, Being seems to be nothing: "The ontological difference is the 'not' between beings and Being" (GA 9: 123/ PM: 97). Before we turn to the lecture—"What Is Metaphysics?" which was Heidegger's inaugural lecture on the occasion of his assuming the chair of philosophy at the University of Freiburg, the very chair that Husserl had occupied[2]—we must get a better sense of the ontological difference.

We can get a sense of this difference if we take up the way Heidegger poses the question of Being in the Introduction to *Being and Time*. Following dogmatic prejudices arising from Aristotle, Heidegger tells us that Being is *first* of all the most universal concept. But pointing in the direction of the paradoxical nature of the difference, Heidegger asserts that Being is not a species or a genus. Indeed, the universality of Being means that it is not the clearest of concepts but the most obscure. So, *secondly,* he tells us that Being is indefinable, which means that it can be neither derived from higher concepts nor represented by lower ones. Notice the negative formula: Being is *not* a being. The ways in which we define a being are *not* applicable to Being. Then *third,* its indefinability implies that Being is self-evident. Because Being is used in all knowing and predicating, there is an average understandability of Being. But this average understandability makes its meaning only more enigmatic. We understand it but we do not know how to speak about it. Therefore, according to Heidegger, the question of the meaning of Being must be retrieved. To retrieve it, however, we must investigate the being that we are, which is *Dasein*. The famous term "*Dasein*" is the center of *Being and Time*. In standard German, "*Dasein*" means existence, but, as is easily seen, it contains the word "*Sein*" or "being." Noticing the "*Sein,*" we see that the term "*Da-sein*" means literally "there-being" or less literally "determinate being." "*Dasein*" refers to the being that is my own or our own, the being that I find myself with, that we find ourselves with. Insofar as "*Dasein*" finds itself determined in a singular way, it is concerned with its being. The being with which we are or I am concerned, according to Heidegger in *Being and Time*, is called "*Existenz*": "We shall call the very being to which *Dasein* can relate itself [*sich verhalten kann*] in one way or another, and somehow always does relate, existence [*Existenz*]" (SZ: 12/BT: 11). The term "*Existenz*" refers not to attributes of the "what" of something like a table; rather, "*Existenz*" refers to the possibilities that *Dasein* finds itself with: "*Dasein is* always its possibility" (SZ: 42/BT: 42; Heidegger's emphasis). These possibilities of existing have always been concealed in everyday life to the point of forgetting the possibilities that most define *Dasein*. "*Existenz*" then must be awakened to the "fundamental possibilities" of *Dasein*, the most important of which is the possibility that *Dasein* will die: "the possibility of impossibility" (SZ: 250/BT: 241).[3] This awakening takes place by means of the mood of anxiety (SZ: 251/BT: 241); anxiety gives one a moment of vision, which makes one's proper or authentic possibilities available to be taken up (SZ: 344/BT: 328). But in this moment of vision, in which one sees the future possibility of death, one also realizes that one's Being, the Being of *Dasein*, is time. Therefore, "the existential analytic of *Dasein*" prepares for the development of the meaning of Being within the horizon of time (SZ: 437/BT: 415). It prepares for the remembrance of the question of Being.

In *Being and Time*, it is the "history of ontology," or more precisely "metaphysics" (a word Heidegger places within scare quotes), that has led to the "forgetfulness" of the question of Being. "What Is Metaphysics?" attempts to bring about remembrance and thereby revive metaphysics by investigating the ground of metaphysics. Therefore Heidegger adopts an image we saw in Husserl.[4] In the *Encyclopedia Britannica* essay, a network of terms appear—"*Boden*" ("soil"), "*Lage*" ("layer"), "*Zweigen*" ("branch"), and "*Begründung*" ("grounding" or "foundation")—that suggest the image of a tree, the sciences being the branches, the natural attitude being the trunk, and transcendental subjectivity being the roots set into the soil. In his 1949 "Introduction" to "What Is Metaphysics?" Heidegger says, "We ask: in what soil [*Boden*] do the roots of the tree of philosophy take hold?" (GA 9: 365/PM: 277). He adopts the tree image because in "What Is Metaphysics?" he asks, "What is happening with us, essentially in the *grounds* of our existence [*Dasein*], when science has become our passion?" (GA 9: 103/PM: 82; my emphasis). Husserl could have asked the same question.

As a passion, an event has happened in which the sciences seem dispersed. "Nonetheless [that is, despite the unity that the university provides for the sciences], the rootedness of the sciences in their essential ground has *died off*" (GA 9: 104/PM: 82–83; my emphasis).[5] It has "died off" because, as Husserl would say, the sciences remain within the dogmatism of positivity. As Heidegger would say and does say, the sciences want beings "and nothing further." This additional clause means that in order for the sciences to fulfill their task in "continuously new ways" (GA 9: 121/PM: 95), that is, in ways that are no longer dead, we must investigate what Heidegger calls "the nothing." The investigation into the nothing is a metaphysical (not a physical) inquiry.

## Summary-Commentary: The Question of Metaphysics[6]

### THE UNFOLDING OF A METAPHYSICAL INQUIRY

Despite the title, we do not find in the lecture a discussion about metaphysics. Rather, Heidegger engages us in a specific metaphysical question so that we shall be "transposed immediately" into metaphysics. As we shall see, we do not need to be transposed since we are already there; the place where we are is only disguised. It must be revealed in an experience. The metaphysical question that will lead us to the experience turns out to be "how is it with the nothing?" (*Wie steht es um das Nichts?*) (GA 9: 106/PM: 84). This question will provide metaphysics with the proper occasion to introduce itself. The plan of the lecture, as Heidegger tells us, is the following: first, the unfolding of a metaphysical inquiry; second, the elaboration of the question; and then, the conclusion, in which a response to the question is presented. Heidegger begins with the unfolding of a metaphysical inquiry.

The "unfolding" (*Entfaltung*) is necessary because the undertaking in which we are engaged is peculiar. It is peculiar especially from the viewpoint of "sound common sense." For Heidegger, "sound common sense" is equivalent to what Husserl calls "the natural attitude." As Heidegger says, "From the point of view of sound common sense, philosophy is in Hegel's words 'the inverted world'" (GA 9: 103/PM: 82). Here Heidegger is alluding to the age-old complaints about philosophy from people not trained in philosophy.[7] Philosophy seems to have inverted the real world into being

an unreal world since philosophy thinks that the real (material) world is
dependent on or is an appearance of more real (spiritual) ideas. As we shall
see, Hegel will return at the end of the lecture. In any case, to unfold the
metaphysical inquiry, we must understand the two characteristics of any
metaphysical interrogation. These are: first, every metaphysical question
encompasses the whole of metaphysical problems; and, second, being the
*whole* of the problems, any metaphysical question includes the questioner
as one of its parts so that it puts the questioner as such into question. The
two characteristics imply that "a metaphysical inquiry must be posed as
a whole and from the essential position of the existence [*Dasein*] which
questions" (GA 9: 103/PM: 82). As we mentioned above, Heidegger claims
that the being that we are today, the way we find ourselves, our "*Dasein*,"
"is determined [*bestimmt*] by science." Science is our passion.[8] But the
sciences lack unity (despite the university structure[9]), with the result that
the "roots of science have died off."[10]

When we follow the sciences' proper intention (despite the dying
off of their roots), we find that "in all the sciences, we relate ourselves
[*verhalten wir uns*] towards beings themselves" (GA 9: 104/PM: 83). This
positive sentence states that in *all* the sciences, no matter how dispersed
or disintegrated they may be, our behavior is always related only to beings.
In the *unfolding* of the metaphysical question, we see that we are moving
from multiplicity (the mani-fold of the sciences) toward simplicity (the
uni-fold of relating ourselves only to beings), and we are moving toward
simplicity by means of a "triplicity" (*Dreifache*). The *first* "fold" of the
triplicity consists in the fact that science does *not* make one field such as
nature take precedence over any other field, nor does it make one way
of treating things such as mathematics dominate others; it relates to the
world as a whole (GA 9: 104/PM: 83). But then, the *second* "fold" moves
from science to the human. It consists in the distinctive world relation to
beings being supported and guided by "*one* freely chosen stance [*Haltung*]
of human existence [*Existenz*]": objectivity (*Sachlichkeit*) (GA 9: 104/PM:
83). In the *third* "fold," we return to the question of what happens when
science is our passion:

> The human being, one being among others, "pursues [*triebt*] science." In
> this "pursuit" [*Treiben*] nothing less happens than the intrusion by one
> being called "the human being" into the whole of beings, indeed in such a

way that in and through this intrusion beings break open [*aufbricht*] and show what they are and how they are (GA 9: 105/PM: 83).

The triplicity, Heidegger says—the relation to the world; stance; and intrusion (*Einbruch*)—in its "radical unity," shows that there is a luminous "simplicity" and "aptness" of *Dasein* to "scientific existence." In other words, through Heidegger's "un-folding" of the question we see clearly the one-foldedness of the three-foldedness, as if we are following the tree down into its roots to the radical ("radical" in the literal sense) unity.[11] The unity, however, consists in the fact that in its relation to the world, in all of its stances, and in the event of its intrusion, scientific existence concerns itself with beings—and nothing beside, nothing further, and nothing beyond (GA 9: 105/PM: 84). The positive statement given above—"in all the sciences we relate to beings themselves"—now has its contrasting clause: "and beyond that, nothing."

What lies beyond beings is nothing, or more precisely, as Heidegger shifts from an adverbial use of "*nicht*" to a nominative use, what lies beyond is "the nothing" (*das Nichts*). Heidegger points out that science, when it seems to be speaking of nothing but beings, speaks of something different, of nothing. Immediately science rejects this nothing as a nullity. The question of the nothing looks to be a mere dispute about words.[12] It wants to know nothing about the nothing since the nothing is a phantasm. But this claim that the nothing is a phantasm implies that science knows about the nothing: "We know it, the nothing, in that we wish to know nothing about it" (GA 9: 106/PM: 84). Nevertheless, in order for science to try to express its own essence, it must call upon the help of the nothing. Therefore Heidegger concludes that with this reflection on our "existence at this moment as an existence determined by science," a question "has already unfolded": "How is it with the nothing?" (GA 9: 106/PM: 84).

So the movement in the first part is the following: From the two characteristics of metaphysical inquiry—the metaphysical inquiry concerning beings as a whole and concerning therefore the being that questions—we go to the question of what is happening with our "*Dasein*" when science becomes the passion; science determines our "*Dasein*" today. This question is then "un-folded." It is unfolded into the multiplicity of the sciences, which have had their roots die off. The dispersion of the sciences "unfolds" into the triplicity, into the three-fold: the relation to the world; the stance; and the event of intrusion. From the three-fold, we go to the "radical unity," to the simplicity, the one-fold. With the move to simplicity, has Heidegger abandoned any notion of multiplicity? We shall return to this question in the "Interpretation." In any case, the simplicity discloses that science concerns beings and nothing else. And here, by speaking about beings and nothing else, science speaks of something other than the beings, "the nothing." Although it rejects the nothing as a nullity, science needs it in order to define itself. Hence our question has unfolded into: When science is our passion, we must ask, "How is it with the nothing?" Beyond beings, this question is a metaphysical inquiry.

## THE ELABORATION OF THE QUESTION

The elaboration of the question revolves around the possibility or impossibility of finding an answer for the question about the nothing. Although science relegates the nothing to what "there is not," Heidegger says, "all the same," we are going to try to ask about the nothing. The first form of the question is: What is the nothing? Yet this form makes us think that the nothing is something, that it "is" such or such. But, as Heidegger says, "that is exactly what the nothing is differentiated from." The question seems to deprive itself of its own object since it turns the nothing into a something. Finding an answer to this question looks to be impossible. Of course, science's rejection of the nothing had indicated this impossibility, but also "universal 'logic' itself" teaches us that contradiction is to be avoided (GA 9: 107/PM: 85).[13] According to "logic," we cannot make the nothing into a "something," into an object. According to "logic," when we ask the question of the nothing, it seems that thinking must act in a way opposed to its essence. Since thinking seems to be always the thought of (or about) the being, the thought of (or about) (the) nothing seems to be impossible. Moreover, "logic" and the intellect (or the faculty of the understanding: *Verstand*) say that the nothing is the "negation" of the "totality" of beings (GA 9: 107–8/PM: 85). Negation is a specific act of the intellect (or the understanding). Is the nothing a particular case of the intellectual act of negation, of the "not"? Or is it the other way around, that negation and the "not" are given only because the nothing is given? Then Heidegger says, "That has not been decided; it has not even been raised explicitly as a question. We assert that the nothing is more original than the 'not' and negation" (GA 9: 108/PM: 86). As already indicated by the scare quotes placed around the word "logic," Heidegger is trying to make us question whether "logic" (formal logic, rules for thinking) really captures the essence of the *logos*, language, and therefore of thinking. In Bergson, we saw a similar criticism of logic (intellectualist thinking or thinking based in the understanding) when he distinguished intuition from analysis. As we shall stress in the "Interpretation" below, Heidegger is always concerned, like Bergson, about how we conceive thinking. Heidegger calls the assertion he just made a "thesis," which implies that it requires a proof. Heidegger will provide something like a "demonstration" (see GA 9: 109/PM: 86), even a "proof" (see GA 9: 117/PM: 92, and GA 9: 120/PM: 95). Such a proof will confirm the thesis and show that the nothing is more original than negation. If the nothing is more original, then negation as an act of the intellect and the intellect itself are dependent on the nothing (GA 9: 108/PM: 86). The intellect cannot hope to decide on the nothing.

So, setting aside "logic" and the intellect, we must not be misled by the formal impossibility of the question (GA 9: 108/PM: 86). For Heidegger, the very fact that we can ask the question of the nothing means that "we must be able to encounter it" (GA 9: 108/PM: 86). Somehow we must already be familiar with the nothing. Indeed, we know the word "nothing" and we seem to be able to provide a "definition" of it. Here is the "definition": "The nothing is the complete negation of the totality of beings" (GA 9: 109/PM: 86). The definition of the nothing implies that the totality of beings is given and then we negate it; it implies that there is an act through which the nothing would manifest itself. As Heidegger points out, the definition still seems to make the act of negation be more original than the nothing. But even if we set aside this concern with the relation between the nothing and negation, another question arises: How should we who are "essentially finite" (*als endliche Wesen:* "as finite essence or being") make the whole of beings in their totality penetrable in themselves and especially for us? We might think, according to Heidegger, that we can attain the whole of beings in their totality through an "idea" (GA 9: 109/PM: 87). Then we would be able to "think" the idea negated. The way of cognitive negation provides "the formal concept of the imagined nothing, but never the nothing itself" (GA 9: 109/PM: 87). But if the nothing is nothing, and if moreover it represents "total indifferentiability" (*Unterschiedlosigkeit*), then no "difference" (*Unterschied*) can obtain between the "imagined" nothing and the "proper" nothing. In fact, Heidegger wonders whether this "proper" nothing is not the "absurd" or "contradictory concept" of a nothing that is (GA 9: 109/PM: 87). We must finally discharge the objections of the intellect; we can question the legitimacy of the intellect's objections only "on the basis of a fundamental experience of the nothing."

The fundamental experience takes place in two phases, two phases that resemble the formal concept of the nothing. First, we must have access to beings as a whole; then they must be negated. Here Heidegger describes famously the moods of, first, boredom (*Langeweile*), then of anxiety (*Angst*). The descriptions presented here in the lecture refer to those found in *Being and Time*, in particular to §§29, 30, 40, and 68; in fact, "What Is Metaphysics?" repeats some of the wording found in §40. The descriptions also refer to Heidegger's 1929–30 lecture course and book called the *Fundamental Concepts of Metaphysics*, where Heidegger provides extensive descriptions of the mood of boredom. As we see in *Being and Time* §29, part of the structure of *Dasein* consists in attunement or disposition, how one finds oneself (*Befindlichkeit*). One finds oneself always with a mood, and that mood, prior to any understanding and conceptualization, discloses the world to us (SZ: 134/BT: 131). So here in the lecture, having finally broken free of "logic" and the intellect, Heidegger starts by stressing that we assuredly cannot "grasp" (*erfassen*, grasp as in a concept [*Begriff*]) absolutely the whole of beings. After all, we are finite beings. Yet "we certainly do find ourselves [*finden wir uns*] stationed in the midst of beings that are revealed somehow as a whole" (GA 9: 110/PM: 87). Thus, between "comprehending" or "grasping" (*Erfassen*) the whole of beings in themselves and finding oneself in the midst of beings as a whole,[14] there is an "essential difference." Comprehending the whole of beings is in principle impossible; finding oneself in the midst of beings, however, "happens" (*geschieht*) all the time in our *Dasein*. Even though we cling to this or that being in our "everyday preoccupations" (*alltägliche Dahintreiben*: in our everyday hustle and bustle), or to this or that region of being (as in the pursuit [*Treiben*] of a science), our everyday existence deals with beings in the unity of the whole, "if only in a shadowy way."

Now we turn to the mood of boredom, the first mood, which is parallel to the "idea" of the totality of beings. When we are *not* actually busy, when we are bored, then beings as a whole overcome us. Yet Heidegger makes a distinction within the mood of boredom. If we are bored with a particular thing, then we are focused on that thing: beings as whole do not manifest themselves. Such boredom with a thing is inauthentic or superficial boredom. We have authentic or profound boredom, not when one is bored *with*, but merely when "one is bored" (*es einem langweilig ist*).[15] Here when *one is bored*, one has no one object of boredom, which is why Heidegger can say that beings as a whole manifest themselves in this mood.[16] Heidegger says, "Profound boredom, drifting here and there in the abysses of our existence like a muffling fog, removes all things and men and oneself along with it into a remarkable indifference [*Gleichgül-tigkeit*, more literally, into their "all-being-the-same-ness"]. This boredom manifests beings as a whole" (GA 9: 110/PM: 87).[17] The indeterminacy of profound boredom (no single determinate object of boredom) allows the world (the whole) to manifest itself. Boredom, however, does not give us the nothing. We need a second, different mood: "It [the nothing] can and does occur, although rarely enough and only for a moment [*Augenblicke*], in the fundamental mood of anxiety [*Angst*]" (GA 9: 111/PM: 88). For Heidegger, as is well known from *Being and Time* (§§30, 40, and 68), anxiety is not fearfulness; fear occurs in the face of one determinate being. So, as we saw with profound boredom, in anxiety there is indeterminacy. More precisely, in anxiety, there is the "essential impossibility" of determination ("*wesenhafte Unmöglichkeit*"), of determining that in the face of and that for which one is anxious. Fear, moreover, is recognized by the fact that in the face of the determinate being, one reacts with confusion. In contrast, with anxiety "a peculiar calm pervades it" (GA 9: 111/PM: 88). This calm or rest is opposed to the preoccupations, the hustle and bustle, the pursuits of everyday life (*Treiben*). Finally, in connection with the calm that results from the indeterminate nature of the anxiety, one feels "uncanny" (*unheimlich*). The negative prefix of "*un-heimlich*" implies the nihilation of the everyday hustle and bustle, the "pursuits" (*Treiben*), the everyday senses of Being in which one feels at home (*heimlich*). In anxiety, according to Heidegger, I am no longer at home (*unheimlich*).

The question becomes: "What is 'it' that makes 'one' feel uncanny" or not at home (GA 9: 111/PM: 88)? Heidegger's response to this question is complicated. In fact, the description he gives (and the wording he uses) of the experience of anxiety extends into the lecture's next section, called "The Response to the Question." Here is the answer he gives to the question of what makes one feel uncanny:

> All things and we ourselves sink into indifference. This [sinking into indifference is meant] however not in the sense of mere disappearance.

Rather, in their very receding, things turn toward us. The receding of beings as a whole that closes in on us in anxiety oppresses us. We can get no hold on things. In the slipping away of beings only this "no" [*kein*, no hold on things] comes over us and remains (GA 9: 111–12/PM: 88).

Heidegger presents the mood of anxiety as the nihilation of the world made manifest by the mood of boredom. The indifference (*Gleichgültigkeit:* the "all-the-same-ness"), however, means the opposite of mere disappearance. In anxiety, the things turn toward us, close in upon us, oppress us; they come close. Nevertheless, in their proximity, we can get no hold on them; they are slipping away. Having no hold on anything, even "we humans who are . . . in the midst of beings slip away from ourselves" (GA 9: 111/PM: 88). It is not the case that you or I feel uncanny, "rather it is this way for some 'one' (*einem*)." Anxiety even robs us of words. So we face ourselves as the "*Da*," the there, the place, the place where silence rings out. As we shall see in the next chapter, the primary characteristic of language, for Heidegger, is silence. In any case, in the mood of anxiety, we try to shatter the empty silence with compulsive talk, which, according to Heidegger, is only "the proof for the presence of the nothing" (GA 9: 112/PM: 88). As Heidegger says, "That anxiety unveils the nothing is immediately confirmed by human beings themselves when anxiety has dissolved. In the lucid vision sustained by fresh remembrance we must say that in the face of which and for which we were anxious was 'properly' nothing. Indeed, the nothing itself—as such—was there [*Da*]" (GA 9: 112/PM: 89). With this mood, we have arrived at the event of nothing in human existence from which the nothing must be interrogated. What has happened in the mood of anxiety is that we have started to transform man into his *Da-sein*, into the fundamental possibilities forgotten in the pursuit of science.

## THE RESPONSE TO THE QUESTION

According to Heidegger, we must complete "the transformation of man into his *Dasein*" in order to be able to answer the question of the nothing (GA 9: 113/PM: 89). In order to complete the transformation, we must examine how the nothing manifests itself. Heidegger reiterates that although the nothing uncovers itself in anxiety, anxiety does not manifest as if the nothing were an object or a being. The nothing "manifests" itself in and through anxiety, but *not* in such a way that the nothing "shows itself" in our uncanniness "apart" ("*neben*": "next to") "from beings as a whole" (GA 9: 113/PM: 89). Rather, and positively, in anxiety, the nothing is encountered "at one with" (*in eins mit*) beings as a whole. As Heidegger says, "Rather [than annihilation], the nothing manifest itself *with* [*mit*] beings and *in* [*an*] beings expressly as a slipping away of the whole" (GA 9: 113/ PM: 90, my emphasis). In the earlier description (in "The Elaboration of the Question"), we recall, Heidegger had spoken of the slipping away of beings as a whole as not being a "mere disappearance." They remain there but the nothing means that they can no longer be understood. Therefore, no kind of annihilation of the whole of beings takes place in anxiety. And there is no negation (as in a judgment or act of will) of beings as a whole. Beings are *not* annihilated by anxiety so that nothing is left, but they are transformed into something "frail" or "powerless" (*hinfällig*: frail, infirm, *kraftlos*, forceless). And in anxiety we are "in utter impotence" (*Ohnmacht*) in regard to beings as a whole (GA 9: 113/PM: 90).

*Powerlessness* brings us to the most important description of the fundamental experience of anxiety:

> In anxiety there occurs a shrinking back before [*Züruckweichen*, yielding] . . . that is surely not any sort of flight but rather a kind of bewildered calm [*gebannte Ruhe*, spellbound rest]. The "back before" has its starting point [*Ausgang*] in the nothing. The nothing itself does not attract; it is essentially repelling [*abweisend*]. But this repulsion [*Abweisung*] is itself a parting gesture [*entgleitendelassen Verweisen*, a letting slip away gesture or pointing] toward the beings, that they are submerging [*versinkende*] as a whole. This wholly repelling gesture [*Verweisung*] toward beings that are in retreat as a whole, which is the action of the nothing that oppresses *Dasein* in anxiety, is the essence of the nothing: nihilation [*Nichtung*]. It is neither an annihilation [*Vernichtung*] of beings nor does it spring from a negation [*Verneinung*]. Nihilation will not submit to calculation in terms of annihilation and negation. The nothing itself nihilates [*Das Nichts selbst nichtet*, the nothing itself nothings] (GA 9: 114/PM: 90).

In the "Interpretation," we shall return to Heidegger's famous sentence, "the nothing itself nihilates," since it implies a kind of immanence. The long quotation, however, revolves around one root word: "*Weisen*," which means "to point," as with a finger of the hand.[18] Indeed, with this word, we are at the basis of the "proof" (*Be-weis*) that the nothing is more originary than negation. There are two words in the quote associated with "*Weisen*": "*Abweisung*" ("repulsion") and "*Verweisen*" ("gesture"). The "repulsion," the "*Abweisung*," of the nothing is a pointing away. It makes the one undergoing anxiety *release* so that there is "a shrinking back before." When one shrinks back before, the hand of the one experiencing anxiety must let go and no longer grasp (*erfasst*). Indeed, Heidegger tells us that in anxiety, there "is no kind of grasping [*Erfassen*] of the nothing" (GA 9: 112/PM: 89). The beings as a whole then slip away out of one's hands: "no hold remains [*es bleibt kein Halt*]" (GA 9: 111/PM: 88). Yet at the same time, there is a gesture, a *Ver-weisung*, to the beings as a whole; the beings are directed to sink away into indifference. As being indifferent, the beings are no longer directed to something else, to the world; they have lost their "fundamental character of the 'for the sake of' [*Umwillen von*]" (see GA 9: 157/PM: 122). In the "*Weisen*" of the nothing, one is "directed [*verweist*] precisely to the beings" (GA 9: 115/PM: 92), but the beings are "frail" (*hinfällig*) and not to be used by our grasping hand in the pursuits. This frailty means that the beings are pointed out *as such*. By gesturing, by the pointing finger of the hand that no longer grasps, the beings as a whole, so to speak, "presence" (*west*). We have already contrasted the mood of anxiety to the mood of boredom by means of the manifestness of the world and the manifestness of the nothing. But now, with the beings presencing as such, we are able to say that in boredom, times takes a long while (*Langeweile*); it concerns the "expanse of the temporal horizon."[19] But in anxiety, we are concerned with the "moment" (*Augenblick*); in anxiety, there is a "moment of vision," in which the beings are manifested "in their full but heretofore concealed strangeness as radically other with respect to the nothing" (GA 9: 114/PM: 90). This moment is an event. Heidegger's insistence on the mood of anxiety being an event anticipates what we shall see in the next chapter (on language and *Ereignis*). Through the manifestness of the nothing in the moment of anxiety, one sees that "they are beings—and not nothing" (GA 9: 114/PM: 90). This "they are" echoes the "nothing nothings": both phrases are positive statements since the action of the nothing is not annihilation. Not being annihilated, the beings as a whole recede only to press in upon us in their being as such. As Heidegger says, "The *essence* [*Wesen*] of the originally nihilating nothing lies in this, that it brings *Da-sein* for the first time before beings *as such*" (GA 9: 114/PM: 90; my emphasis). By means of its nihilating action, the nothing shows that the beings *are* and thus we human *Dasein* can understand, "approach and penetrate," their being, their "as such." Understanding happens only on the ground (*Grunde*) of the original manifestness of the nothing.

But according to Heidegger, since, as we saw with science, *Dasein* in its essence adopts a stance toward all beings, including itself, *Dasein* emerges as such, as *Dasein,* from the manifestness of the nothing. In other words, since the nothing reveals Being, our understanding of our own being comes from the nothing. Thus Heidegger gives us a definition of *Dasein:* "*Dasein* means being held out into the nothing" (GA 9: 115/PM: 91). This "being held out into the nothing" implies being held out over an abyss (an *Abgrund,* literally, a lack of ground). In other words, by having no hold on beings, by being anxious in the face of my own death—anxious at the possibility of impossibility—I am held out into the nothing, beyond beings as a whole, beyond the world. Heidegger calls this "being beyond beings as a whole" "transcendence" (GA 9: 115/PM: 91). We shall return to transcendence below in the "Interpretation," since throughout we have stressed its opposite, immanence. For Heidegger, transcendence, being beyond beings as a whole—including beyond myself as a human being, as a psychological being, as a mundane being—allows *Dasein* to understand what *Dasein* itself is. If *Dasein* were not transcendence in the sense of holding itself out into the nothing, then it could never be related to Being nor even to itself—as such. As Heidegger says, "Without the original manifestness of the nothing, [there would be] no selfhood and no freedom" (GA 9: 115/PM: 91). In other words, insofar as the nothing allows us to understand beings as such, including understanding our own existence, the nothing grants to us our capacities; we learn what we are and what we can do. Without the event of the nothing, we would remain bound to common sense and the predeterminations of historical thought. In short, the nothing makes present. That claim, according to Heidegger, leads us to an answer to the question of how it is with the nothing: "the nothing is neither an object nor any being at all. The nothing comes forward neither for itself nor next to [*neben*] beings to which it would, as it were, adhere" (GA 9: 115/PM: 91). The nothing is not a counterconcept to beings, which would amount to a "next to" relation. The nothing originally belongs to the "essential presencing" (*Wesen*) of beings as such; they presence by means of the nothing. Thus, "In the Being of beings the nihilation [*das Nichten*] of the nothing occurs [*geschieht*]" (GA 9: 115/PM: 91).

We can summarize this complicated development in the following way. As we know from *Being and Time,* anxiety is felt in the face of one's own death. It is the awareness of finitude, or more precisely the awareness of mortality, that enables us to be nothing. In anxiety then, the nothing (of death) manifests with and in the beings; there is no annihilation of the beings. Instead, through anxiety, beings as a whole become frail. In other words, the beings lose their power to be used and so do we; they are slipping away from our hold. How have they slipped away? The nothing is essentially repelling; this is *its* action, not the action of negation. The nothing itself nihilates or, so to speak, "nothings." It is not something else, like the power of the intellect, that does the repelling action. As repellent, the nothing forces one to release the grasp, and that release frees the beings from the "for the sake of" our pursuits. Then there is rest and the hand is free to point. The hand that points and no longer grasps (because it cannot grasp, because it is "utterly impotent") points the beings out as radically other than the nothing. The beings *are*—and are not nothing. The manifestness of the nothing gives *Dasein* access to the beings as such and to itself. Insofar as *Dasein* gains access to itself, it is defined as transcendence: being beyond beings as a whole, held out over (or into) the abyss of nothing. Yet for Heidegger, what the nothing does for all beings including *Dasein* is manifestness. Through the nothing, the beings "presence" as such. The unusual verbal use of the word "presence" refers to Heidegger's use of the noun "*Wesen*" above, which I have rendered as "presencing"; it is the German word usually rendered in English as "essence." But later in his career, as for instance in the 1950 essay "Language," to which we shall turn in the next chapter, Heidegger will use the word as a verb, as "*wesen*": "*es west*," which means "it presences" (see especially GA 12: 190/OWL: 94–95).[20] The verbal use of the German word for essence indicates that Heidegger is not conceiving essence as a permanent concept or general representation. Presencing means that something is coming into being as an event (or singularity) that persists in presence. Therefore, when the beings presence as such, then the ontological difference is established. For Heidegger, Being is presence as such, and not as a present being.

The development we just summarized implies that the nothing makes our relation to beings possible. But if that is true, then, as Heidegger asks, is it not the case that we must "hover" in anxiety constantly in order to be able to exist at all (GA 9: 115/PM: 91)? Yet original anxiety is rare, and we do exist and relate ourselves to beings (including ourselves) without this anxiety. If anxiety is rare, this rarity is, according to Heidegger, due to the fact that at first and for the most part the originating role of the nothing is "distorted." It is distorted because we usually "lose ourselves" among beings. This losing ourselves, according to Heidegger, agrees with the most proper meaning of the nothing. The nothing makes beings open or public; it "directs" (*verweist*) us toward beings (GA 9: 116/PM: 92). Instead of lettings the beings slip away, instead of turning toward the nothing, we grasp the beings and turn toward our "preoccupations" or "machinations" (*Umtrieben*). Below our "hastening into the public superficies of existence [*offentliche Oberfläche des Daseins*], . . . the nothing nihilates incessantly without our really knowing of this event in the manner of our every-day knowledge" (GA 9: 116/PM: 92). According to Heidegger, negation in judgment testifies to this incessant and yet unrecognized nihilation. Yet negation in judgment could not bring the "not" out of itself unless the beings were already manifested, that is, unless the beings "presenced" by means of the nothing. The "not" and negation therefore spring from the nothing, when the nothing itself has been "disengaged from concealment" (GA 9: 116/PM: 92). So the thesis that Heidegger had made earlier has been proven: the nothing is the origin of negation, not vice versa (GA 9: 116–17/PM: 92). This proof shatters the privilege and power of intellect (or the understanding) and of logic.

For Heidegger, however, negation is not the most important phenomenon of nihilative behaviors. He presents other behaviors as being more authoritative witnesses to the manifestness of the nothing that belongs essentially to *Dasein*:

> Unyielding antagonism and stinging rebuke have a more abyssal source than the measured negation of thought: galling pain and merciless prohibition, privation, these require some deeper answer. These possibilities of nihilative behavior [or comportment]—forces in which *Dasein* bears [*trägt*] its thrownness without mastering it—are not types of mere negation (GA 9: 117/PM: 93).

As we shall see in the next chapter, pain (*Schmerz*) plays an important role in Heidegger's discussion of language. Indeed, in "What Is Metaphysics?" Heidegger adds, "That [the lack of mastery of thrownness that pain indicates] does not prevent them [the nihilative behaviors], however, from speaking out in the 'no' and in negation" (GA 9: 117/PM: 93). In short, pain is the origin of speaking. Such speaking testifies to the obscured manifestations of the nothing. It shows that existence (*Dasein*), for Heidegger, is saturated with nihilative behavior. Anxiety is always "there" (*Da*, as in *Da-sein*). Anxiety being "there" leads Heidegger to another definition of *Dasein*:

> Being held out into the nothing—as *Dasein* is—on the ground of con-
> cealed anxiety makes the human being the lieutenant [*Platzhalter,* liter-
> ally, placeholder, lieu-tenant] of the nothing. We are so finite that we
> cannot even bring ourselves originally before the nothing through our
> own decision and will. So deeply [*abgründig,* abyssally] does finitization
> [*Verendlichung*] entrench itself that our most proper and deepest limita-
> tion [*Endlichkeit*] refuses to yield to our freedom (GA 9: 118/PM: 93).[21]

This "finitization"—note the ending: *Verendlichung*—is not a determinate
limit, but a process ("tion" or "*ung*") that grants to *Dasein* its freedom
since it means going over or beyond a limit. We should also note the
prefix, which is ambiguous, meaning both "re-" as in "re-petition" and a
negation, as in "in-finitization" or "de-finitization." We shall see this sort
of receding limit when we turn to Foucault in chapter 7. The nothing is
the abyss over which Dasein is suspended and on the basis of which—the
*Abgrund*—*Dasein* grounds its existence. Heidegger therefore repeats the
earlier definition of *Dasein* as transcendence: "Being held out into the
nothing—as Dasein is—on the ground [*Grunde*] of concealed anxiety is
its surpassing [*Ubersteigen*] of beings as a whole. It is transcendence" (GA
9: 118/PM: 93).

The "surpassing" of beings as a whole allows Heidegger to return
finally to metaphysics. This is a Greek word, of course: *meta ta physika.*
Heidegger says, "This peculiar title was later interpreted as characterizing the inquiry, the *meta* or *trans* extending out 'over' beings as such.
Metaphysics is inquiry beyond or over beings, which aims to recover them
as such and as a whole for our grasp" (GA 9: 118/PM: 93).[22] The question
of the nothing "proves" to be a metaphysical question, since it goes beyond beings as a whole. But to see this proof we must return to the two
characteristics of every metaphysical inquiry. *First,* does the question of
the nothing encompass the whole of metaphysics? In order to answer
this question, Heidegger considers the history of metaphysics in a "brief
memory." So, according to Heidegger, for a long time, metaphysics has
expressed the nothing in this proposition: *ex nihilo nihil fit,* from nothing,
nothing comes ("*fit*" is past participle of the Latin "facio," to make or bring
into existence). According to Heidegger, the ways in which historically this
proposition has been discussed have "expressed the guiding fundamental
conception of beings [*des Seienden*]" (GA 9: 119/PM: 94). First, we have
"ancient metaphysics," which grasps the nothing through the signification of "non-being" (*Nichtseienden*), that is, through the signification of

"unformed matter, matter that cannot itself be formed into a being that
has a form and that would consequently offer an outward aspect (*eidos*)"
(GA 9: 119/PM: 94). For ancient metaphysics, according to Heidegger, the
form exhibiting an outward aspect means that a being is a self-forming
form that presents an image or a spectacle. But, second, we have "Christian
dogma," which transforms the signification of *ex nihilo nihil fit* into *Ex
nihilo fit—ens creatum*. Instead of "from nothing, nothing comes," there is
"from nothing, comes created being." The transformation denies the truth
of the ancient metaphysics' interpretation by claiming that there are no
beings—"the complete absence of beings"—apart from God. The guiding
conception of beings now is that beings could not be without God's creation of them. Rather than formed being, there is *ens creatum*. Where in
ancient metaphysics, nonbeing was the counterconcept to a form presenting an image, here in Christian dogma, nonbeing, "the nothing becomes
the counter-concept to that which properly is, to the *summun ens*, to God
as *ens increatum*" (GA 9: 119/PM: 94). Apart from God and what he has
created, there is no being.

What Heidegger is showing us here is that the question of the nothing stays on the same level as the beings. The question of Being and the
nothing is never posed. The nothing is merely a counterconcept to what
properly is, that is, it is conceived as negation. So, according to Heidegger,
if the nothing is to become a problem at all, we must properly formulate
"the metaphysical question concerning the Being of beings. The nothing
does not remain the indeterminate opposite of beings but reveals itself
as belonging to the Being of beings" (GA 9: 109/PM: 94–95). Here, as he
anticipated with the mention of the "inverted world," Heidegger takes up
Hegel's logic. Hegel too had claimed that being and the nothing belong together. According to Heidegger, this claim is correct, but the correctness of
the proposition does not reveal what the relation is really about. Being and
nothing belong together because "Being itself is essentially finite [*endlich*]
and reveals itself only in the transcendence of *Dasein* which is held out
into the nothing" (GA 9: 120/PM: 95). Being is finite, because it is relative to
*Dasein*, who is finite or mortal (*endlich*). This relativity means that if Being
is itself defined as presence, while the beings are present things, then presence is limited by that which lies beyond it, as death lies beyond *Dasein*.
Presence is limited by nonpresence. By showing the belonging-together
of Being and nothing, and since Being is the encompassing question of

metaphysics, Heidegger "proves" that the question of the nothing embraces the whole of metaphysics. So Heidegger states that the old proposition *ex nihilo nihil fit* contains another sense appropriate to the problem of Being itself: *ex nihilo omne ens qua ens fit* (from the nothing all beings as beings, that is, as such, come to be) (GA 9: 120/PM: 95). As Heidegger says, "Only in the nothing of *Dasein* do beings as a whole, in accord with their most proper possibility—that is, in a finite way—come to themselves" (GA 9: 120/PM: 95). This claim means that things come to an end, that nothing is eternal, but that all things are temporal and in becoming.

The reinterpretation of the "*ex nihil nihil fit*"—from the nothing of *Dasein* comes all beings as such—leads Heidegger to the second characteristic of a metaphysical question: How has this question implicated our questioning *Dasein*? We saw at the beginning that according to Heidegger, our existence is essentially determined by science (GA 9: 105/PM: 83). If the question of the nothing implicates *Dasein* in its existence, then this determination must have become questionable. Scientific *Dasein* relates to beings themselves and only them; it wants to know nothing of the nothing (GA 9: 120/PM: 95). But we have learned that scientific *Dasein* is possible, that is, it understands itself only if it holds itself out into the nothing. As Heidegger says, "Only because the nothing is manifest can science make beings themselves objects of investigation" (GA 9: 121/PM: 95). Therefore, only on the basis of metaphysics can science "fulfill, in ever-renewed ways, its essential task which is not to amass and classify bits of knowledge, but to disclose in ever-renewed fashion the entire region of truth in nature and history" (GA 9: 121/PM: 95). Earlier, Heidegger had said that "the rootedness of the sciences in their essential ground has died off" (GA 9: 104/PM: 83). Now, with the nothing of *Dasein*, the sciences have had their roots revitalized. Thanks to the nothing in the ground of *Dasein*, beings can overwhelm us in their total strangeness. The nothing arouses wonder and makes us, we investigators, ask the question "why?" In wonder, even we ourselves appear strange. We must then ask the question "why?" of ourselves. We must put ourselves in question. Therefore, as Heidegger concludes, "The question of the nothing puts us, the questioners, in question. It is a metaphysical question" (GA 9: 121/PM: 96). Being put in question, we can no longer conceive ourselves as being determined by science, by this possibility of existence. Therefore, Heidegger concludes the lecture by speaking of the human.

Here at the end, as if appealing to the way we have been determined by science and its rigor, to "logic," Heidegger lays out a syllogism (GA 9: 121/PM: 96). First, going beyond beings belongs to the essence of *Dasein*. Second, going beyond beings is metaphysics. Therefore, metaphysics belongs to the essence of the human being. Belonging to the essence of the human being, "metaphysics is the grounding event [*Grundgeschehen*] in our *Dasein*. It is that *Dasein* itself" (GA 9: 121/PM: 96). This claim, for Heidegger, changes the meaning of metaphysics. Metaphysics is not a division of academic philosophy (metaphysics, alongside the areas of epistemology and ethics). The "truth of metaphysics dwells" in *Dasein*, which Heidegger calls a "groundless ground" (*abgründigen Grunde*). Because the truth of metaphysics dwells in the groundless ground of *Dasein*, metaphysics "stands in closest proximity to the constantly lurking possibility of deepest error" (GA 9: 121/PM: 96). The possibility of error makes metaphysics more serious that science. Never concerning itself with the nothing, science does not encounter the possibility of error. Science is certain because it only concerns what has been grounded in groundlessness. Therefore, "philosophy can never be measured by the standard of the idea of science" (GA 9: 121/PM: 96). Heidegger brings forward one last consequence of the syllogism: If the question of the nothing has put us in question, and if the question of the nothing is a metaphysical question, then metaphysics has not been put opposite us like an object and we have not been transported into metaphysics. In other words, if metaphysics belongs to the nature of the human, then "we are always already within it" (GA 9: 122/PM: 96). Because we are always already within it, philosophizing happens in certain ways. But what "we" call philosophy, that is, what Heidegger calls philosophy, is the getting under way of metaphysics so that metaphysics comes to itself and to its explicit tasks. Although we are always already philosophizing in certain ways, "philosophy itself gets under way," for Heidegger, "only by a peculiar insertion of our own existence into the fundamental *possibilities* of *Dasein* as a whole" (GA 9: 122/PM: 96; my emphasis). This comment means that we must be inserted into the fundamental possibility of death as the outside. As Heidegger frequently does in his lectures, he ends with a kind of formula. Here it is. For this insertion, it is of decisive importance that: (1) We allow space for beings as a whole (boredom); (2) we release ourselves into the nothing (anxiety), i.e., we liberate ourselves from those "idols" everyone has and to which everyone holds; and finally (3) we let the sweep of our suspense—as in over an abyss, an *Abgrund*—take its full course, so that it swings back into the basic question of metaphysics that the nothing itself compels: Why are there beings at all and why not nothing?

## Interpretation: The Thought of the Nothing

If the "great French philosophy of the Sixties" functions as the guiding thread for our study, then Heidegger's thought of the ontological differ-ence makes a decisive transition. Indeed, the first proper name to appear in Deleuze's *Difference and Repetition* is "Heidegger." Yet in *Difference and Repetition*, Deleuze levels a serious criticism at Heidegger.[23] Accord-ing to Deleuze, Heidegger does not make Being (*l'être*) be said only of difference and thereby revolve around the being (*l'étant*); he does not conceive the being in such a way that it will be truly disengaged from any subordination to identity and homogenizing mediation. In other words, Heidegger conceives Being as a unifying principle that subordinates the multiplicity of beings. In Heidegger, for Deleuze, there is no continuous heterogeneity. Similarly, Derrida argues in "Geschlecht II: Heidegger's Hand" that "Gathering together (*Versammlung*) is always what Heidegger privileges."[24] For Derrida, Heidegger's privilege of gathering implies that there is no dispersion. As we saw in relation to Husserl, it is perhaps not possible to deny the force of these criticisms. Indeed, the beginning of "What Is Metaphysics?" confirms Deleuze's and Derrida's suspicions. The movement of Heidegger's thought goes from the multiplicity of the sci-ences to the simplicity of the root. As Deleuze (and Guattari) would say, Heidegger's thinking is arborist. Yet it must be said that it would not be possible to formulate these criticisms—and both Derrida and Deleuze would agree with this claim—without Heidegger's thought. Therefore, perhaps, we can now draw out the elements of Heidegger's thought that lead to a genuine thought of multiplicity. The "Interpretation" is guided by the indisputable fact that when Heidegger writes the sentence "the nothing nihilates," he is trying to think Being entirely from itself (and not from the forms of beings and not from the highest being).[25]

At the end of "What Is Metaphysics?" it seems that Heidegger is aim-ing at a renewal of metaphysics (as Bergson and Husserl too had sought) by investigating the ground or soil of metaphysics (GA 9: 121/PM: 96).

But, as we learn in the "Postscript" and in the "Introduction to 'What Is Metaphysics?'" Heidegger aims at an overcoming of metaphysics. As Heidegger says, "Insofar as a thinking sets out to experience the ground of metaphysics . . . , thinking has in a sense left metaphysics" (GA 9: 367/ PM: 279). The ground of metaphysics is not metaphysics; it is beyond and other than metaphysics (GA 9: 367/PM: 279). In the 1949 "Introduction to 'What Is Metaphysics?'" Heidegger tells us that

> Metaphysics . . . speaks continually, and in the most various ways, of Being. Metaphysics gives, and seems to confirm, the appearance that it asks and answers the question concerning Being. In fact, metaphysics never answers the question concerning the truth of Being, for it never asks this question. Metaphysics does not ask this question because it thinks Being only by representing beings as being. . . . From its beginning to its completion, the propositions of metaphysics have been strangely involved in a persistent confusion of beings and Being (GA 9: 370/PM: 281).

The confusion means that metaphysics conceives Being in terms of beings. Dispelling the confusion, the ontological difference means that Being *cannot* be conceived on the basis of the beings. To conceive Being on the basis of the beings means, as we have seen, to conceive it in terms of form and unformed matter or in terms of one being who has the highest form (GA 9: 119/PM: 94). The "not" of the "not in terms of beings" means that the thought of Being is a thought beyond the forms of beings. The "not" therefore liberates the informal so that the beings are not hierarchized, subordinated, or classified: "Being, however, is *not* an existing quality found in beings" (GA 9: 306/PM: 233; my emphasis). Through the nothing, the beings become "all the same" (*Gleichgültigkeit*). The "not" of the "not a being," of the ontological difference, dehierarchizes the beings; it smoothes out the beings into a plane.

We can go further. In "What Is Metaphysics?" Heidegger stresses that the nothing does not annihilate the beings. The nothing is "one with beings." They therefore slip away from our grasp and press in upon us. The beings "presence" as such and not "for the sake of" something else. This "as such" liberates the beings from the pursuits; it lets them be. Despite the expression "one with," which suggests that the nothing is proximate, the nothing is not, according to Heidegger, "next to" (*neben*) "beings as a whole" (GA 9: 113 and 115/PM: 89 and 91). Not being next to or near and yet being one with, the nothing is distant. This distance implies that beings are *not* gathered around a principle. It also implies that the source of their presence is *not* present. Because Being and nothing "belong together," Being is finite (GA 9: 120/PM: 95). As we noted above, presence, or more precisely "presencing," is an event. As an event, Being has not always been permanently (or eternally) present; Being presences in a moment (*Augenblick*) (even a moment that lasts awhile [*Langeweile*]). Beyond that moment, there is nothing. To return to the expression we saw in Bergson, we can say that with Heidegger, the whole is *not* given. As we have seen, this absence is what makes multiplicity possible. This absence makes a plane of immanence.

Yet, famously, from the period of *Being and Time* (the period to which "What Is Metaphysics?" belongs), Heidegger speaks of transcendence. *Dasein,* human existence, is defined by transcendence, the ecstatic, the being outside of itself of existence. To transcend then, in Heidegger, is to be outside. Indeed, in the "Introduction to 'What Is Metaphysics?'" Heidegger says:

> The ecstatic essence of existence [*Existenz*] is . . . still understood inadequately as long as one thinks of it as merely a "standing out," while interpreting the "out" as meaning "away from" the interior of an immanence of consciousness or spirit. For in this manner, existence would still be represented in terms of "subjectivity" and "substance"; while, in fact, the "out" ought to be understood in terms of the "outside itself" of the openness of Being itself. The stasis of the ecstatic consists—as strange as it may sound—in the "out" and "there" of unconcealedness, which prevails as the essence of Being itself (GA 9: 374).

What Heidegger calls transcendence is in fact a movement to immanence.[26] Immanence is not the immanence of consciousness or spirit. It is this "outside itself." With Heidegger immanence becomes immanent to nothing but itself. Being held out into the nothing is to be held out over an *Abgrund,* in the sense of both an "abyss" and, more literally, an "unground." To make this important point again, we must say that the ground of beings is based on nothing but itself; it is no longer based on a subject or substance, on form or matter, on "idols." The sentence "the nothing itself nihilates" attests to the plane of immanence insofar as the action of the nothing is not done by the human intellect (by the faculty of the understanding). The structure of the sentence is a tautology since the subject of the sentence is the same as the verb: nothing is nothing. Heidegger therefore is trying to think the nothing entirely in terms of itself. It does not involve human subjectivity or an external agency. The nothing itself, and not man, nothings. Indeed, the forms of thinking— "logic"—that makes the plane dependent on transcendent beings such as subject and substance are bound up in illusions:[27] "Metaphysics gives, and seems to confirm, the *appearance* that it asks and answers the question concerning Being" (GA 9: 370/PM: 281; my emphasis). Only the overcoming of metaphysics, as Heidegger conceives it, dispels these appearances, which appear like a fog above the plane.

The overcoming of metaphysics transforms thinking. The thought into the ground of metaphysics is the thought of (the) nothing. Thinking is no longer a thinking of this or that being; it is not thinking of their relations and orders. As the thought of nothing, it is open to the greatest errors. It cannot be exact. Exact thinking, according to Heidegger, "binds itself to the calculation of beings and serves this end exclusively" (GA 9: 308/PM: 235). Calculation does not let the beings be since it refuses to let anything appear except what is countable. Such calculative thinking is for Heidegger at the center of contemporary technology and modern science (GA 9: 303/PM: 231): "Calculative thinking compels itself into a compulsion to master everything on the basis of the consequential correctness of its procedure" (GA 9: 309/PM: 235). It is such mastery, which turns all beings into things that can be used for our pursuits, into "standing reserve" (*Bestand*), that must be overcome. In the "Introduction to 'What Is Metaphysics?'" Heidegger asks (GA 9: 368/PM: 279), "Why, however, should such an overcoming of metaphysics be necessary?" It is necessary because metaphysics "continues to prevent the relation of Being to man from lightening up, out of the essence of this relation, in such a way as to bring human beings into a belonging to Being" (GA 9: 69/PM: 280). The overcoming of metaphysics therefore is supposed to transform who we are. The beginning of the transformation appears in "What Is Metaphysics?" when Heidegger describes the mood of anxiety. The experience of anxiety is an experience of powerlessness. We must quote this passage again:

> We are so finite that we cannot even bring ourselves originally before the nothing through our own decision and will. So deeply [*abgründig*, abyssally] does finitization [*Verendlichung*] entrench itself that our most

proper and deepest limitation [*Endlichkeit*] refuses to yield to our freedom (GA 9: 118/PM: 93).

Just as Being is finite, we are subjected to anxiety, in which things are no longer objects determined by our pursuits. Things become strange, and we are no longer at home.

As Freud says, "we have a feeling that something different must be going on here" (GW X: 299/SE XIV: 200). Although Heidegger rejects the association of his descriptions of anxiety to the "familiar assortment of psychic states observed by psychology" (GA 9: 307/PM 234, also GA 9: 371/PM: 282), it is possible to see a similarity between these descriptions and those of Freud. As we saw, in anxiety hysteria, a defense mechanism is established that transfers the source of anxiety from one object to many objects. The result is that the source of anxiety becomes increasingly indeterminate. The transference of the feeling reaches its culmination with the schizophrenic, for whom only the mere similarity of the word conveys the transference. In other words, with the schizophrenic, it is possible to say that anxiety has become truly indeterminate: *Gleichgültigkeit*. But, more importantly, as we stressed, it is the schizophrenic, for Freud, who is on the way to a cure since he or she is able to bring to language the loss of the primary object. Similarly, as we saw, anxiety for Heidegger robs us of our words, leaving us in silence: "the silent voice that attunes us toward the horror of the abyss" (GA 9: 306–7/PM 233). But then, "in the uncanniness of anxiety, we often try to shatter the vacant silence with compulsive talk" (GA 9: 112/PM: 89). In that compulsive talk, we perhaps still speak in the language of metaphysics. A poorer kind of language is required in order to speak otherwise. As Heidegger would say, what is required is mortal speech, a response to the peal of silence.

## Transition

What we have seen in this first chapter on Heidegger is the continuous radicalization of the universal epoché. The mood of anxiety puts in suspense metaphysics as the constant confusion of beings and Being. The "not" (the "not a being") disambiguates Being from beings. It establishes the ontological difference through which the beings are, through which they presence as such. Establishing the ontological difference—Being is not beings—opens the way for a transformation of thinking. The thought of Being (or of the nothing) is a thought not restricted to any of the forms of thinking of beings. Being cannot be conceived as a present or static ground (as subject or substance). Being must be thought as an event; it "presences," it happens. This thought of the event requires a different conception of language, different from the one that conceives language as an expression of man. We see the seeds of the conception in "What Is Metaphysics?" The event of anxiety robs us of words, leaving us in silence. Language must be conceived on the basis of this silence. Just as "the nothing itself nothings," "speech itself speaks."

# 5

## Dwelling in the Speaking of Language:
## Heidegger's "Language" (1950)

We have been building up to this moment, the moment when language itself becomes an issue. In Husserl, we were able to unearth a kind of variation that is not determined by a form. An-exact variation indicates a possibility of language beyond a univocal purpose. In Freud, we found that unconscious drives are exempt from mutual contradiction; his analysis of schizophrenia discloses the a-logical possibilities of language. Yet it is Bergson who most anticipates this moment of language. On the one hand, Bergson recognizes that "the primitive function of language is to establish communication" (CENT 1320–21/CM: 80). On the other, as we saw, he recognizes that the intuition of which he speaks will never find an appropriate language; it requires a fluid concept, enlarged with images indicating that the concept "does not contain the complete experience" (CENT: 1288/CM: 45). For Bergson, thinking is not utilitarian; being incomplete, the concept or word, the speaking, always calls for more thinking—as it does in Heidegger. Heidegger recognizes that when exact thinking dominates, everything becomes unconditionally objectified; "language thereby falls into the service of expediting communication along routes where objectification . . . branches out and disregards all limits" (GA 9: 317/PM: 242). Yet Heidegger also says, "To bring to language ever and again [the] advent [*Ankunft*] of Being . . . is solely what is at issue in thinking" (GA 9: 363/PM: 275). What is at issue, however, in the advent is not just a new or different conception of language. Even more, what is being called forth, what is called to come, for Heidegger, is a transformation of humanity.

The transformation of humanity is what the overcoming of metaphysics really means.

We have selected the 1950 "Language" essay because, just as "What Is Metaphysics?" is emblematic of Heidegger's early thought, "Language" is a compact presentation of Heidegger's later thought (starting around the time of the so-called "turn" in the 1930s). The most important reason for selecting the "Language" essay, however, lies in the fact that it concerns the transformation of language and thus of humanity. In order to bring about this transformation, the essay brings about a reversal. Instead of us having language as a possession over which we have power, language has us. Heidegger states this reversal in the sentence "language speaks." If we are able to listen to the sentence "language speaks," then we can no longer think that man is the origin of language. If we are to think that language speaks, then, according to Heidegger, we must understand what speaking is. To understand speaking we must take up the spoken, something older than man's speech. For Heidegger, what is already spoken is the poem. In the poem, language calls. As we shall see, calling is Heidegger's primary definition of language. Language calls things to come, and when they come, they bear the world. The world, however, is also called, and when it comes, it grants things. What is most called, however, according to Heidegger, is the difference between things and world. We have seen this difference in the last chapter as the ontological difference. Here, however, Heidegger calls the difference "the event of propriation" (*Ereignis*).[1] As Heidegger tells us in his 1959 *On the Way to Language* (in which the "Language" essay is collected), he had been using the word "*Ereignis*" for twenty-five years in his personal notebooks in order to refer to the central issue of his thinking (GA 12: 248n2/OWL: 129n).[2] Heidegger's use of this word refers back to his use of "*Geschehen*" in his early works like "What Is Metaphysics?". But *Ereignis* refers in particular to the difference happening in the middle of thing and world, making each in relation to the other both proper and improper. This difference is not spoken in the poem; it remains in silence. From this silence, language, for Heidegger, rings out, calling, like a bell tolling; it calls not only things and world, but also us. It is in this difference that humans will find their abode. As we shall see now, the essay's purpose lies in helping humans learn "to dwell" (*wohnen*) in the speaking of language (GA 12: 30/PLT 207). As we move forward, we shall see that to dwell in the speaking of language is to dwell in the outside, "to be placed," as Foucault would say, "on the inside of the outside, and vice versa."[3]

## Summary-Commentary: "Language Speaks"[4]

### WHAT ABOUT LANGUAGE ITSELF?

The first sentence—*"Der Mensch spricht"* ("Man speaks") (GA 12: 9/PLT: 187)—sets up a reversal that we do not really see until the end of the essay. The reversal goes from humanity defined as the speaking being to humanity defined as the listening being: "mortals speak insofar as they listen" (GA 12: 29/PLT: 206). Heidegger is able to make this reversal come about by considering language as language: language is language. The attempt to think language on the basis of itself means that Heidegger is not going to provide something like a concept of language (a concept in the sense of a universal representation, an essence). Thus the question of language, for Heidegger, is not what language is. Rather the question is: "What about language itself [*Wie steht es mit der Sprache selbst*]?" In other words, "how does language presence as language [*Wie west die Sprache als Sprache*]" (GA 12: 10/PLT: 188)? Instead of asking about the essence of language, we are asking about the presencing of language.[5] The answer is: "Language speaks," or "speech speaks," *"Die Sprache spricht."* By "discussing" (Heidegger uses the word *"erörtern,"* which includes the word for place, *"Ort"*) what speaking is, we shall "bring to its place of being [*Ort ihres Wesen*] not so much language as ourselves: the gathering into the event of propriation [*Ereignis*]" (GA 12: 10/PLT 188). The word *"Ereignis"* is the central word of the essay. In order to reach the place of language's presence (the *Ereignis*), we must learn what is called speaking or what speaking means (*heisst*) (see also GA 12: 190/OWL 95). When we have learned what speaking is, then we can take up our "abode," "residence," or "dwelling place" (*Aufenthalt*). Only by taking up our abode within the speaking of language will language tell us its way of presencing.

In this reflection on speaking, the "guiding clue" therefore is the sentence "language is language." Heidegger finds a similar tautological sentence in a 1784 letter from Hamann to Herder: "reason is language, *logos.*" For Hamann, this sentence opens up the depth of an abyss (*Abgrund*). We have seen this word before; it refers to the lack of a ground. Heidegger asks, does the abyss consist in that reason resides in language or is language itself the abyss? But we are not asking what reason is. The clue "language is language" does not lead us to something else (such as reason) in which language may be grounded. The tautological sentence "leaves us to hover over an abyss as long as we endure [*aushalten*, hold out into] what it says" (GA 12: 11/PLT: 189). Then we have a famous comment:

> Language speaks. If we let ourselves fall into the abyss [*Abgrund*] named by this sentence we do not go tumbling into emptiness. We fall upward to a height. Its loftiness opens up a depth. The two [loftiness and depth] span a realm [*Ortschaft*] in which we would like to become at home [*heimisch*], so as to find an abode [*Aufenthalt*] for the essence [*Wesen*, presencing] of man. (GA 12: 11/PLT: 189–90)

In other words, by concerning ourselves with language alone, we occupy, get a hold on, a space, a middle that is grounded on nothing else, and this allows us to understand who we are, to understand that we are mortal (see also GA 12: 255/OWL: 134). To think according to language amounts, for Heidegger, to experiencing the speaking of language itself so that this speaking "happens" (*ereignet*); as an event, it grants an abode.

### WHAT DOES IT MEAN TO SPEAK?

In order to start to answer the question of what it means to speak, Heidegger lays out a kind of history that starts with the "current opinion" about language. The current opinion, according to Heidegger, declares that speech is the activation of the organs for sounding and hearing; speech is the audible expression and communication of human feelings, which are accompanied by thoughts. The current view has three presuppositions. First, speaking is expression. This idea of language, according to Heidegger, is the most common. It presupposes that language is the externalization of an internal representation of something. This idea of language as externalization explains language by something other than language; it turns language into something superficial by making it dependent on something internal. Second, speech is one of man's activities. Thus we have to say that man speaks and that he speaks always some specific language. With this presupposition, we cannot say that language speaks. To say that it is language that does the speaking means, as Heidegger says, that "[language brings about and produces [*er-gibt*] man, and so thought, man would be one promise [*ein Versprechen*] of language" (GA 12: 12/PLT: 190). Heidegger hyphenates "*er-gibt*" so that it indicates that language has given man over, as if he were a gift, instead of man producing language. Instead of language being one of man's activities, man is one of language's "products" or even "promises" (*Versprechen*). As we shall see, humans keep the promise—come into their own—by co-responding to the call that defines language (see also GA 12: 170/OWL: 76). Then, third, human expression is always a representing (*Vorstellen*) and a presenting (*Darstellen*) of the real and unreal. Notice that if we define language as human expression, we are defining language by means of something internally present as a representation, a representation that is then merely externalized so that language is a form of mediation from one representation to another, from mine to your representation. And then, there is nothing to think about, as if the thinking has already been formed and completed, as if there is no beginning of thinking. Moreover, the representation is of something real or unreal, actual or in-actual, and thus language is not an event. It is in relation to this third presupposition that Heidegger sets up the discussion of poetic invention that we usually conceive as being concerned with expressing not something real but something unreal.

Now, from this current view, Heidegger moves backward in history. So for a long time, this view of language—language as expression—has been seen as inadequate. Other views may make language divine, as in the Prologue of St. John's Gospel, "in the beginning was the word." Here logic is contested and the metaphorical use of language is emphasized. But in all these views, according to Heidegger, a philosophical anthropology and biology, a sociology and psychopathology, a theology and poetics are used to explain linguistic phenomena more comprehensively. From "time immemorial," language has always appeared to require a ground in something else, and this appearance has set the standard for how we conceive language (GA 12: 13/PLT 191). Heidegger does not deny that these "time-immemorial" ideas about language are correct. Yet they never bring us to language as language. As Heidegger says, "they ignore completely the oldest essential imprint of language" (GA 12: 13/PLT: 191). Again we see the demand that Heidegger is making, that is, that we treat language as language, as such, and not as expression, not as a means of communication, not explained in terms of something other than language. These old

views therefore do not get us to what language is. We must reflect more
on the speaking of language.

Where then do we find the speaking of language? Heidegger tells us
that we find it "most likely [*ehesten*, the "most before" or the "earliest"] in
the spoken [*im Gesprochenen*]" (GA 12: 13/PLT: 191). This comment means
that if we want to get behind or be older than the time-immemorial view,
we must start with something that is past. For Heidegger what is most past
is the spoken. Here we encounter a reversal like the one between language
and man. Usually we think of the spoken (or of something that has been
spoken) as a thing of the past of a speaking, as if it depended on a prior
speaking. But for Heidegger, the spoken comes first. Or, more precisely,
Heidegger argues that speaking comes to its fulfillment in the spoken.
"Fulfillment" (*Vollendung*) means that the spoken is liberated from the
conditions of its utterance (the condition of being uttered by someone
in a particular place and at a particular time) into its "persistence." In
its persistence, the spoken contains concealed possibilities of speaking,
speaking that was never thought by the person who said the word. Indeed,
by "gathering the ways in which [speaking] persists, the spoken allows
speaking to presence, that is, it allows speaking to show itself as it really
is, and not as it has appeared since time immemorial" (GA 12: 14/PLT: 192).

For Heidegger, however, in order to learn what speaking means, the
pastness of the spoken is not enough. The spoken must be something that
is spoken "purely." Heidegger defines the pure in this way: "What is spoken purely is that in which the fulfillment of the speaking that is proper
[*eignet*] to what is spoken is, in its turn, a beginning speaking [*eine anfan-
gende*].[6] What is spoken purely is the poem [*Gedicht*]" (GA 12: 14/PLT: 192).
On the basis of this definition, we can say negatively that impure speaking
is a speaking that is based in something else; it is a speaking that aims at
the communication of an internal representation. In this case, speaking is
not a beginning.[7] The poem, however, for Heidegger, does not communicate an already formed representation because its sense is not immediately
given. One must not just hear the poem but listen to it. In other words, if
"impurely" means expressing an internal, already formed representation,
then *listening* to something spoken must include something unsaid and
unnamed, more precisely, unthought—so that, by listening, we hear a
beginning of thinking. "Pure" in Heidegger means a beginning of thinking; being a beginning is even the purpose of poetry. The spoken as the
fulfillment of speaking must start some other way of thinking than the

time-immemorial way. As we shall see, what is unnamed in the poem is difference, the "*Ereignis*." There is therefore a bond between the speaking of language and thinking. The bond is that genuine thinking (thinking is not the mere having of an internal mental representation) "thoughtfully follows" (*nach-denken*[8]) what presences in language (GA 12: 14/PLT: 192). Guided as we are by the sentence "language speaks," something presences already. We already have a sense of what language is or, at least, what it is *not:* already we know that language is not the externalization of an internal thought, as if language depended on thought. Instead, thought is bound to language since thought depends on the speaking of language. We need a poem to help us reach the speaking of language. Heidegger selects Georg Trakl's "A Winter Evening."[9]

## THE SPEAKING OF LANGUAGE IS TO CALL

### *The First Stanza: Things Bearing World*

Here is the *first* stanza of "A Winter Evening": "Window with falling snow is arrayed, / Long tolls the vesper bell. / The house is provided well, / The table is for many laid." About the first two lines of the first stanza— "Window with falling snow is arrayed, / Long tolls the vesper bell"— Heidegger says, "This speaking names" (GA 12: 18/PLT: 196). What the speaking of the first stanza names is *things,* in particular, the snow that "soundlessly" (*lautlos,* without tolling) strikes the window. The silence of the snowfall allows one thing to be heard, the bell "tolling" (*läuten*). The bell tolling has a temporal sense; it is the church bell tolling the end of the day: "*Abendglocke.*" So, as Heidegger says, "In such a snowfall, everything lasting lasts longer" (GA 12: 18/PLT: 196). "Therefore," although "daily" [*täglich*] the bells rings at its strictly fixed time, now it tolls "longer." So, here in the first stanza, what the things named point to is *time,* time that is *not* the daily time. We recall the description of boredom that we saw in "What Is Metaphysics?"; boredom is "*Langeweile*": everything lasting lasts longer. In a snowfall, time slows down (not the hustle and bustle of pursuits), and beings as a whole, the world appears.

Or, more precisely, in the slowed-down time of the snowfall, things "presence." Indeed, for Heidegger, the naming of the poem calls things to come into presence, but *not* as objects found "present in the lecture hall" (GA 12: 18/PLT: 196). Here Heidegger makes his first of four warnings about the words he is using (GA 12: 19/PLT: 187). The "is" in the second two verses "sounds" as though the two verses are statements about what is present. "Nevertheless," Heidegger says, "[the 'is'] speaks by calling." The naming taking place in the verses does not consist in attaching a word to a thing already present. Naming "calls things into the word" (GA 12: 18/ PLT: 196). Insofar as Heidegger is defining the speaking of language in terms of a naming that calls, he is defining language itself as a call (*Rufen*). What does calling into the word mean for Heidegger? On the one hand, calling calls in here, and thus it calls into nearness and "presence." (Heidegger uses the word "*Anwesen*," which, like "*Wesen*," has a verbal sense of "presencing"; Heidegger will even extend the verbal sense to the German word for "thing," "*Ding*": "thinging.") But on the other hand, in calling here, calling calls over there, and thus it calls out into the distance, out into what remains absent (*Abwesende*). The calling calls the snowfall and the tolling of the evening bell—here and there, here into presence (as the word), there into absence. In other words, structurally, the call consists in this: If a call is to be a call, it must be the case that what is called is present, as that to which the call is directed. If the thing called, however, is entirely present—like the chair in the lecture hall—then it is not necessary to call it; it is already laid out in front of us (*Vorliegende*). Calling necessarily implies presencing and a drawing-near, but a presencing and drawing-near that includes absence and distance. Therefore, the calling does not "wrest" (*entreißt*, wrench with the hand by force) what it calls away from the remoteness in which it is kept by the calling there. So far, Heidegger has defined language itself as a naming-calling, a "*nennen-rufen*." Now we pass to language as "*heißen*," as in "*Wie heißen Sie?*" "What is your name?" Heidegger also defines language itself as a "calling by name." (Hofstadter renders "*heißen*" throughout his English translation as "bidding.") Because the naming-calling (*nennen-rufen*) is not compulsion, it is, for Heidegger, a "calling by name." Calling by name is "inviting" (*Einladen*) (GA 12: 19/PLT 197); it is a gesture of waving in, of welcome: "Come in!" The rest of the first stanza says, "The house is provided well, / The table is for many laid." The bell tolling at the end of the workday, during a snowfall in which everything slows down, invites things in, but it also brings men under the sky that is darkening into the house. The tolling of the evening bell in the darkening night brings the men not as men, but as mortals "before the divine" (*vor das Göttliche*). House and table, Heidegger says, "binds" (*binden*) the mortals to the earth. House and table cannot be set up, except upon the earth; but the earth absorbs all things back into itself. The things and the mortals therefore are called to "the place of advent" (*Ort der Ankunft*). Language itself ("language is language") is not only a naming that calls into presence while keeping at a distance, it is not only an inviting, a welcoming calling by name, it is also a call to come. In the "Interpretation," we shall return to this complicated definition of language.

The place of advent, however, presences in the same way as the things, "a presence [*Anwesen*] concealed in absence [*Abwesen*]." The place of advent is what Heidegger here calls the fourfold:

> The things that were named, thus called, gather to themselves sky and earth, mortal and divinities. The four are an originary-unified intertwining [*ursprünglich-einiges Zueinander*]. The things let the square of the four linger with them. This gathering letting-linger is the thinging of the things. The unitary square of sky and earth, mortals and divinities, which is stayed in the thinging of things, we call the world. In the naming, the things named are called into their thinging. Thinging, they un-fold world, in which things linger and so are the lingering ones. By thinging, things bear the world out (GA 12: 19/PLT 197).

This is a famous passage in Heidegger's later works. It is clear that with the place of advent, we have moved from the things to the world. Yet it is the things that have made this movement possible. They have made it possible only insofar as they have been named in the way Heidegger has just described. Thanks to Heidegger's comment about the "is" in the verses, we know that things presence, but never as objects fully present before us; things are not objects of pursuit or of scientific investigation. As presencing, the things are doing something; they are active. Hence, Heidegger's use of the noun "*Ding*" as a participle, "*Dingend.*" What the named things do is "linger" (*weilen*). As we have seen, time has slowed down due to the evening snowfall. And as lingering—they are the lingering ones in this slowed-down time—they "unfold" the intertwining of the fourfold (earth, sky, mortals, divinities), which is the world. Insofar as they "thing," insofar as they "unfold," the things "bear" the world. Such carrying is *Austragen*, which in Old German, according to Heidegger, is "*bern.*" It is connected to the English word "born." We are indeed in a time of advent, of something coming. By playing, however, on the word for "bearing," Heidegger makes it signify gesturing (GA 12: 19/PLT: 197). What the things do when called, what constitutes their "thinging," is a kind of gesture: from their central point in the fourfold, they point to the world in the distance. Heidegger concludes, "Hence the first stanza names not only things. It simultaneously [*zugleich*] names world. It calls 'the many' who belong as mortals to the world's square. Things be-thing [*be-dingen*] the mortals. This now says: the things at times [*jeweils*] visit mortals properly [*eigens*] with a world" (GA 12: 20/PLT 197). In this passage, we can see that Heidegger also plays on the verb "*bedingen*," which means "to condition"; the things condition the many mortals with the world, locates them properly in it. But also there is a connection between Heidegger's use of "*zugleich*," which means "simultaneously," and "*eigens*," which means "properly" or "literally." The interaction between "*zugleich*" and "*eigens*," indeed, the calling into presence and absence, anticipates the discussion of the difference of "*Ereignis*." The place of advent is also the event of propriation.

### The Second Stanza: World Grants Things

Where the first stanza named the things that point to the world, the *second* stanza names *the world*. The second stanza says, "Wandering ones, more than a few, / Come to the door on darksome courses. / Golden blooms the tree of graces / Drawing up the earth's cool dew." Like the first stanza, the second calls the mortal, but not all of them. Only more than a few are called, those who are wandering on darksome courses; these are the few wandering toward death. Heidegger says, "These mortals are capable of dying as the wandering toward death. In death the highest concealedness of being gathers itself. Death has already overtaken all dying" (GA 12: 20/ PLT: 198). As we know from *Being and Time,* and as we saw in "What Is Metaphysics?" *Dasein* is finite; the mood of anxiety is a mood of death. Therefore, the "more than a few" are those in anxiety. The relation to death itself allows the few to dwell, while the many "are of the opinion that, by merely installing themselves in houses and sitting at tables, they are already conditioned [*be-dingt*, be-thinged] by the things and have arrived at dwelling" (GA 12: 20/PLT 198). What is precisely at stake in the essay is dwelling: to learn to dwell in the speaking of speech or language (GA 12: 30/PLT: 207). That the many do not understand dwelling implies that now we are approaching what dwelling is, even though Heidegger will not mention dwelling again until the end of the essay (GA 12: 30/PLT: 207). And we shall take up the idea of dwelling in the "Interpretation."

As mortals, the wandering ones belong to the world's fourfold. However, the first two lines of the second stanza do not name the world. It is the second two lines that "properly" (*eigens*) name the world. As Heidegger says, "suddenly" they name something "wholly different": "Golden blooms the tree of graces / Drawing up the earth's cool dew." The tree is not a thing like the others. It roots "soundly" (*gediegen*, solid, upright) in the earth, and its bloom opens itself to heaven's blessing. The towering of the tree and its enrootedness mean that "the earth's abated growth and the sky's open bounty belong to one another" (GA 12: 21/PLT: 198/23). This sentence means that the "sky" (*Himmel*, heaven) gives; what it gives is its "bounty" (*Spende*, benefaction). The earth takes the sky's bounty for growth, but the earth's growth is "restrained" (*verhaltenes*). And the tree shelters the unearned fruit that falls: "saving holiness that is smiling upon [*hold ist*] the mortals." (The Hofstadter English translation says, "loving towards the mortals," but the word "*hold*" is synonymous with the German "*gnädig*," "gracing.") In the golden-blossoming tree there "prevail" (*walten*) earth and sky, divinities and mortals: "Their unitary fourfold or square is the world" (GA 12: 21/PLT: 199). The world therefore is in the tree. According to Heidegger, here the word "world" is no longer used in a metaphysical sense: it means neither the universe of nature and history in its secular or theologically conceived creation (*mundus*), nor does it mean simply the whole of beings that are present (*kosmos*).[10] In other words, the world is neither dependent on a supreme being nor is it a collection of beings. For Heidegger, what is proper to the world—what is called "properly" (*eigens*) in the third and fourth verses—is the world's shining through the things like gold (GA 12: 21/PLT: 199).[11] So the second stanza calls the world that shines through all the things, just as the first stanza called things which gesture to the world. Thus Heidegger concludes the discussion of the first two stanzas by saying, "It [*Es, das Rufen*, the call] entrusts world to the things and simultaneously [*zugleich*] shelters the things in the glistening of world. The world grants to things their presence [*Wesen*]. Things bear [*gebärden*] world. World grants [*gönnt*] things" (GA 12: 21/PLT: 199). We can see in this passage a progression from "*zugleich*," "simultaneously," to a division or difference, which is indicated by the period marks. Moreover, these period marks, which indicate a division, also indicate that the relation is reversible; this is why we can represent the fourfold as a chiasm: Things bear [*gebärden*] world. World grants [*gönnt*] things." The word here for "grants" is "*gönnt*" which also means to favor; this word should be connected with "the favor [*Gunst*] of the world" (GA 12: 25/PLT: 203/28).

### Transition to the Third Stanza: Difference

Thus the first two stanzas both speak by calling, calling things to come to the world, calling the world to come to things. Then Heidegger says,

> The two ways of calling are different but not separated. But neither are they also coupled in one another. For the world and things do not subsist alongside one another. They go through one another. Thus, the two traverse a middle. In it they are unified. As unified, they are intimate. In our language [German], the middle of the two is named the between [*das Zwischen*]. The Latin language says: "inter," to which the German "unter" corresponds. The middle of the two is intimacy. The intimacy of world and thing is not a mixture. Intimacy prevails only where the intimate, world and thing, purely divides itself and remains different. [*Innigkeit walte nur, wo das Innige, Welt und Ding, rein sich scheidet und geschieden bleibt.*] In the midst of two, in the between of world and thing, in their "inter," in this "unter," the division prevails [*in diesem Unter-waltet der Schied*] (GA 12: 21–22/PLT: 199).

In the final phrase, Heidegger has split the German word for "difference," "*Unter-schied*," into its two roots. (The splitting of "*Unter-schied*" is why Hofstadter puts the word "difference" at the end of the sentence. In the remaining pages of the essay, Heidegger continues to hyphenate the "*Unter-schied*" so that we see the word "*Schied*" (division). Hofstadter then continuously hyphenates the word "dif-ference," which allows one to see the root "ference." The sense of "ference" as carrying over is not irrelevant to Heidegger's discussion since he speaks of the relation between thing and world as "diaphora.") The final phrase means: inside (*Unter,* inter), that is, in the middle, the departure or division (*der Schied*) prevails (*waltet,* this word also has a sense of violence). By upper-casing and adding the hyphen to the "*Unter-*," Heidegger is showing that this "*Unter*" is to be connected, across the "*waltet*" (prevailing) to "*Schied*" (division). The intimacy of world and thing presences (*west*) in the division of the "between"; it presences in the "*Unter-Schied*," in the "inter-division." The inter-division or difference holds the world and thing "outside of one another" (*aus-ein-ander*), yet on the basis of the difference, the world and thing "go into one another" (*durch-gehen ein-ander*). In short, with the difference, there is also a unity (difference is the unifier [*das Einigende*]); there is both confrontation and intimacy, that is, a carrying (*diaphora*), a carrying *out* (*aus*) of one from another and a carrying *in* of one into another (*das Innige*). The difference bears the world in its worlding and the thing in its thinging. The middle is not the mediation of two separate beings, but rather it "elicits" (*ermittelt*) the "presencing" (*Wesen*) of the world and thing. It bears this unity into the relation they have "to one another" or into their "intertwining" (*zueinander*). Just as the word "world" no longer has its metaphysical meaning, the word "difference" (*Unter-schied*), Heidegger tells us, does not have its usual and customary sense. Difference does not refer to various kinds of difference; it is not a generic concept. It no longer means a distinction between objects "laid out before" (*vor-liegt*), it is not based in objects placed before (*vor-gestellt*), nor is it abstracted by means of our representation (*Vor-stellung*). Here the word "difference" refers only to this one difference (*dieser Eine*); it is unique (*er ist einzig*). What this difference does is make the thing properly a thing while it makes a world properly a world. As Heidegger says, "the dif-ference for world and thing *appropriates* things into bearing a world and *appropriates* world into granting things. [*Der Unter-schied für Welt und Ding ereignet Dinge in das Gebärden von Welt, ereignet Welt in das Gönnen von Dingen*]" (GA 12: 22/PLT: 200; Heidegger's emphasis). The entire purpose of the essay lies in bringing us to the place of the *Ereignis*, the place of propriation. This place is the difference. In the "Interpretation" below, we shall return to this place, which is the outside itself. In any case, what is important in this quotation is that the difference metes out what is *proper* (*eigentlich*) to things and world. The difference therefore is the dimension, according to Heidegger. Just as difference no longer has its usual or customary sense, dimension no longer means an area that is already present. It is a process of measuring out the presence of world and things (GA 12: 23/PLT: 200). Now we see, however, that in the two ways of calling—the calling of the things (bearing the world), the calling of the world (granting the things)—what is "properly" called is the difference. The calling of the difference brings us to the third stanza.

### The Third Stanza: The Event of Propriation (Ereignis)

The *third* stanza says, "Wanderer silently steps within; / Pain has turned the threshold to stone. / There lie, in limpid brightness shown, / Upon the table bread and wine." According to Heidegger's discussion, the wanderer has been called into silence, which is indicated in the "emphatic call" (*betonten Rufen*) of the first line: the wanderer "silently" (*still*) crosses the doorway (GA 12: 23/PLT 201). "Suddenly and strangely," Heidegger continues, "the call sounds." This call is the second line: "Pain has turned the threshold to stone." Heidegger stresses that these are the only words in the poem written in the past tense. As past, the threshold is what is prior to world and thing. Even though it is prior to or comes earlier than world and thing, the threshold is not a thing of the past. It endures. If it did not endure, if it were not dependable, the difference between world and thing would disappear like a line drawn in dirt. The threshold must be as hard as stone; it is the "the ground-beam" (*Grundbalken*) (GA 12: 24/PLT: 201). The second verse "names" pain as what has turned the threshold into stone. The wanderer has been called to pain. Just as with his earlier discussion of moods (as in "What Is Metaphysics?"), here Heidegger warns us not to think of pain psychologically or anthropologically. Heidegger defines pain as what "rends" (*reiß*); it is the "rift" (*Riss*) (which extends the idea of the division [*Schied*]). And yet he insists that pain is the "jointure" (*die Fuge*, "the joining agent") of the rift (GA 12: 24/PLT: 202). Following the idea of a rending (or disjointure) that joins, we can, it seems, think of pain as a cut or incision. Insofar as the pain does not "grow stiff" (*erstarren*), but continues to presence "unflagging" (*ausdauernd*) (GA 12: 24/PLT: 201), we can think of the pain as a scar. Pain cuts or divides and yet as a scar it does not disappear; it continues to gather the cut skin toward itself. Given the understanding of pain as a joining rift (the image of the scar), Heidegger says that "Pain is the dif-ference itself" (GA 12: 24/PLT: 202). The poem calls the difference into presence.

How does the difference presence? The next two verses say: "There lie, in limpid brightness shown, / Upon the table bread and wine" (GA 12: 25/ PLT: 202). In reference to these two verses, Heidegger says,

> The rift of the dif-ference lets the pure brightness glisten. Its luminous jointure [*lichtendes Fugen*] de-cides [*ent-scheidet*] the brightening of the world into its own [*ihr Eigenes*]. The rift of the dif-ference *expropriates*

[*enteignet*] the world into its worlding, which grants things. By the brightening of the world in their golden glistening, bread and wine simultaneously [*zugleich*] come into their own gleaming (GA 12: 25/PLT: 203, my emphasis).

The word "*enteignet*" has been emphasized because it indicates that expropriation (*Enteignis*) is necessarily connected to the event of propriation, to the event of making proper (*Ereignis*). Based on this quote and the earlier one (from GA 12: 22/PLT: 200, "the dif-ference for world and thing appropriates things into bearing a world and appropriates world into granting things"), the formula for the intimacy of appropriation and expropriation is the following: So that the things are themselves properly, they must bear world, but, insofar as they bear world, they must be related to what is not proper to them, that is, to the world; similarly, so that the world is itself properly, it must grant things, but, insofar as it grants things, the world must be related to what is not proper to it, that is, to the things. The difference or interdivision makes this improper propriety happen; it is the event of propriation. In other words, expropriation implies that the world passes out of—it is a process of "worlding" and not a collection of objects, not *mundus* or *cosmos*—what is proper to it into things, which are different from the world and therefore are not what is proper to the world. By the world expropriating itself, the things, however, become proper; things go into their own, into what is proper to them: they shine like gold. Shining like gold, things gather, according to Heidegger, the fourfold to themselves in a simple unity (GA 12: 25/PLT: 203). Gathering to themselves the fourfold, that is, the world, the things expropriate themselves. Expropriation implies that the things pass out of—they too are a process of "thinging" and not objects—what is proper to them into the world, which is different from the things and therefore is not what is proper to things. By the things expropriating themselves, the world however becomes bright. We are able perhaps to get a better sense of what Heidegger means here with pain if we reflect on the things named in the fourth verse. The things are bread and wine. Heidegger calls bread and wine "simple things" (*einfache*); their bearing of the world is fulfilled "immediately" (GA 12: 25/PLT: 203). Although Heidegger does not elaborate on the simplicity and immediacy of bread and wine, it seems that he is referring to the fact that their production cannot be planned and calculated; the harvest of wheat and grapes is dependent on grace. They are the fruits of the heaven and earth, gifts from the divinities to the mortals. But grace can be withheld, and that is pain-ful, even deadly. Thus, although "the third stanza calls world and things into the middle of their intimacy"—the world grants the things as gifts, as holy—"the jointure [*Die Fuge*] of their intertwining [*Zu-einander*] is *pain*" (GA 12: 25/PLT: 203, my emphasis). In the "Interpretation," we shall return to this idea of pain since it indicates the transformation of humanity that is a necessary component of the overcoming of metaphysics.

As we see now, Heidegger devotes the most time to the discussion of the third stanza. Of the three stanzas, it is the "first" that "gathers the calling of the world *and* the calling of the things" (GA 12: 25/PLT: 203, my emphasis). The "first" means the third stanza calls "originarily" (*ursprünglich*) (GA 12: 25/PLT: 203). It is originary calling because it calls the difference by leaving it unspoken. (See also GA 12: 24/PLT: 202, where Heidegger says that the verse calls the difference, but not by name.) Origi-nary calling calls only what is unnamed. Only by leaving the difference unnamed is the poem pure. Only by calling (or inventing) something unnamed does thinking begin, do we have a beginning of thinking. What must be thought is the intimacy that the unnamed difference brings forth, the intimacy of world and thing, each being called into what is proper to them: the bearing and granting. The "originary call" (*ursprüngliche Rufen*), which calls things and worlds in the difference, is then the "proper calling" (*eigentliche Heissen*). As Heidegger says,

> This calling [*Heißen*] is the presence [*Wesen*] of language. Speaking pres-ences [*west*] in what is spoken in the poem. It is the speaking of language. Language speaks. It speaks by calling the called, thing-world, world-thing, to come to the between of the dif-ference. (GA 12: 26/PLT: 203)

Language speaks by calling world and thing into the advent of the differ-ence. Indeed, what is originary, most prior, for Heidegger, is the difference. What is so called, as we saw, is invited, not compelled or forced. But even as invited, what is called is "commanded" (*befohlen*). Heidegger specifies that he is using the word "*Befehlen*" in the sense of "commended" as in the old saying "Commit thy way unto the Lord" or "Put thyself in the care of the Lord!" or "Go with God" (*Gott befohlen!*). The calling of language commands what is called to put itself in the care of the "*Unter-schied*," of the inter-division or difference. Putting the things into the care of the difference means the thing is linked to the world and the world is linked to the thing. By linking the thing to the world, the difference links the thing to what is different from it and not proper to it (the world); the thing becomes improper (GA 12: 26/PLT: 203), the difference "expropriates the thing". However, being linked improperly, the thing is properly a thing since it is "exalted" (*enthebt*) into a gift from the divinities to the mortals and fruit from the heavens and the earth. As a gift of grace, the thing is then at "rest" (*die Ruhe*): "the thinging of the thing rests in the worlding of the world" (GA 12: 26/PLT: 203). Resting means that the thing is "still." As still, the thing is "enough" (*Genüge*). But likewise, the world is stilled so that "the world is content [*begnügen*] in the thing" (GA 12: 26/PLT: 203). With the thing and the world being enough, we no longer speak endlessly of what we do not have. Being enough, the world and thing allow for silence.

### CO-RESPONDING AS THE KEEPING OF THE PROMISE

With this sequence from rest to still to silence, Heidegger plays on the German word "*Stillen*," which means both stillness (at rest) and silence. But, since the essays concern language, what is at stake is really silence. For Heidegger, silence is not the mere opposite of sound. How are we to think about the claim that silence is not the opposite of sound? In everyday life, there is the motion of rushing about for more things and the noise of communication about how to get more things (see GA 12: 155/OWL: 62). Here things and the world never look to be enough. Being driven in this way, no one sees the thing in relation to the world—things seem to be mere objects present before us for use, near enough to grasp—and no one sees the world in relation to things—the world seems to be a mere collection of present objects. In this noisy hurrying about, the difference between world and things is endangered. However, in the slowed-down time of the snowfall and in the moment of wandering across the threshold out of the snow, this motion and sound disappear so that other activities and sounds are possible. Which activities and sounds? Heidegger says that the difference quiets in two ways: the thing in thinging (bearing) and the world in worlding (granting). This movement means that we are able to experience things as gifts of the divinities, thanks to the bounty of the sky and the earth, allowing us mortals not to die. Things and the world are enough. When the things and world are enough, when things are intertwined with the world—"in the simple onefold of the pain of intimacy"—they "save" (*retten*) the difference (GA 12: 27/PLT: 204). The world and things intertwined save the difference by means of the silence made possible by the snowfall. Then, in the quiet of the snowfall, the difference is able to call. Although world and things save the difference, the difference calls them by ringing out of the silence. This ringing is something different from the mere communication of a time of day for the grasping of present objects. It commands that the world and things come forward into presence while remaining out of reach. The command that rings out is, for Heidegger, language:

> Language speaks in that the command of the dif-ference calls world and things into the simple onefold of their intimacy. Language speaks as the peal of silence. Silence silences by the carrying out, the bearing and enduring, of world and thing in their presence [*Wesen*]. The carrying out of world and thing in the manner of silence is the propriating event [*Ereignis*] of the dif-ference. Language, the peal of silence, is, inasmuch as the dif-ference happens [*ereignet*]. Language presences [*west*] as the propriative dif-ference [*ereignende Unter-Schied*] for world and thing (GA 12: 27/PLT: 205).

Language speaks as a calling, but the calling calls to the event of the difference, of the division in the middle of world and things.

We have seen that in the discussion of Trakl's poem, humans were called as mortals to the event of the difference. But the ringing out of the call is, as Heidegger says, "nothing human" (GA 12: 27/PLT: 205). Instead, humans are "linguistic" insofar as their being linguistic "happens" (*ereignet*) out of the speaking of language. In other words, through the event of propriation, language brings man into "its own" (*sein Eigenes*). Instead of humans using and needing language (for communication), the presence of language uses and appropriates the speaking of mortals. It uses the speaking of mortals to sound as the peal of silence for the listening of mortals. The pure calling of world and thing, of the difference, occurs in the poem. Engaging in another reversal, Heidegger claims that poetry is not a higher mode of everyday language; everyday language is a forgotten and used-up poem (GA 12: 28/PLT: 205).

In effect, when Heidegger says that language brings man into his own, makes him proper to what he is, he has returned to the current view of language with which he started. In the current view, language is considered as one of man's activities. But now, thanks to the discussion of the Trakl poem, we see that man is one of language's promises. However, we do not yet see how the promise of man is kept. It is kept insofar as we see that human speech, as mortal speech, is dependent on the speaking of language. In order to understand that dependency, we must think of human speech not as an utterance or expression, the externalization of man's inner thought, but as a co-responding (*Ent-sprechen*) (or echo [GA 9: 310/PM: 236; GA 12: 166/OWL: 72]). The "*Ent-sprechen*" keeps the "*Ver-sprechen*." Co-responding, for Heidegger, is a "holding back" (*Zurück-haltung*), a restraint (keeping quiet) so that it is able to listen to the command of the call. Such responding must be ready for the command. But being ready includes not only the holding back in restraint, not only not speaking so that one may hear the ringing of silence afterward, but also hearing the command beforehand. Mortal speech as listening for the call must anticipate it. It is this anticipating while being restrained that Heidegger calls "dwelling in the speaking of language" (GA 12: 30/PLT: 207).

### Interpretation: Dwelling in the Speaking of Language

Why is an overcoming of metaphysics necessary? Heidegger answers the question in the following way:

> What is to be decided is whether Being itself, out of its own proper truth, can come to pass [*ereignen*] in a relation appropriate to the essence [*We-sen*] of human beings; or whether metaphysics, in turning away from its own ground, continues to prevent the relation of Being to the human from lighting up, out of the essence [*Wesen*] of this very relation, in such a way as to bring human beings into a belonging to Being (GA 9: 369/PM: 280).

What is metaphysics? As Heidegger says, metaphysics does not think "the truth of Being" (GA 12: 369/PM: 280). Here Heidegger is alluding to his many reflections on the ancient Greek word for truth: "*a-letheia*."[12] Heidegger always stresses the literal meaning of the ancient Greek word. Because the "*letheia*" means "concealment," the ancient Greek word can be rendered as "un-concealment" ("*Unverborgenheit*"). For Heidegger, truth is not the adequation of a representation and a thing (or perception). Truth happens when something comes from concealment into unconcealment. Unconcealment, however, is always limited by concealment. Therefore the truth of Being is, as we saw in "What Is Metaphysics?" finitude. If Being is presence or presencing, presence emerges from absence and distance; presence is always limited with non-presence. Not thinking the truth of Being, metaphysics commands all beings to be formed or enframed in representations (*Vorstellung*). This demand for representation is why Heidegger defines metaphysics as the "persistent confusion of beings and Being" (GA 9: 370/PM: 281). Metaphysics always conceives Being on the basis of a prior representation of beings as such. Insofar as it forms beings into representations, metaphysics turns all beings into objects, things present before us (*Vor-stellung*), with no absence and distance. In this way, metaphysics overpowers beings. Under this power, beings become calculable (GA 9: 308–9/PM: 235). According to Heidegger, "calculation refuses to let anything appear except what is countable" (GA 9: 308/PM: 235). In this compulsion to make countable, the thinking that is based in metaphysics "lets all beings count only in the form of what can be set at our disposal and consumed" (GA 9: 309/PM: 235). And not only all beings; the earth itself must appear in "uniformly calculated availability" (GA 12: 200/OWL: 105). So, Heidegger says, "This is why the battle for the dominion of the earth has now entered its decisive phase" (GA 12: 201/OWL: 105). In this decisive phase of overpowering (in the age of what Foucault would call "bio-power"), and against "unbounded calculation" (against what Merleau-Ponty would call "operationalism"), a transformation of humanity is necessary.

If we are to change who we are, then, since we have always conceived ourselves as the ones with language, there must be a transformation of language. Indeed, we must not ask at this point "what is metaphysics?" but, as Heidegger did, "what about language itself?" As with the nothing, Heidegger attempts to think about language itself: "language is language." Such abyssal thinking, in effect, lays out a plane of immanence, making immanence immanent to nothing transcendent, immanent to nothing but itself. Abyssal thinking makes language immanent only to itself. As we saw, in order to think language only from itself, Heidegger effects several reversals, the most important of which is that man does not possess language, language possesses man. The reversal of man and language means that language can no longer be defined as the expression of an internal, already formed, mental representation. In this case, speaking would be human externalization. For Heidegger, however, language itself speaks. This strange sentence means that rather than being a product, language is a calling forth. First and foremost, for Heidegger, language is the place of advent. It calls to come.

What does it call to come? As we saw, in the answer of what language calls to come, Heidegger makes four negative statements (warnings): negative statements for things, world, difference, and pain. These four negations punctuate Heidegger's discussion of language. The Trakl poem calls things to come into the word. But when they come to presence in the word, they do *not* presence like objects in the lecture hall (GA 12: 18/PLT: 196). Not being present like objects, they gesture to absence and distance. They gesture to the world. They bear the world which then presences as the fourfold, as the intertwining of earth, heavens, mortals, and divinities. The "tree of graces," however, names the world specifically. But when it is so named, the world does *not* presence as universe (understood either theologically as creation or secularly, that is, scientifically, as matter) or as the whole collection of present objects (GA 12: 21/PLT: 199). The world presences as that from which things are granted as gifts, as that thanks to which things shine as gold. As we saw, here we have a difference, even though the Trakl poem does not name it: things bear world; world grants things.

Thus what language most calls forth is the difference between world and things. Throughout, we have seen each philosopher eventually arrive at the place of difference. When Husserl describes the parallelism between the psychological and the transcendental, he is using neither "identity" nor "difference" in the natural or habitual sense. Instead of the natural sense, there is, for Husserl, a "complex interpenetration of ontological senses [*Ineinander des Seinsinnes*]" (HUA IX: 294/CH: 173). Similarly, for Heidegger, the difference called forth by language does *not* have its usual and customary sense, as two objects juxtaposed (GA 12: 22/PLT: 200). It too is a unique "*Ineinander*." As the unique difference, the difference is prior to world and things, prior to the fourfold of earth, heavens, mortals (or humans), and divinities. This priority makes the difference almost ultra-transcendental,[13] or, reverting to the terminology of "What Is Metaphysics?" the difference is the nothing. As prior, the difference makes the thing properly a thing while it makes the world properly the world. The place of the difference in Heidegger is the place of the event of propriation (*Ereignis*). The *Ereignis* is the "law" of the propriety of things and world (GA 12: 248/OWL: 128). The structure of the *Ereignis* repeats the structure of the call. Just as the call calls (or invites) into presence while sheltering in absence, the event at once makes proper and improper (*Ereignis* and *Ent-eignis*). The world as worlding goes into its own, which is to grant things; but by granting things, which are different from world, the world becomes something other than itself. The thing as thinging goes into its own, which is to bear world; but by bearing world, which is different from the thing, the thing becomes something other than itself. As a reversible relation between thing and world, the event of propriation makes the thing shelter the world in absence while it makes the world shelter the thing in absence. When things and world are doing what is proper (and improper) to them, they are freed from the rushing about of everyday life. The idea of freeing the world and things from the forms of utility allows us to see, as we did as well in the last chapter, a concept of multiplicity buried under Heidegger's idea of gathering and simplicity. Indeed, that the impropriety of world and things cannot be eliminated, that it is a necessary element in the event of propriation, allows us to claim that the event sets into motion a kind of becoming (continuous variation). Heidegger, however, adds a new facet to the idea of becoming we have been developing. That new facet is messianism: the advent or keeping of the promise of language, the call to come.

Not only does language call the difference of things and world. It also calls the humans. As we saw, at first, it looks as though the many humans are called. Only a few, however, hear the tolling bell. The few who hear the call are those who experience themselves as mortals, who experience themselves as capable of dying. Mortality means, according to "What Is Metaphysics?" that the few experience themselves as powerless. In the mood of anxiety, things slip away and become strange, uncanny, or, more precisely, "un-homely" (*unheimlich*). Just as the many are reduced to the few, the few are reduced to the one, the one wanderer. We might say that the wanderer, in Heidegger, is a kind of "conceptual persona" for the event of propriation.[14] In experiencing mortality, the wanderer undergoes pain. Heidegger's reference to pain is not surprising since we saw that in "What Is Metaphysics?" Heidegger speaks of "galling pain" as having an abyssal source in the nothing. The reference to pain brings us to Heidegger's fourth negative statement in "Language." Just as things are not present objects, just as the world is not a collection of objects, and just as the difference is not the generic difference between objects, pain is *not* to be conceived psychologically or anthropologically. What is being experienced is not a feeling relative to a human being or to the body of a human being; it is not a subjective state of mind. What is being experienced is the fundamental "rift" or "tear" (*Riss*) of Being itself, that is, it is the experience of the difference that joins in disjointure. Being internal to Being, this pain cannot be eliminated. As we said above, it resembles a scar. The image of the scar suggests that we might think of this experience as the pain of the "heart."[15] No matter how near the beloved is, that "person" is never able—this is a necessity that cannot be changed—to be present completely, properly, in person.[16] Even in proximity, the beloved is always distant. The pain of distance (the rift), however, is a pain in which the one from whom you are separated is nevertheless always present in your heart (the jointure). With this memory (present), there is always forgetfulness (separation).

Having the pain always in his heart, the wanderer lives differently than the many who think that love includes nothing but the enjoyment of someone's presence. Instead, the wanderer loves the slipping away of the beloved, of all things; he loves their absence. The wanderer lives then in the uncanny, in the unhomely, but the unhomely has become for him homeliness; the strange resides, with him, within the familiar. As Heidegger says, speaking of Heraclitus' fragment 119 (which is usually translated as "A man's character is his daimon"), "The (familiar) abode [*Aufenthalt*] for humans is the open region for the presencing of god (the unfamiliar one)" (GA 9: 356/PM: 271).[17] Having the presence of the god—the daimon—in one's heart, in the familiar, makes the abode ("*Aufenthalt*" being Heidegger's translation of the Greek word "*ethos*") unfamiliar and other. The god remains distant in the heart. Heidegger's messianism is therefore a messianism without a messiah; it is always incomplete or unfinished, always still to come, insofar as the other always remains unfamiliar, absent, improper, never coming in person. Thus, dwelling in the speaking of language means to wait for the other or the god to come. Heidegger had indirectly spoken of waiting when he described dwelling as the restraint of listening to the call while anticipating the call. Of course, waiting is also related to the mood of boredom. We recall that in "What Is Metaphysics?" Heidegger had distinguished between superficial boredom (when one is bored with a specific thing) and profound boredom (when one is bored with everything). In his 1929–30 lecture course and book *The Fundamental Concepts of Metaphysics*, Heidegger had provided extensive descriptions of profound boredom. Through these descriptions Heidegger aims to show that human *Dasein* is fundamentally attuned to the world in profound boredom. Even if we do not experience profound boredom, it is "asleep" in us. However, for profound boredom to be "awake" in us, we must not, according to Heidegger, "counteract" it. The demand not to counteract profound boredom means:

> neither this nor that bustling activity, it means neither this passivity nor that activity, but something this side of the two: *Dasein's keeping to itself,* which is a *waiting.* This waiting is not indeterminate, but is *directed out toward an essential questioning of itself.*[18]

In other words, if the mood of profound boredom is to become awake, then we must ask: "Who are we?" Now we are able to see how the description of the wanderer provides us with the idea of a transformation of humanity, the very transformation that defines the overcoming of metaphysics. In the discussion of the second stanza, Heidegger had said that the few are called to come across darksome courses not for themselves but for the many (GA 12: 20/PLT: 198). Listening to and anticipating the call of language, the few are those who demand of us that we ask this question of ourselves. They are waiting for the question to be asked; they are waiting for an answer; they are waiting for the promise of language to be kept, the promise that is man. Language, for Heidegger, is not determined by the aim of communication, but it does call forth a community. It calls forth a people, who, being powerless to stop the things from slipping away—as Merleau-Ponty would say, they no longer conceive themselves as the "manipulandum"—this powerless people dwell with the uncanny, they dwell in the home that has become unhomely. Like the god who is never able to appear in person, this people is always still to come.

The transformation of humanity is supposed to occur out of a transformation of our understanding of language. The principal transformation is that language speaks, not man. When Heidegger writes this tautological sentence ("language is language"), he is trying to show that the traditional view of language as expression is not adequate to the being of language. Viewing language as expression, it seems as though man first forms an internal representation, which he then externalizes. To think about language only from language (language based on nothing else), however, implies that language speaks on the basis of silence. In Heidegger, silence functions in two ways. First, silence is the quieting of the snowfall, which eliminates what Heidegger in *Being and Time* had called "*Gerede*," "idle talk." Minimally, idle talk refers to the discourse of the rushing about for pursuits; it is communication. But more precisely, idle talk refers to a past of speaking; it contains the intelligibility of things that had already been expressed. Idle talk is a "spoken speaking" (*gesprochene Sprache*) (SZ: 168/BT: 162). In its first function, silence eliminates spoken language. The eliminative silence leaves behind the tolling of the bell, the call. We came to this call (the call of language or language as a call), however, through what Heidegger calls the "pure spoken" (*rein Gesprochenes*), which is the poem (GA 12: 14/PLT: 192). How are we to think of the spoken, of the poem, when, like idle talk, the spoken refers to a past of speaking (*Gerede* and *Gesprochene*)? We know that for Heidegger, the poem is not a "higher mode of everyday speech"; rather, everyday discourse is a "used-up poem" (GA 12: 28/PLT: 205). As used up, everyday discourse does not speak truly since it communicates only what has already been said. Not being communication, the poem, however, speaks something that was hitherto unspoken: "everything spoken [*Das Gesprochene*] stems in a variety of ways from the unspoken" (GA 12: 240/OWL: 120). It is not a repetition of what has already been spoken; rather, it is a beginning. In order to be a beginning, the speaking of the spoken must speak from silence. This speaking from the unspoken, a beginning speaking, is the second function of silence in Heidegger. This second function of silence turns the spoken into a "trait" (*Zug*) (GA 12: 240/OWL: 121) or a "trace" (*Spur*) (GA 12: 245/OWL: 125). What we must learn to do is to dwell within this "whole of traits" (GA 12: 240/OWL: 121). Another name for this whole of traits is the outside.

~

## Transition

By 1969, in *The Archeology of Knowledge*, Foucault calls the outside "the archive." Here too, he has stopped speaking of the outside as a "murmur" that is quieter (like a bell tolling) than opinions and things said.[19] Indeed, in *The Archeology of Knowledge*, he separates what he thinks is the primary "atom" of language, "the statement" (*l'énoncé*), from silence.[20] Nevertheless, we cannot avoid noticing the resemblance between the spoken in Heidegger and the statement in Foucault. We see this similarity especially if we stress the pastness of the statement and render "*l'énoncé*" as "the stated." There is also a conceptual similarity insofar as Foucault conceives the statement as starting from a lack.[21] Just as Bergson says that "the whole is not given," Foucault says that the analysis of statements "is based on the principle that everything is never said."[22] And, although Foucault consciously distances himself from phenomenology, and from Merleau-Ponty in particular, in *The Archeology of Knowledge*, this lack ("everything is never said") is what, for Merleau-Ponty, allows artworks to institute possibilities, to institute a future that remains incomplete.[23] As we shall see now, however, in order to reach the institution of this open future, we must, as with Heidegger, return to a tautological sentence. Just as with Heidegger speech speaks, with Merleau-Ponty vision sees.

# 6

## Dwelling in the Texture of the Visible:
## Merleau-Ponty's "Eye and Mind" (1961)

The speech which speaks in us (*die Sprache spricht*), what does it say about language? That it is without foundation, *Abgrund*.

Coming from Merleau-Ponty's 1959–60 course at the Collège de France called "Husserl at the Limits of Phenomenology," this quotation shows the important role Heidegger plays in Merleau-Ponty's final thinking. Heidegger's importance does not, however, diminish the role that Husserl's thought plays in Merleau-Ponty's final thinking: "Husserl never stopped speaking of *Bewußtsein* [consciousness], never stopped believing in the possibility of an intentional analytic, but converges with Heidegger through the idea of *Verflechtung* [interweaving], of the *Ineinander* [the "in-one-another"]."[1] Freud too remains important: "Positing the unconscious not as a primary consciousness that has been masked, not as a forgotten adequation (postulate of the priority of conventional thought, of the priority of the thinking subject), but as indirect consciousness or consciousness without exactitude or thinking for itself, near to itself, according to systems of weakly articulated signs, of 'near' equivalences. Consciousness can be 'unconscious,' if it is not intellectual adequation, but a signifying or speaking subject" (NC 59–61: 151). And Heidegger, for Merleau-Ponty, does not diminish Bergson: "The truth of the matter is that the experience of a coincidence can be, as Bergson often says, only a 'partial coincidence.' But what is a coincidence that is only partial? It is a coincidence always past or always future, an experience that remembers an impossible past, anticipates an impossible future, that emerges from Being or that will incorporate itself into Being" (VIF: 163–64/VIE: 122–23). Indeed, Merleau-Ponty is the inheritor of all the figures we have been following. But more than that, Merleau-Ponty's final thinking draws together all the conceptual components we have been assembling for the research agenda called continental philosophy.

The research agenda starts (1) with the universal epoché, which opens up a non- or presubjective level of experience. Following Deleuze, we have called this experience "immanence." Immanence is not immanent to the subject or to the "I." Using Heideggerian formulas, we can say that immanence is not a being; it is (the) nothing, or immanence is immanent to nothing but itself. Being ungrounded or abyssal, immanence is the same. Merleau-Ponty, however, makes the tautology explicit when he describes vision in terms of the seer-seen relation, in terms of a relation of auto-affection.[2] Throughout our investigations, auto-affection has been in the background of immanence. Below reflection, and as the origin of reflection, is spontaneous self- or auto-experience.[3] For Merleau-Ponty, auto-experience takes place in the sensible itself, or, as Heidegger would say, in Being itself. More importantly, (2) Merleau-Ponty transforms auto-affection into hetero-affection. Auto-experience is never self-adequate; it always contains latency and invisibility. In a word, it includes concealment. Even though it is auto, the same, there is a division. Indeed, Merleau-Ponty defines auto-affection by "in-division," which resembles Heidegger's "*Unter-Schied*." Ultimately, as we shall see, the Merleau-Pontean division consists in a multiplicity since what is concealed is a surplus veiled in silence. Silence leads to language. Clearly, (3) Merleau-Ponty conceives language as expression. However, Merleau-Ponty explicitly refers to Heidegger's "Language" essay when he says that "[speech] falls towards the height."[4] Merleau-Ponty's taking up of the Hamann passage, as quoted in Heidegger, means that there is no prior, already formed, internal representation to be expressed (it falls into the abyss); rather, the lack of ground (*Ab-grund*) allows speech to say more, to say what has never been expressed before (it ascends toward the height). As Merleau-Ponty says, "Language is neither *Äußerung* [externalization] of the organism, nor *Ausdruck* [expression] of life, nor even sign, nor even *Bedeutung* [meaning], but *the advent of Being*" (NC 59–61: 148; my emphasis). The liberation of language from representation implies (4) the overcoming of metaphysics.

To claim that Merleau-Ponty is engaged in the project of overcoming metaphysics is perhaps controversial. Although his final courses at the Collège de France indicate this trajectory for his thinking, we cannot know for certain due to his untimely death. Nevertheless, it is clear that throughout the 1950s, Merleau-Ponty refers to his own thinking as an "archeology."[5] A philosophical archeology digs into the soil of metaphysics, just as we saw Heidegger do in "What Is Metaphysics?" Always reacting to Cartesianism, Merleau-Ponty digs specifically into the depth of the mixture of mind and body, a mixture that must be understood through the visible. But that is not all. Like Heidegger (and here we must note that despite Merleau-Ponty's continuous interest in and writings on the politics of his time, he did not make a political mistake), Merleau-Ponty thinks that the overcoming of metaphysics also brings forth a transformation of humanity.[6] Humans must learn to dwell in the texture of the visible.

We have selected the 1961 essay "Eye and Mind" because it provides— through a published text—a clear view of Merleau-Ponty's mature and final thought.[7] More importantly, in "Eye and Mind," we see Merleau-Ponty in effect overcome the metaphysics of contemporary science (at least science as it is found in the middle of the twentieth century). The metaphysics of science is objectivism insofar as science attempts to determine the object in general in its separation from the subject; but it is also a subjectivism insofar as the object in general comes about by means of scientific operations. This metaphysics is one result of the dismemberment of Descartes' philosophy. For Merleau-Ponty, however, there is another result. The other result comes from Descartes' idea of the mixture of mind and body. By retrieving this other part, Merleau-Ponty aims to put science back upon the soil of the sensible world. In other words, beyond metaphysics, for Merleau-Ponty, lies vision, the seer-seen relation. As we have already indicated, the seer-seen relation is auto-affective because the seer sees with his or her eyes, that is, vision is corporeal. That vision takes place with fleshy eyes (and not with the mind) means that the one who sees can be seen. Although there is sameness in this relation, the sameness does not allow for a clear and distinct representation. In vision, specifically in the painter's vision, there are always shadows, things concealed behind one another. What the painter does, according to Merleau-Ponty, is express that concealment. The painter makes the invisible visible.[8] Indeed, this making visible of the invisible is the painter's "silent science."

The science arose as soon as some human being scratched lines in a cave. The cave lines gave rise to what Merleau-Ponty in "Eye and Mind" calls a "hidden historicity."

## Summary-Commentary: Hidden Historicity[9]

### SCIENCE, PHILOSOPHY, AND PAINTING

For the final Merleau-Ponty, the painter is opposed to the scientist, at least to the contemporary scientist (science as Merleau-Ponty found it in 1960, but perhaps also still today). Like Heidegger in "What Is Metaphysics?" Merleau-Ponty in "Eye and Mind" is asking what happens to us when science has become our passion. The basic answer to this question is that we have become "the manipulandum" that we think we are (OE: 12/MPR: 352). The basic question is indicated by the first sentence of "Eye and Mind": "science *manipulates* things and gives up dwelling in them" (OE: 9/MPR: 351; my emphasis). The word "manipulates" literally means to grasp with the hand. For Merleau-Ponty, grasping by the hand is a way of thinking, in which "thought is deliberately reduced to the set of collecting and capturing techniques that thought invents" (OE: 10/MPR: 351). So reduced, thinking, that is, scientific thinking in the contemporary epoch, operates by constructing internal models of the thing. The operation turns the thing into what Merleau-Ponty calls an "acquisition," that is, into a positivity with no distance and no indeterminacy. Then, having the internal models, that is, having "indices and variables" of the thing, the contemporary scientist makes transformations based on the definitions of the indices and variables. Not only, for Merleau-Ponty, does the scientist make things too close—his operations make things too close by making internal models of them—but also, as he turns things into mental representations, he ends up operating only on those representations or ideas, separating himself farther and farther from the things; science therefore "confronts the actual world only from a greater and greater distance" (OE: 9/MPR: 351). In its distance from the world, "the philosophy of science" is a "surveying thought" (OE: 12/MPR: 352). Surveying thought sets up at once an ontology of extreme objectivism (what is present before the gaze is all that it is, present, an ontology of acquisition) and an ontology of an extreme subjectivism (the subject's operations, really the subject's power, determine what is absolutely). "All beings" then, as Merleau-Ponty says, look to be "nothing to us" (that is, independent from us, an object in general) and yet "discovered [to be] predestined for our artifices" (that is, in agreement with our operations) (OE: 9/MPR: 351). Through this "operationalism," contemporary science conceives itself up as autonomous. As Merleau-Ponty says, "To say that the world *is*, by nominal definition, the object *x* of our operations is to adjust the scientist's epistemic situation to the absolute, as if everything that was and is has never existed but in order to enter the laboratory" (OE: 11–12/MPR: 352; Merleau-Ponty's emphasis). Contemporary science therefore reverses the relation of the relative and the absolute, of the dependent and independent. Merleau-Ponty says that the reversal of contemporary science is "entirely new" (OE: 10/MPR: 351) because the "classical science" of the modern epoch (the epoch of Descartes to Kant) "kept the feeling of the opacity of the world." Classical science conceived itself as dependent on something else.[10]

The comparison between contemporary science and classical science is important for Merleau-Ponty, as we shall see later in "Eye and Mind." Even here, however, at the beginning, we see that classical science's self-conception as dependent on something else (in its case, on a transcendent God) motivates the entire essay. Merleau-Ponty wants to place the thought of science back in the "soil of the sensible world and in that of the worked-on world [that is, cultural world]" (OE: 12/MPR: 352). This is the world in which we live. And we live in it with the actual body we call "mine" (OE: 13/MPR: 352). The body I call mine will also call up "associated bodies," that is, others who "haunt me and whom I haunt" (OE: 13/MPR: 352). Here, as we shall see, with the actual body (which Merleau-Ponty will call the flesh [*la chair*]), there will be a kind of proximity and distance that is different from that of the thought of science: the proximity of touch is always intertwined with a distance (and otherness), and what remains distant (and other) is always intertwined with a proximity. This intertwining precedes the thought of science. Here Merleau-Ponty calls it "primordial historicity" (OE: 13/MPR: 352); later he will call it "hidden historicity" (*historicité sourde*) (OE: 90/MPR: 377). If the thought of science places itself back in this historicity, then it "will learn to expatiate upon the things themselves and upon itself, and will once more become philosophy" (OE: 13/MPR: 352).

Unlike the thought of science, art and especially painting draw from "this pool of raw sense" (OE: 13/MPR: 352). For Merleau-Ponty, it is the painter in particular who is able to hold the world in suspense, that is, the painter puts all opinions and beliefs out of play. To use Husserl's term, the painter for Merleau-Ponty performs the epoché. Here, however, Merleau-Ponty is not only interested in the metaphysical beliefs underlying contemporary science, he is also interested in political opinions. Indeed, as Merleau-Ponty points out, "activism wants to know nothing" of this raw sense. Only the painter, for Merleau-Ponty, is able to draw upon the implacable source of sensations without the burden of having to offer opinions and advice.[11] The painter is able to "waive the responsibilities of the speaking man" (OE: 14/MPR: 353). The painter is not even accused of escapism when he dodges politics. He is responding, according to Merleau-Ponty, to an urgency that passes beyond every other urgency. What he does, using his only "'technique,' . . . the one that his eyes and hands are given by means of seeing, by means of painting" (OE: 15/MPR: 353), is pull canvases from the world. No one complains about the painter's work, even though his canvases add hardly anything to "the hopes and angers of humans" (OE: 15/MPR: 353). So what we must now investigate is the painter's "secret science." We must ask, "What is this fundamental of painting, this fundamental perhaps of all culture" (OE: 15/MPR: 353)?

## "THIS STRANGE SYSTEM OF EXCHANGES"

As we have seen, according to Merleau-Ponty, the ontology of contemporary science posits a mind that gazes upon a representation of the world, a world of ideality (OE: 17/MPR: 354).[12] In this ontology, vision is "an operation of thought" (OE: 17/MPR: 354), "a gaze from inside, a third eye" (OE: 24/MPR: 356). For Merleau-Ponty, such an ontology forgets "the working actual body [le corps opérant et actuel]" (OE: 16/MPR: 353); it forgets "the fleshy eyes" (nos yeux de chair) (OE: 25/MPR: 356). If we consider, however, the working actual body, we experience it not as a "chunk of space," not as "extension," but as "my body." Experiencing it as my body, we experience the body as "an intertwining of vision and movement" (OE: 16/MPR: 353).

In order to explain this intertwining, Merleau-Ponty tells us, on the one hand, that it is enough to see something in order to know how to reach it (OE: 16/MPR: 353). Why? Because my body counts among the visible things. As one among many visibles, I can direct my body in the visible. Yet on the other hand, vision depends on movement. Merleau-Ponty means that one sees only because one looks away from something to look at something else. One sees only that at which one looks, that is, we see only based on the movements of our eyes. I can see because I move my eyes (I am looking at this and away from that), and I can move my eyes because I can see (seeing my eyes, I know how to move them). This "extraordinary overlapping" means that movement is not "a decision made by a mind" (*une décision d'esprit*) and the body that moves (and the world in which it moves) is not "in itself or matter" (OE: 18/MPR: 354). But this "extraordinary overlapping" appears in one more way: "My body moves *itself*" (OE 18/MPR: 354; Merleau-Ponty's emphasis).

Self-movement leads Merleau-Ponty to present an important description about the self. The enigma of my body derives from the fact that my body is "simultaneously" seeing and visible. Because the seer is a visible thing, can be looked at, he is able to recognize, "in what he sees then, the 'other side' of his seeing potentiality" (OE: 18/MPR: 354). This "other side" is that the seer is looked at. There is passivity at the center of the self-relation. Just as I am moved by myself, I am seen by myself, and I am touched by myself. For Merleau-Ponty, the self-relation is not coincidence. The self is not a self by transparency like thought, but a self by confusion, "narcissism," a self caught up in things, having a front and a back, a past and a future. As he says, "This initial paradox cannot but produce others" (OE: 19/MPR: 354). Visible and mobile, my body is a thing, *and yet* because it sees itself and moves itself, it holds things in a circle around itself; "they are incrusted in its flesh" (OE: 19/MPR: 354). Thus the things are prolongations of the body; the whole world is of "the very stuff as the body." All these reversals and antinomies "are different ways of saying" that "a visible" starts to see, becomes visible for itself. It starts to see through the fact that the other things see me, by means of the vision that emanates from all things. There is an "in-division of the sensing and the sensed," "like the original fluid in the crystal" (OE: 20/MPR: 354). Alluding to the self, Merleau-Ponty calls this "original fluid in the crystal" "interiority" (OE: 20/MPR: 355).[13] Merleau-Ponty is trying to show that this interiority does not precede the material makeup of the human body, but neither is it caused by the material makeup. The contingencies that make up the human body do not, by themselves, bring about a human being alone. In other words, the accidental character of the makeup of the human body is a necessary condition, but not a sufficient condition for the human to appear. If the body could not have a self-reflection (Merleau-Ponty mentions *the mirror,* which anticipates the later discussions in "Eye and Mind"), there would be no human beings: the human is doubled. As Merleau-Ponty says, "A human body is present when, between seeing and visible, between touching and touched, between one eye and the other, between the hand and the hand, a kind of crossover is made, when the spark of the sensing-sensible is lit, when the fire starts to burn that will not stop until some accident of the body unmakes what no accident would have sufficed to make" (OE: 21/MPR: 355). In the "Interpretation" below, we shall return to the "crossover" of the sensing-sensible, which here Merleau-Ponty calls "this strange system of exchanges."

"This strange system of exchanges"—auto-affection—brings forward, according to Merleau-Ponty, all the problems of painting (just as the problems of painting bring forth those of the body): "These problems illustrate the enigma of the body and the enigma justifies the problems [of painting]" (OE: 21/MPR: 355). Because of the seer-seen reversibility, because I can *be* seen, like a thing, I am made of the "same stuff" as the things. Since things and my body are made of the same stuff, it is necessary that my body's vision be made somehow in them, or that their visibility doubles itself in my body. Their being seen "awakens" in me "a secret visibility," "an echo," "an internal equivalence," which can be made visible; when made visible, this internal equivalence, for Merleau-Ponty, is painting. Painting is a visible "to the second power" (*à la deuxième puissance*), "a carnal essence or icon of the first [visible]" (OE: 22/MPR: 355). Even though painting is the double of the visible, painting is not another thing, like a "faded double"; paintings are, as Merleau-Ponty says, "the halos of Being." To explain the status of painting, Merleau-Ponty refers to the cave paintings at Lascaux: "the animals painted on the walls of Lascaux are not there in the same way as are the fissures and limestone formations. Nor are they *elsewhere*" (OE: 22/MPR: 355; Merleau-Ponty's emphasis). If they were as the fissures are, they would be things. Merleau-Ponty does not say what the painted animals would be if they were elsewhere. Instead, he admits that we are hard-pressed to say where they are.

The neither-thing-nor-elsewhere status of the painting or picture leads Merleau-Ponty to the problem of the image and the imaginary. He says that the word "image" is in ill repute because we have "thoughtlessly" believed that "a drawing is a tracing" (OE: 23/MPR: 356).[14] This belief has then made us think as well that a "mental image" is a drawing like a decal (nothing but a copy). The only difference between the mental image and the physical one is that the mental image belongs to "our private bric-a-brac." In short, with either the mental or the physical, we have conceived the image as a "second thing," a second thing through which we aim at things in their absence, and, similarly, we have conceived the mental image, since it is a traced outline of things, an occasion to rethink the constitutive relations of things. Merleau-Ponty, however, argues that the image is not a traced copy. As Merleau-Ponty says, "[The image, the picture, and the drawing] are the inside of the outside and the outside of the inside, which the duplicity of sensing makes possible and without which we would never understand the quasi-presence and imminent visibility which make up the whole problem of the imaginary" (OE: 24/MPR: 356). This comment means that the imaginary provides "a diagram" in my body of the actual, that is, not the presence of the life of the actual but its "quasi-presence." In other words, it provides the premises—the shadows, contrasts—that make the actual be visible. But also, the imaginary provides "traces of the vision of the inside" of the actual, what "clothes vision internally," that is, it provides the interior in an imminent visibility, a "not yet" visibility of the invisible that animates the visible. The imaginary, according to Merleau-Ponty, offers to the look "the imaginary texture of the real" (OE: 24/MPR: 356). Although Merleau-Ponty does not say this, we would have to call this imaginary "the true imaginary," in opposition to "the false imaginary" he will describe at the end of "Eye and Mind."

Does the (true) imaginary, however, require that we speak of a "third eye"? According to Merleau-Ponty, there is no need to posit such a mental eye. Our "fleshy eyes" are much more than passive receptors for light. Merleau-Ponty calls them "computers [*computeurs*] of the world." With this comparison (which is obscure), Merleau-Ponty seems to mean that "fleshy eyes" are active in the sense that they transform (and do not merely copy) what they passively receive, just as a calculator provides a sum from the numbers put into it. But then, Merleau-Ponty changes the image from a sort of calculator: the fleshy eyes "have the gift for the visible as we say that the inspired person has the gift for languages" (OE: 25: MPR: 357). This comparison too implies an activity: the inspired person speaks one language, but transforms it and responds in another. But again, we must ask, what exactly do the fleshy eyes transform? Merleau-Ponty says:

> The eye sees the world, and it sees what the world lacks in order to be a painting, and what the picture lacks in order to be itself, and, on the palette, the colors for which the painting is waiting; and it sees, once it is

done, the picture that responds to all these lacks, and it sees the painting of others, the other responses to other lacks. It is no more possible to make a restrictive inventory of the visible than it is to catalog the possible usages of a language or even its vocabulary and turns of phrase (OE: 25–26/MPR: 356).

The fleshy eyes transform lacks into something nearly visible. What is important in vision and language are the lacks. The lacks in vision (hidden sides or profiles, invisibles) allow for the endless variability of responses, either linguistic or in paintings: "Painting celebrates no other enigma but that of visibility" (OE 26/MPR: 357).

Merleau-Ponty admits that saying that the enigma of visibility is what painting celebrates is a truism; of course, the painter's world is a visible world. Yet painting carries the "delirium" of vision to "its highest power" (*sa dernière puissance*). This highest power of vision is "having at a distance." For Merleau-Ponty, the painter extends having at a distance "to all the aspects of Being" (OE: 27/MPR: 357). This "strange" way of possessing does not mean (Merleau-Ponty mentions the art critic Bernard Berenson) that painting evokes tactile values. For Merleau-Ponty, painting neither evokes nor is it tangible. What painting does is "give visible existence to what profane vision believes to be invisible" (OE 27/MPR: 357). Profane vision, that is, everyday vision, is the potency of the eye reduced to the one function of recognition (just as language can be reduced to the function of communication). As recognition, profane vision believes that what it sees is a mere copy of a mental representation or a concept (in the proper sense); therefore it does not or cannot see that the thing emerges from invisibility, that sides and profiles of the thing remain invisible. Painting makes these invisibles *exist,* that is, painting makes them affect our vision. These invisibles, which painting gives us to "have," provide the visible with a sort of "voluminosity" and "texture." Merleau-Ponty concludes: "The eye *dwells* in this texture as man dwells in his house" (OE 27/MPR: 357; my emphasis). As with Heidegger, with Merleau-Ponty we shall return, in the "Interpretation" below, to the idea of dwelling. Here, Merleau-Ponty defines dwelling as interrogation.

When the painter (such as Cézanne) makes a mountain be seen, what does he ask of the mountain? Merleau-Ponty responds, "To unveil the means, which are nothing but visible means, by which the mountain makes itself into a mountain before our eyes. Light, lighting, shadows, reflections, color, all these objects of the investigation are not entirely real beings; like ghosts, they have only visual existence. In fact, they exist only at the threshold of profane vision; they are not commonly seen" (OE: 29/MPR: 357). These ghostly visibles allow us to see things, but they efface themselves in the vision (OE: 30/MPR: 358). To see the thing, it was necessary not to see the play of shadows and light around it. Then Merleau-Ponty says, "The visible in the profane sense forgets its premises" (OE: 30/MPR: 358). The interrogation of painting aims to make us remember this secret and feverish genesis of things in our body. The interrogation is not the schoolmaster's question; it is not the question from someone who knows to someone who does not know. It is the reverse of this kind of question: a question from someone who does not know to a vision that knows everything, a vision that we do not make but which is made in us. As Merleau-Ponty says, making painting and language (or more precisely poetry) parallel:

> Max Ernst (and surrealism) is right to say, "just as the role of the poet since [Rimbaud's] famous *Letter of the Visionary* consists in writing under the dictation of what is being thought, of what articulates itself in him, the painter's role is to circumscribe and project what is making itself seen within himself." The painter lives in fascination. (OE: 30/MPR: 358)

The gestures of the painter—those gestures of which he alone is capable since others, the many, do not have the same lacks as he does—seem to emanate from the things themselves, and thus the roles between the painter and the visible reverse. Merleau-Ponty quotes Paul Klee, saying, "In a forest, I have felt many times over that it was not I who looked at the forest. Some days I felt that the trees were looking at me, were speaking to me. . . . I was there listening" (OE: 31/MPR: 358). From the voice of the trees, the painter gives birth to what was, previously, virtually visible; the painter gives birth to pictures. We shall return to Merleau-Ponty's quote from Paul Klee in the "Interpretation" below.

In the pictures themselves, we could seek, Merleau-Ponty says, a "figured philosophy of vision" (OE: 32/MPR: 359). The philosophy of vision Merleau-Ponty has been describing is a "pre-human vision"; it is a vision prior to recognition, prior to "profane vision." If painting "figures" this philosophy of vision, then we should be able to find "the painter's way of looking" in the paintings. The painter's way of looking appears when painting contains pictures of mirrors, as in Dutch paintings. Merleau-Ponty's discussion of mirrors here alludes back to the seer-seen relation, in which the seer sees something like himself since he is also, as a corporeal seer (the fleshy eyes), something seen; "there is a reflexivity of the sensible." "The specular image," however, according to Merleau-Ponty, "more completely than lights, shadows, and reflections, draws, within things, the work of vision. Like all other technical objects, such as tools and signs, the mirror has sprung up along the open circuit running from the seeing body to the visible body. Every technique is a 'technique of the body.' The technique figures and amplifies the metaphysical structure of our flesh" (OE: 33/MPR: 359). Containing the first nominative occurrence of Merleau-Ponty's technical term "the flesh," "*la chair*," this quotation means that "the metaphysical structure of the flesh" is the origin of technology. Technology originates in the flesh because all the things that humans produce are things that are visible. As visible, they are extensions of the visible body, of the flesh; but also, as extensions, they are ways of having access to things, ways of looking back at things. Therefore, the mirror, as one of the technical things, is a paradigmatic example of the metamorphosis of the seeing and the visible that "defines both our flesh and the painter's vocation." Painters love to paint themselves painting because of the reversibility of seer and seen; Merleau-Ponty calls this reversibility here "a total or absolute vision" (OE: 34/MPR: 359). Merleau-Ponty finally draws the most radical conclusion from the absolute vision (the reversibility of the seer and seen to which all other ways of looking are relative): "Essence and existence, imaginary and real, visible and invisible—painting blurs all our categories, spreading out before us its oneiric universe of carnal essences, efficacious resemblances, muted meanings" (OE: 35/MPR: 359–60). We shall return, in the "Interpretation" below, to this conclusion and "the metaphysical structure of our flesh."

## DESCARTES' CLASSICAL ONTOLOGY[15]

Profane vision, however, does not conceive the relations between essence and existence, the imaginary and the real, the visible and the invisible as blurred; it conceives these relations as separations. As we anticipated in the opening discussion of science, the separation leads to two complementary mistakes in the conception of vision; these complementary mistakes are "fusion and survey" (VIF: 169/VIE: 127).[16] Manipulation implies that one conceives vision (or, more broadly, sensing) as fusion: the immediate grasping with the hand. In this case, sensing takes place in an absolute proximity somewhere; one coincides with and touches pure facts. If one conceives sensibility, however, as survey (*survol*)—the view from nowhere—one intuits and sees pure essences; in this case, sensing takes place at an infinite distance everywhere (VIF: 169/VIE: 127). In other words, according to Merleau-Ponty, profane vision is at once too close to the thing seen and too far away from it. The mistakes reside *both* in the purity of touch, fusion, and absolute proximity, *and* in the purity of vision (which in *The Visible and the Invisible* Merleau-Ponty calls the "*kosmotheoros*" [VIF: 32/VIE: 15]), survey, and infinite distance.

It is this double mistake that orients Merleau-Ponty's analysis of Descartes' *Optics* conception of vision in Part III of "Eye and Mind." What Merleau-Ponty is trying to show is that Descartes' conception moves from one mistake to the other. Because Descartes is interested only in how vision works so that he can correct it with artificial organs, he conceives light as a mechanical cause. Descartes, according to Merleau-Ponty, considers not the light that we see but the light that makes contact with, the light that touches and enters into our eyes from the outside (OE: 37/MPR: 360). In other words, Descartes considers light as a cause outside that makes real effects inside of us. Merleau-Ponty says, "In the world there is the thing itself, and outside this thing itself there is that other thing which is only reflected light rays and which happens to have an ordered correspondence with the real thing; there are two individuals, then, *connected by causality from the outside*" (OE: 38/MPR: 360, my emphasis). For Merleau-Ponty, the proximity of cause has two interrelated consequences. *First,* and this is most important, causal contact eliminates resemblance; even the resemblance of the mirror image becomes a projection of the mind onto things. For the Cartesian, according to Merleau-Ponty, the image in the mirror is an effect of the mechanics of things. For Merleau-Ponty, because Descartes wants to conceive light on the basis of causality, a conception that requires no resemblance between a cause and an effect, we do not in fact have an image in vision, but rather a representation. A representation, such as an etching, works as signs do; signs in no way resemble the things they signify. Here, in the signs that do not resemble, we see the origin of the indices with which, as we saw, today's science works (OE: 9/

MPR: 351). Merleau-Ponty says, "The magic of intentional species—the old idea of efficacious resemblance so strongly suggested to us by mirrors and paintings—loses its final argument if the entire power of the picture is that of a text to be read, a text totally free of promiscuity between the seeing and the visible" (OE: 40/MPR: 361).[17] This citation brings us to the *second* consequence of Descartes' conception of light as causal contact: vision in Descartes is the decipherment of signs. This move, which starts with the conception of light through causality, to vision as decipherment, leads to surveying thought. Since vision is the decipherment of signs, it *thinks* in terms of a flat surface; signs on the page for instance (like writing) are flat. But also, according to Merleau-Ponty, the representation, which is the effect of the mechanical light, immobilizes the figure so that it can be abstracted from the background.[18] Descartes takes only the external envelope of things, and this abstraction of the figure from the field is why for Descartes, according to Merleau-Ponty, drawing is what defines pictures (OE: 42/MPR: 362). Because the flat representation presents only the outlined figure, for Descartes, depth is a false mystery (OE: 45/MPR: 363). Cartesian space is in itself, one thing outside of another, *partes extra partes,* and thus depth is really width. If we think we see depth, this is because we have bodies (which are the source of deceptions); therefore depth is nothing. Or if there is depth, it is my participation in God; the being of space is beyond every particular point of view (OE: 46/MPR: 363). God then, who is everywhere and has no perspective, sees all things, without one hiding another; thus God creates, or, better, draws, a "geometral," a surveying plan.[19] So we can see now that Merleau-Ponty's analysis of vision in Descartes' *Optics* goes from fusion, at one extreme, to the other extreme, surveying thought (OE 48/MPR: 363).

Here then is a reduced presentation of Merleau-Ponty's analysis of vision in Descartes' *Optics.* According to Merleau-Ponty, Descartes starts from the conception of light as a cause contacting the eyes. The contact of light with the eyes is the absolute proximity of fusion. Because the contact with the eyes is causal, there is no resemblance between the image and the thing. Instead of images that resemble, we have signs. Signs are the figure without the background, immobile, and they are flat, like writing or a drawing. Vision then in Descartes becomes the decipherment of signs. And the decipherment of signs leads to the intellectual surveying plan, the geometral. The geometral is a drawing according to rectilinear perspective, with nothing hidden. It is surveying thought. Therefore, this double mistake—at once too close (contact) and too far (survey)—concerns the conception of space. As Merleau-Ponty says (clearly appropriating Heideggerian wording), "Like all classical ontologies, this one elevates certain properties of beings into a structure of Being, and in so doing it is both true and false" (OE: 47/MPR: 363). This quotation means that Descartes (following, as Merleau-Ponty points out, "the perspectival techniques of the Renaissance" [OE: 49/MPR: 364]) idealizes space. The idealization is even necessary according to Merleau-Ponty, if thought is too empirically dominated. Descartes was right to make space clear, manageable, and homogeneous so that thought is able to survey it. "His mistake," according to Merleau-Ponty, "was to erect it into a positive being, beyond all points of view, all latency and depth, devoid of any real thickness" (OE: 48/MPR: 364). Something about space evades our attempts to survey it from above.[20]

"Yet" (*cependant*)—this "yet" is important for Merleau-Ponty— "Descartes would not have been Descartes if he thought to *eliminate* the enigma of vision" (OE: 51/MPR: 365; Merleau-Ponty's emphasis). To show this, Merleau-Ponty considers what happens when we want to understand how we see the situation of objects. It seems as though we have no other recourse than to suppose that the soul is able (knowing where the parts of its body are) to transfer its attention to all the points of space to which its body extends. Here we see vision being turned into the mind's inspection (like a pilot in a vessel), judgment and recognition, a reading of signs. With this first conception of vision, it looks as though thought alone (and not the fleshy eyes) is enough to see. Yet, Merleau-Ponty asks, "how does the soul know that space of its body which it extends toward things, that primary *here* from which all the *theres* will come?" (OE: 53/MPR: 365; Merleau-Ponty's emphasis). The primary here is not just another mode of extension. It is the place the soul calls "'mine,' a place in which the soul dwells" (OE: 53/MPR: 365). Here we have the "mystery of passivity." Without reflection, the eyes converge and the soul sees a certain distance. The soul then "thinks according to the body, not according to itself" (OE: 53/MPR: 365). The vision that results from this "immemorial thought inscribed in our inner workings" is the vision that actually occurs. As Merleau-Ponty concludes, "The enigma of vision is not eliminated; it is referred from the 'thought of seeing' to actual vision" (OE: 54/MPR: 366).

Merleau-Ponty stresses that vision as it in fact happens (not idealized vision) does not overthrow Descartes' philosophy.[21] The practices of actual vision refer, for Descartes, to an order of existence that we are not burdened to think. We are not burdened to think it because factual vision is a thought united with a body. As so united, it cannot by definition be thought. Merleau-Ponty says, "The truth is that it is absurd to submit to the pure understanding [*l'entendement*: the intellect] the mixture of the understanding and the body" (OE: 55/MPR: 366). The clarity of thought and the obscurity of the mixture are, for Descartes, grounded in a Truth (that is, God), a truth that Merleau-Ponty also calls an "abyss" (OE: 56/MPR: 366). Our position as created beings disqualifies us from investigating this ground. "The secret of the Cartesian equilibrium" is that there is a limit to what can be thought, but this limit does not disqualify the enterprises of thought. The Cartesian equilibrium is "a metaphysics which gives definitive reasons to do metaphysics no longer" (OE: 56/MPR: 366). Today, as Merleau-Ponty says, it seems that the Cartesian equilibrium between science and obscurity "has been lost and lost for good" (OE: 56/MPR: 366). "Our science" has rejected both the justification and the restrictions that Descartes made for its domain. "The detour into metaphysics that Descartes had to make at least once in his life," science manages to do without (OE: 57/MPR: 366). The "technized" thought of science is no longer doubled with an unfathomable God. Operational thought, according to Merleau-Ponty, even claims for itself, in the name of psychology, "that domain of contact with oneself and with the world which Descartes reserved for a blind but irreducible experience" (OE: 57/MPR: 366). Clarifying his criticism of science, Merleau-Ponty continues, "Operational thought [contemporary science] is fundamentally hostile to philosophy as thought in contact" (OE: 57/MPR: 366). Science continues to conceive all things as "constructa" (that is, as constructs of its own operations), while "philosophy maintains itself against such operationalist thought" (OE: 57/MPR: 367). Lacking such an equivalence, "Our science and our philosophy are two faithful and unfaithful offshoots of Cartesianism, two monsters born of its dismemberment" (OE: 58/MPR: 367).

From "our science," Merleau-Ponty turns to "our philosophy." Indeed, Merleau-Ponty lays out a sequence of investigations: the actual world, the body, space, light, vision, questioning, and thinking. Our philosophy must be not the inspection, but the "prospection" of the actual world, which means that it must investigate the compound of body and mind that we are. The body then becomes not the means, but the depository of vision and touch. The body moves itself; so we must think of space not as geometry does (as homogeneous), but as starting from me as the zero point, from space as I live it from the inside, as I am immersed in it. As Merleau-Ponty says, "the world is around me, not in front of me" (OE: 59/ MPR: 367). Starting from the actual world, light is different. It is no longer the action of contact, but action at a distance. Vision then "assumes its fundamental power of manifestation, of showing more than itself" (OE: 59/MPR: 367). Vision is no longer the reading mind, a mind that might never have "dwelled in a body." What is at issue, for Merleau-Ponty, is no longer to "speak about space and light, but to make the space and light that are there speak" (OE: 59/MPR: 367). This change in the address (making space and vision address us) also changes questioning. All questions are open since what is addressed is itself a question. What are addressed in the question are depth, light, and Being. What are they, not for the mind cut off from the body, but for the mind suffused throughout the body? And not only for the mind, but also for themselves? For Merleau-Ponty, this prospective philosophy is still to be made. Yet this philosophy starts to come into existence when the painter turns his vision into gestures that produce a picture, when a painter "thinks in painting" (OE: 60/MPR: 368).

## SILENT SCIENCE: DEPTH, COLOR, LINE, AND MOVEMENT

The discussion of contemporary science with which we were just concerned alluded to something like the death of God, as Nietzsche announced it at the end of the nineteenth century. In the twentieth century, flat technicized science is no longer doubled with the depth of God. Therefore, Merleau-Ponty opens the next part by speaking of the modern, that is, twentieth-century, history of painting. This history discloses an effort by painting to break with illusionism, that is, to break with the view that painting must copy reality. In other words, twentieth-century painting is anti-Platonistic, which explains why Merleau-Ponty says that twentieth-century painting has a "metaphysical significance" (OE: 61/MPR: 368). The claim that twentieth-century painting has a metaphysical sense cannot, according to Merleau-Ponty, be demonstrated. The obstacle to the demonstration does not lie in the fact that an artwork is a historical event, and it does not lie in the fact that an artwork generates a plurality of interpretations. No demonstration (in the strict sense) can be given because the "metaphysics" of which Merleau-Ponty is thinking is, like modern painting, not Platonistic, that is, it is not a collection of separate ideas for which inductive justification could be sought in experience. Instead the metaphysics is in experience, in the flesh. Indeed, as Merleau-Ponty says here (and he is alluding to the crucial idea, in his final thinking, of institution), there is a structure in the contingency (which he calls an event) of the flesh and a "virtue" (in the sense of a virtuality, a potentiality) that makes the event a "durable theme of historical life" and gives it "a right to philosophical status" (OE: 62/MPR: 368). So there are grounds for a philosophical meditation on art. Merleau-Ponty admits that such a meditation would require the training of an art historian. But since the potency of artworks outstrips all causal and filial relations, it is permissible for a layperson (that is, for Merleau-Ponty) to register "a profound discordance between the human and Being, when he brings a universe of classical thought into confrontation with the investigations of modern painting" (OE: 63/MPR: 368).

Modern painting's attempt to break with illusionism guides Merleau-Ponty's discussion of the painter's vision. Because it does not aim at recognition, the painter's vision must be distinguished from what Merleau-Ponty calls "profane vision" (OE: 27/MPR: 357) or "ordinary vision" (OE: 70/MPR: 371). Like Descartes' conception of vision, profane vision consists in two extreme views. On the one hand, there is the view from the airplane, which allows us to see an interval, without any mystery, between the trees nearby and those far away. Yet on the other hand, there is "the sleight of hand" by means of which one thing is replaced by another, as in a perspective drawing (OE: 64/MPR: 369). With these two views, once again, we have the proximity of fusion (the contact through the hand) and the infinite distance of surveying thought (the distance from the airplane). Both the sleight of hand and the view from the airplane separate things and make them be *partes extra partes*. This maneuver and this aerial view are the opposite of the interweaving in which the enigma of vision consists. Here is Merleau-Ponty's description of the enigma of vision: "The enigma is that I see things, each in its place, precisely because they eclipse one another; it is that they are rivals before my sight precisely because each one is in its own place. The enigma is their exteriority known in their envelopment, and their mutual dependence in their autonomy. Once *depth* is understood in this way, we can no longer call it a third dimension" (OE 64–65/MPR: 369, my emphasis). We can see the oxymoronic formulas by means of which Merleau-Ponty is defining the enigma: exterior—known, they are *partes extra partes*—and yet in envelopment—dependent. But we can see as well the reversibility. Each thing is in its own place—exterior to one another—because they hide one another—envelopment; they are rivals—mutually dependent—because each is in its own place—autonomous. While for Descartes depth was a false problem, for Merleau-Ponty, as this quote indicates, depth is the whole question. Indeed, the enigma of vision is the enigma of depth. It is not by accident that Merleau-Ponty quotes Giacometti: "I believe Cézanne was seeking *depth* all his life" (OE: 64/MPR: 369; my emphasis). For Merleau-Ponty, depth is the first dimension or the source of all dimensions; it is "dimensionality" (OE: 48/MPR: 364), "voluminosity" (OE: 27/MPR: 357), the "one same space" (OE: 85/MPR: 375), the "one same Being" (OE: 17/MPR: 354); depth is the experience of the reversibility of dimensions, of a global "locality," where all the dimensions are at once (OE: 65/MPR: 369).

From depth, the figure comes next. The figure is generated by color and line. What is at issue is the dimension of color, the dimension that creates lines, identities, and differences, a something. Like all the other dimensions, color and line are not based in a "recipe," as Merleau-Ponty says, for the visible. It is not a question of adding other dimensions to the two of the canvas. The lack of a recipe means that for Merleau-Ponty painting, or more generally pictures, do not imitate nature. It is not a question of making simulacra of the colors of nature, just as it is not a question of copying the "prosaic line," the line that divides a field from a forest, for example, that a pencil or a brush would only have to reproduce (OE: 87/MPR: 370). As we saw with the discussion of the Lascaux cave paintings, Merleau-Ponty is rejecting the traditional concept of imitation, which implies an external relation between the representation and the represented. For Merleau-Ponty, the painter is not viewing something else from an interior to an exterior. Art, for Merleau-Ponty, is not a "skillful relation, from the exterior, to a space and a world." Instead, the painter is born in the things by the concentration and coming to itself of the visible; the picture is "auto-figurative" (OE: 69/MPR: 370).[22] Here, Klee plays an important role. Merleau-Ponty quotes Michaux saying that Klee's colors seem to have been born slowly upon the canvas, to have emanated from "a primordial ground," "exhaled at the right spot like a patina or mold" (OE: 70/MPR: 370). According to Merleau-Ponty, in Klee, the line is the genesis of the visible. Klee has painted two holly leaves *exactly* in the way they are generated in the visible, and yet they are indecipherable precisely because the painting does not imitate the empirical object called holly leaves. Klee then, as Merleau-Ponty says, "leaves it up to the *title* to designate by its prosaic name the being thus constituted, in order to leave the painting free to function more purely as a painting" (OE: 75/MPR: 372; Merleau-Ponty's emphasis).[23] The lines of the holly leaves do not pre-exist; the lines emerge from the colors and the colors emerge from the depth.

From the figure, line, and color comes movement. Just as twentieth-century painting contests the prosaic line with the latent line, it also creates a movement by vibration or radiation in opposition to change of place (or locomotion). Painting might suggest change of place by presenting—this is what photography does according to Merleau-Ponty—instantaneous frames of motion, of changes of place, suspended between a "before" and an "after." It would present in a picture an isolated instant. But in this kind of picture—here, unlike Bergson, Merleau-Ponty does not criticize cinema[24]—we would not have something moving itself (OE: 78/MPR: 373). For a picture to make a successful instantaneous view of movement, we would have to compose "an image in which the arms, the legs, the trunk, and the head are each taken at a different instant," an image that portrays the body in an attitude which it never at any one instant really held, an image, finally, that imposes fictive links between the parts. It is as if, according to Merleau-Ponty, the mutual confrontation of things that are not possible together make passage and duration well up in bronze or on the canvas. As Merleau-Ponty says, "The picture makes movement visible by its internal discordance. Each member's position, precisely by virtue of its incompatibility with that of the others (according to the body's logic), is dated differently, and since all of them visibly remain within the unity of one body, it is the body which comes to bestride duration" (OE: 79–80/MPR: 374). Here Merleau-Ponty is implying that the same internal discordance that defines movement defines the experience of time, the duration: "painting is never altogether outside of time, because it is always within the carnal" (OE: 81/MPR: 374).

Thanks to this discussion of modern, that is, twentieth-century, painting's attempt to break with illusionism, we now have, according to Merleau-Ponty, a better sense of what is involved in seeing: "Vision is not a certain mode of thought or presence to self; it is the means given me for being absent from myself, for being present from the inside at the fission of Being only at the end of which do I close up into myself" (OE: 81/ MPR: 374). Merleau-Ponty adds that "painters have always known this." Indeed, Merleau-Ponty cites Da Vinci and Rilke speaking of Rodin, both of whom speak of a kind of science, a "silent science," that speaks in works by bringing forth the forms of things that have not yet been subject to operationalist thought. The silent science of painting comes from the eye and it is addressed to the eye. The eye, for Merleau-Ponty, is truly the window of the soul, in the sense that the eye opens the soul to what is not soul. A Cartesian cannot believe this since, for him, the eye does not see; it only receives light. Yet we must take literally what the eye teaches us: "we touch the sun and the stars, that we are everywhere at once, and that even our powers to imagine . . . borrow from vision" (OE: 83/MPR: 375). Even a secondary quality like a color ("a visual qualia") is in fact a texture, since it is "a concretion of a universal visibility," since it is the result of "the dehiscence of Being" (OE: 85/MPR: 375). As Merleau-Ponty says, "what defines the visible is to have a lining of invisibility in the strict sense, which [the visible] makes present as a certain absence" (OE: 85/MPR: 375). Merleau-Ponty has already mentioned the eye "touching" and now he speaks of the hand; the hand of the painter who responds to the incitement of the visible "is nothing but the instrument of a distant will" (OE: 86/MPR: 376). Because the painter is nothing more than an instrument, through him "silent Being itself comes to show forth its sense" (OE: 87/ MPR: 376). As we can see, Merleau-Ponty is defining vision ontologically, which he makes explicit in the following formula: vision is the "precession" of what is upon what one sees and makes seen, and of what one sees and makes seen upon what is. In other words, vision is the reversibility of seeing and Being.

## THE FALSE IMAGINARY

On the basis of this reversibility, Merleau-Ponty, in the final pages of "Eye and Mind," outlines what he calls "a false imaginary" (OE: 92/MPR: 378). In other words, he outlines a way of living that lives according to a false idea. The false idea is that of "intellectual adequation" (OE: 91/MPR: 377). In other words, the false imaginary lives in a false idea of truth, truth as adequation. Truth as adequation consists in forming a representation that is empty or unfulfilled. It is fulfilled or realized with a positive content (an intuition or an action), that is, with a "positivity" (OE: 92/MPR: 378). According to Merleau-Ponty, the classical idea of adequation seems to derive from two other ideas. On the one hand, there is "utilitarian activity," in which goals are conceived (represented); they are conceived clearly so that they define the means necessary for the attainment (the realization) of those goals (OE: 90/MPR: 377). On the other hand, there is "speaking thought" (OE: 91/MPR: 377). With speaking thought, the support of thought (in this case, sounds) becomes "manipulable," and, as manipulable, the support can be "exhaustively" determined, made to be "objective," that is, completely present (OE: 91/MPR: 377). The primary implication of the intellectual adequation is the conception of Being as "acquisition" (OE: 89/MPR: 377). We can see that in Merleau-Ponty, the concepts of positivity and acquisition overlap. Both are exhaustively determined, completely present, with no latency; they refer back to the ontology of contemporary science. Yet the concept of acquisition affects how one thinks of problems, and thus of history. As with the idea of a goal (as in utilitarian activity), the idea of a problem (in the ontology of acquisition or objectivism) must be clearly represented to oneself so that it will determine the means necessary for its solution. If one conceives the solution as an acquisition, that is, as completely and permanently present, as a "stable treasure" (OE: 91/MPR: 377), it looks as though once the solution is found, the problem is done, at an end, never to return. Thus as the solutions "accumulate," it looks as though real progress, "progress in itself," is being achieved (OE: 91/MPR: 377). It also looks as though there is a hierarchy of partial problems and partial solutions leading to the goal of a complete solution. In relation to the history of painting, for Merleau-Ponty—but he is also thinking of history in general—the false imaginary includes "the idea of universal painting, of a totalization of painting, of painting's being totally realized" (OE: 90/MPR: 377). The person who lives under this false imaginary, when he or she is confronted with something less than adequation, less than positivity, less than acquisition, less than real progress moving toward totalization, this person asks "what, is that all there is?" (OE: 92/MPR: 377; the French for the question is: "*quoi, n'est-ce que cela,*" which can be rendered more literally as "what, is it only that?").

For Merleau-Ponty, in contrast to this person, there is the painter. The painter imagines otherwise, because the painter "does not regret not being everything [*tout*]" (OE: 92/MPR: 378). He has learned that the truth is never adequate. Because the painter knows that "Being is never complete" (OE 92/MPR: 378), nothing is ever a positivity. The emptiness of an intention is not therefore something that must be fulfilled. In the painter's thinking, the emptiness itself is a positive phenomenon. What the painter "wants is less than [*en deçà*] goals and means"; the painter wants what "commands all our *useful* [*utile*] activities from up above" (OE: 90/MPR: 377; Merleau-Ponty's emphasis). The painter's imaginary derives no more from utilitarian calculation than it does from the privilege of spoken thought. The painter's thinking is "mute" (OE: 91/MPR: 377). As mute, the support of this thinking is not manipulable, just as the lines in the cave paintings are neither the limestone nor second things. The painter knows that "nothing is ever an acquisition" (OE: 89/MPR: 377). Nothing is ever exhaustively determined, completely present, and therefore over and done with. For the painter, there is no accumulation of solutions: "At the moment he acquires a certain '*savoir-faire*,' he sees that he has reopened another field where everything he has been able to express must be said again in a different way" (OE: 89/MPR: 377). The painter knows that problems return and unexpected convergences seem to resolve other problems that he had forgotten. These returns and forgettings mean that the history of painting and history in general "advances through the labyrinth by detours, transgressions, slow encroachments and sudden thrusts" (OE: 90/MPR: 377). There is no progress in itself, no hierarchy or movement toward total realization. Without real progress, it seems as though history is stationary; yet the soil beneath our feet is always shifting because "the very first painting went to the furthest reach of the future" (OE: 92/MPR: 378). This stationary but shifting soil may not be enough for science, but for the painter "only that" (*que cela*) is enough. Unlike the *manipulandum* that man seems to have become, the painter has learned to dwell within this "hidden historicity" (OE: 90/MPR: 377). But the question for Merleau-Ponty is: Do any painters remain (OE 90/MPR: 377)?[25]

## Interpretation: Dwelling in the Texture of the Visible

At the same time as "Eye and Mind," Merleau-Ponty is teaching, at the Collège de France, a course called "Cartesian Ontology and Ontology Today" (1960–61). Even more than "Eye and Mind," this course shows explicitly how much Merleau-Ponty's thought (like that of Husserl) owes to Descartes. In "Cartesian Ontology and Ontology Today," Merleau-Ponty frequently criticizes his colleague at the Collège de France, Martial Gueroult, for reducing Descartes' philosophy down to "the order of reasons," to "a series of positive truths, in a linear order" (NC 59–61: 222).[26] For Merleau-Ponty, however, Descartes' philosophy is "a philosophy of experience" (NC 59–61: 254). Merleau-Ponty says, "The discovery of the Cartesian epoché, of the universe of the *cogitatio,* is not idealism, but the advent of a dimension of experience" (NC 59–61: 261). That the *cogitatio* is a dimension of experience does not mean, however, that Merleau-Ponty is asserting empiricism in opposition to rationalism. As Merleau-Ponty specifies in *The Visible and the Invisible,* "we are not opposing to an interior light an order of things in themselves into which it could not penetrate. There can be no question of fitting together passivity before a transcendent with an activity of immanent thought" (VIF: 67/VIE: 43). Instead, "the fiber of Cartesian Being," for Merleau-Ponty, is "an ambiguous relation of light and feeling, of the invisible and the visible, of the positive and the negative. It is this relation or this mixture that it would be necessary to investigate" (NC 59–61: 222). Cartesian Being is "a certain way of identifying and differentiating" (NC 59–61: 223), which "does not involve the cleavage of one and many" (NC 59–61: 262). Importantly, Merleau-Ponty adds in "Cartesian Ontology and Ontology Today" that the relation is a "mirroring" (NC 59–61: 245 and 251).

To define the dimension of the *cogitatio* as a mirroring transforms the concept of immanence. It transforms the concept in two ways. On the one hand, because mirroring necessarily includes identity, mirroring means that immanence is no longer immanent *to* consciousness, as if consciousness were a separate ground for immanence. Mirroring turns immanence into a groundless self-relation, into auto-affection. Yet on the other hand, the mirroring means that immanence is in fact *not* a self-relation. The mirroring relation takes place across "a minuscule hiatus" (*un écart infime*), which cannot be closed. The minuscule hiatus turns auto-affection into hetero-affection. The auto-affective relations of seeing-oneself-seeing or touching-oneself-touching are differentiated even in self-identity. When I touch myself touching, I touch myself. I am never able, however, to touch myself solely in the active phase of touching. When I hold my left hand in my right, I hold my left hand as a passive thing. My left hand as an active feeler is always out of reach, distant and invisible. Yet, it is *my* left hand, and it can immediately transform itself into a feeling left hand. But then my right hand disappears as a feeling hand and becomes a felt hand. Coincidence is impossible. The minuscule hiatus, for Merleau-Ponty, makes coincidence in auto-affection always and only imminent (VIF: 194/VIE: 147). In auto-affection, there is always invisibility and intangibility. This invisibility, intangibility, difference, and distance, within visibility, tangibility, identity, and proximity, is, as Merleau-Ponty says, "the metaphysical structure of the flesh" (OE: 33/MPR: 359). Even more, the irreducible invisibility included in auto-affection (the "hetero") opens the inside of immanence to the outside. As Merleau-Ponty says in "Eye and Mind," "I live it from within [*du dedans*]; I am immersed in it" (OE: 59/MPR: 367). The irreducible distance makes immanence be (within) the outside. Now immanence is no longer complete intuitive self-knowledge. Like Heidegger, Merleau-Ponty calls the outside "transcendence" (VIF: 248/VIE: 195) because he conceives immanence only on the basis of classical Husserlian phenomenology (VIF: 140/VIE: 103).[27] We are no longer, however, dealing with the phenomenological concept of immanence. The movement toward the outside is not a movement beyond—transcending—one point to another point at which the movement would stop; the movement toward the outside is a movement in place that never stops. As Merleau-Ponty says, it is stationary and yet the soil beneath our feet is moving.[28]

In Merleau-Ponty, the outside is called depth (*profondeur*), the background (*fond*). We can see better how depth works if we turn to an example of auto-figuration that Merleau-Ponty provides in "Eye and Mind." It is the example of the painter's vision of the swimming pool. Here is the description:

> If I saw, without this flesh, the geometry of the tile, then I would stop seeing the tiled bottom as it is, where it is, namely: farther away than any identical place. I cannot say that the water itself—the aqueous power, the syrupy and shimmering element—is *in* space; all this is not somewhere else either, but it is not in the pool. It dwells in it, is materialized there, yet it is not contained there; and if I lift my eyes toward the screen of cypresses where the web of reflections plays, I cannot contest that the water visits it as well, or at least sends out to it its active and living essence. This inner animation, this radiation of the visible, is what the painter seeks beneath the names of depth, space, and color (OE: 70–71/MPR: 371; Merleau-Ponty's emphasis)

In order to understand the description, we must recall that for Merleau-Ponty, the painter's vision is not a gaze from an interior upon an exterior; the painter's vision is fleshy and therefore it participates in the water as another visible. We must imagine that the painter is *within* the swimming pool. But why a swimming pool? Merleau-Ponty selects the vision of a swimming pool because, it seems, any swimming pool has to have depth so that one might be able to swim in it. The depth is the water, which is not in space or in the pool; the water "dwells in it," as Merleau-Ponty says, but "dwelling" (*habiter*) means that the water is not contained in the pool. Rather, dwelling means that the water lets something happen. Without the water, we would be able to grasp the tiles with our hands and hold them in one identical place, but then we would not see their "geometry," or, more precisely, geometry. The water lets us see the geometry, since the water's distortions function as a sort of variation of the spatio-temporal individual. The variation means that the geometry is "farther away than any identical place." Several implications follow from this description.

*First,* the water is prior to both the idea and spatio-temporal individual. In other words, the water is a blur of essence and existence. Insofar as the water is based on nothing but itself—it is a plane of immanence—it is tautological: water is water. Once again, we can see that the auto-affective relation in Merleau-Ponty is in-division. But, *second,* as the water differentiates through the variation it makes possible, the water makes the idea come into being; as Merleau-Ponty says, alluding to Heidegger, we have a "*Wesen* in the sense of a verb" (VIF: 154/VIE: 115; also VIF: 309/VIE: 255). The water, in other words, "*west,*" "presences." It brings forth an essence as an event, but as an event, it is incomplete. In other words, the essence advents, is always coming. *Third,* the event of the essence is always still coming because the water is auto-figurative. It does not copy a prior form. Although Merleau-Ponty here speaks of geometry (as if he were writing about the origin of geometry), there is no limit-form for the water to approximate; as Bergson would say, "the whole is not given." Being midway, the fleshy water means that the geometry is not so far away as to exist in a second world of forms without any support from the visible (cf. OE: 91/ MPR: 377). The geometry reaches only as low as the bottom of the syrupy element and only as high as the screen of cypresses. The generativity of the essence Merleau-Ponty calls a "power" or "potentiality" (*puissance*). So, *fourth,* since the water is grounded on nothing but itself, since the water, in other words, is auto-figurative, this potentiality is not the power to trace or to copy. For the water and the painter who dwells in it, no form can be found. It is the lack of power that opens up the potentiality of the water. It is a powerlessness that allows for the water's power of variation. Its potency is a variability without an original form and without an ultimate purpose. Then *fifth*, the water's power of indefinite continuous variation is why Merleau-Ponty calls water an "element." In *The Visible and the Invisible*, Merleau-Ponty also calls the flesh an element, saying "to designate the flesh, we would need the old term 'element,' in the sense it was used to speak of water, air, earth, and fire, that is, in the sense of a general thing, midway between the spatio-temporal individual and the idea" (VIF: 184/ VIE: 139). Like the water, the flesh is "one 'element' of Being" (VIF: 139/ VIE: 184). Here we can see that since it is only one of the elements, the fleshy water refers to Being as a multiplicity.

For Merleau-Ponty, like water, language is one of the elements. As early as the *Phenomenology of Perception* and as late as *The Visible and the Invisible* (VIF: 189/VIE: 144), Merleau-Ponty defined language as expression.[29] We have already mentioned that Merleau-Ponty seems to be aware of Heidegger's criticisms of language as expression since he cites the "Language" essay in his final courses at the Collège de France. We must assume that Merleau-Ponty thinks that his conception of expression is different from the one that Heidegger attacks. Despite Heidegger's criticisms (expression reduces language down to an externalization of an internal complete thought), it seems that Merleau-Ponty retains the word "expression" in order to define language because he thinks it agrees with the idea of the visible and the invisible. In *The Visible and the Invisible*, speaking of translation into available meanings, Merleau-Ponty says that what the philosopher does is make vision "pass into the expressed," but "vision remains his measure and model" (VIF: 58/VIE: 36).[30] This comment seems to mean that in Merleau-Ponty, we must not conceive vision on the model of expression, but expression on the model of vision. So, just as vision includes the passivity of being looked at and therefore includes the invisibility of that other look's interiority, expression must include passivity and therefore the "inlinguisticality" of the other's speech. That "inlinguisticality" would be silence. In relation to this silence, it is necessary to quote again what Klee says: "In a forest, I have felt many times over that it was not I who looked at the forest. Some days I felt that the trees were looking at me, were speaking to me. . . . I was there listening" (OE: 31/MPR: 358). The passivity of expression is listening, but that to which one listens is, as Klee says, here the trees, or it is the "voice of light." Or, borrowing from Paul Valéry's poem "*la Pythie*," as Merleau-Ponty does, it is "the voice of no one, the voice of the woods and waves." In "Cartesian Ontology and Contemporary Ontology," Merleau-Ponty comments on Valéry's poem by saying that "the visible and what the poem means [are] interwoven" (NC 59–61: 186).[31] From that listening, vision passes into the "inarticulate cry," which is art and literature (OE: 70/MPR: 370). We must notice that the Klee quote says "listening" ("*écoutant*"), not hearing. The voice of the woods and waves, the voice of light, the voice of silence, is not easily heard. All the utilitarian speech of everyday communication pushes it into the background, making it nearly inaudible and invisible. Instead, just as "hidden historicity" (*la historicité sourde*) is hidden because it expresses itself in "a muffled voice" (*une voix sourde*), these voices make no more noise than a murmur.

We have isolated in Merleau-Ponty three of the four conceptual components of the project of what we are calling "continental philosophy": immanence, multiplicity, and language. Does Merleau-Ponty, the final Merleau-Ponty, call for an overcoming of metaphysics? As we anticipated at the beginning of this chapter, no certain answer can be established for this question since we do not have a complete version of *The Visible and the Invisible*. Yet let us assemble some evidence that might point in the direction of an answer. In "Eye and Mind," it seems as though Merleau-Ponty aims at a renewal of metaphysics when he claims that "every theory of painting is a metaphysics" (OE: 42/MPR: 361). He makes a similar comment when he says, "The entire history of painting in the modern period [the twentieth century], with its efforts to detach itself from illusionism and acquire its own dimensions, has a metaphysical significance" (OE: 61/MPR: 368). As we have already noted, he seems to suggest that his thinking in this phase could be called a "metaphysics of the flesh," since he speaks of the "metaphysical structure of the flesh" (OE: 33/MPR: 359). Even more, in "Eye and Mind," Merleau-Ponty also speaks of "a metaphysics of depth" (OE: 56/MPR: 367). Yet the context for this phrase—"a metaphysics of depth" being another possible name for Merleau-Ponty's final thought—is Merleau-Ponty's discussion of Descartes. What Merleau-Ponty is saying is that we have to push Descartes so far that he is made to speak of "a Truth that grounds its own obscurity as well as our own lights." As we noted above, for Descartes, according to Merleau-Ponty, it is futile to probe this truth (here called "God," but Merleau-Ponty also calls it an "abyss"). Then Merleau-Ponty says, "That is the secret of the Cartesian equilibrium: a metaphysics which gives us definitive reasons to do metaphysics no longer" (OE: 56/MPR: 366). Therefore the metaphysics of depth is a metaphysics that gives us definitive reasons to do metaphysics no longer. In other words, the metaphysical structure of the flesh—its non-self-coincidence—pushes us so far as to overcome metaphysics. After all, in *The Visible and the Invisible,* Merleau-Ponty says simply: "metaphysics remains coincidence" (VIF: 169/VIE: 127). Or, as he says at the beginning of the 1958–59 course "Philosophy Today," "The aim is even more generally ontology (in the modern [contemporary] sense), i.e., the consideration of the whole and its articulations, beyond the categories of substance, subject-object, cause, i.e., metaphysics in the classical sense" (NC 59–61: 37). Perhaps what is most indicative are his comments at the beginning of the 1960–61 course, "Philosophy and Non-Philosophy Since Hegel": "what is at issue is a philosophy that wants to be philosophy by being non-philosophy . . . , which opens access to the absolute not as 'beyond,' as a second order positive, but as another order which requires the 'this side,' the double, another order which is accessible only by means of the 'this side'—the true philosophy makes fun of philosophy, it is a-philosophy" (NC 59–61: 275). In other words, the true philosophy is a negation (the privative "a-") of *the* philosophy—meta-physics—the philosophy that posits a second order beyond, another world, like Platonism.[32]

Despite the unfinished status of *The Visible and the Invisible,* it is clear that Merleau-Ponty's final thought fits the definition of the overcoming of metaphysics with which we have been working: this "a-philosophy" is a thought that aims at the creation of concepts not oriented by the idea that all things are defined by the ready availability of what is present before our eyes, that is, by static forms and teleological genesis. Therefore, for us, Merleau-Ponty's thinking is definitively antimetaphysical. But, as we saw, starting in particular with Heidegger (but we think Husserl and Bergson were approaching this idea), the project of the overcoming of metaphysics really concerns a transformation of humanity. More important than Merleau-Ponty's "a-philosophy" is the fact that his thinking aims to dispel the illusion of the "false imaginary." The false imaginary sets up the "profound discordance" "between humans and Being" (OE: 63/MPR: 368). It sets up the cultural regime that Merleau-Ponty calls a nightmare, the cultural regime of the human being who understands himself as the *manipulandum*.

As we saw above in the closing discussion of the "false imaginary," for Merleau-Ponty, the painter's mode of life is opposed to that of the scientist. Not only is the ontology of the scientist one of acquisition, but also the mode of his existence is one of grasping from above: at once as close as possible and as far as possible. His mode of existence is one determined by power. In contrast, the painter lives differently. In short, his mode of existence is one determined by powerlessness. He (or she) undergoes, as Klee says, the gaze of the trees; he (or she) experiences that the visible looks at the painter. This passivity, however, is generated by the minuscule hiatus in the visible, the distance through which alone vision happens at all. This distance cannot be closed. In the powerlessness of this "cannot be closed," the painter at once lets things go and remains among the things. As one of the visibles, the painter is not a *manipulandum*. The distance necessary for vision protects the things from the painter, from the painter completely grasping them. Certain sides and profiles of the thing remain in absence, as lacks. And yet the painter has access to the things—they have a presence or they "presence"—insofar as the painter sees them. This presencing in absence does not make the painter ask, "what, is that all there is?" The false imaginary makes the scientist think—makes us think who share his mode of existence—that the things are not enough; it makes us think that the absences that infect their presence must be fulfilled; it makes us think that their being must be grounded in a permanent form. For the painter, however, who dwells in the true imaginary, the things are grounded in nothing but themselves. As groundless, their presencing in absence is "enough." In fact, it is more than enough. The "true imaginary" of the painter allows the things to be grounded in nothing but themselves, to be elements, *not* acquisitions. At this point, the final Merleau-Ponty seems very close to the later Heidegger. For Heidegger, as we saw in chapter 5, things are "enough" when they are gifts of grace, when they are holy. In Merleau-Ponty, there is no explicit mention of the things in the painter's vision being holy. However, we could say that things are holy since Merleau-Ponty opposes the painter's vision to "profane vision" (OE: 27/MPR: 357). This opposition suggests that the painter's vision is "sacred." This suggestion of the sacred could be seen as an extension of the idea of the flesh, which is a religious idea. The painter and the poet dwell in the flesh, which makes their canvases and words sacred, which makes their canvases and poems themselves gifts. These gifts are enough, that is, they are not copies of and approximations to positive being or forms. In fact, since they do not approximate, they are more than enough. They are let free to be an-exact and vary indefinitely and continuously. From the powerlessness of the distance comes all the potency of the image. To borrow again from the Klee quote, we can say that the mode of existence of the painter is "listening." The painter listens to "the undecided murmur of colors" (OE: 43/MPR: 362); the painter listens to what "commands from above all of our utilitarian activity" (OE: 90/MPR: 377). Listening to this commandment is what it means to dwell.

At the end of his life, Merleau-Ponty is fond of quoting Paul Claudel saying:

> From time to time, a man lifts his head, sniffs, listens, considers, recognizes his position: he thinks, he sighs, and, drawing his watch from the pocket lodged against his chest, looks at the time. *Where am I?* and, *What time is it?* Such is the inexhaustible question from us to the world (VIF: 140/VIE: 103; also NC 59–61: 356; Claudel's emphasis).[33]

Just as the question "what do I know?" asks for an enumeration of things that I know, these questions ask for landmarks and reference events. This kind of question asks for answers that are positive indicative sentences. They ask for a positive order of Being that lies in certainty beyond our perplexities (NC 59–61: 356). We could, however, pursue the question more and ask: where are these landmarks and when are those events? As Merleau-Ponty says in *The Visible and the Invisible*, "[these questions] refer us to others, and the answers satisfy us only because we do not attend to it, because we believe we are 'at home'" (VIF: 141/VIE: 104). This comment means that if we were no longer satisfied with the answer given by these reference marks (places and events), that is, if we attended and listened to the things, to their potentiality, the question would arise again and indeed would be inexhaustible, "nearly insane" (VIF: 141/VIE: 104). Then we would no longer believe we were at home. The questions become inexhaustible only when "life is threatened" (VIF: 141/VIE: 104). These inexhaustible questions, according to Merleau-Ponty, are questions that "the sick person" puts to himself during the moments when the illness has left him some calm. Like the painter, the sick person is responding to "the call for totality to which no objective being [*être*] gives a response" (VIF: 141/VIE: 104). Unlike the scientist, the sick person and the painter have not given up dwelling in the things (OE: 9/MPR: 351). Unlike the scientist, however, the painter has learned to dwell in "the central question that is ourselves" (VIF: 141/VIE: 141). To dwell (*habiter*) therefore, in Merleau-Ponty, is not to question but to be put in question; it is to be at home in the question to which the responses are only more questions. It is to be at home in the stationary but shifting soil of the texture of the visible.³⁴

## Transition

Merleau-Ponty's final thought revolves around the visible that is prior to, older than, the lines drawn in the caves at Lascaux. Being grounded in nothing but itself, the ancient visible is auto-affective. It therefore resembles interior monologue. For Merleau-Ponty, however, the ancient visible is also inseparable from the imaginary (VIF: 21–22/VIE: 6–7). Therefore, as he says in "Eye and Mind," the visible is an "oneiric universe" (OE: 35/ MPR: 359–60). Combining these two aspects of the visible, Merleau-Ponty says in the 1955 course at the Collège de France that "The 'interior monologue' [is] an extremely approximate account of this oneirism." Then he reproduces the following quote from Maurice Blanchot's "Death of the Last Writer":

> There is also chatter and what has been called interior monologue, which does not in the least, as we well know, reproduce what a man says to himself, for man does not speak to himself, and the deepest part of man is not silent but most often mute, reduced to a few scattered signs. Interior monologue is a coarse imitation, and one that imitates only the apparent traits of the un-interrupted and incessant flow of unspeaking speech. Let us recall that the strength of this speech is in its weakness; it is not heard, which is why we don't stop hearing it; it is as close as possible to silence, which is why it destroys silence completely. Finally, interior monologue has a center, the "I" that brings everything back to itself, while that other speech has no center; it is essentially wandering and always outside.³⁵

The writer of modern literature (that is, late nineteenth- and twentieth-century literature), for Blanchot, is always tempted to come closer to this incessant flow of "unspeaking speech." Indeed, like Blanchot's unspeaking speech, the ancient visible, this silence to which not only the modern writer but also the modern painter listens is still present. As Merleau-Ponty saw, it is only concealed beneath the chatter, only barely audible, nothing more than a "murmur."

# 7

Enveloped in a Nameless Voice: Foucault's
"The Thought of the Outside" (1966)      ⁼/ο′

If, like Foucault, we had started our investigation earlier, farther back
than the beginning of the twentieth century, we would have traced out
a development that went from transcendence in the Middle Ages (from
the transcendence of God or another world), across the Classical epoch,
to immanence in the nineteenth century (to the immanence of subjective
experience), and then from immanence to—to what, today? A transformation of immanence into what Foucault calls "screams and fury."[1] Like
Heidegger, he also calls this transformed immanence "the nothing," "the
void." Following Bergson, we have called this empty space "multiplicity."
Like Merleau-Ponty, Foucault—as we see in his description of Velasquez'
*Las Meninas* painting (MC: 19–31/OT: 3–16)—discovers the multiplicity
by means of the mirror relation. Or, more precisely, as Foucault says at
the end of his career in *The Hermeneutics of the Subject*, "[to constitute
an ethics of the self] is perhaps an urgent, fundamental, and politically
indispensable task, if it is true that there is no first or final point of resis-
tance to political power other than in *the relationship one has to oneself*."[2]
We encountered the self-relation, in a word, auto-affection, in Heidegger
when he coined tautological sentences like "the nothing nothings" and,
especially, "language is language." What Heidegger discovers within this
tautology is the threshold, the difference. Foucault too finds what he calls
"a minuscule hiatus" in the middle of this relation (MC: 351/OT: 340).
This "out of joint" self-relation requires a reform not only of psychology,
as Foucault showed in his first great book, *The History of Madness*, but

also a reform of philosophy, indeed, an overcoming of metaphysics. As Foucault says in *The Order of Things*, "Modern thought [thought in the twentieth century] . . . will contest even its own metaphysical impulses, and show that reflections upon life, labor, and language . . . express the end of metaphysics" (MC: 328/OT: 317). Or, as he says in "What Is Enlightenment?" "[critique] is no longer going to be practiced in the search for formal structures with universal value. . . . It is not seeking to make possible a metaphysics that has finally become a science. . . . It will separate out, from the contingency that has made us what we are, the possibility of no longer being, doing, thinking what we are, do, or think."[3] As we see here, for Foucault, the end of metaphysics does not eliminate philosophy. Instead, it calls for a history of thought that aims to invent new forms of thought. Such new forms must be a thinking that is beyond logic, even beyond reason. It calls for a thought of the murmur, it calls for a thought of the outside. It is contemporary literature, for Foucault, that most displays this new form of thought. For Foucault, as for Heidegger and Merleau-Ponty, literature and poetry show that it is language who speaks, not man.

Thus, in our final chapter we shall examine Foucault's 1966 essay on Maurice Blanchot's writings, which is called "The Thought of the Outside." As Foucault says, "Blanchot . . . [represented] for me . . . an invitation to call into question the category of the subject, its supremacy, its foundational function."[4] Thus "The Thought of the Outside" begins with a movement beyond Cartesianism. Perhaps more than any other text we have examined, "The Thought of the Outside" demonstrates the transformation of immanent subject experience ("lived experience," "*Erlebnis*," as Husserl would say) into multiplicity. As we have seen, however, starting with Heidegger this transformation also includes a transformation of who we are. Although Foucault does not speak of dwelling in "The Thought of the Outside," the essay concerns an experience. The experience of the outside transforms our thinking about the past and the future. Foucault suggests this new mode of thinking under the Blanchotian title of "awaiting-forgetting."[5] Awaiting-forgetting, however, amounts to me "wanting to be enveloped by speech and carried well beyond every possible beginning. [It amounts to me] loving to see in myself, at the moment of speaking, a nameless voice that was preceding me for a long time."[6] Awaiting-forgetting "enmeshes" us, makes us be "lodged" in the non-formal voice of no one. This amounts to a transformation of us, of man. In order to lead us to this transformative experience, Foucault begins "The Thought of the Outside" with a paradox coming from the ancient Greeks. As we shall see in a minute, it is not this paradox, however, in which Foucault is interested. He is interested in a simple sentence that "opens up a domain of questions that is perhaps unlimited."

## Summary-Commentary: "I Speak"[7]

### "I LIE, I SPEAK"

Although the title is "The Thought of the Outside," Foucault's essay begins with the inside, with a self-referential relation. Indeed, the entire essay unfolds as a way of undoing interiority. It aims to show that the "auto" or "self" of auto-affection really includes something else or other. As we just mentioned, Foucault introduces the self-referential relation by means of the paradox of the Cretan Epimenides.[8] Epimenides' paradox consists in his saying, "All Cretans are liars." But since Epimenides is a Cretan, it must be the case that he is lying about lying; therefore, is he contradicting himself and in fact telling the truth?[9] According to Foucault, although Greek truth trembled by means of this paradox, the paradox is "master-able" (DE 1: 546/EWF 2: 147). Within Epimenides' discourse it is necessary to distinguish two propositions "of which [dont] one is the object of the other" (DE 1: 546/EWF 2: 147). Even though Epimenides' argument artificially gathers itself into a kind of unity, the grammatical configuration of the paradox cannot suppress this "essential duality" of propositions. Alluding to Bertrand Russell, Foucault says, "Every proposition must be of a higher 'type' than the one that serves as its object" (DE 1: 546/EWF: 147).[10] Making this distinction in propositions allows us to understand the logic of the paradox. Now we are able to reformulate the paradox as "I am lying *about* another proposition." The paradoxical nature of the assertion had come from the fact that the two propositions—the designating proposition and the object proposition, that is, the proposition *about* which ("*dont*," this is the French relative pronoun based in the preposition "*de*") Epimenides is lying, the proposition *of* which ("*dont*") Epimenides is speaking—have the same content. It comes from the sole fact that "the speaking subject is the same as the one of which it is speaking" (DE 1: 547/ EWF: 147). The separation of the proposition into two "types," however, the second of which is the content for the first, stops the assertion "I lie" from being self-referential. If "I lie" is not self-referential, then it is possible to determine its truth value by making it correspond to the second proposition. So the Cretan paradox is mastered by giving its "simple form" a separate object-proposition; it is mastered, in other words, by means of the content, by means of the transitivity of the statement, by means of the "*de*" (making use of the French preposition): "I am lying about (*de*). . . ." According to Foucault, however, when I plainly say "I speak," I am not threatened by any of the dangers associated with the Cretan paradox (DE 1: 547/EWF 2: 147). "I speak" says just what it says. As Foucault says, "It is therefore true, undeniably true, that I speak when I say that I am speaking. But things may not be so simple" (DE 1: 547/EWF: 148). Unlike the Cretan paradox, which concerned content, the sentence "I am speaking" really concerns form.

Foucault's simple sentence consists of two principal steps. *First*, language is stripped down to the point of an "I speak"; the stripping down is done by eliminating any object or content from the sentence. It does not say "I am speaking *about* or *of* something" (there is no "*je parle de . . .*"). The elimination of the content means that the supporting discourse "about which" the sentence might speak is "in default." The "I speak" seems to be gathered up into itself, closed up on itself, like a "fortress." Certain consequences seem to follow from this gathering up into sovereignty of a fortress. The supporting discourse does not pre-exist the moment in which I say "I speak"; it flickers into existence at that moment alone, and if I fall silent, the supporting discourse disappears. But also, if I speak "of" ("*de*") something, then the supporting discourse again disappears since the object of the sentence—the addition of content—removes all the other possibilities of language, all the other possibilities of this formal statement. As Foucault says, elaborating on the image of the fortress, "The desert surrounds [this "I speak"]" (DE 1: 547/EWF 2: 148). Prior to my speaking, when I am silent there is no supporting discourse. When I speak without an object, it comes into existence but only for that moment; as soon as I speak "about" ("*de*") something it disappears since I have determined its content. The desert surrounding the fortress brings us to the *second* step in Foucault's analysis. The second step starts with Foucault saying "unless." We would have to say that in order to grasp itself, language has gathered itself into an "extreme fineness," in a mere "singular and thin point" (DE 1:

547/EWF 2: 148). Language has gathered itself into a point, unless the void (or desert) in which the "I speak" manifests itself "is an absolute openness by means of which language is able to expand to infinity" (DE 1: 547/EWF 2: 148), *unless* the formality of the "I speak" is an opening that scatters the speaking subject to infinity. If language has its place, becomes what it is in the solitary sovereignty of the "I speak," then, Foucault says, "nothing in principle can limit it—not the one to whom it is addressed, not the truth of what it says, not the values or systems of representation it utilizes" (DE 1: 547/EWF: 148). In other words, lacking a supporting discourse—there is no "of"—the "I speak" is able to speak of any and all things. Language is no longer, according to Foucault, "discourse or the communication of sense"; language is only the "spreading forth of language in its raw being, an unfolding of pure exteriority" (DE 1: 547/EWF 2: 148). The speaking subject is no longer the one responsible for the discourse; rather he is "the inexistence in whose void the indefinite outpouring of language pursues itself." The "power" of this assertion is indeed different from the power of the Cretan assertion (DE 1: 546/EWF 2: 148). While truth is at issue in the Cretan paradox, what is at issue in the "I speak" is the uncertainty of the existence of the subject.

The assertion of "I speak" puts, according to Foucault, modern fiction to the test. Normally (at this time in the 1960s, at the time of the new novel), we think that modern fiction is defined by this doubling back of self-designation or self-reference, as in "I am lying about my lying." This self-reference would turn modern fiction at once into an interiorization (saying nothing but literature) and a sign of what literature is. Yet, according to Foucault, what we call "literature" in the strict sense (as the word "literature" was especially used at this time[11]) is an interiorization only in a superficial way. In fact, Foucault claims, "literature" is not interiorization, but "a passage to the 'outside'" (DE 1: 548/EWF 2: 148). In "literature," language escapes from discourse understood as representation. In representation, as we saw with Heidegger, language is conceived merely as a medium for communication, and thereby it is conceived as being always dependent on something else such as a thought, a sense, or an object. So, insofar as "literature" opposes the representational conception, we might think of language as self-designation. However, it is neither the same (as itself) nor is it other (than itself). Indeed, here, Foucault is trying to point to a different distribution of same and other. As Foucault says, "literary speech is developed on the basis of itself, forming a network whose every point, distinct from the others, at a distance from its closest neighbors, is situated in relation to all of them in a space which simultaneously houses them and separates them" (DE 1: 548/EWF 2: 149). Language "develops on the basis of itself," and yet it forms a space of points "at a distance from its closest neighbor." This space—distance and sameness—is the outside. Being neither one nor the other, literature is language making itself—the same—as distant from itself as possible—other. According to Foucault, language's proper being is less a "folding over" (*repli*) of itself, which would make it the same, than a "hiatus" (*écart*), which would insert distances into it, making it other than itself. It is not a return of signs upon themselves. The "subject" of literature, according to Foucault, would be the void, in which the "subject" discovers its space when it states itself in the indeterminate formality of the "I speak" (DE 1: 548/EWF: 149).

This "neutral" space characterizes contemporary Western fiction. As Foucault says, "The reason it is so necessary to think this fiction—while earlier it was necessary to think truth—is that 'I speak' functions as if against the grain of 'I think'" (DE 1: 548/EWF: 149). The "I speak" disperses the certainty of the "I think." The subjectivity that is inside the outside (or that experiences itself outside of the outside) is a subject of uncertainty; the existence is "maybe." We must note how often Foucault uses the word "*peut-être,*" "maybe" or "perhaps" in this essay; in this neutral space, we are not in a domain of certainty, but in a domain of "maybe." It looks as though thought about thought should lead us to the deepest interiority. But speech about speech leads us to the outside in which the speaking subject disappears. As Foucault concludes, "No doubt that is why Western thought took so long to think the being of language: as if it had a premonition of the danger that the naked experience of language poses for the self-evidence of the 'I am'" (DE I: 548/EWF 2: 149). So in this first section, we have passed from the ancient Greeks to modern fiction, but we end with Descartes.[12]

## THE EXPERIENCE OF THE OUTSIDE

Here Foucault lists several points in culture where the experience of a breakthrough to a language from which the subject is "excluded" is being brought to light, where "the perhaps irremediable incompatibility" between the being of language and self-consciousness in its identity is starting to appear. The points are: the gesture of writing as an attempt to formalize language; the study of myths in psychoanalysis; and, finally, the search for a "*Logos* that would be like the birthplace of all of Western reason" (DE 1: 549/EWF 2: 149). More importantly, Foucault here gives us a clearer idea of what the outside is. As he says, "we are standing at the edge of an abyss that has long been invisible: the being of language appears only with the disappearance of the subject" (DE 1 549/EWF: 149). But this disappearance of the subject does not move us to an exteriority (despite Foucault's own use of the word "exterior"). Instead, the question is: How are we to gain access to this "strange relation" between the appearance of language in its being and the disappearance of the subject? It seems that we are able to do this through a kind of thinking that stands "outside" (*hors*) of all subjectivity, setting the limits of subjectivity as though from the exterior, "by stating the end of the subject," by making its dispersion and absence shine forth. Yet it is a form of thinking that stands on the threshold of all positivity in order *not* to grasp the foundation or justification of positivity, but to regain the space of positivity unfolding itself; this form of thinking wants to find the void serving as the place of positivity.[13] So we gain access to this "strange relation," we experience it, in a form of thinking that on the one hand exits from interiority. But on the other hand, it is an experience that does *not* rush into the exteriority of positivity's foundation; Foucault does not specify how we are to think of this foundation, but it is clear that it could not be conceived as something like a substance (as opposed to subject), or causal relations such as physical causes described by contemporary science or causal relations such as social causes given to us by Marxism (at least in its most classical form). The form of thinking that Foucault is outlining here does not think of these kinds of foundations. Instead of this kind of exteriority, thinking moves toward the space and void in which positivity develops. Anticipating the final section of the essay, we can say that this thinking is "neither one nor the other." It is necessary to use a formula of negative theology to describe this thought of the outside. So Foucault suggests that the origin of this experience probably lies in negative theology, but negative theology is still really concerned with a "dazzling interiority" (DE 1: 549/EWF 2: 150). He then lists other writers who have described this experience: Hölderlin, Sade, Nietzsche, Mallarmé, Bataille, Klossowski (the experience of the double, the simulacra), and then, of course, Maurice Blanchot. According to Foucault, Blanchot is the thought from the outside itself; he is its invisible presence (DE 1: 550–51/EWF 2: 151).

If the linguistic strategies of negative theology betray the thought of the outside by referring to an interiority, then, as Foucault states, it is extremely difficult to find a language faithful to this thought (DE 1: 551/EWF 2: 151). Both the language of reflection (as we find in the early Merleau-Ponty and in Husserl) and the vocabulary of fiction repatriate the dimension of the outside to an interiority or consciousness. Inevitably reflection develops the dimension through "a description of lived-experience" (*du vécu*, of *Erlebnis*, as in Husserl), where the outside is thought of as the experience of the body, of space, of the limits of the will, and the ineffaceable presence of the other (DE 1: 551/EWF 2: 152). Although Foucault does not say this, it is clear that he thinks that these "exteriors" (which we find in the phenomenological tradition, particularly in Merleau-Ponty) are still not outside enough; they maintain their dependence on interiority or consciousness. Turning from reflective language, Foucault sees that in fiction there are images that suggest ready-made meanings. The ready-made meanings allow the images to weave together the old network of interiority. Hence, for Foucault, we must convert both reflective language and fictive language.

First, Foucault takes up reflection. We must use reflective language (one of the traditional languages of philosophy), but reflective language must not be directed toward some sort of internal confirmation, that is, it must not be directed toward "a sort of central certitude from which one cannot be dislodged" (DE 1: 551/EWF 2: 152). Instead, reflective language must be turned toward an extremity where it always needs "to contest itself" (DE 1: 551/EWF 2: 152). In his 1963 essay on Bataille, "A Preface to Transgression," where he also mentions Blanchot, Foucault says that "contestation does not imply a generalized negation, but an affirmation that affirms nothing, a radical break of transitivity" (DE 1: 266/EWF 2: 74–75). This comment means that when reflection reaches the extremity or limit, it must realize that it is reflecting not on something, but on *nothing*. Indeed, if it finds itself to be still a thought *of* something, then it must take that something and make it more extreme so that it breaks free from the "of" of transitivity: "To contest is to go as far as the empty core where being attains its limit and where the limit defines being" (DE 1: 266/EWF 2:

75). For Foucault, being is not a being (it is not any of the things that are), which allows being to be conceived as the void (of beings): "being attains its limit." But also, insofar as being is not any of the things that are, it is always defined as that which is over the limit of any being whatsoever: "where the limit defines being." Although these formulas recall "What Is Metaphysics?" and the ontological difference, Foucault does not mention Heidegger.[14] Instead, he stresses that contestation is not equivalent to negation in the Hegelian dialectic. Negation in the Hegelian dialectic brings what one has negated into the "restless interiority of spirit" (DE 1: 551/EWF 2: 152). Contestation, however, goes in the opposite direction. When he negates his own discourse, Blanchot makes it "lose the grasp" (dessaisir) not only on what it just said but also on "its very power [pouvoir] to enunciate" (DE 1: 551/EWF 2: 152). Here, in Foucault (where he is again echoing Heidegger through Blanchot), we encounter a kind of powerlessness; in the experience of the outside, the hand no longer grasps. We shall return to this powerlessness below in the "Interpretation." When language loses its grasp, the grasp made possible by past meaning, when it loses even its power to enunciate, then language no longer internalizes; it has truly passed to the outside. Going in the opposite direction of internalization, contestation therefore is no longer the internalizing memory we find in Hegel; it becomes forgetfulness (DE 1: 551/EWF 2: 152). As forgetfulness, contestation realizes that language must be left behind since it has always referred to interiority or to the exteriority of interiority (or the exteriority relative to and dependent on interiority). Leaving this language of interiority behind, contestation makes language "hollow itself out," that is, it frees language of the already-said of language so that it is able to say something other than what it has said before. In this way, contested language is, as Foucault says, "a pure origin since it has itself and the void for its principle" (DE 1: 551/EWF 2: 152). But, it is also, as Foucault notes, "a re-beginning since it is past language which, by hollowing itself out, has liberated this void" (DE 1: 551/EWF 2: 152). The contested language of reflection is a beginning and a re-beginning. We have, as Blanchot says, and Foucault quotes him at length, "not speech, but barely a murmur, barely a tremor, less than silence," that is, less than the silence of a truth ultimately illuminating itself; but also, we have more, we have "the fullness of the void, something we cannot silence, occupying all of space, the uninterrupted, the incessant, a tremor and already a murmur, not a murmur but speech" (DE 1: 552/EWF 2: 152).

A conversion symmetrical to the conversion of philosophical discourse is required of fictive language. Fictive language must no longer be a "power" (*pouvoir*) to produce images. Instead, it must become the "potency" (*puissance*) to "un-knot" images from the way they have already been charged and weighed down. To enact this kind of release of the images, fictive language must divest the images of a reference to anything else, anything else like an interiority or foundations of positivity. So freed, the images become transparent. Then they refer to the weightlessness of "the unimaginable" (DE 1: 552/EWF 2: 153). In other words, like the words, the images must be hollowed out of their already-made significations so that they are able to present what can never be imagined. For Foucault, following Blanchot, fiction is not supposed to help us imagine new people or things; it is not supposed to be a fiction *of* something. This transitivity too must be broken. Then the fictitious is found "in the impossible similitude of what is between them: encounters, proximity of the most distant, absolute dissimulation where we are. Fiction consists therefore not in making the invisible be seen, but in making us see how much the invisibility of the visible is invisible" (DE 1: 552/EWF 2: 153). This phrase—"the invisibility of the visible"—is reminiscent of the later Merleau-Ponty, to whom Foucault is so close at times. But in fact what Foucault is pointing to with this phrase amounts to a radicalization of Merleau-Ponty. Indeed, the radicalization amounts to following the trajectory of an overcoming of metaphysics. We shall return to this radicalization in the "Interpretation" below. The proximity to Merleau-Ponty (and to Heidegger again) can be seen insofar as the fictitious concerns what is between or the "between." Therefore, the fictitious has, according to Foucault, a profound kinship with space; "space," Foucault says, "is to fiction as the negative is to reflection" (DE 1: 554/EWF 2: 153). This comparison means that space is not to be conceived as a determinate place; it is always an "elsewhere." All of Blanchot's writings then concern "placeless places" (DE 1: 554/EWF 2: 153). These non-places, like "beckoning thresholds, closed forbidden space that are nevertheless exposed to the wind," consist of a closeness hollowed out by distance, and a distance that indefinitely comes close.

For Foucault, Blanchot's writings make these two discourses, that of reflection (or philosophy) and that of fiction (or the imaginary), intersect. The result of this intersection, after reflection negates determinations and after fiction undoes its images, is a discourse without conclusion and image, a discourse free of any center and fatherland, a discourse that constitutes its own space "as the outside toward which, and outside of which it speaks" (DE 1: 552–53/EWF: 153). What is the status of Blanchot's discourse? Foucault answers that it is "commentary" (DE 1: 553/EWF 2: 153). Commentary is nothing more than "the repetition of what the outside has never stopped murmuring" (DE 1: 553/EWF 2: 153). But as a repetition of the outside, commentary is openness. It welcomes the outside into its words; or it is an "incessant advance towards the absolutely fine light which has never received language" (DE 1: 553/EWF 2: 153–54). This welcoming in and advancing out toward what has never received language gives Blanchot's discourse, according to Foucault, its "singular mode of being" (DE 1: 553/EWF 2: 154). Indeed, the singular mode of being of his discourse is the "place common" to all of Blanchot's different kind of works. The different kinds of works—"novels," "narratives," or "criticisms"—engage in a kind of thinking that no longer interiorizes itself. When it no longer interiorizes itself, thought becomes language about the outside of all language, it becomes speech about the invisible side of words. What is required for this transformation of language is an "attention to what already exists in language, what has already been said, printed, made manifest"; it requires a listening not so much to what has been pronounced in language but to "the void that circulates between the words, the murmur that does not stop unmaking language" (DE 1: 553/EWF 2: 154). In Blanchot's writings, language itself is allowed to speak—here Foucault refers to Blanchot's "novel" *Awaiting, Forgetting*, which is one of his main references throughout "The Thought of the Outside"—"the one who is no one, who is neither fiction nor reflection, neither already said nor never yet said" (DE 1: 553/EWF 2: 154).

### BEING ATTRACTED AND NEGLIGENT

According to Foucault, the attention required for Blanchot's discourse is called "attraction." Foucault says that "attraction" is for Blanchot what desire is for Sade, what force is for Nietzsche, what the materiality of thought is for Artaud, and what transgression is for Bataille: "the pure and most naked experience of the outside" (DE 1: 553/EWF 2: 154). More important than these comparisons to different authors is the fact that Foucault describes attraction in this way: "To be attracted is not to be invited by the attraction from the exterior; it is rather to undergo [*éprouver*, also to feel and to suffer], in the void and nudity, the presence of the outside, and, connected to this presence, the fact that one is irremediably outside of the outside" (DE 1: 553–54/EWF 2: 154). This is an important quote, with its use of the verb "*éprouver,*" to which we shall return in the "Interpretation" below. In any case, one must feel *not* that one is internal (protected and clothed) being attracted to something external. Rather, one must feel naked and defenseless so that one undergoes the presence of the outside, that is, one must be *in* the void, naked and defenseless, and yet undergo the feeling that one is still not inside the outside. One must suffer that one is "irremediably" outside of the outside. The outside, Foucault explains, is not the call to an interiority from an other interiority with which the calling interiority is supposed to be reconciled. In this way we see that the outside is not an exteriority into which one must enter; if it were such an exteriority, it would harbor an interiority. In fact, the outside has no interiority. The outside is not an enclosure, which means that there can be no question of finding an entrance to it. Nevertheless, the experience of attraction manifests that the outside is "there, open, with neither protection nor reserve" (DE 1: 554/EWF 2: 154). Unfolding itself to infinity, the outside never offers up its essence; it is not a positive presence. In other words, as Foucault says, the outside is not "something inwardly illuminated by the certainty of its own existence—but [it offers itself] merely as an absence that pulls itself [*se retire,* withdraws] as far away from itself as possible, hollowing itself in the sign that it makes so that one advances towards it as if it were possible to rejoin it" (DE 1: 554/EWF 2: 155). The sign is a gesture signaling to the infinite void, a gaze calling one forward, so it seems, to death.

In Blanchot, according to Foucault, negligence is the necessary counterpart of attraction. In order to be susceptible to attraction, "man" (*l'homme*) must be negligent, "essentially negligent with total disregard for what one is doing . . . and with the attitude that one's past and kin and that the whole other life is non-existence, thus relegating them to the outside" (DE 1: 554/EWF 2: 155). It is clear that negligence is a kind of indifference. Yet this negligence is only the other side of a sort of zeal, of a sort of obstinate diligence of "letting oneself be attracted by attraction, or more precisely," as Foucault adds, "(since attraction has no positivity) to being the aimless movement without a moving body of attraction itself in the void" (DE 1: 554–55/EWF 2:155). But this zeal does not remain awake and on guard; it forgets so that its movement is one of distraction and error. Consequently, zeal amounts to neglecting this negligence so that it becomes "courageously negligent care" (DE 1: 556/EWF 2: 157).[15] Zeal cares too much; it multiplies its steps. But then it ends up going in advance of attraction when attraction has said "imperiously" that one should stay behind (DE 1: 555/EWF 2: 156). Zeal then undergoes so much uncertainty, it undergoes the pressure of "maybe."[16] According to Foucault, there is so much uncertainty because "carelessness reigns in the house" (DE 1: 555/EWF 2: 156). This carelessness, however, is equivocal. Despite the appearance of carelessness, the signs can be deciphered as intentional. Characters in Blanchot's "novels" think that the law concerns them, that they are being watched, even constrained. Yet the law binds no one, since if it did "it would itself be bound to this bind, and then it would no longer be the pure open attraction" (DE 1: 556/EWF 2: 156). To be the pure open attraction, the outside must be negligent; it can be none of the things that have already been coded by actual laws.

### WHERE IS THE LAW, AND WHAT DOES IT DO?

As we have seen, each time Foucault attempts to define the outside, he first makes use of negative formulas. So, in the case of the law, he tells us that if the law was obvious to the heart, it would be the "sweet interiority of conscience" (DE 1: 556/EWF 2: 157). Likewise, if the law was written down in books, it would have "the solidity of external things" (DE 1: 556/EWF 2: 157). If the law was available and present in this way, then we would be able to follow it or disobey it. But if the law is to have the power and force that makes it venerable, then it must be neither internal nor external. "In fact," according to Foucault, "the presence of the law is its concealment [*dissimulation*]" (DE 1: 556/EWF 2: 157). What defines the law is its invisibility, or, more precisely, its manifestation in dissimulation. The question for Foucault is: How are we to make the law visible? How are we to undergo it?

To make the law appear what is required is zeal, or, as Foucault alludes again to Bataille, transgression. Zeal is required when one has read decrees from afar, believing them to apply not to oneself but to others. In other words, one thinks that one understands the decrees. By understanding them, one makes the enforcement of the decrees circulate, makes them work upon others. At that moment, Foucault says, one is "closest to the law" because the law applies to others, not to oneself (DE 1: 556/EWF 2: 157). In other words, one is outside the law with the law. Yet how can one be certain that one has understood the decree? Maybe (again "maybe") it means something else. As Foucault says, this perpetual manifestation [of the law] never illuminates what one is saying or what the law wants" (DE 1: 556–57/EWF 2: 157). The law is not the principle or internal prescription of actions; the law envelopes actions and "makes them escape from all interiority" so that the singularity of the actions is turned back "into the gray monotony of the universal" (DE 1: 557/EWF 2: 157). The potency of the law—making actions either legal or illegal—is universality. Universality keeps the law invisible and withdrawn. One believed that one had understood the decree. If one behaved this way, then, it seemed, one was outside the law's enforcement. But its universality includes even these conducts. One would then have misunderstood the law. A kind of zealous attention is clearly required to understand this dissimulating law. In the zealous manifestation of the law, it is dissimulated (hiding its universality). Transgression for Foucault, however, is not the same as zeal. It is not the attempt to understand the law; it is nothing less than breaking the law. But in the violation of a law, one may undertake to break the law in order to make the law punish oneself. One then attracts the law to oneself. If this provocation of the law into punishment is the purpose of the action, then the law becomes something one can touch, it becomes subject to one's will. The one who violates becomes "master of the law's shadows and light" (DE 1: 557/EWF 2: 158). Being master of the law is not the aim of transgression. By violating an interdiction, transgression undertakes to attract the law not to the one doing the violation; it lets the law be attracted to the law itself. In other words, transgression "lets itself be attracted to the essential withdrawal of the law" (DE 1: 557/EWF 2: 158). Transgression violates a law in order to show that law cannot be reduced to this one determination of this law, edict, interdiction, or statute. Thus transgression, "madly," as Foucault says, aims to venerate the law; it aims to reinforce the "weakness of the law," meaning that it aims to show that the law is always less determinate than one particular statute or interdiction (DE 1: 557/EWF 2: 158). The law is made up of "an invincible weightlessness" (DE 1: 557/EWF 2: 158). In the transgressive dissimulation of the law, the law is made manifest (as never appearing merely as one law).

According to Foucault, two of Blanchot's novels form a diptych in relation to the invisibility of the law: while *Aminadab* dissimulates the law while manifesting it, *The Most High* manifests the law while dissimulating it.[17] The primary character in *Aminadab* is called Thomas; he makes his way into a house that is under the rule of a law that no other tenant in the house knows. The law's proximity and absence is recalled constantly by the forbidden doors and openings in the building. Yet when some of the tenants want to track the law down, to make it appear by violating it, by transgressing it, they are confronted only with the monotony of the place where they were already. Then they experience violence and resign themselves to the place. The result of this transgression, according to Foucault, is not punishment; it is profound forgetfulness (of all the particular laws) (DE 1: 557–58/EWF 2: 158). In contrast, the primary character in *The Most High* is Henri Sorge (DE 1: 558/EWF 2: 158). Sorge is an office worker for the state, a cog in a machine that turns individual existences into an institution, places births into an archive; he orders other people's existence. Then he does not do his duty; he takes a vacation, but it is not certain that he is not doing his duty when he leaves. His departure is a quasi-withdrawal, which results in confusion in the office. Thus when Sorge leaves state service, "he erases his singular existence and subtracts it from the universality of the law" (DE 1: 558/EWF 2: 158). Even so, when he seems to elude the classificatory power of the law, he does not go outside the law. Instead, he forces the law to manifest itself at the empty place he abandoned. In other words, the law manifests itself as withdrawal, as strictly universal (and thereby indeterminable), insofar as the ensuing chaos in the office implies that the law can never be reduced to any one law or any one set of laws. Sorge (whose name in German means care, and this is an allusion by Blanchot to Heidegger), therefore, *caring* more for the law than others, "exalts the law" (DE 1: 558–59/EWF 2: 159).

These transgressions or "provocations," as Foucault says, of the law make the law respond by means of a withdrawal. For Foucault, each transgression, even the most violent or revolutionary, does not make the law withdraw into a more profound silence. Instead, the law remains in "its identical immobility" (DE 1: 559/EWF 2: 159–60). This means that the law never changes. The law is never equal to a singular law or statute, to a singular decree. So we can say, as Foucault says, that the law is already dead, but this is a death that never ends (DE 1: 559/EWF 2: 160). So each time one tries to kill a form of the law, one finds that the new form is still not equal to the law; the new form is a way of killing the law, but only to find itself as a form of the law that must be overcome or sent into the grave. If each attempt to overcome a form of the law only results in another form to be overcome, then all one can ask is "where is the law, what does it do?"

It is always elsewhere (than the form we are in) and it does nothing (in particular). The promise to answer these questions is never fulfilled. Or, more precisely, it responds to these questions by saying, "I speak, I speak now" (DE 1: 558/EWF 2: 160). The lack of an object to these sentences indicates the law's essential indeterminacy, its amorphous (in the literal sense non-formal) presence. The lack of an object to these sentences indicates that there is an essential silence within this language through which the law responds indefinitely.

## EURYDICE AND THE SIRENS

According to Foucault, the figures of Ulysses and the sirens and Orpheus and Eurydice are "profoundly interwoven" in Blanchot's writings.[18] The two figures are related to one another in terms of an idea of the promise. The promise attracts. In the case of the sirens' song, it is the promise of a song of Ulysses' exploits; in the case of Eurydice's face, it is the promise of her face being shown to Orpheus. However, just as the law is unable to manifest itself without dissimulation, the promise of the sirens' song and the promise of Eurydice's face are at once deceptive and veridical. On the one hand, the sirens' song is deceptive since all those who let themselves be seduced by it will encounter only their own death. On the other hand, it is true since only through death will the song arise that will recount, to infinity, the hero's adventure. Similarly, according to Foucault, Orpheus's gaze takes place at the "oscillating threshold of death," promising life while delivering death (DE 1: 561/EWF 2: 162). Each, however, approaches this threshold without crossing it. Both Ulysses and Orpheus hear the song and see the face but each also keeps himself tied up and turns back so that each loses the song in the waves and the face in the shadows. Foucault says in fact that Ulysses lost the song by remaining tied up; Orpheus, by turning about to see Eurydice, so to speak, "untied" himself, thereby losing her face (DE 1: 561/EWF 2: 162). But the point is that each does not die. In this way, as Foucault says, "the voice is liberated: for Ulysses, it is the salvation, the possible narration of the marvelous adventure; for Orpheus, it is the absolute loss, it is the lament that will have no end" (DE 1: 561/EWF 2: 162). The voice that has been liberated through the gaze of Orpheus is a pure voice, the sirens' song that sings only the song's own withdrawal.

## THE COMPANION

As the sirens and Eurydice indicate, the outside appears as a kind of figure, which Blanchot, according to Foucault, calls the companion. The companion is the result of the outside intruding on interiority. The outside draws interiority out of itself, making a double that remains at a distance, a resemblance who accosts (DE 1: 562/EWF2: 163). As Foucault says,

> The moment interiority is attracted outside of itself, an outside hollows out the place into which interiority customarily has its recesses [repli] and the possibility of its recesses: a form arises—less than a form, a kind of stubborn and non-formal [informe] anonymity—that dispossesses the subject of its identity, scoops it out, and distributes it into two twin figures that are not super-posable, dispossesses it of its immediate right to say "I," and raises against its discourse a speech that is indissociably echo and negation (DE 1: 562/EWF 2: 163).

As we can see in this passage, the companion is "the other of the same" (DE 1: 562/EWF 2: 163), the "double" of the subject. This double is the informal anonymity, which is, in fact, the most precise definition of the outside. Indeed, where the outside of attraction, of the law, of the pure voice and gazeless face were distant, this outside is the outside that is closest to interiority. In other words, the companion in Foucault is what results from auto-affection (the mirror relation in the subject folds itself over—*le repli*—into the same) becoming hetero-affection. The formulas presented here in the section called "The Companion" are the most important in "The Thought of the Outside," as they allude to the doubles of "Man and his Doubles" in *The Order of Things* (MC: 323–46/OT: 312–35). We shall return to these formulas below in the "Interpretation." Because the companion is the outside (the informal anonymity) at its closest to interiority, it is also at the height of its dissimulation (DE 1: 563/EWF 2: 163). The companion presents itself as a pure, close, redundant presence. But more importantly, Foucault describes the companion "as one figure too many; . . . it repels [*repousse*, pushes back and away] more than it attracts, one must keep it at a distance, there is always the danger that one will be absorbed by it and compromised by it in boundless confusion" (DE 1: 562/EWF 2: 163). The companion haunts interiority as a demand to which one is never equal and a weight one would like to get rid of. One is bound to the companion with "an invincible connection," and yet it is necessary to find some other kind of connection than the connection to its "faceless form of absence" (DE 1: 562/EWF 2: 164). Foucault concludes that the companion is a figure that is "indefinitely reversible": attractive and repellent, too close and too far, a demand and a burden (DE 1: 562/ EWF 2: 164).[19] With this mention of reversibility, Foucault speaks of the flesh, but, despite the allusion to Merleau-Ponty, this is a flesh that will be the cry of death that contests the flesh (that rends it) and affirms it (the tearing of it indicates the flesh is nothing but flesh) (DE 1: 564/EWF 2: 165).

This cry takes us back to language. It is when language pivots between contestation and affirmation that the companion is most manifest. The companion is not "a privileged interlocutor, not some other speaking subject" (DE 1: 564/EWF 2: 165). The companion is the "nameless limit that language reaches" (DE 1: 564/EWF 2: 165). Foucault adds that this limit is in no way positive. The limit not being positive means that language does not refer to things. Insofar as it does not refer in this way, language is able to be itself, "to return identical to itself, the echo of a different discourse that says the same thing, of the same discourse, saying something different" (DE 1: 564/EWF 2: 165). Because the companion, who is the outside, is nameless, anonymous, the companion is an "*il*," but one that is as close as possible to the "*je*," as in the sentence, "*je parle*"; or, using English pronouns, within—but as the outside—every "I speak," there is a "he (or it) speaks." In other words, within every person (within every personal pronoun) there is something like an "imperson" (an impersonal pronoun). And the bond between the "I" and this "it" is not positive enough to make a bond that could be untied. There is a "pact" that attaches the "it" to the "I." But they are "powerfully bound by a constant interrogation . . . and by the uninterrupted discourse that manifests the impossibility of responding" (DE 1: 565/EWF 2: 165). Blanchot's narratives, Foucault concludes, take place in the thin line that separates the companion from the narrator with whom it is indissociably connected. The narrative then opens up a boundless, unlimited, "placeless place" (DE 1: 565/EWF 2: 165).

### NEITHER ONE NOR THE OTHER

At the end of "The Thought of the Outside," Foucault returns to the kind of experience that is the experience of the outside. As he had already noted earlier in the essay, the experience of the outside is close to an experience of mysticism, but it does not consist in opening a difficult communication with the positivity of an existence (in a word, God). The experience of the outside is an experience neither of the word nor of silence; it does not concern "the visibility that is free of all figures" (DE 1: 565/EWF 2: 166). Instead, as Foucault says,

> The movement of attraction and the withdrawal of the companion lay bare what precedes all speech, what underlies all silence: the continuous streaming of language. A language spoken by no one [*personne*]: any subject it may have is no more than a grammatical fold. A language not resolved by any silence: any interruption is only a white stain on its seamless sheet. It opens a neutral space in which no existence can take root. (DE 1: 565/EWF 2: 166)

No existence can take root, since what defines the being of language, as Foucault quotes Blanchot, "is the void of repetition" (DE 1: 565/EWF 2: 166). Repetition empties out what is being said and the one who speaks so that the being of language is the visible erasure of the one who speaks. According to Foucault, all the experiences Blanchot narrates lead to a murmuring space, which is less an endpoint than a place without geography for the possible re-beginning of these experiences. Thanks to these experiences, language finds itself freed from all the old myths from which our consciousness of words, discourse, and literature has been formed (DE 1: 566/EWF 2: 167).

The quote from Blanchot about language being defined by repetition, for Foucault, challenges in particular the myth that language has mastery over time. We believed that language acted both as the connection of a given word to the future and as memory and recitation connected to the past. We believed, in other words, that language was prophecy and history, both the eternal and the visible body of truth, both the form of words and the breath that animates them. Instead, according to Foucault, "language is nothing but a non-formal and streaming murmur [*rumeur informe et ruissellement*], its force is in its dissimulation. That is why it is one with the erosion of time; it is depthless forgetting and the transparent void of waiting" (DE 1: 566/EWF 2: 167). This comment means that it is neither memory nor promise; or it is both forgetfulness and waiting. Foucault explains this couple of awaiting-forgetting—from the title of Blanchot's "novel"—in this way. In each of its words, language is really directed toward the contents that are prior to it. But in its very being and provided it maintains itself closest to its being, language "deploys itself only in the purity of waiting" (DE 1: 566/EWF 2: 167). As Foucault says, "waiting is directed at nothing, for the object that would come to fill it in could only erase it" (DE 1: 566/EWF 2: 167). In other words, if we think that language is merely to be fulfilled with the object of which the words are speaking (as in the sentence "I am speaking of . . ."), then the being of language is no longer independent. Its own being is a waiting that never ends. Similarly, if we think that language is merely the expression of interior thoughts, then again the being of language is no longer independent. In these two cases, we are not thinking language as language; in these two cases, language is not language. The dispersal of interiority—the repetition extends beyond any living speaker—means that while language's being is a pure wait (not a waiting for something), its being is also a pure forgetfulness. Foucault stresses that this forgetfulness is not sleepiness or distraction. It is extreme attention or even extreme waiting (since the French word for "waiting" is *"attente"*; thus "attention" and *"attente"* are connected, being attentive and waiting) (DE 1: 566/EWF 2: 167). This attentive waiting is so extreme that it erases any face; as soon as a form is determinate, it is "at once too old and too new" (DE 1: 567/EWF 2: 167). Or it is attention to what is radically new without any bond of resemblance and what is most profoundly old, older than anything for which it is waiting.

So, as Foucault says, alluding to the title of this section, "Language . . . is *neither* truth *nor* time, *neither* eternity *nor* man; it is instead the always undone form of the outside" (DE 1: 567/EWF 2: 168; my emphasis). Always undone, language places the origin in contact with death. The origin of speech and death are in an "indefinite oscillation." The perpetually re-begun outside of death never allows truth to take shape, and the outside of the origin never solidifies into a positivity. The origin takes on the transparency of what has no end; death opens interminably onto the repetition of the beginning. Language in its being is this pure voice; it is "the weakness at the heart of and around all things and all faces, which bathes them with one identical neutral clarity—at once day and night— the delayed effort of the origin and the dawnlike erosion of death" (DE 1: 567/EWF 2: 168).

Thus the conclusion of the essay returns to the Cretan paradox. When language was the place of truth, it was put in danger by the Cretan Epimenides' assertion that all Cretans were liars. But now we have a different paradox. Foucault says, "when language is revealed to be the reciprocal transparency of origin and death, there is not one existence that, in its sole affirmation of the 'I speak,' does not receive the threatening promise of its own disappearance, of its future appearance" (DE 1: 567/EWF 2: 168).

## Interpretation: Being Enveloped in a Nameless Voice

In *The Order of Things*, starting from the Middle Ages and going to the twentieth century, Foucault lays out an archeology of anthropology. As a completion of the archeology, Foucault lays out a "quadrilateral" of man (in the famous ninth chapter, "Man and His Doubles"). Each point of the quadrilateral shows that man is constituted by means of doublets that make the figure of man ambiguous. The first point of the quadrilateral is the fact that man is finite both in the sense that positive sciences such as biology, economics, and philology tell him that he is finite and in the sense that the positive sciences themselves are grounded in man, who being finite makes them finite (MC: 325–26/OT: 314–15). Second, as this first point indicates, man as ground and man as grounded, man is at once empirical and transcendental; knowledge of what makes all knowledge possible (including knowledge about man) will be found in man (MC: 329/ OT: 318). Third, if man is the foundation of knowledge of man, then man can neither be posited in the immediate and sovereign transparency of a *cogito* nor in an inert object that has no self-consciousness; man thinks the unthought, what is alien to thought and yet related to it (MC: 335/OT: 324). Finally, fourth, man is ambiguous in the sense that his origin lies always farther back in the development of life; yet man is the opening through which all time flows and therefore the origin might be recovered farther out in the future (MC: 342–43/OT: 332). The concept of man is ambiguous as a subject of knowledge and an object of knowledge, as empirical and transcendental, as thought and unthought, and as retreat and return of the origin. For Foucault, the anthropological quadrilateral has dominated our thinking so much in the twentieth century that we are not able to think in any other way. It has made us enter into a kind "anthropological slumber."[20] In fact, Foucault says that the dogmatism of "modern [that is, twentieth-century] philosophy" takes place at two levels, which reciprocally support one another. On the one hand, there is the precritical analysis, in the positive sciences, of what man is essentially; on the other, there is all of what can be given in general (transcendentally) to human experience

(MC: 352/OT: 341). In other words, in modern thought, we encounter an "empirical-critical reduplication through which one attempts to make man . . . serve as the foundation of his own finitude" (MC: 352/OT: 341). It is in "this Fold" of doubling that the transcendental comes to coincide with the empirical, and inversely, the empirical contents are animated by a discourse that bears their transcendental presumption farther and farther. The anthropological slumber then consists in this fold being folded over (*repli*) into the same. In order to awaken from the anthropological slumber, we must, Foucault says, "*destroy* the anthropological quadrilateral in its foundation" (MC: 353/OT: 341; my emphasis). Indeed, he says that any attempt to think in a new way must take on this quadrilateral. Published at the same time as *The Order of Things*, "The Thought of the Outside" is such a destruction of the quadrilateral. The destruction takes place with the simple sentence: "I speak."

Let us return to the development of the "I speak," as Foucault presents it in "The Thought of the Outside." As we noted, Foucault associates the "I speak" with the image of a fortress. The image comes about because the "I speak" suspends (in the sense of an epoché) both the content of the sentence and the supporting discourse of the sentence. It is the suspension of transitivity in general. Transitivity being suspended results in the sentence being entirely formal. The suspension of transitivity adds another detail to the image: now it looks as though a desert surrounds the fortress. What the image and the suspension indicate is an interiorization—the "I speak" seems to stand all alone, independent, sovereign, like the Cartesian "I think"—"unless" the desert, which Foucault of course calls a "void" (*vide*, also "emptiness"), is "an absolute opening" (DE 1: 547/EWF 2: 148). Notice the wording: "absolute opening." On the one hand, the phrase "absolute *opening*" indicates that the fortress is not closed off; the suspension of transitivity—that the sentence has no object, that nothing follows the "about" or the "of," that the sentence does not say "I am speaking of ..." —opens the sentence, opens the thinking to what is not interior and what can never be interiorized. It opens the speaking to the outside. As we have seen, the outside for Foucault—but the outside is the very subject matter of this book, the very subject matter of what we have been calling continental philosophy—is language. Language, however, is neither a supporting discourse (transcendental) nor is it content (empirical); it is neither subject nor object. So, on the other hand, the phrase "*absolute* opening" indicates that the void itself is absolute. No longer is the foundation the Cartesian *cogito*, no longer is the foundation transcendental conditions of possible experience, no longer is the foundation man in his finitude. Rather, and here we can see the first impact of Freud on Foucault, the foundation—if we can call a void a foundation—is language "in its raw being" expanding itself "to infinity."[21] In other words, by means of the suspension of transitivity, Foucault has transformed the immanence of interiority—the "I" of the "I speak"—into the immanence of the outside. Immanence is now immanent to the outside that is nothing (or the nothing)—nothing but the flow of language. Foucault sets up therefore what Deleuze (inspired by Bergson) would call a plane of immanence: a movement to infinity that precedes the division into thought and matter.[22]

The establishment of a plane of immanence means that with the outside, Foucault is involved in a project not only of the destruction of anthropology, but also of metaphysics. As we saw at the beginning of our study, the nineteenth century brought about a decline of metaphysics into psychology. The decline moved from a kind of Platonism, in which there was a second world transcendent to this world, to the immanence of this world where immanence meant the human psyche. The human psyche then is understood in terms of ambiguous "both-and" formulas, the formulas of what Foucault calls the anthropological quadrilateral. Earlier, we saw Husserl speak of a "paradoxical ambiguity." With Foucault and with the project of "continental philosophy" that we are outlining, the movement now goes from the ambiguous formulas of sameness (phenomenological formulas) to disambiguous formulas of difference. In short, with Foucault we have a transformation of the "both-and" into the "neither-nor." The outside in Foucault is the outside of subjectivity, but that does not turn the outside into the foundation of positivity; the outside is neither subject nor substance. It is neither the luminous interiority of God nor the gray interiority of man. We must not overlook the fact that Foucault appropriates in "The Thought of the Outside" formulas of negative theology. These formulas make the outside at least parallel to what Heidegger calls the holy and Merleau-Ponty's suggestion of sacred vision.[23] Other formulas for the outside, however, more directly allude to Merleau-Ponty and Heidegger. For Foucault, the outside is an invisibility that "presences" without ever becoming visible. It is a stubborn invisibility. As we saw with the law, the outside is a presence that is never manifest, that always dissimulates itself. Indeed, the formulas for the outside that Foucault composes indicate that it cannot be defined by simple presence that is readily available. As well, for Foucault, the outside is not a being, not an individual thing that is; the outside is being where the limit defines being. The outside is a limit extending itself to infinity, a universality, really a universalization that exceeds every singularity, while never attaining a positive form. The outside is a repetition that at the same time differentiates (MC: 351/OT: 340).[24] Besides a placeless place, Foucault also calls it a neutral space. It is a multiplicity.

It is important to recognize that what we are calling a multiplicity refers to what Foucault calls "language in its raw being" [son être brut]. Language in its raw being means that Foucault, like Heidegger, is not defining language by its customary concepts. It is not discourse, not representation; it is not defined by the function of communication (which would make it the speaking of man); it is not even literature in the sense of a self-referential discourse. To indicate the unusual status of language in Foucault, we must put the word between quotation marks. Foucault is conceiving "language" as a space of dispersion (see also AS: 173/AK: 131). Dispersion implies that "language" is not organized around a central meaning, either originary or teleological. As Foucault says, it is language getting as far away from itself as possible, getting away from itself in the sense of getting away from the customary senses of "language," but also in the sense of getting away from the pre-established meaning of words, phrases, and statements. "Language" hollows itself out from these already-given meanings. Like the law, its universalization exceeds anyone and any one statement of it. Exceeding any one statement of it, "language" is informal. Exceeding all individuality, "language" therefore is not spoken by someone. "Language" makes a network that is anonymous and informal. The network that "language" forms—the outside—is prior to the forms of subjectivity and to the forms of objectivity. Although Foucault calls this plane of the outside archeological, we could call it ultra-transcendental. The absence of no one and no meaning means that "language" has a kind of silence to it. But the silence gives way, as we have seen, to a murmur. This murmur, "language" for Foucault, calls—or better, attracts—like the sirens' song and Eurydice's face.

Eurydice and the sirens are companions, doubles. As we noted above, the formulas in the section called "The Companion" are the most important in "The Thought of the Outside." In this section, Foucault transforms the experience of auto-affection into that of hetero-affection. When I think, when I engage in interior monologue, when I experience my own body, in short when I have an immanent subjective experience (interiority), I experience something other than myself; I hear voices other than my own. Merleau-Ponty would say the same: the touching-touched relation never achieves unity. The left hand is never quite the same as the right hand; it remains other. Yet Foucault adds something to this unclosable relation that we have not seen before. Foucault conceives the auto-affective relation as one of *violence* (and therefore of power).[25] Perhaps Heidegger had anticipated this addition when he spoke of anxiety, of the nothing that repels in "What Is Metaphysics?" Or he anticipated the violence when he spoke in "Language" of the "prevailing" (*walten*) in the dif-ference of things and world, the pain of the threshold. But it is Freud's conception of the relation between the unconscious and the conscious as a battlefield that most anticipates the violence. And if there is something like a concept of the flesh in Foucault, the violence of the relation makes the concept different from that of Merleau-Ponty. In Foucault, the flesh contains the cry of death. In Foucault, the elemental in Merleau-Ponty, the element of water, becomes "an obscure aquatic element, a dark, disordered shifting chaos, the germ and death of all things."[26] For Foucault, because the companion is the outside at its closest to interiority, it is at the height of its dissimulation. What does the height of dissimulation mean? It means that the companion (who looks to be a double of me, as Eurydice and the sirens look to be doubles or reflections of Orpheus and Ulysses) is a power that "pushes back and away," and therefore it is dangerous, a menace. One must keep it at a distance—the companion does not accompany—since the companion might absorb and plunge one into "boundless confusion" (DE 1: 562/EWF 2: 163), in a word, into madness.[27] The companion is not a person with an interiority; it is impersonal. Although the companion is not a privileged interlocutor—it is a mere "it"—it is a demand, to which one is never equal and a weight one would like to be free of. The companion is the imperative of a law that can never be obeyed. One is connected to the companion with "an invincible connection," and yet one senses the need to find some other kind of connection than the connection one has to its "faceless form of absence." Thus even as the companion, the double, Eurydice and the sirens push back and away, they also attract.

Attraction is not a call if calling is defined as an invitation from one interiority to another interiority. The outside is the outside and when it attracts, it makes one undergo the presence of the outside, and importantly, that one is "irremediably" outside of the outside. One is irremediably outside of the outside because the outside is "weak." It is not a thing with which one can do something; it is not a statute that can be enforced or applied; it does nothing since it is nothing.[28] One is irremediably outside of the outside because the outside is not an inside to which one could find an entrance. The outside is not a place like that. The irremediable impossibility of gaining access to the outside brings us once more to the experience we have encountered before: the experience of powerlessness. Indeed, with the verb "*éprouver*," Foucault is suggesting that experience is even one of suffering. One suffers because as one advances toward the outside, it withdraws from the place toward which one has advanced. Because the outside pushes back and away, because it eludes our grasp and withdraws, we who are attracted must, as Foucault says, be negligent. Negligence is the negation and transgression of any singular form. These singular forms (thoughts already thought, meanings already made, institutions already constructed) must be forgotten. As forgetfulness, negligence resembles the experience of dying; these singular forms must be destroyed if one is to try to reach the outside. But like Orpheus and Ulysses, the experience is not death. One must approach as closely as possible without entering into the danger of madness. Thus while forgetting, one must wait. As we saw, on the other side of forgetting is awaiting. Here Foucault is again quite close to Heidegger. Waiting for Foucault must be a "pure waiting," that is, it must be a waiting for nothing in particular, just as profound boredom for Heidegger is boredom with nothing in particular. Because one is waiting for nothing in particular, it is not certain that what comes is that for which one is really waiting. Thus one must be zealous, even attentive, and multiply the efforts to wait for what is radically new or so old that it has never been seen before. Such an event, however, never happens as such. As soon as the event appears, it appears as someone, as something, and then it is no longer an event of the outside; appearing as something or someone, the outside is no longer the outside. We must not expect the origin to return. The promise is never fulfilled. Thus, as we saw with Heidegger, Foucault too suggests a kind of messianism without a messiah.

The experience to which Foucault is leading us is the experience of attraction-withdrawal. In the experience, one responds with awaiting-forgetting. Awaiting-forgetting is therefore a specific sort of discourse or thinking. We saw Foucault describe this discourse when he spoke of commentary in Blanchot. Commentary, Foucault says, welcomes the outside into its words; it lets them enter. Thus, like Heidegger and Merleau-Ponty, this discourse is based on a kind of attentive listening to a voice that is nearly mute. This voice is what Merleau-Ponty, quoting Valéry, called "the voice of no one." As Foucault says, commentary, the kind of writing or speaking required for awaiting-forgetting, is nothing more than "the repetition of what the outside has never stopped murmuring" (DE 1: 553/ EWF 2: 153). The discourse faithful to awaiting-forgetting engages in a kind of thinking that no longer interiorizes itself. What is required then is a thought of (the) nothing, nothing formal or singular. Or, more precisely, what is required is a thought of a singularity that immediately unravels itself, that immediately makes itself continuous with other singularities. As we already noted, the thought of the outside is the thought of multiplicity. In order to think the outside, one must not say "I am thinking *of* my thoughts." What is required is not the "folding over," the "*repli*," of the "of." What is required is the unfold, the "*dépli*," of "I am thinking . . ." In the openness of the unfold, one is thinking of or listening to or writing about the murmuring voices. In the thought of the outside, therefore, one finds oneself "enveloped in a nameless voice."[29]

## Transition

Since we have reached the apex of our study, let us recapitulate the four features that define the project of what we are calling continental philosophy. The four features are: (1) the starting point in immanence (where immanence is understood first as internal, subjective experience, but then, due to the universality of the epoché, immanence is understood as ungrounded experience); (2) difference (where difference gives way to multiplicity, itself emancipated from an absolute origin and an absolute purpose; being so emancipated, multiplicity itself becomes the absolute); (3) thought (where thought is understood as language liberated from the constraints of logic, and language is understood solely in terms of its own being, as indefinite continuous variation); and (4) the overcoming of metaphysics (where metaphysics is understood as Platonism and overcoming is understood as the creation of a new mode of thought, a new people, and a new land). Like the thought of Derrida and Deleuze at this moment (at the end of the 1960s), Foucault's "The Thought of the Outside" makes these four features explicit.

(1) In the first section of "The Thought of the Outside," we saw Foucault enact something like a universal suspension, an epoché, by means of the simple but enigmatical sentence "I speak."[30] By suspending its transitivity, the sentence forces us to abandon our presuppositions about the being of language. Prior to the suspension, we believed that language externalized the interiority of the speaking subject. Through the suspension, we see that language has no support but itself; it is a void, an abyss, or *Abgrund*. In other words, as Heidegger says, "language is language." Instead of language being in the subject, the subject is in language. We are not in an experience of the inside but in (immanent to) an experience of the outside. (2) Because the outside, for Foucault, is defined by "neither-nor" formulas (neither the interiority of God nor the exteriority of substantial positivity), it is ontologically differentiated from all beings. As Foucault says repeatedly, the outside is a space of dispersion in which positive things develop; it is a neutral space, a placeless place, a non-place. As we saw in particular with the law, the outside is a universality that exceeds any singular limit in which it is placed. Therefore, as a constantly mobile limit (always withdrawing, a violent distancing from itself, a "*dépli,*" not a "*repli*"), the outside is neither an origin nor an end; or it has neither an origin nor an end. The outside is a multiplicity. (3) In "The Thought of the Outside," Foucault shows that what modern literature concerns cannot be captured by the logical paradox of lying about lying. Modern literature goes beyond logic. Blanchot's literature presents us with language as nothing more than an indefinite murmur, something less than words, sentences, propositions, and meanings. Thought then becomes not the thought of forms but the thought of the informal. Thought becomes the repetition of this informality, which means it develops concepts and images that negate their formality, that show themselves to be less than a form, as if the form is incomplete, like Bergson's incomplete concepts. (4) The thought of the outside is a non-metaphysical thought. On the one hand, as immanentist thought, it is anti-Platonistic. On the other, as a thought of what is stubbornly invisible, of non-presence, it

overcomes metaphysics. But more importantly, Foucault's early thought, captured here in "The Thought of the Outside," opens up an experience that transforms who we are. Not being able to reach the outside—since it is not an enclosed interiority—we undergo and suffer powerlessness. The powerlessness, however, does not render us paralyzed. Instead, it makes us more zealous in our attempt to neglect the forms (such as the form of man) that have imprisoned us. We become more attentive to the attraction of what lies outside these forms. We transgress the limits imposed by the forms in order to free us for what has not yet come.

We began both this chapter and the entire book with a quote from Foucault's 1984 essay "What Is Enlightenment?" Let us repeat it here as we approach the conclusion. He is speaking of the purpose of critique. In full he says,

> [The purpose of critique] will not be to deduce from the form of what we are what it is impossible for us to do and know [as in Kant]; but it will separate out, from the contingency that has made us what we are, the possibility of no longer being, doing, or thinking what we are, do, or think. It is not seeking to make possible a metaphysics that has finally become a science; it is seeking to reopen as far and as wide as possible, the indefinite work of freedom.[31]

This indefinite work of freedom, by means of which we become other than what we were, by means of which we transform our thinking and our lives, is the very project of what we call continental philosophy. It is perhaps the only project worthy of the name "philosophy."

# Further Questions

The research agenda for what we have been calling "continental philosophy" can be summed up in one sentence. This kind of philosophy aims to construct a discourse that leads us to an experience that puts ourselves in question. In other words, it aims to invent concepts that lead us to an experience that transforms how we think of ourselves, that transforms who we are and what we do. The experience is the experience of powerlessness. Leading us to the transformative experience, we must *first* negate and destroy anything that might count as a simple, undifferentiated, pure, and static presence. That is, we must deconstruct anything that might count as an origin or an end, anything that might count as a foundation or ground, such as God, truth, the good, or nature. Anything that suggests the metaphysics of presence must be criticized and overcome. We must *then* affirm non-presence and groundlessness, which means that we must affirm immanence. Our starting point then is no different from that of Descartes in the first two meditations: "I am thinking, I am thinking about . . . , I am thinking about my own ideas." The starting point therefore is auto-affection. Auto-affection is not a deliberate act of reflection through which an object called the self is given in a representation. Below reflection and as its origin is the basic experience of my own thoughts. Since Plato's *Theaetetus,* thinking has been defined by means of an interior monologue (189e–190a): hearing oneself speak. The auto-affection called "hearing oneself speak" seems to include two aspects. On the one hand, I seem to hear myself speak *at the very moment* that I speak and *without* delay, and on the other I seem to hear *my own self* speak and *not* someone or something other. Let us now examine the particular experience of hearing oneself speak.

When I engage in interior monologue, when, in short, I think—it *seems* as though I hear myself speak at the very moment I speak. It seems as though my interior voice is not required to pass outside of myself, as though it is not required to traverse any space, not even the space of my body. So my interior monologue seems to be immediate, immediately present, and not to involve anyone else. Interior monologue seems therefore to be different from the experience of my speaking to another and different from the experience of my looking at myself in the mirror, where my vision has to pass through, at the least, the portals of my eyes. It is important to hear the "seems" in the preceding sentences. We are now going to *deconstruct* the appearances in order to expose the essential structure or process below what is apparent or believed. So the problem with the belief that interior monologue (in a word, thought) is different from other experiences of auto-affection is twofold. On the one hand, the experience of hearing oneself speak is temporal (like all experience). The "timing" of interior monologue means that the present moment involves a past moment, which has elapsed and which has been retained. It is an irreducible or essential necessity that the present moment comes after, a little later; it is always involved in a process of mediation. The problem therefore with the belief that interior monologue happens immediately (as if there were no mediation involved) is that the hearing of myself is never immediately present in the moment when I speak. The hearing of myself in the present comes a moment later; there is a delay between the hearing and the speaking. This conclusion means that my interior monologue in fact resembles my experience of the mirror image in which my vision must traverse a distance that differentiates me into seer and seen. I cannot; it is impossible for me to hear myself immediately.

But there is a further implication. The distance or delay in time turns my speaking *in the present moment* into something coming second. Temporalization implies that the present is not an origin all alone; it is compounded with a past so that my speaking in the present moment is no longer *sui generis*. Therefore it must be seen as a kind of response to the past. The fact that my speaking is a response to the past leads to the other problem with the belief that interior monologue is my own. Besides the irreducible delay and distance involved in the experience of auto-affection, there is the problem of the voice. In order to hear myself speak at this very moment, I must make use of the same phonemes as I use in communication (even if this monologue is not vocalized externally through my mouth). It is an irreducible or essential necessity that the silent words I form contain repeatable traits.[1] This irreducible necessity means that when I speak to myself, I speak with the sounds of others. In other words, it means that I find in myself other voices, which come from the past; the many voices are in me. I cannot—here we encounter the experience of powerlessness—it is impossible for me to hear myself speak all alone. There is a multivocality, a sort of murmur or clamor coming from the past. Others' voices contaminate the hearing of myself speaking.[2] Just as my present moment is never immediate, my interior monologue is never simply my own.

This description shows that auto-affection is based on a formal structure at work in the "timing," but also, the "spacing" of auto-affection, a structure consisting of two contradictory elements. On the one hand, there is always a present moment, a kind of event, a point, a singularization. Each thought I have, as I speak it, has a kind of novelty to it, giving it a singular location. On the other, however, the singularity of the thought is connected back to some other thoughts in the past or in some other place. As the description shows, each thought is necessarily composed of traits already used in the past, traits standing nearby. Time temporalizes or endures and space spatializes or distances by means of two forces, the force of repetition and the force of singularization, the force of universality and the force of event. These two elements of repetition (or universality) and singularization (or event) are irreducibly connected to one another, but without unification. In other words, these two forces are necessarily bound to one another and necessarily disunified. The paradoxical relation of the two elements or forces implies that auto-affection is really, necessarily, hetero-affection. It implies that immanence dissolves into multiplicity; that the inside is in the outside (or the outside contaminates the inside); that instead of an "I," there is a "we"; and that instead of our thinking we have the power to hear ourselves speak (the very ground of autonomy), we find ourselves in an experience of inability. The necessity of these two forces is so strong that we are powerless not to obey their commands, even though their commands cannot be reconciled. We must singularize and we must universalize.

Let us be more precise about implications that follow from this deconstruction. *First,* experience as the experience of the present is never a simple experience of something present over and against me, right before my eyes in a clear intuition; there is always another force, another element, another agency there. Repetition contains what has passed away, distant, and no longer present, and what is about to come, from a distance, and is not yet present. The present therefore is always complicated by non-presence. Above, we called this minimal repeatability a trait; the trait refers to a kind of proto- and informal linguisticality that refers back to nothing but other traits. *Second,* if the experience of the present is always complicated, then nothing is ever given as such in certainty. Whatever is given is given as other than itself, as already past or as still to come. What becomes "foundational," we might say is this "as." Or what becomes "foundational" is the "of" of "the thought of . . . nothing (present as such)." That is, what becomes foundation is a transitivity that, suspending its object, goes to infinity. Instead of the certainty of something given as such, we have the "maybe" of something given incompletely. *Third,* if the "foundation" is transitivity to infinity, then the proto-linguisticality of the trait is nothing but an informal (below the forms of meanings and propositions) murmur, a collectivity of voices. Instead of a unified "I," an "auto," we find a "we" that remains incomplete and absent. *Fourth,* the fact that transitivity to infinity (the two forces of event and repetition) has become foundational has disturbed the traditional structure of transcendental philosophy, which consists in a linear relation between foundational conditions and founded experience. In traditional transcendental philosophy (as in Kant, but we noted above that Husserl's transcendental phenomenology is different from Kant's transcendental philosophy), an empirical event such as what is happening right now is supposed to be derivative from or founded upon conditions that are not empirical. Yet the deconstruction shows that the empirical event is a non-separable part of the structural or foundational conditions. Or, in traditional transcendental philosophy, the empirical event is supposed to be an accident that overcomes an essential structure. But we see now that this accident cannot be removed or eliminated. *Fifth,* if the "accident" cannot be eliminated, if the "accident" has always already taken place, then we cannot speak of an origin in the traditional sense, a principle (or *arché*), a unitary starting point, complete in itself, an unprecedented beginning. Instead, the origin is always origin-heterogeneous, that is, the origin is heterogeneous from the start or what starts is itself heterogeneous to the very idea of origin. Likewise, if the "accident" cannot be eliminated, if the "accident" always remains, then we cannot speak of an end in the traditional sense, a purpose (or *telos*), a unitary stopping point, complete in itself, with nothing left over. Instead, the end is always end-heterogeneous, that is, the end is heterogeneous finally or what finishes is heterogeneous to the very idea of end. *Sixth,* if there is no original principle and if there is no final purpose, then every experience contains an aspect of lateness and an aspect of earliness. Every experience is the experience of awaiting-forgetting. It seems as though I am late for the origin since it seems already to have disappeared; it seems as though I am early for the end since it seems still to come. Every experience then is not quite on time or in the right place. Experience, the experience exposed only by deconstruction, is "out of joint." Being "out of joint," commanding in ways that are irreconcilable, the experience is one of powerlessness, but, more explicitly, it is one of violence and injustice.

It is precisely this "out of jointness" of the relation that raises *further questions.* Here is the most obvious and maybe the most pressing question. Is it necessary to conceive the relation of the two forces as one of violence? Is some other conception of the relation possible? It seems that we cannot conceive the relation strictly as peace or non-violence since the idea of peace, balance, equality, reconciliation, seems to imply a bringing to an end (or at least it implies the imagination of an end; this claim itself raises a question of whether we can indeed imagine an end in the strict sense). If peace means the end of experience, then reacting to the imbalance of the two forces with perfect peace seems to be the very worst sort of violence, complete violence, the end of everything. The question of the conception of the relation as violence leads to the question of reaction. Let us imagine—maybe we can imagine nothing else—that the relation between event and repetition remains forever unjust. The pain of loss in one's heart always remains; we continue to suffer the anxiety, with neither protection nor reserve, almost to the point of madness, that the injustice is irremediable. Then, we must ask, how do we react to this necessary violence, this irreducible pain, this insane anxiety? As we just realized, it seems that we cannot react with perfect and complete peace.

We must become something other than the reaction of the worst violence. Therefore, the question: Is there then some other reaction hiding behind the "non" of non-violence? Is there some other power hiding behind the absence of power? Perhaps there is, and it amounts to this: If we cannot stop the violence of repetition on the event, we can let it happen; if we cannot stop the violence of the event on repetition, we can let it happen. This letting happen means that we have the ability—the power maybe—to be unable. We are able to obey the law of repetition (we must always await the repetition in each event, obligated thereby to forget each event); we are able to obey the law of singularization (we must always forget all the repetitions of events, obligated thereby to wait for another event). Is this obedience a listening to the murmur of the outside? Is this obedience a welcoming of all the events across the border that divides while binding, welcoming all repetitions across the threshold that binds while dividing? Maybe this obedience would do the least violence. Nothing is certain, however, since the least violence would come from chance or grace.

In this reaction of the least violence, we have opened the border of who we are to others, to all the others that haunt us from the past (they keep coming back to us) and to all the others that wait for us in the future (they keep coming toward us). How are we to conceive this "we"? Even if we could do the very least violence, there would still be other events violated by repetition, there would still be other repetitions violated by the event. Because of this irremediable violence—but must it be irremediable?—this "we" cannot be unified and identical. A unified and identical "we," a community at peace with itself, can never, therefore, be accomplished. The people are lacking. They are therefore, always, still a people, a "*demos*," to come. Unlike us, we who are dominated by the pursuits of science, the hustle and bustle of everyday life, the noise of business and globalization, would this people to come be negligent; would they abandon grasping and be content with the things that are given to them by grace or chance? Would this people to come ever ask, "what, is that all there is?" This people to come, however, would question itself, its "we." In this self-interrogation, the people to come would always become other than it is, going over border and limits or opening borders and limits. Will the people to come, therefore, include everyone, the whole world, and therefore the foreign, the migrating, the vagrant, the homeless, and even the beastly—in a word, will the people to come include the enemies? How can there be something like a society of friends that includes the enemies? And if we can imagine such a hyperbolic society of "friends" (including the whole world), of what are they friends? We cannot imagine any society that does not dwell on a land. There can be no people, no nation, no democracy, without a land. They must have a place to dwell and be enveloped. Just as the people are always to come, the land, soil, the earth, is still to come. There is always more depth, more distance, more dimensions, to infinity. How are we to imagine this earth to come? Is it *terra firma*, or is the soil shifting beneath our feet? Is it a utopia or a dystopia, a heterotopia? What is its element? Is it a desert or an ocean? Is the land an ark floating on the water or a fortress sitting on the sand? Is it a countryside or a city? Is it a terrain of pastures or mountains? Is it a finely segmented city or a city of porous walls? Does it have a name? Do the people who might dwell on this land have a name? If they have a name, can we call them forth? How? Can we imagine an artform, a literature, a letter, that addresses them? Can we invent concepts, create beliefs, a name that will make these dispersed living beings come together?

There are no clear answers to these questions of violence, of a people to come, and a land to come. Yet if we have been exposed to the experience of powerlessness, we sense that these questions have force. Like a law, they command us to think. Indeed, these questions have been formulated with the hope that they will bring about a renewal of thinking. As we have argued, such a renewal is the very project of what we have been calling continental philosophy. Perhaps these questions lead us "beyond continental philosophy." Perhaps the attempts to answer them constitute something like "post–continental philosophy." Whatever we call the next step in thinking, however, does not matter, as long as we remember the potentiality of these conceptual elements: (1) the starting point in immanence (where immanence is understood first as auto-affection, but then, when its appearances are deconstructed, it becomes the powerlessness of hetero-affection); (2) difference (where the relation in hetero-affection is conceived as violence between the forces of repetition and the forces of singularization); (3) thought (where the language in which we think is understood as a threatening murmur); and (4) the overcoming of metaphysics (where metaphysics is understood as a mode of thinking that reacts to the murmur with the worst violence, and overcoming is understood as the creation of a new mode of thinking, imagining, and inventing that calls forth a people to come, friends of the least violence, dwelling in a land to come). If we do not forget the potentiality of these elements, if we hold to a remembering that obliges us to forget the forms of them, then perhaps continental philosophy has a future.

# A Note on the Idea of Immanence

The discourse of anti-Platonism or of the overcoming of metaphysics requires the use of the term "immanence." The *first* sense of the word must
be opposed to the transcendent. In the reversal of Platonism, we are no
longer concerned with a second, transcendent world; our concern is not
with transcendent ideas. Our gaze is now turned back to this world and to
our ideas. Cartesianism is the necessary outcome of anti-Platonism. Both
Bergson and especially Husserl embraced the necessity of Cartesianism. If
we are overcoming metaphysics, where the "meta" of "metaphysics" means
a transcendent realm of ideas "beyond" this world and our experiences,
then we must reflect on our experience, on "inner experience." Yet both
Husserl and especially Bergson (through respectively absolute time consciousness and the duration) recognized that inner experience is not an
enclosure. The fact that inner experience is fundamentally temporal opens
the inside to the outside. In other words, due to the structure of temporalization, that is, due to the fact that every present moment is retained and
repeatable, there is a sort of becoming in inner experience. Becoming is
the *second* and more profound sense of "immanence."

Deleuze (or Deleuze and Guattari) have especially stressed that philosophy, in order to be genuine, must be a philosophy of immanence.[1] They
define immanence in this way, taking their inspiration from Spinoza and
Bergson:

> Immanence does not refer back to the Spinozist substance and modes,
> but, on the contrary, the Spinozist concepts of substance and modes re-
> fer back to the plane of immanence as their presupposition. This plane

presents two sides to us, extension and thought, or rather its two potentialities, the potentiality of being and the potentiality of thinking. Spinoza
is the vertigo of immanence from which so many philosophers try in vain
to escape. Will we ever be mature enough for a Spinozist inspiration?
It happened once with Bergson: the beginning of *Matter and Memory*
marks out a plane that slices through the chaos—at once the infinite
movement of a matter that continuously propagates itself, and the image
of a thought that everywhere continuously spreads an in principle pure
consciousness (immanence is not immanent "to" consciousness but the
other way around).[2]

In reference to this passage, we must note that in Deleuze and Guattari,
the plane of immanence is neither matter nor consciousness. Immanence
cannot be immanent to matter or to consciousness. If Deleuze and Guattari call the plane of immanence at times "nature," they mean nature in a
sense entirely distinguished from, as they say above, Spinozist substance.
As they say in *A Thousand Plateaus*, "This plane [as opposed to the plane
of transcendence] is necessarily a plane of immanence and univocity. We
therefore call it a plane of Nature, although nature has nothing to do with
it, since on this plane there is no distinction between the natural and the
artificial. However many dimensions it may have, it never has a supplementary dimension to that which happens upon it. That alone makes it
natural and immanent."[3] It bears repeating: "*That alone* makes [the plane
of immanence] natural and immanent [*par là meme il est naturel et immanent*]" (my emphasis). Nature is not the plane of immanence. It has no
"supplementary dimension." Therefore, the plane of immanence is based
on nothing but itself, which gives it the status of being that which precedes
subjectivity and objectivity. In this sense of precedence to subjects and
objects (prior to the two potentialities mentioned above), it is "natural"
(or "vital"). It is not natural in the sense of objective laws, material forces,
chemical processes and causes, or neurochemical processes and causes.
To reduce the plane of immanence to these scientific entities (to these beings, as Heidegger would say) distorts the very concept of immanence. The
plane of immanence cannot be the matter of nature. One misunderstands,
it seems to me, the conceptual core of Deleuze and Guattari's plane of immanence if one identifies their thinking with naturalism or materialism.
In fact, such an identification makes Deleuze's thought compromise with
modes of thought that are *inferior* to it.

We just mentioned transcendence, which leads us back to the second and more profound sense of immanence. The plane of immanence is a becoming. It becomes because it has "no supplementary dimension." In other words, it is infinite, in the sense of having no absolute endpoint and no absolute starting point. It is based on no principle (no *arché*) and on no purpose (no *telos*). It may be that we distinguish transcendence from the transcendent. Thereby, with transcendence we can say that the other transcends me *but* is still of this world or of this experience. The transcendence of the other is indeed an opening of inner experience. It does not however open the inside *enough*. In the transcendence of the other, we conceive the other as another subject, as a face with a form. In other words, we conceive the other as an always hidden subjectivity, the form of his or her experiences being always hidden from my gaze by that face, but still there somewhere, like a secret. If we conceive the transcendence of the other in this way, then we have set up a starting point or an endpoint to becoming.[4] Hyperbole cannot be limited and must not be limited. The difference between transcendence and immanence is the difference between the other and becoming-other (not just the "alter," but alteration). Transcendence is a point at which we could imagine stopping moving (if we were finally to reach the secret life of the other), while immanence is a vanishing point (*une ligne de fuite*) toward which one never stops moving. The unlimited movement of becoming is why we must really imagine immanence as a plane. At the horizon (we are never certain how far or near it is), there is a point toward which I can make a beeline and fly (*une ligne de fuite*).

## APPENDIX 2

# What Is a Trait?

We must not confuse a trait with the traditional ways in which we have thought about language.[1] It is not a sense or meaning; it is not a proposition; it is not even a sentence, phrase, or a word. A trait is smaller than these linguistic forms; if we say that it is a kind of form, it is one that is minimal or micrological. But it is best to say that a trait is non-formal; it is not yet or no longer a unit or a unity. A trait is non-linguistic insofar as traits do not necessarily carry a meaning; a trait is prelinguistic (or proto-linguistic) insofar as language is made of traits and contains them. A trait is not invisible, but it is frequently covered over by maximum or macrological units such as words, phrases, and sentences. A trait therefore is a very small (abstract) element such as a cry or a murmur.[2] It is a singularity or an event. In this regard, a trait is material or corporeal. It has something to do with a body and a location: a trait of a face, a tic, or the trait of a voice, a lilt. A trait, however, is also variable, repeatable, or transformable, which makes it incorporeal or spiritual. The repeatability of the trait is what makes it haunt anyone who encounters it. The cry of the wolf in the night recurs in a nightmare. It is the repeatability of the trait that makes it retreat or withdraw; a trait, so to speak, "retraits." Retreating, the trait becomes; it becomes a multiplicity. It has always been a multiplicity, prior to any subject who might speak it. Traits are the voices of no one, or, more precisely, they are voices of everyone: a clamor. Traits refer back to past uses and ahead to future uses, but also they refer across, down, or up to other traits. But they never refer to an absolute origin or an absolute purpose. They are inherently mobile. They never refer back to a repressed content. They never refer to "something" unthought, even [ə] though their withdrawal gives us more to think about. What there is more to think in the trait is its indeterminacy; it remains indeterminate in its uses or occurrences. A trait is undecidable.

Traits then are not forms but functions. Being large, a form is composed of many functions. Functions are informal; they have only little, micrological details. We already mentioned that a face, for example, has a form, but it is composed of many traits or features; besides a tic, there is a mole. A poem, for example, has a form, its verses and the spatial arrangements of words and punctuation. But within the poem, there are functions of rhyme and alliteration. These poetic traits may be extracted and repeated differently than they were in the poem; repeated into a different milieu or repeated more rapidly or more slowly, they may be used differently and then they produce different outcomes. Because the traits are informal, each function is indeterminately plural. For instance, the function of disguising oneself contains at least two possible uses: exhibition and concealment. We see the undecidability of the function of disguise in animals. Animals disguise themselves at times in order to exhibit themselves so that, through the exhibition, they are able to attract something that can serve as a mate; at other times, they disguise themselves in order to conceal themselves so that, through the concealment, they are able to attack something that can serve as nourishment. A warrior therefore dresses himself for battle in a way that he may hide from the enemy.[3] The function of disguise is inherently variable, without an absolute purpose or origin. Although the warrior extracts the function of disguise from the animals, he does not become an animal. The warrior becomes a woman, since women too disguise themselves. So the warrior becomes woman so that woman may become something else. What does the woman become? The woman does not become a man. Disguising herself, she becomes an animal who exhibits herself, not so that she may attract a mate, but so that she may be able to attack an enemy. She becomes a warrior-animal. This sequence is only one possible line of becoming in the disguising function. We must note that in the sequence, in any sequence whatsoever, there is no reciprocity. In its undecidability, the animal function of disguise does not result in man becoming woman and woman becoming man. Man becomes woman and then woman becomes animal. But woman becomes animal so that animal as well becomes something else. In fact, this is a necessary step in becoming generally: What one becomes must become something else. In this sequence, the animal becomes other as warrior; the warrior becomes other as woman; the woman becomes other as animal. Next, the animal must become other. What does the animal become? There is no clear answer to this question, except to say that the function of disguising has other possible uses, other possible milieus, than the ones we have just outlined. Perhaps disguising is a function of marking, a function of tracing; disguising is perhaps a way of writing. Then we could say that the animal becomes a tale. Traits therefore are not concepts, but we can make concepts and discourses out of them.

# NOTES

## Introduction

The text that is the basis for this introduction was written in 1999. It is the oldest part of Early Twentieth-Century Continental Philosophy. All other chapters, the preface, the conclusion, the appendices were written at Penn State University in 2010. However, the book is based on a course I taught at the University of Memphis called "Recent Continental Philosophy." (I taught the same course one time at Penn State University in the fall of 2009 under the title "Twentieth-Century Philosophy.") Teaching that course (several times at the University of Memphis, starting in 1999) forced me to think about what continental philosophy might mean; it led to the idea of writing this book.

1. Gilles Deleuze, *Foucault* (Paris: Minuit, 1986), p. 124, English translation by Seán Hand as *Foucault* (Minneapolis: University of Minnesota Press, 1988), p. 116. See also Gilles Deleuze, *Différence et répétition* (Paris: Presses Universitaires de France, 1968), p. 188n1, English translation by Paul Patton as *Difference and Repetition* (New York: Columbia University Press, 1994), p. 144; this note is left untranslated in the English translation. Deleuze's book on Foucault has played an enormous role in the writing of *Early Twentieth-Century Continental Philosophy*.

2. These four formulas do not correspond to the four features presented in the preface.

3. Deleuze, *Différence et répétition*, p. 258; *Difference and Repetition*, p. 199.

4. Deleuze, *Différence et répétition*, p. 196; *Difference and Repetition*, p. 151.

5. Deleuze, *Différence et répétition*, p. 173; *Difference and Repetition*, p. 132.

6. Deleuze, *Différence et répétition*, p. 205; *Difference and Repetition*, p. 158.

7. Michel Foucault, *Surveiller et punir* (Paris: Gallimard, 1975), English translation by Alan Sheridan as *Discipline and Punish* (New York: Vintage, 1995). See also Gilles Deleuze and Félix Guattari, *Capitalisme et schizophrénie 2. Mille plateaux* (Paris: Minuit, 1980), p. 244, English translation by Brian Massumi as *A Thousand Plateaus: Capitalism and Schizophrenia* (Minneapolis: University of Minnesota Press, 1987), p. 224.

8. See chapter 7 below for the introduction of violence into the self-relation.

9. Jean Hyppolite, *Logique et existence* (Paris: Presses Universitaires de France, 1952), p. 230, English translation by Leonard Lawlor and Amit Sen as *Logic and Existence* (Albany: The State University of New York Press, 1997), p. 176.

10. Andrew Cutrofello has noted not only the importance of Nietzsche but also of Heidegger for the development of twentieth-century continental philosophy. His overall orientation, however, comes from appropriations of Kant. Cutrofello's *Continental Philosophy: A Contemporary Introduction* (London: Routledge, 2005) is by far the best introduction to continental philosophy written to date. Lee Braver has also made an admirable presentation of continental philosophy in his *A Thing of this World: A History of Continental Anti-Realism* (Evanston, Ill.: Northwestern University Press, 2007).

11. Martin Heidegger, *Sein und Zeit* (Tübingen: Niemeyer, 1979 [1927]), p. 344, English translation by Joan Stambaugh, revised and with a foreword by Dennis J. Schmidt as *Being and Time* (Albany: The State University of New York Press, 2010), p. 328.

12. See Leonard Lawlor, "The Beginnings of Thought: The Fundamental Experience in Derrida and Deleuze," in *Thinking Through French Philosophy: The Being of the Question* (Bloomington: Indiana University Press, 2003), pp. 123–41.

13. Eugen Fink, "Die Phänomenologische Philosophie E. Husserl in der Gegenwärtigen Kritik," originally published in *Kantstudien,* Band, XXXVIII, 3/4 (Berlin, 1933); collected in Eugen Fink, *Studien zur Phänomenologie* (Den Haag: Nijhoff, 1966), p. 105n1, English translation as "The Phenomenological Philosophy of Edmund Husserl and Contemporary Criticism," in *The Phenomenology of Husserl,* ed. R. O. Elveton (Chicago: Quadrangle Books, 1970), p. 99n11.

14. For more on Husserl and phenomenology, see chapter 3.

15. Gilles Deleuze and Félix Guattari, *Qu'est-ce que la philosophie* (Paris: Minuit, 1991), p. 103, English translation by Hugh Tomlinson and Graham Burchell as *What Is Philosophy* (New York: Columbia University Press, 1994), p. 108.

16. G. W. F. Hegel, *Phänomenologie des Geistes* (Hamburg: Meiner, 1952), p. 32, English translation by A. V. Miller as *Phenomenology of Spirit* (Oxford: Oxford University Press, 1979), p. 21.

17. Hegel, *Phänomenologie des Geistes,* pp. 24–26; *Phenomenology of Spirit,* pp. 14–15.

18. Maurice Merleau-Ponty, "Philosophie et non-philosophie depuis Hegel," in *Notes de cours 1958–1959 et 1960–1961* (Paris: Gallimard, 1996), p. 278, English translation by Hugh J. Silverman as "Philosophy and Non-Philosophy Since Hegel," in *Philosophy and Non-Philosophy Since Merleau-Ponty,* ed. Hugh J. Silverman (New York: Routledge, 1988), p. 12. See also Mauro Carbone, *The Thinking of the Sensible: Merleau-Ponty's A-Philosophy* (Evanston, Ill.: Northwestern University Press, 2004); Martin Heidegger, *What Is Called Thinking,* trans. J. Glenn Gray (New York: Harper Colophon, 1968).

19. See Edward S. Reed, "The Separation of Psychology from Philosophy: Studies in the Sciences of Mind, 1815–1879," in *Routledge History of Philosophy, Volume VII: The Nineteenth Century,* ed. C. L. Ten, pp. 297–356 (London: Routledge, 1994).

20. See Edmund Husserl, "Prolegomena zur reinen Logik," in *Logische Untersuchungen, I* (Tübingen: Niemeyer, 1968), chapters 3–10, English translation by J. N.

Findlay, edited by Dermot Moran as "Prologomena to Pure Logic," in *Logical Investigations*, vol. 1 (London: Routledge, 2001), chapters 3–10. These chapters concern Husserl's extensive criticisms of psychologism.

21. Husserl, *Logical Investigations*, vol. 1, p. 176. This is the original 1901 comment on phenomenology, which Husserl replaced for the second edition in 1913. For the characterization of phenomenology as transcendental, see Husserl, *Ideen zu einer reinen Phänomenologie und phänomenologischen Philosophie. I. Buch: Einführung in die reine Phänomenologie*, Husserliana Band III (Den Haag: Martinus Nijhofff, 1976), §33, English translation by Fred Kersten as *Ideas Pertaining to a Pure Phenomenology and to a Phenomenological Philosophy. First Book* (The Hague: Martinus Nijhoff, 1982), §33.

22. Sigmund Freud, *Aus der Anfängen der Psychoanalyse* (London: Imago, 1950), English translation by Eric Mosbacher and James Strachey as *The Origins of Psychoanalysis* (New York: Basic Books, 1954). See also Paul Ricœur, *Freud and Philosophy: An Essay on Interpretation* (New Haven, Conn.: Yale University Press, 1970), pp. 69–70.

23. See CENT: 37–51/DI: 55–74 for Bergson's criticisms of Delbœuf and Fechner.

## 1. Thinking beyond Platonism

1. It is clear that Bergson has not considered the Kant of *The Critique of Judgment*.

2. See Jacques Derrida, *De l'esprit* (Paris: Galilée, 1987), p. 103, English translation by Geoffrey Bennington and Rachel Bowlby as *Of Spirit* (Chicago: University of Chicago Press, 1989), p. 64. Here Derrida notes that now we know that Heidegger read Bergson more than Heidegger's texts indicate.

3. Gilles Deleuze, "Postface pour l'édition Américaine: Un retour à Bergson," in *Deux régimes de fous* (Paris: Minuit, 2003), pp. 314–15, English translation by Ames Hodges and Mike Taormina as "Postscript to the American Edition: A Return to Bergson," in Gilles Deleuze, *Two Regimes of Madness*, ed. David Lapoujade, pp. 336–37 (New York: Semiotext(e), 2006).

4. Georges Canguilhem, *La connaissance de la vie* (Paris: Vrin, 1965), p. 13, my translation. The introduction to *La connaissance de la vie* is interesting in comparison to Bergson's "Introduction to Metaphysics." Canguilhem states that knowledge is based in analysis, but then claims that the living (*le vivant*) may require something else to be known, "*de nous sentir bêtes.*" Perhaps Bergson would agree that one side of intuition is that we sense like animals.

5. The French edition contains paragraph breaks where new themes start. There are also titles for each section at the top of the page. Here is the "table of contents" for "Introduction to Metaphysics." I. Analysis and Intuition (CENT: 1392–96/CM: 159–62); II. Duration and Consciousness (CENT: 1396–1403/CM: 162–69); III. Component Parts and Partial Expression (CENT: 1403–6/CM: 169–73); IV. Empiricism and Rationalism (CENT: 1406–11/CM: 173–78); V. The Real Duration (CENT: 1411–18/CM: 178–88); VI. Reality and Mobility (CENT: 1418–19/CM: 188–89); VII. The Alleged Relativity of Knowledge (CENT: 1419–26/CM: 188–93); VIII. Metaphysics and Modern Science (CENT: 1426–32/CM: 194–200). The last two sections concern precisely Kant and modern philosophy. Later in the 1934 introductions to *La*

*pensée et le mouvant,* Bergson will develop the intuitive method precisely as a differentiation within a mixture (given to us ahead of time in language) along the natural articulations (CENT: 1270/CM: 29).

6. See also the course Bergson taught in 1902, the year before the publication of "Introduction to Metaphysics." *Cours de Bergson au Collège de France,* "Histoire de l'idée de temps" (1902), in *Annales bergsoniennes I* (Paris: Presses Universitaires de France, 2002), pp. 25–68.

7. Husserl makes a similar distinction between "pieces" or "independent parts" and "parts" or "dependent parts." See Edmund Husserl, *Logische Untersuchungen; Logical Investigations,* vol. 2, third investigation, paragraphs 1 and 2.

8. Bergson's criticism of symbolism is similar to Husserl's insofar as the manipulation of symbolic formulas produces the crisis of European sciences. See Edmund Husserl, *Die Krisis der Europäischen Wissenschaft und die Transzendentale Phänomenologie, Husserliana VI* (The Hague: Martinus Nijhoff, 1976), p. 52, English translation by David Carr as *The Crisis of European Sciences and Transcendental Phenomenology* (Evanston, Ill.: Northwestern University Press, 1970), p. 51.

9. The original Andison English translation renders the word "sympathise" with "harmony"; in the revised translation, it is "sympathy."

10. Whenever we see this word "translation" in Bergson, we should keep in mind that translations can always be perfected.

11. See Gilles Deleuze, *Le pli. Leibniz et le Baroque* (Paris: Minuit, 1988), p. 28, English translation by Tom Conley as *The Fold: Leibniz and the Baroque* (Minneapolis: University of Minnesota Press, 1993), p. 20.

12. See also Martin Heidegger, *The Metaphysical Foundations of Logic,* trans. Michael Heim (Bloomington: Indiana University Press, 184), p. 203.

13. See Deleuze, *Le pli. Leibniz et le Baroque,* p. 88; *The Fold: Leibniz and the Baroque,* p. 65.

14. In regard to this image, we should read this comment from the first introduction to *The Creative Mind* (CENT: 1261/CM: 19): "Try, for instance, to call up today the act you will accomplish tomorrow, even if you know what you are going to do. Your imagination perhaps evokes the movement to be gone through; but what you will think and feel in doing it you can know nothing of today, because your state tomorrow will include all the life you will have lived up until that moment, with what that particular moment is to add to it. To fill this state in advance with what it should contain you will need exactly the time which separates today from tomorrow, for you cannot shorten psychological life by a single instant without modifying its content."

15. As far as I know, no Bergson commentator has stressed the role of component parts in Bergson's conception of intuition. Jean-Louis Vieillard-Baron, however, says that "[L'intuition] nous donne une connaissance absolue, mais *partielle*" (*Bergson* [Paris: Presses Universitaires de France, 1991], p. 107, my emphasis). The following texts have been consulted in the writing of this chapter. Marie Cariou, *Bergson et le fait mystique* (Paris: Abier Montaigne, 1976), especially, pp. 21–85. Marie Cariou, *Lectures bergsoniennes* (Paris: Presses Universitaires de France, 1990), especially, pp. 112–18. Bernard Gilson, *La revision bergsonienne de la philosophie de l'esprit* (Paris: Vrin, 1992). Jean-Christophe Goddard, *Mysticisme et folie* (Paris: Desclée de Brouwer, 2002). Vladimir Jankélévitch, *Henri Bergson* (Paris: Presses Universitaires de France, 1959). Frédéric Worms, "La conception bergsonienne du temps," in *Philosophie,* no.

54 (1 juin 1997): pp. 73–91. Frédéric Worms, "Intuition," in *Le vocabulaire de Bergson* (Paris: Ellipses, 2000), pp. 37–39. Frédéric Worms, *Annales bergsoniennes II: Bergson, Deleuze, la phénoménologie* (Paris: Presses Universitaires de France, 2004).

16. The term "element" in Bergson has nothing to do with what we shall call, in chapter 6, "the elemental" in Merleau-Ponty's thought. Merleau-Ponty's elemental is in fact Bergson's duration.

17. Cf. Jacques Lacan, *Les quatre concepts fondamentauz de la psychanalyse* (Paris: Seuil, 1973), p. 88, English translation by Alan Sheridan as *The Four Fundamental Concepts of Psycho-analysis* (New York: Norton, 1981), p. 75.

18. Bergsonian becoming is the basis of Deleuze and Guattari's concept of becoming. See Deleuze and Guattari, *Mille plateaux*; *A Thousand Plateaus*, see all of plateau ten.

19. Cf. Deleuze and Guattari, *Mille plateaux*, p. 291; *A Thousand Plateaus*, p. 238.

20. See also Bergson's discussion of color in "The Life and Work of Ravaisson," in *The Creative Mind*, CENT 1455/CM 225. See also Gilles Deleuze, "La conception de la différence chez Bergson," in *L'île déserte et autres textes* (Paris: Minuit, 2002), p. 60, English translation by Michael Taormina as "Bergson's Conception of Difference," in *Desert Islands and Other Texts* (Los Angeles: Semiotext(e), 2004), p. 43.

21. We shall return to this claim about Cartesianism several times in the chapters that follow.

22. Although he is not interested in Bergson's idea of fluid concept, that is, although he is more interested in Bergson's theory of general ideas (concepts in the proper sense) and whether there is a conceiving tendency in life itself, Canguilhem's "Le concept et la vie" contains an important discussion of conceptualization in Bergson. See Georges Canguilhem, "Le concept et la vie," in *Etudes d'histoire et de philosophie des sciences concernant les vivant et la vie* (Paris: Vrin, 2002), pp. 335–81.

23. Merleau-Ponty in his 1955 "Everywhere and Nowhere" (collected then into *Signs*) says, "Husserl had understood: our philosophical problem is to open the concept without destroying it." See Maurice Merleau-Ponty, "Partout et nulle part," in *Signes* (Paris: NRF Gallimard, 1960), p. 174, English translation by Richard C. McCleary as "Everywhere and Nowhere," in *Signs* (Evanston, Ill.: Northwestern University Press, 1964), p. 138.

24. Bergson also says, now from the first introduction to *The Creative Mind*, "For lack of precision is commonly the including of a thing in too wide a genus, things and genera corresponding moreover to pre-existing words. But if one begins by casting off ready-made concepts, if one professes to have a direct vision of reality, if one sub-divides this reality taking into account its articulations, the new concepts one must form in order to express oneself will now be cut to the exact measure of the object; lack of precision will arise only from the extension of these concepts to other objects which they would include equally in their generality, but which will have to be studied in themselves, outside of these concepts, when one wishes to know them in their turn" (CENT: 1270/CM: 29). He makes a similar comment in "Introduction to Metaphysics," "[True empiricism] cuts out for the object a concept which can as yet hardly be called a concept, since it applies to this one thing" (CENT: 1408/CM: 175).

25. For more on the idea of a trait, see appendix 2.

26. See Gilles Deleuze, *Bergsonisme* (Paris: Presses Universitaires de France, 1968),

p. 108, English translation by Hugh Tomlinson and Barbara Habberjam as *Bergsonism* (New York: Zone Books, 1991), p. 104.

27. Merleau-Ponty sees that it is partial. See Maurice Merleau-Ponty, *Le visible et l'invisible* (Paris: Tel Gallimard, 1964), p. 163, English translation by Alphonso Lingis as *The Visible and the Invisible* (Evanston, Ill.: Northwestern University Press, 1968), p. 122.

28. Merleau-Ponty says, "One has to believe, then, that language is not simply the contrary of the truth, of coincidence, a manner of making the things themselves speak—and this is what [the philosopher] seeks. It would be a language of which he would not be the organizer, words he would not assemble, that would combine through him by virtue of a natural intertwining of their sense, through the occult trading of the metaphor—where what counts is no longer the manifest sense of each word and of each image, but the lateral relations, the kinships that are implicated in their transfers and their exchanges. It is indeed a language of this sort that Bergson himself required for the philosopher." Merleau-Ponty, *Le visible et l'invisible*, p. 167; *The Visible and the Invisible*, p. 125.

29. For an important discussion of Bergson's relation to metaphysics, see Camille Riquier, *Archéologie de Bergson. Temps et métaphysique* (Paris: Presses Universitaires de France, 2009).

## 2. Schizophrenic Thought

1. The texts that make up *Metapsychological Writings of 1915* are: 1. "Instincts and their Vicissitudes" (1915); 2. "Repression" (1915); 3. "The Unconscious" (1915); 4. "Metapsychological Supplement to the Theory of Dreams" (1916); 5. "Mourning and Melancholia" (1917); then we have *Beyond the Pleasure Principle* (1920). These papers belong to Freud's "speculative" work. On Freud's use of the word "speculation," see his essay "Zur Einführung des Narzißmus," in *Gesammelte Werke, Zehnter Band, Werke aus den Jahren 1913–1917* (London: Imago Publishing Company, 1949), pp. 138–70, especially p. 142, English translation by Cecil M. Baines as "On Narcissism: An Introduction," in *General Psychological Theory*, ed. Philip Rieff (New York: Simon & Schuster, 1997), pp. 56–82, especially pp. 59–60.

2. If we spoke like Lacan, we would say that the relation is the bar between the signifier and the signified. Jacques Lacan, "L'instance de la letter dans l'inconscient ou la raison depuis Freud," in *Écrits* (Paris: Seuil, 1966), p. 501, English translation by Alan Sheridan as "The Instance of the Letter in the Unconscious," in *Écrits: The First Complete Edition in English* (New York: Norton, 1977), pp. 417–18. See also Jean-Luc Nancy and Philippe Lacoue-Labarthe, *The Title of the Letter: A Reading of Lacan*, translated by François Raffoul and David Pettigrew (Albany: The State University of New York Press, 1992), p. 36.

3. See chapters 5, 6, and 7, respectively.

4. Deleuze and Guattari, *Mille plateaux*, p. 39; *A Thousand Plateaus*, p. 27.

5. There are several translation problems when dealing with Freud's texts. The German word "*Trieb*" plays a central role in Freud's thought. The *Standard Edition of the Complete Psychological Works of Sigmund Freud* frequently renders this word as "instinct." The word "*Trieb*," however, is probably better rendered in English as

"drive" (the French translation renders the German word as "*pulsion*"). In "The Unconscious," Freud distinguishes between drives and instincts by saying, "If inherited psychical formations exist in the human being—something analogous [*Analoges*] to instincts [*Instinkt*] in animals—these constitute the nucleus of the Ucs" (GW X: 294/SE XIV: 294/195). A fuller account of the Freudian concept of drive would have to take into account his essay "Instincts and their Vicissitudes," in GW X: 210–32/SE XIV: 117–40. "The Unconscious" starts Freud's dualistic theory of the drives, which culminates in *Beyond the Pleasure Principle,* in *The Standard Edition of the Complete Psychological Works of Sigmund Freud, Volume XVII* (1920–1922), trans. James Strachey (London: The Hogarth Press, 1981); see especially p. 53 for the discussion of the dualistic theory. The German can be found in *Studienausgabe: Psychologie des Unbewussten* (Zürich: Buchclub Ex Libris, 1975), p. 262. The "working hypothesis" in "Instincts and their Vicissitudes" is that there are ego or self-preservative drives and sexual drives. The ego-drives are narcissistic, while the sexual drives have other objects. Here he distinguishes drives from external stimuli. Freud describes a drive as a "need" (in scare quotes) requiring "satisfaction" (also in scare quotes) (GW X: 212/SE XIV: 212/118–19). A drive's need is constant force, not momentary as a stimulus is. A drive has pressure (*Drang*) (the pain of the need); aim (satisfaction in release: pleasure); object (that through which the aim is going to be achieved); and source (*Quelle*), which Freud locates in a bodily organ. However the drive is never known directly in consciousness, only its aim. The drive is a "borderline concept" between the psychical and the physical. The destinies of the drives come from the different ways that the aim can be achieved, even though the ultimate aim remains unchangeable. Freud presents four destinies (*Schicksale*): reversal into its opposite, turning around upon the subject's own self, repression, and sublimation. For an exhaustive study of Freud's concept of drive, see Adrian Johnston, *Time Driven: Metapsychology and the Splitting of the Drive* (Evanston, Ill.: Northwestern University Press, 2005), pp. 156–59.

Second, there is the term "*Vorstellung,*" which is rendered as "representation" or "idea." Then there is the word "*Aufhebung.*" The *Standard Edition* renders this word sometimes as "abrogation" and at other times as "lifting." It would be surprising, however, if Freud was unaware of its use in Hegel's work. Therefore, it is probably better rendered in English with a term associated with Hegel's thought of *Aufhebung*: "sublation." Finally, and most importantly, there is the word "*Besetzung.*" The *Standard Edition* renders the word with the Greek "*cathexis*" (a word based on the Greek verb for "to occupy"), while the French translations render it as "*investissement.*" (See Sigmund Freud, *Métapsychologie,* traduit de l'allemand par Jean Laplance et J.-B. Pontalis [Paris: NRF Gallimard, 1940].) The word "*Besetzung*" is based on the verb "*setzen,*" "to place" or "to put." The term therefore is connected to a network of terms found in "The Unconscious": "*Ubersetzung,*" "translation"; "*Umsetzung,*" "transposition." All of these terms have a spatial sense, which links them to the idea of a psychic topography. Like the spatial sense of these terms, "*Besetzung*" has a sense of occupation, like an occupying military force in a foreign country. Indeed, when a drive "*besetzt,*" it places a "charge" of energy in a representation; it also "invests" that energy insofar as placing it in the representation might lead to the satisfaction of the drive (or need), and therefore to its discharge in the affect of pleasure. So, depending on the context, we shall avoid the Greek term "*cathexis*" and use the more common English words "charge," "occupation," or "investment." In general, in the commentary and interpretation of "The Unconscious," we shall use these modified translations.

6. The table of contents for "The Unconscious" is:

I. The Process of Repression (I have assigned this title to the untitled opening section, GW X: 264/SE XIV: 166)

II. The Justification of the Unconscious (section 1, GW X: 264–70/SE XIV: 166–71)

III. The Various Meanings of the Unconscious and the Topological Viewpoint (section 2, GW X: 270–75/SE XIV: 172–76)

IV. Unconscious Feelings (section 3, GW X: 275–79/ SE XIV: 177–79)

V. Topology and Dynamics of Repression (section 4, GW X: 279–85/ SE XIV: 180–85)

VI. The Special Characteristics of the System Ucs (section 5, GW X: 285–88/SE XIV: 186–89)

VII. Communication between the Two Systems (section 6, GW X: 288–94/SE XIV: 190–95)

VIII. The Recognition of the Unconscious (section 7, GW X: 294–303/ SE XIV: 196–204)

7. The standard English translation of this German phrase is "ideational presentation."

8. For Freud's discussions of speculation, see "On Narcissism: An Introduction," SE XIV: 141–42/76–77: "And secondly, if we concede to the ego a primary cathexis [investment] of libido [erotic energy], why is there any necessity for further distinguishing a sexual libido from a non-sexual energy pertaining to the ego-instincts? Would not the assumption of a uniform mental energy save us all the difficulties of differentiating the energy of the ego-instincts from ego-libido, and ego-libido from object-libido? . . . To be required to give a definite answer to the second question must occasion perceptible uneasiness in every psychoanalyst. One dislikes the thought of abandoning observation for barren theoretical discussions, but all the same we must not shirk an attempt at explanation. Conceptions such as that of an ego-libido, an energy pertaining to the ego-instincts, and so on, are certainly neither very easy to grasp nor is their content sufficiently rich; a speculative theory of these relations of which we are speaking would in the first place require as its basis a sharply defined concept. But I am of the opinion that that is just the difference between a speculative theory and a science founded upon constructions arrived at empirically. The latter will not begrudge to speculation its privilege of a smooth, logically unassailable structure, but will itself be gladly content with nebulous, scarcely imaginable conceptions, which it hopes to apprehend more clearly in the course of its development, or which it is even prepared to replace by others. For these ideas are not the basis of science upon which everything rests: that, on the contrary, is observation

alone. They are not the foundation-stone, but the coping of the whole structure, and they can be replaced and discarded without damaging it. The same thing is happening in our day in the science of physics, the fundamental notions of which as regards matter, centers of force, attraction, etc. are scarcely less debatable than the corresponding ideas in psychoanalysis." See also *Beyond the Pleasure Principle,* in SE XIV: 24/*Studienausgabe: Psychologie des Unbewussten* 234: "What follows is speculation, far-fetched speculation, which the reader will consider or dismiss according to his individual predilection. It is further an attempt to follow out an idea consistently, out of curiosity to see where it leads. Psychoanalytic speculation takes as its point of departure the impression, derived from examining unconscious processes, that consciousness may be, not the most universal attribute of psychical processes, but only a particular function of them." See also Jacques Derrida, *La carte postale de Socrate à Freud et au-delà* (Paris: Aubier-Flammarion, 1980), p. 296, English translation by Alan Bass as *The Postcard from Socrates to Freud and Beyond* (Chicago: University of Chicago Press, 1987), p. 277.

9. In section six, Freud says that he is trying to construct a "theory" that is "adequate" to observations, that is, to clinical observations (GW X: 289/SE XIV: 190). The observations require that the theory be "complicated," especially when we consider the relations between the different localities of the psyche.

10. The German verb rendered by "link up" is "*verknüpfen,*" literally "knot up"; this word will appear in §§3 and 7 as a way of speaking of the sublation of the unconscious idea of the object and the conscious idea of the word. As we shall see, schizophrenic thought unties this knot. It goes in a different direction than a higher organization of the psyche.

11. The German word rendered as "derivatives" is "*Abkömmlingen,*" offspring or descendant; this term should be associated with "*Herkunft,*" which means source or place of emergence (GW X: 289/SE XIV: 190). See also J. Laplanche and J.-B. Pontalis, *Vocabulaire de la psychanalyse* (Paris: Quadrige Presses Universitaires de France, 2009), p. 403 (entry for "*rejetons*"), English translation by Donald Nicholson-Smith as *The Language of Psycho-Analysis* (New York: Norton, 1973), p. 116 (entry for "derivative"). Laplanche and Pontalis use the French word "*rejeton*" ("offshoot") because it suggests a primary characteristic of the unconscious; it is always active, like something botanical that keeps coming back.

12. The word "repression" renders the German "*Verdrängung,*" which literally means "to drive out pressure" (*Drang,* pressure).

13. In *Beyond the Pleasure Principle,* Freud distinguishes anxiety (*Angst*) from fright (*Schreck*) and fear (*Furcht*) in the following way: "Anxiety describes a particular state of expecting the danger or preparing for it, even though it may be an unknown one. Fear requires a determinate object of which to be afraid. Fright, however, is the name we give to the state a person gets into when he has run into danger without being prepared for it; it emphasizes the factor of surprise." See *Beyond the Pleasure Principle,* in SE XVIII 12/*Studienausgabe: Psychologie des Unbewussten,* p. 222. This distinction anticipates the one we see in Heidegger; see chapter 5.

14. Freud distinguishes repression proper from primary or primal repression. Repression proper is the repression of the idea that is preconscious or of the conscious

idea that has come to be associated with the drive-impulse ("libido"); primal repression is repression of the ideas of the drive-impulse itself.

15. Freud, *Beyond the Pleasure Principle*, in SE XVIII 34; *Studienausgabe: Psychologie des Unbewussten*, p. 244.

16. Jacques Lacan, *Écrits* (Paris: Seuil, 1966), p. 511, English translation by Bruce Fink as *Écrits: The First Complete Edition in English* (New York: Norton, 2006), p. 425. See also Alphonse de Waehlens, *Schizophrenia*, trans. W. Ver Eecke (Pittsburgh, Pa.: Duquesne University Press, 1978), p. 94.

An important analysis of language in terms of metaphor and metonymy can be found in Roman Jakobson and Morris Halle, *Fundamentals of Language* (The Hague: Mouton, 1971), especially part II, "Two Aspects of Language and Two Types of Aphasic Disorder."

17. Freud, *Beyond the Pleasure Principle*, in SE XVIII 28; *Studienausgabe: Psychologie des Unbewussten*, p. 238.

18. Freud, *Métapsychologie*, p. 101.

19. The development of Freud's concept of the ego (*Ich*, "I" or "*moi*" in the French translation) is complicated. It seems to reach the highest clarity in 1923 in "The Ego and the Id," in *The Standard Edition of the Complete Psychological Works of Sigmund Freud, Volume XIX (1923–1925)*, trans. James Strachey (London: The Hogarth Press, 1978), pp. 13–59, especially pp. 23–24; German in *Studienausgabe: Psychologie des Unbewussten*, pp. 273–325. In *Beyond the Pleasure Principle*, Freud says, "We shall avoid a lack of clarity if we make our contrast not between the conscious and the unconscious but between the coherent ego and the repressed. It is certain that much of the ego is itself unconscious, and notably what may be described as its nucleus; only a small part of it is covered by the term 'preconscious.'" SE XVIII, pp. 19–20; *Studienausgabe: Psychologie des Unbewussten*, pp. 229–30. See also Laplanche and Pontalis, *Le vocabulaire de la psychanalyse*, pp. 241–55 (entry for "*moi*"); *The Language of Psycho-Analysis*, pp. 130–43 (entry for "ego").

20. According to Freud, the patient was under the care of "Dr. Victor Tausk of Vienna," who shared his observations with Freud. Tausk published a paper on the female patient in 1919.

21. Freud repeats this answer in *The Ego and the Id*. See *The Ego and the Id*, in SE XIX, p. 20; German in *Studienausgabe: Psychologie des Unbewussten*.

22. Here Freud refers to his earlier *The Interpretation of Dreams*, in which he had already realized the importance of words for expressing unconscious drives. See *The Interpretation of Dreams*, in *The Standard Edition of the Complete Psychological Works of Sigmund Freud, Volumes IV and V (1900–1901)*, trans. James Strachey (London: The Hogarth Press, 1958), vol. V, p. 617.

23. The interpretation I am proposing here is based primarily on the work of Deleuze and Guattari. See Gilles Deleuze and Félix Guattari, *Capitalisme et schizophrénie 1, Anti-Œdipe* (Paris: 1972/1973), English translation by Robert Hurley, Mark Seem, and Helen R. Lane as *Anti-Oedipus: Capitalism and Schizophrenia* (New York: The Viking Press, 1977); *Mille plateaux; A Thousand Plateaus*. Their reading is based on Lacan's reading of Freud. See, in particular, Deleuze and Guattari, *Mille plateaux*, pp. 38–52; *A Thousand Plateaus*, pp. 26–38. Deleuze and Guattari say that "if the unconscious knows nothing of negation, it is because there is nothing negative in the

unconscious, only indefinite movements toward and away from zero, which does not at all express lack but rather the positivity of the full body as support and prop." The contradictory impulses form an inclusive (not exclusionary) disjunction. Deleuze and Guattari, *Anti-Œdipe*, pp. 70, 389; *Anti-Oedipus*, pp. 60, 333. The dualism of drives has the purpose of thrusting aside the viewpoint of functional multiplicity that alone is economic. Also, Deleuze, *Différence et répétition; Difference and Repetition*. The interpretation is also based on Derrida's *The Postcard*, Nancy and Lacoue-Labarthe, *The Title of the Letter*, and Alain Juranville, *Lacan et la philosophie* (Paris: Presses Universitaires de France, 1984), especially chapter 1.

24. Freud, *Métapsychologie*, p. 109. Strachey renders the term as "assessment," while Philip Rieff renders it as "recognition" in Sigmund Freud, *General Psychological Theory* (New York: Simon & Schuster, 1997), p. 142. See also Jean Laplanche, *The Unconscious and the Id*, trans. Luke Thurston with Lindsay Watson (London: Rebus Press, 1999), pp. 83, 107.

25. Freud, *Beyond the Pleasure Principle*, in SE XVIII, p. 36/*Studienausgabe: Psychologie des Unbewussten*, p. 246.

26. Deleuze, *Différence et répétition*, pp. 146-52; *Difference and Repetition*, pp. 111-15. Also Juranville, *Lacan et la philosophie*, p. 230.

27. Freud, *Beyond the Pleasure Principle*, in SE XVIII, p. 36/*Studienausgabe: Psychologie des Unbewussten*, p. 246.

28. Freud, *Beyond the Pleasure Principle*, in SE XVIII, p. 34/*Studienausgabe: Psychologie des Unbewussten*, p. 244.

29. The entire purpose of Adrian Johnston's excellent *Time Driven: Metapsychology and the Splitting of the Drive* lies in determining in what sense the unconscious drives are timeless.

30. See Michel Foucault, "La folie, l'absence d'œuvre," in *Dits et écrits I, 1954-1975* (Paris: Quarto Gallimard, 2001), pp. 440-48, English translation by Jonathan Murphy and Jean Khlafa as "Madness, the Absence of an Œuvre," in *History of Madness* (London: Routledge, 2006), pp. 541-49. See especially, *Dits et écrits I*, p. 445; *History of Madness*, p. 546: "That modification [of madness from being forbidden speech] only really came about with Freud, when the experience of madness shifted toward the last form of language prohibitions," that is, the prohibition of a language doubled on itself, that is play, not work.

31. Ricœur, *De l'interprétation*, p. 126; *Freud and Philosophy*, p. 122.

## 3. Consciousness as Distance

1. The term "phenomenology" enters philosophical discourse for the first time in 1764, when J. H. Lambert uses it in his *Neues Organon*. See J. H. Lambert, "La Phénoménologie comme doctrine de l'apparence," first article of the fourth part of *Neues Organon, Alter* no. 5 (1997): pp. 223-39. Cited in Françoise Dastur, *La Phénoménologie en questions* (Paris: Vrin, 2004), p. 243n1. In a 1770 letter to Lambert, Kant defines the term as a "negative science," presupposed by metaphysics, in which the principles of sensibility would be determined. For this letter see Ernst Cassirer, *Kant's Life and Thought*, trans. James Haden (New Haven, Conn.: Yale University Press, 1981), p. 113.

2. Husserl, *Logische Untersuchungen, I,* pp. 17–18; *Logical Investigations, Volume I,* pp. 175–76.

3. Edmund Husserl, *Die Idee der Phänomenologie. Fünf Vorlesungen, Husserliana, Band II,* edited by Walter Biemel (The Hague: Martinus Nijhoff, 1973), p. 10; English translation by Walter P. Alston and George Nakhnikian as *The Idea of Phenomenology* (Dordrecht: Kluwer Academic Publishers, 1995), p. 7.

4. Thomas Sheehan and Richard Palmer, eds., *Edmund Husserl: Psychological and Transcendental Phenomenology and the Confrontation with Heidegger (1927–1931)* (Dordrecht: Kluwer, 1997), contains the English translation of all the drafts and an English translation of Husserl's "Amsterdam lectures" (composed between April 7 and 17, 1928, delivered on April 23 and 29, 1928); it also contains useful philological data on the various texts and letters associated with the *Britannica* essay. In the preface, Sheehan and Palmer report that Husserl wrote the *Encyclopedia Britannica* essay between September 1927 and April 1928 for the 14th Edition of the *Encyclopedia Britannica.* The final version therefore is an expression of Husserl's mature thought, since he becomes emeritus professor on March 31, 1928. The *Encyclopedia Britannica,* however, published a free and paraphrased English translation in 1929 by Christopher V. Salmon of Oxford. The final version that Husserl wrote was not published during his lifetime, not until 1962. So scholars have long challenged the legitimacy of designating Salmon's published version of the entry as a "text by Husserl." See pp. xi–xii. Palmer, in his introduction to the "Amsterdam lectures," calls the *Encyclopedia Britannica* essay a "highly condensed statement of Husserl's thinking." See p. 205. More importantly, Palmer reports "Husserl's high regard for the *Encyclopedia Britannica* article": "Clearly, Husserl intended the *Britannica* article to be not just a statement for an internationally known reference work but also to function as a programmatic outline for his future endeavors. It was in essence to be an outline of his phenomenology and therefore could provide the inclusive introduction he wanted for [the Amsterdam] lectures." See pp. 201–2. For more on this text, see Steven Galt Crowell, *Husserl, Heidegger, and the Space of Meaning* (Evanston, Ill.: Northwestern University Press, 2001), pp. 167–81. Joseph Kockelmans has written a thorough commentary on the *Encyclopedia Britannica* essay, but he does not stress the collaboration with Heidegger. See Joseph J. Kockelmans, *Edmund Husserl's Phenomenology* (West Lafayette, Ind.: Purdue University Press, 1994).

5. For the part Heidegger wrote, see HUA IX: 256–63/CH: 107–16.

6. Here is the table of contents for the entry:

Husserl's Untitled Introduction (HUA IX: 277/CH: 159)

I. Part I: Pure Psychology: Its Field of Experience, Its Method, and Its Function (HUA IX: 278–87/CH: 160–67)
  A. Pure Natural Science and Pure Psychology (§1: HUA IX: 278–79/CH: 160)
  B. The Purely Psychical in Self-Experience and Community Experience. The Universal Description of Intentional Experiences (§2: HUA IX: 279–81/CH: 160–62)
  C. The Self-Contained Field of the Purely Psychological-Phenomenological Reduction and True Inner Experience (§3: HUA IX: 281–84/CH: 163–64)

D. Eidetic Reduction and Phenomenological Psychology as an Eidetic Science (§4: HUA IX: 284–85/CH: 165).

E. The Fundamental Function of Pure Phenomenological Psychology for an Exact Empirical Psychology (§5: HUA IX: 285–87/CH: 165–67)

II. Part II: Phenomenological Psychology and Transcendental Phenomenology (HUA IX: 287–96/CH: 167–75)

A. Descartes' Transcendental Turn [*Wendung*] and Locke's Psychologism (§6: HUA IX: 287–88/CH: 167–68)

B. The Transcendental Problem (§7: HUA IX: 288–90/CH: 168–70)

C. The Solution by Psychologism as a Transcendental Circle (§8: HUA IX: 290–92/CH: 170–71)

D. The Transcendental-Phenomenological Reduction and the Transcendental Semblance [*Schein*] of Duplication (§9: HUA IX: 292–95/CH: 171–74)

E. Pure Psychology as Propaedeutic to Transcendental Phenomenology (§10: HUA IX: 295–96/CH: 174–75)

III. Part III: Transcendental Phenomenology and Philosophy as Universal Science with Absolute Foundations (HUA IX: 296–301/CH: 175–79)

A. Transcendental Phenomenology as Ontology (§11: HUA IX: 296–97/CH: 175)

B. Phenomenology and the Crisis in the Foundation of the Exact Sciences (§12: HUA IX: 297/CH: 176)

C. The Phenomenological Grounding of the Factual Sciences in Relation to Empirical Phenomenology (§13: HUA IX: 298/CH: 176–77)

D. Complete Phenomenology as Universal Philosophy (§14: HUA IX: 298–99/CH: 177)

E. The "Ultimate and Highest" Problems as Phenomenological (§15: HUA IX: 299/CH: 177–78)

F. The Phenomenological Resolution of all Philosophical Antitheses (§16: HUA IX: 299–301/CH: 178–79)

7. For an analysis of the ways into phenomenology, see Iso Kern, "The Three Ways to the Transcendental Reduction in the Philosophy of Edmund Husserl," in *Husserl: Expositions and Appraisals*, ed. Frederick A. Elliston and Peter McCormick, pp. 126–49 (South Bend, Ind.: University of Notre Dame Press, 1977).

8. Martin Heidegger, *The History of the Concept of Time*, trans. Theodore Kisiel (Bloomington: Indiana University Press, 1985), pp. 29–46.

9. One must note that here Husserl also says that psychology has for its task the investigation of all the types of intentionality, including those of communities, and he speaks of the experience of others (*Fremderfahrung*). Husserl expands at length on the idea of the experience of others in the Fifth Cartesian Meditation. See Edmund Husserl, *Cartesianische Meditationen und Pariser Vorträge*, ed. S. Strasser (The Hague: Martinus Nijhoff, 1963), English translation by Dorian Cairns as *Cartesian Meditations* (The Hague: Martinus Nijhoff, 1969). The Fifth Cartesian Meditation is very

important for the development of Derrida's thought, to which we shall turn below. In the Fifth Cartesian Meditation, Husserl shows that the experience of the other is always a *Vergegewärtigung*, a presentification or representation, and never a *Gegenwärtigung*, an immediate presentation. See Jacques Derrida, "Violence et métaphysique," in *L'Écriture et la différence* (Paris: Seuil, 1967), pp. 173–96, English translation by Alan Bass as "Violence and Metaphysics," in *Writing and Difference* (Chicago: University of Chicago Press, 1978), pp. 118–33.

10. Edmund Husserl, *Ideen zu einer reinen Phänomenologie und phanomenologischen Philosophie. I. Buch: Einführung in die reine Phänomenologie. Husserliana Band III*, ed. Karl Schuhmann (The Hague: Martinus Nijhoff, 1976), English translation by F. Kersten as *Ideas Pertaining to a Pure Phenomenology and to a Phenomenological Philosophy* (The Hague: Martinus Nijhoff, 1982).

11. Husserl discovered the reduction as early as 1907 in *The Idea of Phenomenology*. See Edmund Husserl, *Die Idee der Phänomenologie; The Idea of Phenomenology*. See also Dastur, *La Phénoménologie en question*, pp. 83–99.

12. Husserl first introduced the terminology of *noesis* and *noema* in *Ideas I*, in 1913.

13. "The Amsterdam Lectures," in Sheehan and Palmer, *Edmund Husserl: Psychological and Transcendental Phenomenology and the Confrontation with Heidegger*, p. 231.

14. Husserl takes up this entire discussion again in great detail in *The Crisis*, section 9.

15. Edmund Husserl, *Die Krisis der Europäischen Wissenschaften und die transzendentale Phänomenologie: Eine Einleitung in der phänomenologische philosophie, Husserliana VI*, edited by Walter Biemel (The Hague: Martinus Nijhoff, 1954), English translation by David Carr as *The Crisis of European Sciences and Transcendental Phenomenology: An Introduction to Phenomenological Philosophy* (Evanston, Ill.: Northwestern University Press, 1970).

16. The phrase "Descartes' transzendentale Wendung" is part of the title of §6.

17. The same discussion appears in the Amsterdam lectures, section 11.

18. See Kockelman's comment on difference and Fink, in *Edmund Husserl's Phenomenology*, p. 240.

19. See Maurice Merleau-Ponty, "L'œuvre et l'esprit de Freud, Préface à l'ouvrage de A. Hesnard, L'œuvre et l'esprit de Freud et son importance dans le monde modern," in *Parcours deux 1951–1961* (Lagrasse: Verdier, 2000), p. 276: "Comme vue du monde, la psychanalyse *converge* avec d'autres tentative, avec la phénoménologie" (English translation: "as a worldview, psychoanalysis *converges* with other attempts, with phenomenology"; my emphasis). This entire text attempts to bring Freudian psychoanalysis into "agreement" with Husserlian phenomenology (p. 283 in particular).

20. Phenomenology is extended in the direction of the unconscious in Roger Chambon, *Le monde comme perception et réalité* (Paris: Vrin, 1974). See also Dan Zahavi, *Self-Awareness and Alterity: A Phenomenological Investigation* (Evanston, Ill.: Northwestern University Press, 1999), where he also examines phenomenology in relation to the unconscious; see pages 203–20, especially p. 208.

21. See Leonard Lawlor, *Derrida and Husserl: The Basic Problem of Phenomenology* (Bloomington: Indiana University Press, 2003), chapter 1.

22. Fink uses the same language of "destruction" in his famous 1933 *Kantstudien* article. See Fink, "The Phenomenological Philosophy of Edmund Husserl and Contemporary Criticism."

23. In chapter 7, we shall see that Foucault's concept of experience is not that of lived experience (*Erlebnis*, rendered in French as "*vécu*"). Experience turns to the outside, for Foucault.

24. Deleuze and Guattari, *Qu'est-ce que la philosophie?* p. 50; *What Is Philosophy?* p. 49.

25. Carnap also made this famous claim in response to Heidegger's 1929 "What Is Metaphysics?" See Rudolf Carnap, "The Overcoming of Metaphysics through Logical Analysis of Language," in *Heidegger and Modern Philosophy*, ed. Michael Murray, pp. 23–34 (New Haven, Conn.: Yale University Press, 1978). We shall of course take up Heidegger's "What Is Metaphysics?" in the next chapter.

26. "Postface pour l'édition américaine: Un retour à Bergson," in *Deux régimes de fous* (Paris: Minuit, 2003), p. 315, English translation by Ames Hodges and Mike Taormina as "Postscript to the American Edition: A Return to Bergson," in *Two Regimes of Madness*, ed. David Lapoujade (New York: Semiotext(e), 2006), p. 337.

27. Edmund Husserl, *Formale und transzendentale Logik, Husserliana, Band XVII* (The Hague: Martinus Nijhoff, 1974), p. 84, English translation by Dorian Cairns as *Formal and Transcendental Logic* (The Hague: Martinus Nijhoff, 1978), p. 95.

28. Husserl, *Formale und transzendentale Logik, Husserliana, Band XVII*, p. 84; *Formal and Transcendental Logic*, p. 96. See also Edmund Husserl, *L'origine de la géométrie, traduction et introduction par Jacques Derrida* (Paris: Presses Universitaires de France, 1962), p. 40; English translation by John P. Leavey, Jr., as *Edmund Husserl's Origin of Geometry An Introduction* (Lincoln: University of Nebraska Press, 1989 [1978]), p. 54.

29. Jacques Derrida, *La voix et le phénomène* (Paris: Presses Universitaires de France, 1967), p. 6, English translation by Leonard Lawlor as *Voice and Phenomenon* (Evanston, Ill.: Northwestern University Press, 2011), pp. 6–7. Here Derrida mentions Fink.

30. Husserl, *Formale und transzendentale Logik, Husserliana, Band XVII*, p. 19; *Formal and Transcendental Logic*, p. 21.

31. See Jacques Derrida, *Voyous* (Paris: Galilée, 2003), pp. 179–80, English translation by Pascale-Anne Brault and Michael Naas as *Rogues* (Stanford, Calif.: Stanford University Press, 2005), p. 128.

32. Husserl, *Ideen Buch I; Ideas*, §74.

33. Here Husserl also speaks of "*Limes-Gestalten,*" but these are liminal shapes of colors.

34. This discussion of the an-exact is inspired by Derrida and by Deleuze and Guattari. See Jacques Derrida, *L'Écriture et la différence* (Paris: Seuil Points, 1967), p. 241–42, English translation by Alan Bass as *Writing and Difference* (Chicago: University of Chicago Press, 1978), p. 162. See Deleuze and Guattari, *Mille plateau*, pp. 507–8; *A Thousand Plateaus*, 407–8.

### 4. The Thought of the Nothing

1. We are adopting the convention of using "Being" (with the uppercase "B") to render the German "*Sein*," while using the lowercase "being" or "beings" to render "*Seiende*."

2. Heidegger presented "What Is Metaphysics?" on July 24, 1929, approximately two years after the publication of *Sein und Zeit*. It is his inaugural address as he assumed the chair in philosophy from which Husserl had just retired. Six months later (in the middle of the writing of the *Encyclopedia Britannica* essay) Husserl becomes emeritus professor (March 31, 1928).

3. Jacques Derrida has provided an important study of this "possibility of impossibility." See Jacques Derrida, *Apories* (Paris: Galilée, 1992), pp. 113-27, English translation by Thomas Dutoit as *Aporias* (Stanford, Calif.: Stanford University Press, 1993), pp. 62-72.

4. Heidegger had already adopted this image in *Being and Time*. See SZ: 13/BT: 12.

5. For the image of roots, see also Martin Heidegger, *Die Grundbegriffe der Metaphysik: Welt, Endlichkeit, Einsamkeit. Gesammtausgabe Band 29/30* (Frankfurt am Main, Klostermann, 1992), p. 52, English translation by William McNeill and Nicholas Warren as *The Fundamental Concepts of Metaphysics: World, Finitude, Solitude* (Bloomington: Indiana University Press, 1995), p. 35.

6. Here is the table of contents of Heidegger's "What Is Metaphysics?" (1929):

> I. "What Is Metaphysics?": The Untitled Opening Section (GA 9: 103/ PM: 82)
>
> II. The Unfolding [*Entfaltung*] of a Metaphysical Inquiry [*Fragens*] (section 1, GA 9: 103-6/PM: 82-84)
>
> III. The Elaboration [or Working-out] of the Question (section 2, GA 9: 106-12/PM: 85-89)
>
> > A. The Formal Impossibility of the Question (GA 9: 106-9/PM: 85-87)
> >
> > B. The Event of the Nothing (GA 9: 109-12/PM: 87-89)
>
> IV. The Response to the Question (section 3, GA 9: 113-22/PM: 89-96)
>
> > A. The Nothing Nothings (GA 9: 112-14/PM: 89-91)
> >
> > B. Finitization (GA 9: 114-17/PM: 91-93)
> >
> > C. Meta ta physika and the Question (GA 9: 117-21/PM: 93-96)

7. Merleau-Ponty begins *The Visible and the Invisible* in the same way. See Merleau-Ponty, *Le visible and l'invisible*, pp. 41-48; *The Visible and the Invisible*, pp. 14-27.

8. Heidegger also speaks of this passion in his rectorship address, "The Self-Assertion of the German University," in Martin Heidegger, *The Heidegger Reader*, trans. Jerome Veith (Bloomington: Indiana University Press, 2009), p. 111.

9. On GA 9: 104/PM: 83, Heidegger uses the word "*Fächer*" for "departments" (Krell renders it as "discipline"), but the word is part of the image of fold he is developing here since it more literally means "each little fold."

10. This comment is so important for Heidegger that he repeats it in the 1966 *Der Spiegel* interview. See Martin Heidegger, "Supplement 1: *Der Spiegel* Interview with Martin Heidegger," in *The Heidegger Reader*, p. 315. Heidegger's self-quotation from

"What Is Metaphysics?" appears in relation to a discussion of his rectorship at the University of Freiburg. He explicitly links "What Is Metaphysics?" to the "The Self-Assertion of the German University." The difficult relation between these two lectures cannot be addressed here in the detail it requires.

11. See Heidegger's discussion of root in "The Nature of Language," in GA 12: 165/ OWL: 71.

12. Indeed, this is how Carnap interprets Heidegger's discourse on the nothing. See Carnap, "The Overcoming of Metaphysics," pp. 23–34.

13. There is a strange logic to the question, and this illogicality is what Carnap criticizes in his "The Overcoming of Metaphysics." See also Hans-Georg Gadamer, "What Is Metaphysics?" in *Heidegger's Ways*, trans. John W. Stanley (Albany: The State University of New York Press, 1994), p. 46.

14. *Die Grundbegriffe der Metaphysik*, p. 153; *The Fundamental Concepts of Metaphysics*, p. 102.

15. *Die Grundbegriffe der Metaphysik*, pp. 220–23; *The Fundamental Concepts of Metaphysics*, pp. 147–48.

16. Here, in "What Is Metaphysics?" Heidegger, strangely, gives us another possibility of such a revelation: joy in the present existence (*Dasein*) of a human being whom we love. The idea here seems to be that the joy of love makes beings as a whole appear because one's world is different.

17. *Die Grundbegriffe der Metaphysik*, p. 116; *The Fundamental Concepts of Metaphysics*, 77.

18. This passage clearly refers back to *Being and Time* §17, whose title is "Reference and Signs" ("Verweisung und Zeichen").

19. Heidegger will take up the lengthening of time in "Language," as we shall see in the next chapter.

20. See Heidegger's note to the 1949 fifth edition of "What Is Metaphysics?": "Essence, verbally; essential unfolding of being." PM: 91nf. Merleau-Ponty will appropriate this use of "*Wesen*" as a verb. See Merleau-Ponty, *Le visible et l'invisible*, p. 154; *The Visible and the Invisible*, p. 115. See also: GA 12: 164/OWL: 70.

21. See Michel Haar, *Heidegger and the Essence of Man*, trans. William McNeill (Albany: The State University of New York Press, 1993), p. 52.

22. See Otto Pöggeler, *Martin Heidegger's Path of Thinking*, trans. Daniel Magurshak and Sigmund Barber (Atlantic Highlands, N.J.: Humanities Press, 1987), p. 74.

23. Gilles Deleuze, *Différence et répétition*, pp. 89–91; *Difference and Repetition*, pp. 64–66.

24. Jacques Derrida, "La Main de Heidegger (*Geschlecht* II) (1984–1985)," in *Psyché* (Paris: Galilée, 1987), p. 439, English translation by John P. Leavey, Jr., as "*Geschlecht* II: Heidegger's Hand," in *Deconstruction and Philosophy*, ed. John Sallis, p. 182 (Chicago: University of Chicago Press, 1987). See also Jacques Derrida, *Mémoires pour Paul de Man* (Paris: Galilée, 1988), p. 136, English translation by Cecile Lindsay, Jonathan Culler, and Eduardo Cadava as *Memoires for Paul de Man* (New York: Columbia University Press, 1986), p. 141. Here Heidegger cites Heidegger's use of the term "*Versammlung*" in *What Is Called Thinking?*

25. In his *Truth and Genesis*, Miguel de Beistegui proposes a profound similarity between the thought of Heidegger and Deleuze. Miguel de Beistegui, *Truth and*

*Genesis: Philosophy as Differential Ontology* (Bloomington: Indiana University Press, 2004).

26. For more on immanence and transcendence, see appendix 1.

27. Deleuze and Guattari, *Qu'est-ce que la philosophie?* p. 50; *What Is Philosophy?* p. 49.

## 5. Dwelling in the Speaking of Language

1. For an excellent discussion of *Ereignis*, see Françoise Dastur, "Language and *Ereignis*," in *Reading Heidegger: Commemorations*, ed. John Sallis, pp. 355–69 (Bloomington: Indiana University Press, 1993). In particular, Dastur stresses that in *Being and Time* (§34) Heidegger makes language a derivative phenomenon from discourse. But later in *On the Way to Language*, language is originary.

2. Heidegger is referring to a manuscript that is now available. Martin Heidegger, *Contributions to Philosophy (From Enowning)*, trans. Parvis Emad and Kenneth Maly (Bloomington: Indiana University Press, 1999). See also GA 9: 316Na/PM: 241Nb: "Only a pointer in the language of metaphysics. For '*Ereignis*,' 'event of appropriation,' has been the guiding word of my thinking since 1936." See also Richard Capobianco, *Engaging Heidegger* (Toronto: University of Toronto Press, 2010), pp. 35–37.

3. Michel Foucault, *L'histoire de la folie à l'âge classique* (Paris: Tel Gallimard, 1972), p. 26; English translation by Jonathan Murphy and Jean Khlafa as *The History of Madness* (New York and London: Routledge, 2006), p. 11.

4. "Language" does not contain any divisions. It can however be outlined in the following way:

I. "Man speaks" (GA 12: 9/PLT: 187)

II. What About Language Itself? (GA 12: 9–11PLT: 187–90)

III. "What does it mean to speak?" (GA 12: 11–18/PLT: 190–95)

IV. The Speaking of Language Is to Call (*rufen*) (GA 12: 18–23/PLT: 195–203)
    A. The First Stanza of "A Winter's Evening": Thinging Bears World (GA 12: 18–20/PLT: 196–98)
    B. The Second Stanza: Worlding Grants Things (GA 12: 20–21/PLT: 198–200)
    C. The "*Unter-Schied*" (GA 12: 21–23/PLT: 200–1/24–26)
    D. The Third Stanza: Pain and Silence (GA 12: 23–26/PLT: 201–4)

V. Conclusion: Dwelling in Speaking of Language (GA 12: 26–30/PLT: 204–8)

5. See chapter 4 for an explanation of Heidegger's use of "*Wesen*" ("essence") as a verb.

6. In "The Postscript to 'What Is Metaphysics?'" Heidegger says, "Originary thinking [*Das anfängliche Denken*] is the echo of Being's favor, of a favor in which a singular event is cleared and lets come to pass [*sich ereignen*]: that beings are. This echo is the human response to the word of the silent voice of Being."

7. In "The Letter on 'Humanism,'" Heidegger says, "In order to experience the . . .

essence of thinking *purely,* and that means to carry it through, we must free ourselves from the technical interpretation of thinking" (GA 9: 314/PM: 240; my emphasis). Here, in "Language," we would have to free ourselves from the technical interpretation of language, that is, the interpretation of language as expression.

8. The French translation of *"nachdenken"* is *"penser en suivant."* See Martin Heidegger, *Acheminement vers la parole,* trans. Jean Beaufret, Wolfgang Brokmeier, and François Fédier (Paris: Tel Gallimard, 1976), p. 16.

9. Here is Trakl's poem first in German:

Ein Winterabend

Wenn der Schnee ans Fenster fällt,
Lang die Abendglocke läutet,
Vielen ist der Tisch bereitet
Und das Haus ist wohlbestellt.

Mancher auf der Wanderschaft
Kommt ans Tor auf dunklen Pfaden.
Golden blüht der Baum der Gnaden
Aus der Erde kühlem Saft.

Wanderer tritt still herein;
Schmerz versteinerte die Schwelle.
Da erglänzt in reiner Helle
Auf dem Tische Brot und Wein.

Heidegger also reproduces Trakl's first version of the last two verses of the second stanza and the third stanza:

Seine Wunde voller Gnaden
Pflegt der Liebe sanfte Kraft.

O! des Menschen bloße Pein.
Der mit Engeln stumm gerungen,
Langt, von heiligem Schmerz bezwungen,
Still nach Gottes Brot und Wein.

This is Hofstadter's English translation:

A Winter Evening

Window with falling snow is arrayed,
Long tolls the vesper bell,
The house is provided well,
The table is for many laid.

Wandering ones, more than a few,
Come to the door on darksome courses.

Golden blooms the tree of graces
Drawing up the earth's cool dew.

Wanderer quietly steps within;
Pain has turned the threshold to stone.
There lie, in limpid brightness shown,
Upon the table bread and wine.

Then the first version:

Love's tender power, full of graces,
Binds up his wounds anew.

O! man's naked hurt condign.
Wrestler with angels mutely held,
Craves, by holy pain compelled,
Silently God's bread and wine.

10. In "The Letter on 'Humanism,'" Heidegger says, "'World' does not in any way imply earthly as opposed to heavenly being, nor the 'worldly' as opposed to the 'spiritual.' For us 'world' does not at all signify beings or any realm of beings but the openness of Being" (GA 9: 350/PM: 266).

11. Here Heidegger recalls a poem by Pindar (*Isthmia 5*). The Pindar poem speaks of the mother of the sun, which graces mortals.

12. See §44 of *Sein und Zeit*, and "Vom Wesen der Wahrheit."

13. Jacques Derrida has used this phrase to refer to a difference that is prior to all differences.

14. See Deleuze and Guattari, *Qu'est-ce que la philosophie?; What Is Philosophy?* chapter 2.

15. Heidegger also discusses pain in his other Trakl essay; see GA 12: 57–61/OWL: 180–84. In *Being and Time* (§6), Heidegger had said, "The ostensibly new beginning of philosophizing [in Descartes] betrays the imposition of a fatal prejudice. On the basis of this prejudice later times neglect a thematic ontological analysis of 'the mind' [*Gemüt*] which would be guided by the question of Being." "*Gemüt*" may also be rendered in English as "heart." See especially, *What Is Called Thinking?* pp. 140–41, 203–4. See also Derrida, *De l'esprit; Of Spirit*.

16. This never completely present in unhidden-ness is the truth of Husserl's Fifth Cartesian Meditation.

17. See also Heidegger's statement in *Hölderlin's Hymn "The Ister"*: "The unhomely being homely of human beings up in the earth is 'poetic.'" Martin Heidegger, *Hölderlin's Hymn "The Ister,"* trans. William McNeill and Julia Davis (Bloomington: Indiana University Press, 1996), p. 120.

18. Heidegger, *Die Grundbegriffe der Metaphysik*, pp. 240; *The Fundamental Concepts of Metaphysics*, pp. 160–61.

19. Michel Foucault, *L'archéologie du savoir* (Paris: NRF Gallimard, 1969), p. 171, English translation by A. M. Sheridan Smith as *The Archeology of Knowledge* (New York: Pantheon Books, 1972), p. 129.

20. Foucault, *L'archéologie du savoir*, p. 147; *The Archeology of Knowledge*, p. 112.

21. Foucault, *L'archéologie du savoir*, p. 145; *The Archeology of Knowledge*, p. 110.

22. Foucault, *L'archéologie du savoir*, p. 156; *The Archeology of Knowledge*, p. 118.

23. Perhaps what motivates Foucault to valorize the word *"énoncé"* is Merleau-Ponty's denigration of it. See, for example, VIF: 145/VIE: 107. Yet what unifies Foucault's and Merleau-Ponty's views of language is that language is prior to human speaking, that language is abyssal.

## 6. Dwelling in the Texture of the Visible

The epigraph is from Maurice Merleau-Ponty, *Notes de cours sur L'origine de la géométrie de Husserl* (Paris: Presses Universitaires de France, 1998), p. 64, English translation by Leonard Lawlor with Bettina Bergo as *Husserl at the Limits of Phenomenology* (Evanston, Ill.: Northwestern University Press, 2002), p. 52.

1. Merleau-Ponty, *Notes de cours sur L'origine de la géométrie de Husserl*, p. 60; *Husserl at the Limits of Phenomenology*, pp. 49–50.

2. Heidegger seems to be the origin of the idea of auto-affection. See Martin Heidegger, *Kant und das Problem der Metaphysik* (Frankfurt am Main: Klostermann, 1998), §34, pp. 188–95, English translation by Richard Taft as *Kant and the Problem of Metaphysics* (Bloomington: Indiana University Press, 1990), pp. 129–33. It is Derrida, however, who most thematizes auto-affection, starting in 1967 with the publication of *La voix et le phénomène*. See Jacques Derrida, *La voix et le phénomène; Voice and Phenomenon*, chapter 6.

3. See Plato's *Theaetetus*, 189e–190a, where we find thinking defined by means of an interior monologue. See *Plato: Collected Dialogues*, ed. Edith Hamilton and Huntington Cairns (Princeton, N.J.: Princeton University Press, 1961), p. 895.

4. Merleau-Ponty, *Notes de cours sur L'origine de la géométrie*, p. 64; *Husserl at the Limits of Phenomenology*, p. 52.

5. Maurice Merleau-Ponty, "Un inédit de Maurice Merleau-Ponty," in *Parcours deux, 1951–1961* (Paris: Verdier, 2000), p. 40, English translation by Arleen B. Dallery as "An Unpublished Text By Merleau-Ponty," in *The Primacy of Perception* (Evanston, Ill.: Northwestern University Press, 1964), p. 5. Merleau-Ponty also uses the word "archeology" in a 1960 note on Claude Simon. See Maurice Merleau-Ponty, *Texts and Dialogues*, ed. Hugh J. Silverman and James Barry, Jr. (Atlantic Highlands, N.J.: Humanities Press, 1991), p. 142. See also the summary for the course called "The Sensible World and Expression," in *In Praise of Philosophy and other Essays*, trans. John Wild, James Edie, and John O'Neill (Evanston, Ill.: Northwestern University Press, 1988), p. 72. Also, Maurice Merleau-Ponty, "le philosophe et son ombre," in *Signes* (Paris: Gallimard, 1960), p. 208, English translation by Richard McCleary as "The Philosopher and his Shadow," in *Signs* (Evanston, Ill.: Northwestern University Press, 1964), p. 165. Also Merleau-Ponty, *Notes de cours sur L'origine de la géométrie*, p. 81; *Husserl at the Limits of Phenomenology*, p. 67.

6. This claim can be supported only by an interpretation of Merleau-Ponty's *Adventures of the Dialectic*. Maurice Merleau-Ponty, *Les aventures de la dialectique* (Paris: Folio Essais Gallimard, 1955), English translation by Joseph Bien as *Adventures of the Dialectic* (Evanston, Ill.: Northwestern University Press, 1973).

7. "Eye and Mind" is the last text Merleau-Ponty published while he was alive, having written it during the summer of 1960 while he was vacationing near Aix en Provence, in Tholonet, where Cézanne had also lived. See Claude Lefort's preface to Maurice Merleau-Ponty, L'Œil et l'esprit (Paris: Folio Essais Gallimard, 1964), p. 1. The essay appeared in the first volume (Spring 1961) of a journal called Art de France. During that spring semester (1961) at the Collège de France, Merleau-Ponty was teaching a course called "l'ontologie cartesienne et l'ontologie aujourd'hui" (Cartesian Ontology and Ontology Today), the notes for which are published in Notes de cours, 1959–61. Any interpretation of Merleau-Ponty's final and incomplete thought (incomplete due to his premature death on May 3, 1961) must utilize the many now published course notes and of course The Visible and the Invisible. However, in order for the interpretation to be relatively accurate, it is necessary to use the final published works (such as "Eye and Mind") as a guide.

8. As we shall see, this is a thought that Foucault will radicalize.

9. "Eye and Mind" contains five parts, which bear no titles. There is a rhythm to "Eye and Mind" since Merleau-Ponty moves in two directions at once. He wants to show that the metaphysics of science is rooted in the body (the elements) and at the same time that the painter (not the poet) is the one who most knows this experience of the body, or, more precisely, this experience called vision. The result is that part II concerns the body and the painter, part III concerns Descartes' metaphysics, and part IV returns to painting. It is possible to outline "Eye and Mind" and assign titles to the parts in the following way:

I. Science, Politics, and Art (Part I) (OE: 9–15/MPR: 351–53)

II. "This Strange System of Exchanges" (Part II) (OE: 16–35/MPR: 353–60)
   A. Auto-affection (OE: 16–21/MPR: 353–55)
   B. A Visible to the Second Power: Painting (OE: 21–27/MPR: 355–57)
   C. The Premises of Profane Vision (OE: 28–30/MPR: 357–58)
   D. The Mirror (OE: 30–35/MPR: 359–60)

III. Descartes' Classical Ontology (Part III) (OE: 36–60/MPR: 360–68)
   A. Descartes' Double Mistake (OE: 36–45/MPR: 360–62)
   B. Two Monsters Born of Descartes' Dismemberment (OE: 45–60/MPR: 362–68)

IV. Silent Science: Depth, Color, Line, Movement (Part IV) (OE: 61–87/MPR: 368–76)

V. The False Imaginary (Part V) (OE: 88–93/MPR: 376–78)

10. Contemporary science refers to what Merleau-Ponty called "little rationalism" (le petit rationalisme) in his 1955 "Everywhere and Nowhere." In "Everywhere and Nowhere," Merleau-Ponty stresses that "little rationalism" is the heritage of "great rationalism," which is exemplified by Descartes' philosophy; in "Eye and Mind," he says that contemporary science is the result of a dismemberment of Cartesianism. Merleau-Ponty, "Partout et nulle part," p. 185; "Everywhere and Nowhere," p. 147.

11. Writing, but also music, plays a large role in "Cartesian Ontology and Ontology Today"; Merleau-Ponty stresses that writing is not copied off the visible, but is a way of "fashioning" (façonner) the visible (NC 59–61: 218–20).

12. At this point, Merleau-Ponty also says "a world of immanence," but with "immanence" he means experience being immanent to a subject.

13. See also VIF: 290/VIE: 237.

14. At the same moment, in 1960, Gadamer too is trying to rehabilitate the image. See Hans-Georg Gadamer, *Wahrheit und Methode*, 4. Auflage (Tübingen: Mohr, 1975), pp. 128–36, English translation by Joel Weinsheimer and Donald G. Marshall as *Truth and Method*, 2nd rev. ed. (New York: Crossroads, 1990), pp. 134–43. Weinsheimer and Marshall render *"Bild"* as "picture."

15. In "Cartesian Ontology and Ontology Today," Merleau-Ponty says that what he is seeking in Descartes is to discover "a fiber of Being, a nexus not of reasons or thoughts, but in experience, in contacts with Being." Also, he says, "these diverse meanings being not related to one another in a certain moment of the order of reasons, but connected together in a texture of Cartesian Being" (NC 59–61: 223). The phrase "order of reasons" refers to Martial Gueroult. In "Eye and Mind," Merleau-Ponty seems to discuss the "texture of Cartesian Being" when he turns away from Descartes' *Optics* toward the enigma that Descartes could not eliminate.

16. In *Le visible et l'invisible*, Merleau-Ponty says, *"on se tromperait,"* "one would be mistaken."

17. It is well known that Descartes tried consciously to break with the Scholastic tradition and used the *Summa Philosophica Quadripartita* of Eustache de Sancto Paulo as his guide to Scholastic philosophy. An intentional species for the Scholastics, according to Eustache, is a mental image, but not a copy of an individual thing; it is an exemplar or species, an *eidos*, the Greek equivalent of species. Apparently, the discussion of ideas throughout the Scholastic period always referred to painters, or more generally, artists. The model would be the exemplar or idea of intentional species, while the painting would be the image, the particular. Referring back to the *Timaeus*, this discussion conceived God as an artificer. See Roger Ariew, *Descartes and the Last Scholastics* (Ithaca, N.Y.: Cornell University Press, 1999), pp. 64–69. What is important for our purposes is that the concept of intentional species implies some sort of resemblance relation.

18. In the 1960–61 course "Cartesian Ontology and Contemporary Ontology," Merleau-Ponty says, "This presence of the figure is all that [Descartes] retains from vision. The rest of the field is composed of such figures that are not present. The visible world is for me [that is, for a Cartesian] a world in itself upon which the light of the gaze is projected and from which the gaze cuts out [*découpe*] present figures. That eliminates the relation to the background which is a different kind of relation" (NC 59–61: 229).

19. For more on Merleau-Ponty and the geometral, see Lacan, *Les quartes concepts fondamentaux de la psychanalyse; The Four Fundamental Concepts of Psycho-Analysis*, chapter 2.

20. The previous two paragraphs are based on Leonard Lawlor, "Un écart infime (Part II): Merleau-Ponty's Mixturism," in *The Implications of Immanence: Toward a New Concept of Life* (New York: Fordham University Press, 2006), pp. 76–77.

21. In "Cartesian Ontology and Ontology Today," Merleau-Ponty says, "If Descartes' philosophy consists in this, the establishment of a natural intelligible light in opposition to the sensual human and the visible world, then [if it consists in] the relative justification of feeling by the natural light, it must contain (if Descartes' philosophy is not, in its second moment, the simple denial of the first) an ambiguous

relation of light and feeling, of the invisible and the visible, of the positive and the negative. It is this relation or this mixture that it would be necessary to seek" (NC 59–61: 222).

22. It seems to me that pages (OE: 69–72/MPR: 370–71) are the heart of the essay; they overlap with the final pages of chapter 4 of *The Visible and the Invisible*. Deleuze, in his book on Foucault, cites these final pages of *The Visible and the Invisible* (VIE 201–2/153–54). See Deleuze, *Foucault*, p. 119n39; *Foucault*, p. 149n38.

23. In the course "Cartesian Ontology and Contemporary Ontology," Merleau-Ponty also speaks of the role of the title in Klee, saying that the title "disburdens the picture of resemblance [here Merleau-Ponty means imitation] in order to allow it to express, to present an alogical essence of the world which . . . is not empirically in the world and yet leads the world back to its pure ontological accent, it puts in relief its way of *Welten* [worlding], of being world" (NC 59–61: 53).

24. See Henri Bergson, *L'evolution créatrice*, in *Œuvres*, Édition du Centenaire, pp. 752–54, English translation by Arthur Mitchell as *Creative Evolution* (Mineola, N.Y.: Dover, 1998 [1911]), pp. 304–6.

25. This question probably anticipates the original last line of "Eye and Mind." The last line did not appear in the printed version, although it appears in the last draft Merleau-Ponty made. The original last line is: "Le peintre est aussi loin du désespoir que de la suffisance, et l'on doit souhaiter à l'humanité beaucoup de l'hommes qui comme lui solidairement contemplent le monde et le transforment." A possible English translation is: "The painter is as far from despair as from self-importance, and we must wish for humanity many men like him who contemplate the world with solidarity and transform it." See Galen Johnson, *The Retrieval of the Beautiful* (Evanston, Ill.: Northwestern University Press, 2010), p. 20, and p. 20n7.

26. Martial Gueroult, *Descartes' Philosophy Interpreted According to the Order of Reasons*, 2 vols., trans. Roger Ariew (Minneapolis: University of Minnesota Press, 1984). The French publication date is 1952.

27. For more on Merleau-Ponty's relation to the thought of the outside, see Françoise Dastur, "Merleau-Ponty and Thinking from Within," in *Merleau-Ponty in Contemporary Perspectives*, ed. Patrick Burke and Jan Van Der Veken, pp. 25–36 (Dordrecht: Kluwer Academic Publishers, 1993).

28. For more on the concept of immanence and transcendence, see appendix 1.

29. Maurice Merleau-Ponty, *Phénoménologie de la perception* (Paris: Tel Gallimard, 1945), English translation by Colin Smith, rev. Forrest Williams, as *Phenomenology of Perception* (London: Routledge and Kegan Paul, 1981). See part I, chapter 6: "The Body as Expression and Speech."

30. As we have seen, Merleau-Ponty's final course at the Collège de France, "l'ontologie cartesienne et l'ontologie aujourd'hui" (Cartesian Ontology and Ontology Today [NC 59–61: 159–268]), sheds light on "Eye and Mind." The lectures for the course (the last of which was to be pronounced on May 4, 1961, the day after Merleau-Ponty died) fell into two parts: fundamental thought given in art and Descartes' ontology. These two themes set up the rhythm of "Eye and Mind." At the beginning of the course, Merleau-Ponty quotes the same Cézanne saying as the epigraph to "Eye and Mind": "What I am trying to translate for you is more mysterious; it is entwined in the very roots of Being, in the impalpable source of sensations" (NC 59–61: 167). In the epigraph, we can see the importance of translation for Merleau-Ponty's final

thought. As is well known, Cézanne never stopped being a touchstone for him. In his 1945 "Cézanne's Doubt," Merleau-Ponty says, "Cézanne did not think he had to choose between sensation and thought, as if he were deciding between chaos and order. He did not want to separate the stable things which appear before our gaze and their fleeting way of appearing. He wanted to paint matter as it takes on form, the birth of order through spontaneous organization. He makes a basic distinction not between 'the senses' and 'intelligence,' but rather between the spontaneous order of perceived things and the human order of ideas and sciences. We perceive things; we agree about them; we are anchored in them; and it is with 'nature' as our base that we construct the sciences. Cézanne wanted to paint this primordial world, and this is why his pictures give us the impression of nature at its origin, while photographs of the same landscapes suggest man's works, conveniences, and imminent presence. Cézanne never wished to 'paint like a savage.' He wanted to put intelligence, ideas, sciences, perspective, and tradition back in touch with the world of nature which they were intended to understand. He wished, as he said, to confront the sciences with the nature 'from which they came.'" Maurice Merleau-Ponty, "Le doute de Cézanne," in *Sens et non-sens* (Paris: NRF Gallimard, 1966), pp. 18–19, English translation by Hubert L. Dreyfus and Patricia Allen Dreyfus as "Cézanne's Doubt," in *The Merleau-Ponty Reader*, ed. Ted Toadvine and Leonard Lawlor, p. 73 (Evanston, Ill.: Northwestern University Press, 2007).

31. "L'entrelacs—le chiasme" is, of course, the title of *The Visible and the Invisible*'s fourth chapter.

32. The best discussion of Merleau-Ponty's idea of "a-philosophy" can be found in Carbone, *The Thinking of the Sensible*.

33. Merleau-Ponty cites Paul Claudel, *Art poétique*, Mercure de France, p. 9. Merleau-Ponty does not provide the publication date in Mercure de France; it is 1907. For a more current citation, see Paul Claudel, *Art poétique* (Paris: NRF Gallimard, 1984), p. 36.

34. Since "Eye and Mind" opens with a criticism of the cultural regime of the *manipulandum* and ends with the claim that we cannot establish a hierarchy of civilizations, it must be said that "Eye and Mind" is a political text, even though it does not provide any positive policies or calls for reform or revolution. Or, at least, we must say that because of the beginning and end of "Eye and Mind," the middle of it, that is, the discussions of vision, Descartes' philosophy, and twentieth-century art, is supposed to have political implications. We can understand the political philosophy implied by "Eye and Mind" if we recall that in *Adventures of the Dialectic,* Merleau-Ponty continuously argues against the view that history has a final positive truth. Instead, he argues that political activity is always in the process of bringing truth about, the advent of truth (*Les Aventures de la dialectique,* p. 200; *Adventures of the Dialectic,* p. 143: "revolution is the advent of an inter-world"). Such advents, such comings, are what the "adventures of the dialectic" concern. Perhaps it is necessary to speak of a kind of messianism in Merleau-Ponty's thought. Perhaps it is also necessary to speak of a kind of democracy to come in Merleau-Ponty: "Like Weber's heroic liberalism, it [the liberalism of which Merleau-Ponty is speaking] makes even what contests it enter its universe, and it is justified in its own eyes only when it understands its opposition" (*Les Aventures de la dialectique,* p. 313; *Adventures of the Dialectic,* p. 226). This comment implies a kind of openness to society. Even though in "Eye and Mind"

Merleau-Ponty says that we cannot make a hierarchy of civilizations, earlier in the course "Institution in Personal and Public History" at the Collège de France in 1954, he had considered the sense of the true civilization, calling it an "open society." For Merleau-Ponty, the open society—he says in a sense different from Bergson's sense of open society (in *The Two Sources of Morality and Religion*)—"plays the mysterious game which consists in putting all humans into the game, in attempting to make the intermingling truly universal." The open society, he continues, follows the spirit of institution, "which consists in not being limited, prohibited, enclosed on an island of customs. The spirit of institution consists in setting an unlimited historical labor under way." Maurice Merleau-Ponty, *L'institution, La passivité. Notes de cours au Collège de France (1954–1955)* (Paris: Belin, 2003), p. 119, English translation by Leonard Lawlor and Heath Massey as *Institution and Passivity: Course Notes from the Collège de France (1954–1955)* (Evanston, Ill.: Northwestern University Press, 2010), p. 72.

35. Merleau-Ponty refers to "Mort du denier écrivain," *Nouvelle Revue française*, March 1955. The text can be found in Maurice Blanchot, *Le livre à venir* (Paris: Folio Essais Gallimard, 1959), p. 302, English translation by Charlotte Mandell as *The Book to Come* (Stanford, Calif.: Stanford University Press, 2003), pp. 222–23.

## 7. Enveloped in a Nameless Voice

1. Michel Foucault, *L'histoire de la folie à l'âge classique* (Paris: Tel Gallimard, 1972), p. 656, English translation by Jean Khalfa and Jonathan Murphy as *The History of Madness* (London: Routledge, 2006), p. 532.

2. Michel Foucault, *L'herméneutique du sujet. Cours au Collège de France. 1981–1982* (Paris: Gallimard Seuil, 2001), p. 241, English translation by Graham Burchell as *The Hermeneutics of the Subject* (New York: Picador, 2005), p. 252; my emphasis.

3. Michel Foucault, "What Is Enlightenment?" ("Qu'est-ce que les Lumières?"), in *Dits et écrits, IV. 1980–1988* (Paris: NRF Gallimard, 1994), p. 574, English translation by Catherine Porter as "What Is Enlightenment?" in *The Essential Works of Foucault, Volume I: Ethics, Subjectivity and Truth* (New York: The New Press, 1997), pp. 315–16.

4. Michel Foucault, "Entretien avec Michel Foucault," in *Dits et écrits 1954–1988, Tome IV, 1980–1988* (Paris: NRF Gallimard, 1994), p. 48.

5. Maurice Blanchot, *L'attente, l'oubli* (Paris: L'imaginaire Gallimard, 1962), English translation by John Gregg as *Awaiting Oblivion* (Lincoln: University of Nebraska Press, 1997).

6. Michel Foucault, *L'ordre du discours* (Paris: NRF Gallimard, 1971), p. 7, English translation by A. M. Sheridan Smith as "The Discourse on Language," in *The Archeology of Knowledge* (New York: Pantheon Books, 1972), p. 215.

7. "The Thought of the Outside" contains eight sections:

I. I Lie, I Speak (DE 1: 546–48/EWF 2: 147–49)

II. The Experience of the Outside (DE 1: 549–51/EWF 2: 149–51)

III. Reflection, Fiction (DE 1: 551–53/EWF 2: 151–54)

IV. Being Attracted and Negligent (DE 1: 553–56/EWF 2: 154–57)

V. Where Is the Law, and What Does it Do? (DE 1: 556–59/EWF 2: 157–60)

VI. Eurydice and the Sirens (DE 1: 560-62/EWF 2: 160-63)

VII. The Companion (DE 1: 562-65/EWF 2: 163-65)

VIII. Neither One nor the Other (DE 1: 565-67/EWF 2: 166-68)

8. Epimenides was a Cretan seer of the sixth century BC.

9. Foucault also refers to the Epimenides paradox in *The Archeology of Knowl-edge*. See Foucault, *L'archéologie du savoir*, p. 108; *The Archeology of Knowledge*, p. 81. He also referred to the paradox, without mentioning Epimenides' name, in "Madness, the Absence of an Œuvre." See Michel Foucault, "La folie, absence d'œuvre," in *Dits et écrits I, 1954-1975* (Paris: Quarto Gallimard, 2001), p. 447, English translation by Jonathan Murphy and Jean Khlafa as "Madness, the Absence of an Œuvre," in *The History of Madness* (London and New York: Routledge, 2006), pp. 548-49.

10. Bertrand Russell, "Mathematical Logic as Based on the Theory of Types," in *Logic and Knowledge* (New York: Putnam, 1971), p. 57.

11. The word "literature" really became part of Derrida's lexicon. See Jacques Derrida, *Dissemination* (Paris: Seuil, 1972), English translation by Barbara Johnson as *Dissemination* (Chicago: University of Chicago Press, 1981). See also Rodolphe Gasché, *The Tain of the Mirror: Derrida and the Philosophy of Reflection* (Cambridge, Mass.: Harvard University Press, 1986).

12. Foucault has many discussions of Descartes throughout his writings. Probably the most famous is the one found in *The History of Madness*. See Foucault, *Histoire de la folie*, pp. 67-70; *History of Madness*, pp. 44-47. These pages became famous because of Derrida's article on them. See Jacques Derrida, "Cogito et histoire de la folie," in *L'écriture et la différence* (Paris: Seuil, 1967), pp. 51-90, English translation by Alan Bass as "The Cogito and the History of Madness," in *Writing and Difference* (Chicago: University of Chicago Press, 1978), pp. 31-63.

13. As Foucault develops his thinking, he will insist on being a positivist. But his "happy positivism" is not the positivism of measurable things; it is always a positivism based on the void or space of the outside. See AS: 164-65/AK: 125; also *L'ordre du discours*, p. 72; "The Discourse on Language," p. 234.

14. Foucault does not follow the convention of capitalizing the first letter of the word "being" ("*Sein*," "*être*"), as we did in chapters 4 and 5 (the two Heidegger chapters). So we have not followed the convention here in chapter 7, on Foucault.

15. Citing Pierre Klossowski, Foucault points out that one of Blanchot's characters (in *The Very High*) is called Sorge, care. The character being called Sorge is of course a reference to Heidegger's *Being and Time*. At the end of his career, Foucault will speak a great deal about care. See Michel Foucault, *Histoire de la sexualité III. Le souci de soi* (Paris: Tel Gallimard, 1984), English translation by Robert Hurley as *The Care of the Self: The History of Sexuality*, vol. 3 (New York: Vintage Books, 1988). Care of the self is also a theme in *The Hermeneutics of the Subject*.

16. In this discussion (DE 1: 555/EWF 2: 156), Foucault uses the word "*peut-être*" seven times.

17. Maurice Blanchot, *Aminadab* (Paris: Gallimard, 1942), English translation by Jeff Fort as *Aminadab* (Lincoln: University of Nebraska Press, 2002). Maurice Blanchot, *Le très haut* (Paris: Gallimard, 1948), English translation by Allan Stoekl as *The Most High* (Lincoln: University of Nebraska Press, 1996).

18. Foucault refers to Blanchot's article "Le regard d'Orphée" and his "La rencontre de l'imaginaire." See Maurice Blanchot, *L'espace littéraire* (Paris: Folio Essais Gallimard, 1955), pp. 225–32, English translation by Ann Smoch as *The Space of Literature* (Lincoln: University of Nebraska Press, 1989), pp. 171–76. Blanchot, *Le livre à venir,* pp. 9–18; *The Book to Come,* pp. 3–10. Novels that contains these figures, according to Foucault, are Maurice Blanchot, *L'arrêt de mort* (Paris: Gallimard, 1948), English translation by Lydia Davis as *Death Sentence* (Barrytown, N.Y.: Station Hill Press, 1978), and Maurice Blanchot, *Au moment voulu* (Paris: Gallimard, 1951), English translation by Lydia Davis as *When the Times Comes* (Barrytown, N.Y.: Station Hill Press, 1985).

19. Here again Foucault discusses *Aminadab* and *The Most High.*

20. In fact, Foucault says that the dogmatism of "modern philosophy" takes place at two levels, which reciprocally support one another. On the one hand, there is the precritical analysis of what man is essentially; on the other, there is all of what can be given in general to human experience (MC: 352/OT: 341).

21. Foucault's relation to Freud is ambiguous. But it is clear that in the *History of Madness,* the importance that Foucault attributes to Freud and psychoanalysis lies in its return to a linguistic relation to madness. See Michel Foucault, *L'histoire de la folie,* p. 428; *The History of Madness,* p. 339. Here Foucault says, "we must do justice to Freud. . . . Freud took up madness at the level of its *language* [Foucault's emphasis], reconstituting one of the essential elements of an experience that positivism had reduced to silence." Later in the *History of Madness (L'histoire de la folie,* p. 616; *The History of Madness,* p. 497), Foucault will associate this language with a more narrow language of guilt, which is perhaps the source of his more severe criticism of Freud in *History of Sexuality I.* Derrida has commented on Foucault's relation to Freud and psychoanalysis. See Jacques Derrida, "'To do Justice to Freud': The History of Madness in the Age of Psychoanalysis," in *Foucault and his Interlocutors,* ed. Arnold Davidson, pp. 57–96 (Chicago: University of Chicago Press, 1997).

22. See Deleuze and Guattari, *Qu'est-ce que la philosophie?* p. 50; *What Is Philosophy?* pp. 48–49. I shall return to this important definition of immanence below in appendix 1.

23. For an interesting assessment of Foucault and religion, see Jeremy Carrette, *Foucault and Religion: Spiritual Corporeality and Political Spirituality* (London: Routledge, 2000).

24. In *The Archeology of Knowledge,* Foucault uses the word "*remanence*" to refer to repetition. See AS: 162/AK: 123.

25. Foucault will locate violence within power. See Michel Foucault, *Le pouvoir psychiatrique. Cours au Collège de France. 1973–1974* (Paris: Hautes Études Gallimard Seuil, 2003), pp. 15–16, English translation by Graham Burchell as *Psychiatric Power. Lectures at the Collége de France. 1973–1974* (New York: Palgrave Macmillan, 2006), p. 16.

26. Foucault, *L'histoire de la folie,* p. 27; *The History of Madness,* p. 12.

27. In *The Order of Things,* Foucault says, "[man] is taken within a power that disperses him" (MC: 345/OT: 334).

28. For formulas very similar to these in Foucault, see Derrida's discussion of Heidegger in his 1964 essay on Levinas, "Violence and Metaphysics." Derrida, "Violence

et métaphysique," pp. 196–224, especially 207–8; "Violence and Metaphysics," pp. 134–151, especially 141.

29. Foucault, L'ordre du discours, p. 7; "The Discourse on Language," p. 215.

30. See AS: 159–60/AK: 121, where Foucault uses the word "suspension," but is unhappy with its phenomenological association (suspension of existence). However, he then uses the word "neutrality," which still has the sense of suspension. In the 1984 text called "Preface to the History of Sexuality, Volume II," Foucault speaks of a "'nominalist' reduction." See Michel Foucault, "Préface à l'histoire de la sexualité," in *Dits et écrits. 1954–1988. IV. 1980–1988* (Paris: NRF Gallimard, 1994), p. 579, English translation by William Smock as "Preface to The History of Sexuality, Volume II," in *The Essential Works of Michel Foucault 1954–1988, Volume I: Ethics, Subjectivity and Truth* (New York: The New Press, 1997), p. 200.

31. Foucault, "What Is Enlightenment?" ("Qu'est-ce que les Lumières?"), in *Dits et écrits, IV,* p. 574; "What Is Enlightenment?" in *The Essential Works of Foucault, Volume I,* pp. 315–16.

## Conclusion

1. For more on the trait, see appendix 2.

2. Fred Evans has developed an important conception of the voice in *The Multivoiced Body: Society and Communication in the Age of Diversity* (New York: Columbia University Press, 2008); see especially pp. 144–68 and 280–82.

## Appendix 1

1. Although the term "immanence" does not belong to Derrida's lexicon, we must conceive him as a philosopher of immanence. His criticisms of Levinas in "Violence and Metaphysics" are made in the name of immanence; the other must be within the same in order to speak about it: "For it is impossible to encounter the alter ego (in the very form of the encounter described by Levinas), impossible to respect it in experience and in language, if this other, in its alterity, does not appear for an ego (in general)" (Jacques Derrida, "Violence et métaphysique," p. 181; "Violence and Metaphysics," p. 123). The term "immanence" is also not part of Foucault's lexicon. However his conception of language in *The Archeology of Knowledge* leaves no room for the idea that language is based on something other than itself. It is, as he says there, "a general, unlimited, and apparently formless, field of discourse." See Foucault, *L'archéologie du savoir,* p. 106; *The Archeology of Knowledge,* p. 79.

2. Deleuze and Guattari, *Qu'est-ce que la philosophie?* p. 50; *What Is Philosophy?* pp. 48–49.

3. Deleuze and Guattari, *Mille Plateaux,* p. 326; *A Thousand Plateaus,* p. 266. Deleuze and Guattari capitalize the word "nature."

4. Derrida must be classified as a philosopher of immanence, if we recall these sentences from one of his first publications: "Let me clarify: when I refer to the forced entry into the world of that which is not there and is supposed by the world . . . , or when I say that this reduction to intraworldiness is the origin and the very meaning of what is called violence, making possible all straitjackets, I am not invoking another

world, an alibi or evasive transcendence. That would be yet another possibility of violence, a possibility that is, moreover, often the accomplice of the first one." See Jacques Derrida, "Cogito et histoire de la folie," p. 88; "Cogito and the History of Madness," p. 57.

## Appendix 2

1. The term "trait" can be found most often in Derrida's works, but it is also found in Deleuze and Guattari. In Derrida see, in particular, "Le retrait de la métaphore," in *Psyche: Inventions de l'autre* (Paris: Galilée, 1987), pp. 63–94, English translation by Peggy Kamuf and Elizabeth Rottenberg as "The Retrait of Metaphor," in *Psyche: Inventions of the Other, Volume 1* (Stanford, Calif.: Stanford University Press, 2007), pp. 48–80. Here Derrida uses the French word *"trait"* to translate Heidegger's terms *"Zug"* and *"Riss,"* and he uses *"retrait"* to render Heidegger's *"Entziehung"* (withdrawal). See, in particular, "Le retrait de la métaphore," p. 87; "The Retrait of Metaphor," pp. 73–74. The French word *"trait"* may also be rendered in English as "feature." In Deleuze and Guattari, see *Mille Plateaux,* pp. 343–44; *A Thousand Plateaus,* p. 280: "To reduce oneself to an abstract line, *a trait,* in order to find one's zone of indiscernability with other traits, and in this way enter the haecceity and impersonality of the creator. One is then like grass: one has made the world [*du monde*], everybody [*tout le monde*], into a becoming, because one has made a necessarily communicating world, because one has suppressed in oneself everything that prevents us from slipping between things and growing in the midst of things" (my emphasis). The ways in which Derrida and Deleuze use the term makes it resemble what Foucault calls a statement. See Foucault, *L'archéologie du savoir,* p. 138; *The Archeology of Knowledge,* p. 105: "[A statement] is endowed with a certain modifiable heaviness, a weight relative to the field in which it is placed, a constancy that allows of various uses, a temporal permanence that does not have the inertia of a mere trace or mark, and which does not sleep on its own past. Whereas an enunciation may be *begun again* or *re-evoked,* and a (linguistic or logical) form may be reactualized, the statement may be *repeated*—but always in strict conditions. This repeatable materiality, which characterizes the enunciative function, makes the statement appear as a specific and paradoxical object" (Foucault's emphasis).

2. See Jakobson and Halle's idea of "distinctive features." See Jakobson and Halle, *Fundamentals of Language,* p. 14: "Linguistic analysis gradually breaks down complex speech units into *morphemes* as the ultimate constituents endowed with proper meaning and dissolves these smallest semantic vehicles into their ultimate components, capable of differentiating morphemes from each other. These components are called *distinctive features*" (Jakobson and Halle's emphasis).

3. See Deleuze and Guattari, *Mille plateaux,* pp. 340–41; *A Thousand Plateaus,* pp. 277–78.

# BIBLIOGRAPHY

## Texts by Bergson

Cours de Bergson au Collège de France: "Histoire de l'idée de temps." 1902. In *Annales bergsoniennes I*. Paris: Presses Universitaires de France, 2002, pp. 25–68.

*Les données immediate de la conscience*. In *Œuvres*, Édition du Centenaire. Paris: Presses Universitaire de France, 1959, pp. 1–157. English translation by F. L. Pogson as *Time and Free Will*. Mineola, N.Y.: Dover Publishing Company, 2001 [1913].

*L'evolution créatrice*. In *Œuvres*, Édition du Centenaire. Paris: Presses Universitaire de France, 1959, pp. 487–809. English translation by Arthur Mitchell as *Creative Evolution*. Mineola, N.Y.: Dover, 1998 [1911].

*Matière et mémoire*. In *Œuvres*, Édition du Centenaire. Paris: Presses Universitaire de France, 1959, pp. 161–382. English translation by N. M. Paul and W. S. Palmer as *Matter and Memory*. New York: Zone Books, 1994 [1910].

*La pensée et le mouvant*. In *Œuvres*, Édition du Centenaire. Paris: Presses Universitaire de France, 1959. English translation by Mabelle L. Andison as "Introduction to Metaphysics." In *The Creative Mind*. New York: The Citadel Press, 1992 [1946].

## Texts by Foucault

*L'archéologie du savoir*. Paris: NRF Gallimard, 1969. English translation by A. M. Sheridan Smith as *The Archeology of Knowledge*. New York: Pantheon Books, 1972.

"Ceci n'est pas une pipe." In *Dits et écrits I, 1954–1969*. Paris: NRF Gallimard, 1994, pp. 635–50. English translation by James Harkness as *This Is Not a Pipe*. Berkeley: University of California Press, 1982.

"La folie, l'absence d'œuvre." In *Dits et écrits I, 1954–1975*. Paris: Quarto Gallimard, 2001. English translation by Jonathan Murphy and Jean Khlafa as "Madness, the Absence of an Œuvre." In *History of Madness*. London: Routledge, 2006.

*L'herméneutique du sujet. Cours au Collège de France. 1981–1982*. Paris: Gallimard Seuil, 2001. English translation by Graham Burchell as *The Hermeneutics of the Subject*. New York: Picador, 2005.

*L'histoire de la folie à l'âge classique.* Paris: Tel Gallimard, 1972. English translation by Jean Khalfa and Jonathan Murphy as the *History of Madness.* London: Routledge, 2008.

*Histoire de la sexualité, I, la volonté de savoir.* Paris: Tel Gallimard, 1976. English translation by Robert Hurley as *The History of Sexuality. Volume I: An Introduction.* New York: Vintage, 1990.

*Histoire de la sexualité III. Le souci de soi.* Paris: Tel Gallimard, 1984. English translation by Robert Hurley as *The History of Sexuality. Volume 3: The Care of the Self.* New York: Vintage Books, 1988.

*Les mots et les choses.* Paris: Tel Gallimard, 1966. Anonymous English translation as *The Order of Things.* New York: Vintage Books, 1994.

*L'ordre du discours.* Paris: NRF Gallimard, 1971. English translation by A. M. Sheridan Smith as "The Discourse on Language." In *The Archeology of Knowledge.* New York: Pantheon Books, 1972), pp. 215–37.

*Le pouvoir psychiatrique. Cours au Collège de France. 1973–1974.* Paris: Hautes Études Gallimard Seuil, 2003. English translation by Graham Burchell as *Psychiatric Power: Lectures at the Collège de France. 1973–1974.* New York: Palgrave Macmillan, 2006.

"Préface à l'histoire de la sexualité," in *Dits et écrits. 1954–1988. IV. 1980–1988.* Paris: NRF Gallimard, 1994, pp. 578–84. English translation by William Smock as "Preface to the History of Sexuality, Volume II." In *The Essential Works of Michel Foucault 1954–1988, Volume I: Ethics, Subjectivity and Truth.* New York: The New Press, 1997, pp. 199–206.

*Sécurité, Territoire, Population. Cours au Collège de France, 1977–1978* (Paris: Hautes Études Gallimard Seuil, 2004), p. 244. English translation by Graham Burchell as *Security, Territory, Population: Lectures at the Collège de France, 1977–1978* (New York: Palgrave MacMillan, 2007), p. 238.

*Surveiller et punir.* Paris: Gallimard, 1975. English translation by Alan Sheridan as *Discipline and Punish.* New York: Vintage, 1995.

"The Thought from Outside." Translated by Brian Massumi. In *Foucault/Blanchot.* New York: Zone Books, 1987.

"The Thought of the Outside." Translated by Brian Massumi (revised). In *Essential Works of Foucault, 1954–1984, Volume 2: Aesthetics, Method, and Epistemology.* Paul Rabinow, series editor. New York: The New Press, 1998.

"What Is Enlightenment?" ("Qu'est-ce que les Lumières?"). In *Dits et écrits, IV. 1980–1988.* Paris: NRF Gallimard, 1994, pp. 562–77. English translation by Catherine Porter as "What Is Enlightenment?" In *The Essential Works of Foucault, Volume I: Ethics, Subjectivity and Truth.* New York: The New Press, 1997, pp. 303–19.

### Texts by Freud

*Aus der Anfängen der Psychoanalyse.* London: Imago, 1950. English translation by Eric Mosbacher and James Strachey as *The Origins of Psychoanalysis.* New York: Basic Books, 1954.

*Beyond the Pleasure Principle,* in *The Standard Edition of the Complete Psychological Works of Sigmund Freud, Volume XVII. 1920–1922.* Translated by James Strachey. London: The Hogarth Press, 1981.

"The Ego and the Id." In *The Standard Edition of the Complete Psychological Works of Sigmund Freud, Volume XIX, 1923–1925.* Translated by James Strachey. London: The Hogarth Press, 1978), pp. 13–59.

"Zur Einführung des Narzißmus." In *Gesammelte Werke, Zehnter Band, Werke aus den Jahren 1913–1917.* London: Imago Publishing Company, 1949. English translation by Cecil M. Baines as "On Narcissism: An Introduction." In *General Psychological Theory,* ed. Philip Rieff. New York: Simon & Schuster, 1997.

*General Psychological Theory.* Edited by Philip Rieff. New York: Simon & Schuster, 1997.

*The Interpretation of Dreams,* in *The Standard Edition of the Complete Psychological Works of Sigmund Freud, Volumes IV and V, 1900–1901.* Translated by James Strachey. London: The Hogarth Press, 1958.

*Métapsychologie.* Traduit de l'allemand par Jean Laplance et J.-B. Pontalis. Paris: NRF Gallimard, 1940.

*Studienausgabe: Psychologie des Unbewussten.* Zürich: Buchclub Ex Libris, 1975.


## Texts by Heidegger

*Acheminement vers la parole.* Translated by Jean Beaufret, Wolfgang Brokmeier, and François Fédier. Paris: Tel Gallimard, 1976.

*Contributions to Philosophy (From Enowning).* Translated by Parvis Emad and Kenneth Maly. Bloomington: Indiana University Press, 1999.

*Einführung in die Metaphysik.* Tübingen: Niemeyer, 1987. English translation by Gregory Fried and Richard Polt as *Introduction to Metaphysics.* New Haven, Conn.: Yale University Press, 2000.

*Die Grundbegriffe der Metaphysik: Welt, Endlichkeit, Einsamkeit. Gesamtausgabe Band 29/30.* Frankfurt am Main, Klostermann, 1983. English translation by William McNeill and Nicholas Warren as *The Fundamental Concepts of Metaphysics: World, Finitude, Solitude.* Bloomington: Indiana University Press, 1995.

*The Heidegger Reader.* Translated by Jerome Veith. Bloomington: Indiana University Press, 2009.

*The History of the Concept of Time.* Translated by Theodore Kisiel. Bloomington: Indiana University Press, 1985.

*Hölderlin's Hymn "The Ister."* Translated by William McNeill and Julia Davis. Bloomington: Indiana University Press, 1996.

*Kant und das Problem der Metaphysik.* Frankfurt am Main: Klostermann, 1998. English translation by Richard Taft as *Kant and the Problem of Metaphysics.* Bloomington: Indiana University Press, 1990.

*The Metaphysical Foundations of Logic.* Translated by Michael Heim. Bloomington: Indiana University Press, 1984.

*Sein und Zeit.* Tübingen: Niemeyer, 1979. English translation by Joan Stambaugh (revised and with a foreword by Dennis J. Schmidt) as *Being and Time.* Albany: The State University of New York Press, 2010.

"Vom Wesen der Wahrheit (1930)." In *Gesamtausgabe. 1. Abteilung: Veröffentlich Schriften 1910–1976. Band 9. Wegmarken.* Frankfurt am Main: Klostermann, 2004. English translation by John Sallis as "On the Essence of Truth." In *Pathmarks,* ed. William McNeil. New York: Cambridge University Press, 1998.

*What Is Called Thinking?* Translated by J. Glenn Gray. New York: Harper Colophon, 1968.

*Zollikon Seminars: Protocols, Conversations, Letters.* Edited by Medard Boss. Translated by Franz Mayr and Richard Askay. Evanston, Ill.: Northwestern University Press, 2001.

## Texts by Husserl

"The Amsterdam Lectures." In *Edmund Husserl: Psychological and Transcendental Phenomenology and the Confrontation with Heidegger (1927–1931)*, ed. Thomas Sheehan and Richard Palmer. Dordrecht: Kluwer, 1997.

*Cartesianische Meditationen und Pariser Vorträge.* Edited by S. Strasser. The Hague: Martinus Nijhoff, 1963. English translation by Dorian Cairns as *Cartesian Meditations.* The Hague: Martinus Nijhoff, 1969.

*Formale und transzendentale Logik, Husserliana, Band XVII.* The Hague: Martinus Nijhoff, 1974. English translation by Dorian Cairns as *Formal and Transcendental Logic.* The Hague: Martinus Nijhoff, 1978.

*Die Idee der Phänomenologie. Fünf Vorlesungen, Husserliana, Band II.* Edited by Walter Biemel. The Hague: Martinus Nijhoff, 1973. English translation by Walter P. Alston and George Nakhnikian as *The Idea of Phenomenology.* Dordrecht: Kluwer Academic Publishers, 1995.

*Ideen zu einer reinen Phänomenologie und phänomenologischen Philosophie. I. Buch: Einführung in die reine Phänomenologie. Husserliana Band III.* Edited by Karl Schumann. The Hague: Martinus Nijhofff, 1976. English translation by F. Kersten as *Ideas Pertaining to a Pure Phenomenology and to a Phenomenological Philosophy. First Book.* The Hague: Martinus Nijhoff, 1982.

*Die Krisis der Europäischen Wissenschaft und die Transzendentale Phänomenologie, Husserliana VI.* Edited by Walter Biemel. The Hague: Martinus Nijhoff, 1976. English translation by David Carr as *The Crisis of European Sciences and Transcendental Phenomenology.* Evanston, Ill.: Northwestern University Press, 1970.

*Logische Untersuchungen, I–II.* Tübingen: Niemeyer, 1968. English translation by J. N. Findlay as *Logical Investigations Volumes I–II.* Translation edited by Dermot Moran. London: Routledge, 2001.

*L'origine de la géométrie, traduction et introduction par Jacques Derrida.* Paris: Presses Universitaires de France, 1962. English translation by John P. Leavey, Jr., as *Edmund Husserl's Origin of Geometry: An Introduction.* Lincoln: University of Nebraska Press, 1989 [1978].

*Phänomenologische Psychologie, Vorlesungen Sommersemester 1925.* The Hague: Martinus Nijhoff, 1968.

## Texts by Merleau-Ponty

*Les aventures de la dialectique.* Paris: Folio Essais Gallimard, 1955. English translation by Joseph Bien as *Adventures of the Dialectic.* Evanston, Ill.: Northwestern University Press, 1973.

"Le doute de Cézanne." In *Sens et non-sens.* Paris: NRF Gallimard, 1966, pp. 13–33. English translation by Hubert L. Dreyfus and Patricia Allen Dreyfus as "Cézanne's

Doubt." In *The Merleau-Ponty Reader*, ed. Ted Toadvine and Leonard Lawlor. Evanston, Ill.: Northwestern University Press, 2007, pp. 69–84.

"Un inédit de Maurice Merleau-Ponty." In *Parcours deux, 1951–1961*. Paris: Verdier, 2000. English translation by Arleen B. Dallery as "An Unpublished Text By Merleau-Ponty." In *The Primacy of Perception*. Evanston, Ill.: Northwestern University Press, 1964.

*L'institution, La passivité. Notes de cours au Collège de France. 1954–1955*. Paris: Belin, 2003. English translation by Leonard Lawlor and Heath Massey as *Institution and Passivity: Course Notes from the Collège de France. 1954–1955*. Evanston, Ill.: Northwestern University Press, 2010.

*Notes de cours 1959–1961*. Paris: NRF Gallimard, 1996.

*Notes de cours sur L'origine de la géométrie de Husserl*. Paris: Presses Universitaires de France, 1998. English translation by Leonard Lawlor with Bettina Bergo as *Husserl at the Limits of Phenomenology*. Evanston, Ill.: Northwestern University Press, 2002.

"L'œuvre et l'esprit de Freud, Préface à l'ouvrage de A. Hesnard, L'œuvre et l'esprit de Freud et son importance dans le monde modern." In *Parcours deux 1951–1961*. Lagrasse: Verdier, 2000, pp. 276–84.

"Partout et nulle part." In *Signes*. Paris: NRF Gallimard, 1960. English translation by Richard C. McCleary as "Everywhere and Nowhere." In *Signs*. Evanston, Ill.: Northwestern University Press, 1964.

*Phénoménologie de la perception*. Paris: Tel Gallimard, 1945. English translation by Colin Smith, revised by Forrest Williams, as *Phenomenology of Perception*. London: Routledge and Kegan Paul, Ltd., 1981.

"Le philosophe et son ombre." In *Signes*. Paris: Gallimard, 1960, p. 208. English translation by Richard McCleary as "The Philosopher and his Shadow." In *Signs*. Evanston, Ill.: Northwestern University Press, 1964.

"Philosophie et non-philosophie depuis Hegel." In *Notes de cours 1958–1959 et 1960–1961*. Paris: Gallimard, 1996. English translation by Hugh J. Silverman as "Philosophy and Non-Philosophy Since Hegel." In *Philosophy and Non-Philosophy Since Merleau-Ponty*, ed. Hugh J. Silverman. New York: Routledge, 1988.

*In Praise of Philosophy and other Essays*. Translated by John Wild, James Edie, and John O'Neill. Evanston, Ill.: Northwestern University Press, 1988.

*Texts and Dialogues*. Edited by Hugh J. Silverman and James Barry, Jr. Atlantic Highlands, N.J.: Humanities Press, 1991.

*Le visible et l'invisible*. Paris: Tel Gallimard, 1964. English translation by Alphonso Lingis as *The Visible and the Invisible*. Evanston, Ill.: Northwestern University Press, 1968.

## Other Texts

Al-Saji, Alia. "Vision, Mirror and Expression: The Genesis of the Ethical Body in Merleau-Ponty's Later Works." In *Interrogating Ethics: Embodying the Good in Merleau-Ponty*, ed. James Hatley, Janice McLane, and Christian Diehm, pp. 39–63. Pittsburgh, Pa: Duquesne University Press, 2006.

Ariew, Roger. *Descartes and the Last Scholastics*. Ithaca, N.Y.: Cornell University Press, 1999.

Banham, Gary, ed., *Husserl and the Logic of Experience*. London: Palgrave MacMillan, 2005.

Barbaras, Renaud. *The Being of the Phenomenon: Merleau-Ponty's Ontology*. Translated by Ted Toadvine and Leonard Lawlor. Bloomington: Indiana University Press, 2004.

———. *Introduction à la philosophie de Husserl*. Chatou: Transparence, 2004.

Beistegui, Miguel de. *Truth and Genesis: Philosophy as Differential Ontology*. Bloomington: Indiana University Press, 2004.

Bernasconi, Robert. *Heidegger and the Question of Language*. Atlantic Highlands, N.J.: Humanities Press, 1985.

Bernet, Rudolf, Iso Kern, and Eduard Marbach. *An Introduction to Husserlian Phenomenology*. Evanston, Ill.: Northwestern University Press, 1993.

Blanchot, Maurice. *Aminadab*. Paris: Gallimard, 1942. English translation by Jeff Fort as *Aminadab*. Lincoln: University of Nebraska Press, 2002.

———. *L'arrêt de mort*. Paris: Gallimard, 1948. English translation by Lydia Davis as *Death Sentence*. Barrytown, N.Y.: Station Hill Press, 1978.

———. *L'attente, l'oubli*. Paris: L'imaginaire Gallimard, 1962. English translation by John Gregg as *Awaiting Oblivion*. Lincoln: University of Nebraska Press, 1997.

———. *L'espace littéraire*. Paris: Folio Essais Gallimard, 1955. English translation by Ann Smoch as *The Space of Literature*. Lincoln: University of Nebraska Press, 1989.

———. *Le livre à venir*. Paris: Folio Essais Gallimard, 1959. English translation by Charlotte Mandell as *The Book to Come*. Stanford, Calif.: Stanford University Press, 2003.

———. *Au moment voulu*. Paris: Gallimard, 1951. English translation by Lydia Davis as *When the Times Comes*. Barrytown, N.Y.: Station Hill Press, 1985.

———. *Le très haut*. Paris: Gallimard, 1948. English translation by Allan Stoekl as *The Most High*. Lincoln: University of Nebraska Press, 1996.

Bossert, Philip J. "A Common Misunderstanding Concerning Husserl's Crisis Text." *Philosophy and Phenomenological Research* 35, no. 1 (September 1974): pp. 20–33.

Braver, Lee. *A Thing of This World: A History of Continental Anti-Realism*. Evanston, Ill.: Northwestern University Press, 2007.

Bruzina, Ronald. *Edmund Husserl and Eugen Fink: Beginnings and Ends in Phenomenology 1928–1938*. New Haven, Conn.: Yale University Press, 2004.

Bubner, Rudiger. *Modern German Philosophy*. Cambridge: Cambridge University Press, 1981.

Buckley, R. Philip. *Husserl, Heidegger and the Crisis of Philosophical Responsibility*. Dordrecht: Kluwer, 1992.

Burke, Patrick, and Jan Van Der Veken, eds. *Merleau-Ponty in Contemporary Perspectives*. Dordrecht: Kluwer Academic Publishers, 1993.

Canguilhem, Georges. *La connaissance de la vie*. Paris: Vrin, 1965.

———. *Etudes d'histoire et de philosophie des sciences concernant les vivant et la vie*. Paris: Vrin, 2002.

Capobianco, Richard. *Engaging Heidegger*. Toronto: University of Toronto Press, 2010.

Carbone, Mauro. *The Thinking of the Sensible: Merleau-Ponty's A-Philosophy*. Evanston, Ill.: Northwestern University Press, 2004.

———. *An Unprecedented Deformation*. Albany: The State University of New York Press, 2010.

Cariou, Marie. *Bergson et le fait mystique*. Paris: Abier Montaigne, 1976.

———. *Lectures bergsoniennes*. Paris: Presses Universitaires de France, 1990.

Carnap, Rudolf. "The Overcoming of Metaphysics through Logical Analysis of Language." In *Heidegger and Modern Philosophy*, ed. Michael Murray, pp. 23–34. New Haven, Conn.: Yale University Press, 1978.

Carr, David. *Phenomenology and the Problem of History*. Evanston, Ill.: Northwestern University Press, 1974.

Carrette, Jeremy. *Foucault and Religion: Spiritual Corporeality and Political Spirituality*. London: Routledge, 2000.

Cassirer, Ernst. *Kant's Life and Thought*. Translated by James Haden. New Haven, Conn.: Yale University Press, 1981.

Chambon, Roger. *Le monde comme perception et réalité*. Paris: Vrin, 1974.

Chase, James, and Jack Reynolds. *Analytic versus Continental: Arguments on the Methods and Values of Philosophy*. Durham, N.C.: Acumen, 2010.

*Chiasmi International: Trilingual Studies concerning Merleau-Ponty's Thought*. Memphis: University of Memphis, 1999–.

Claudel, Paul. *Art poétique*. Paris: NRF Gallimard, 1984.

Cobb-Stevens, Richard. *Husserl and Analytic Philosophy*. Dordrecht: Kluwer, 1990.

Crowell, Steven Galt. *Husserl, Heidegger, and the Space of Meaning*. Evanston, Ill.: Northwestern University Press, 2001.

Cutrofello, Andrew. *Continental Philosophy: A Contemporary Introduction*. London: Routledge, 2005.

Dastur, Françoise. *Husserl, Des mathématiques à l'histoire*. Paris: Presses Universitaires de France, 1995.

———. "Language and Ereignis." In *Reading Heidegger: Commemorations*, ed. John Sallis, pp. 355–69. Bloomington: Indiana University Press, 1993.

———. "Merleau-Ponty and Thinking from Within." In *Merleau-Ponty in Contemporary Perspectives*, ed. Patrick Burke and Jan Van Der Veken, pp. 25–36. Dordrecht: Kluwer Academic Publishers, 1993.

———. *La Phénoménologie en questions*. Paris: Vrin, 2004.

Davidson, Arnold, ed., *Foucault and His Interlocutors*. Chicago: University of Chicago Press, 1997.

Davis, Bret W. *Heidegger and the Will*. Evanston, Ill.: Northwestern University Press, 2007.

Deleuze, Gilles. *Bergsonisme*. Paris: Presses Universitaires de France, 1968. English translation by Hugh Tomlinson and Barbara Habberjam as *Bergsonism*. Cambridge, Mass.: Zone Books, 1991.

———. "La conception de la différence chez Bergson." In *L'île déserte et autres textes*. Paris: Minuit, 2002, pp. 43–72. English translation by Michael Taormina as "Bergson's Conception of Difference." In *Desert Islands and Other Texts*. Los Angeles: Semiotext(e), 2004, pp. 32–51.

———. *Différence et répétition*. Paris: Presses Universitaires de France, 1968. English translation by Paul Patton as *Difference and Repetition*. New York: Columbia University Press, 1994.

———. *Foucault*. Paris: Minuit, 1986. English translation by Seán Hand as *Foucault*. Minneapolis: University of Minnesota Press, 1988.

———. *Le pli. Leibniz et le Baroque*. Paris: Minuit, 1988. English translation by Tom Conley as *The Fold: Leibniz and the Baroque*. Minneapolis: University of Minnesota Press, 1993.

———. "Postface pour l'édition américaine: Un retour à Bergson." In *Deux régimes de fous*. Paris: Minuit, 2003. English translation by Ames Hodges and Mike Taormina as "Postscript to the American Edition: A Return to Bergson." In *Two Regimes of Madness*, ed. David Lapoujade. New York: Semiotext(e), 2006.

Deleuze, Gilles, and Félix Guattari. *Capitalisme et schizophrénie 1, Anti-Œdipe*. Paris: Minuit, 1972/1973. English translation by Robert Hurley, Mark Seem, and Helen R. Lane as *Anti-Oedipus: Capitalism and Schizophrenia*. New York: The Viking Press, 1977.

———. *Capitalisme et schizophrénie 2, Mille plateaux*. Paris: Minuit, 1980. English translation by Brian Massumi as *A Thousand Plateaus: Capitalism and Schizophrenia*. Minneapolis: University of Minnesota Press, 1987.

———. *Qu'est-ce que la philosophie?* Paris: Minuit, 1991. English translation by Hugh Tomlinson and Graham Burchell as *What Is Philosophy?* New York: Columbia University Press, 1994.

Derrida, Jacques. *L'animal que donc je suis*. Paris: Galilée, 2006. English translation by David Wills as *The Animal that Therefore I Am*. New York: Fordham University Press, 2008.

———. *Apories*. Paris: Galilée, 1992. English translation by Thomas Dutoit as *Aporias*. Stanford, Calif.: Stanford University Press, 1993.

———. *L'autre cap*. Paris: Minuit, 1991. English translation by Pascale-Ann Brault and Michael Naas as *The Other Heading*. Bloomington: Indiana University Press, 1992.

———. *La carte postale de Socrate à Freud et au-delà*. Paris: Aubier-Flammarion, 1980. English translation by Alan Bass as *The Postcard from Socrates to Freud and Beyond*. Chicago: University of Chicago Press, 1987.

———. "Cogito et histoire de la folie." In *L'écriture et la différence*. Paris: Points Seuil, 1976, pp. 51–98. English translation by Alan Bass as "Cogito and the History of Madness." In *Writing and Difference*. Chicago: University of Chicago Press, 1978, pp. 31–63.

———. *Dissemination*. Paris: Seuil, 1972. English translation by Barbara Johnson as *Dissemination*. Chicago: University of Chicago Press, 1981.

———. *L'Écriture et la différence*. Paris: Seuil Points, 1976. English translation by Alan Bass as *Writing and Difference*. Chicago: University of Chicago Press, 1978.

———. *De l'esprit*. Paris: Galilée, 1987. English translation by Geoffrey Bennington and Rachel Bowlby as *Of Spirit*. Chicago: University of Chicago Press, 1989.

———. "Et cetera . . . (and so on, und so weiter, and so forth, et ainsi de suite, und so überall, etc.)." In *Jacques Derrida*, ed. Marie-Louise Mallet et Ginette Michaud, pp. 21–34. Paris: Editions de l'Herne, 2004. English translation in *Deconstruction: A User's Guide*, ed. Nicolas Royle, pp. 282–305. London: Palgrave Macmillan, 2000.

———. *Force de loi*. Paris: Galilée, 1994. English translation by Mary Quaintance as "Force of Law: The Mystical Foundation of Authority." In *Deconstruction and the Possibility of Justice*, ed. Drucilla Cornell, Michael Rosenfeld, and David Gray Carlson, pp. 3–67. New York: Routledge, 1992.

———. "La Main de Heidegger. *Geschlecht* II. 1984–1985." In *Psyché*. Paris: Galilée, 1987, pp. 415–52. English translation by John P. Leavey, Jr., as "*Geschlecht* II: Heidegger's Hand." In *Deconstruction and Philosophy*, ed. John Sallis, pp. 161–96. Chicago: University of Chicago Press, 1987.

———. *Marges de la philosophie*. Paris: Minuit, 1972. English translation by Alan Bass as *Margins of Philosophy*. Chicago: University of Chicago Press, 1982.

———. *Mémoires pour Paul de Man*. Paris: Galilée, 1988. English translation by Cecile Lindsay, Jonathan Culler, and Eduardo Cadava as *Memoires for Paul de Man*. New York: Columbia University Press, 1986.

———. *L'origine de la géométrie, traduction et introduction par Jacques Derrida*. Paris: Presses Universitaires de France, 1962. English translation by John P. Leavey, Jr., as *Edmund Husserl's Origin of Geometry: An Introduction*. Lincoln: University of Nebraska Press, 1989 [1978].

———. "Positions." In *Positions*. Paris: Minuit, 1972, pp. 51–133. English translation by Alan Bass as "Positions." In *Positions*. Chicago: University of Chicago Press, pp. 37–96.

———. "Le retrait de la métaphore." In *Psyche: Inventions de l'autre*. Paris: Galilée, 1987, pp. 63–94. English translation by Peggy Kamuf and Elizabeth Rottenberg as "The Retrait of Metaphor." In *Psyche: Inventions of the Other, Volume 1*. Stanford, Calif.: Stanford University Press, 2007, pp. 48–80.

———. *Séminaire. La bête et le souverain. Volume I. 2001–2002*. Paris: Galilée, 2008. English translation by Geoff Bennington as *The Beast and the Sovereign, Volume I*. Chicago: University of Chicago Press, 2009.

———. *Spectres de Marx*. Paris: Galilée, 1993. English translation by Peggy Kamuf as *Specters of Marx*. New York: Routledge, 1994.

———. "'To Do Justice to Freud': The History of Madness in the Age of Psychoanalysis." In *Foucault and his Interlocutors*, ed. Arnold Davidson, pp. 57–96. Chicago: University of Chicago Press, 1997.

———. "Violence et métaphysique." In *L'Ecriture et la différence*. Paris: Seuil, 1967, pp. 173–96. English translation by Alan Bass as "Violence and Metaphysics." In *Writing and Difference*. Chicago: University of Chicago Press, 1978, pp. 118–33.

———. *La voix et le phénomène*. Paris: Presses Universitaires de France, 1967. English translation by Leonard Lawlor as *Voice and Phenomenon*. Evanston, Ill.: Northwestern University Press, 2011.

———. *Voyous*. Paris: Galilée, 2003. English translation by Pascale-Anne Brault and Michael Naas as *Rogues*. Stanford, Calif.: Stanford University Press, 2005.

Descombes, Vincent. *Modern French Philosophy*. Cambridge: Cambridge University Press, 1980.

Dillon, Martin C. *Merleau-Ponty's Ontology*. Bloomington: Indiana University Press, 1988.

Diprose, Rosalyn. "What Is (Feminist) Philosophy?" *Hypatia* 15, no. 2 (Spring 2000): pp. 115–32.

Dodd, James. *Crisis and Reflection: An Essay on Edmund Husserl's Crisis of the European Sciences*. Dordrecht: Kluwer/Springer, 2004.

Dreyfus, Hubert, and Paul Rabinow. *Michel Foucault: Beyond Structuralism and Hermeneutics*. Chicago: University of Chicago Press, 1983.

Embree, Lester, et al., eds., *Encyclopedia of Phenomenology*. Dordrecht: Kluwer, 1997.

Evans, Fred. *The Multivoiced Body: Society and Communication in the Age of Diversity*. New York: Columbia University Press, 2008.

Farber, Marvin, ed. *Philosophical Essays in Memory of Edmund Husserl*. New York: Greenwood Press, 1968.

Fink, Eugen. "The Phenomenological Philosophy of Edmund Husserl and Contemporary Criticism." In *The Phenomenology of Husserl*, ed. R. O. Elveton. Chicago: Quadrangle Books, 1970, pp. 70–139.

Flynn, Thomas R. *Sartre, Foucault, and Historical Reason: Toward an Existentialist Theory of History.* Chicago: University of Chicago Press, 1997.

Fóti, Véronique. *Heidegger and the Poets.* Amherst, N.Y.: Humanity Books, 1992.

Franck, Didier. *Chair et corps.* Paris: Minuit, 1981.

Friedman, Michael. *A Parting of the Ways: Carnap, Cassirer, and Heidegger.* Chicago: Open Court, 2000.

Gadamer, Hans-Georg. *Heidegger's Way.* Translated by John W. Stanley. Albany: The State University of New York Press, 1994.

———. *Wahrheit und Methode.* 4. Auflage. Tübingen: Mohr, 1975. English translation by Joel Weinsheimer and Donald G. Marshall as *Truth and Method.* 2nd rev. ed. New York: Crossroads, 1990.

Gasché, Rodolphe. *The Tain of the Mirror: Derrida and the Philosophy of Reflection.* Cambridge, Mass.: Harvard University Press, 1986.

Gilson, Bernard. *La revision bergsonienne de la philosophie de l'esprit.* Paris: Vrin, 1992.

Goddard, Jean-Christophe. *Mysticisme et folie.* Paris: Desclée de Brouwer, 2002.

Gros, Frédéric. *Foucault et la folie.* Paris: Presses Universitaires de France, 1997.

———. *Michel Foucault.* Paris: Presses Universitaires de France, 1996.

Guerlac, Suzanne. *Thinking in Time: An Introduction to Henri Bergson.* Ithaca, N.Y.: Cornell University Press, 2006.

Gueroult, Martial. *Descartes' Philosophy Interpreted According to the Order of Reasons.* 2 vols. Translated by Roger Ariew. Minneapolis: University of Minnesota Press, 1984.

Gurwitsch, Aron. *Phenomenology and the Theory of Science.* Edited by Lester Embree. Evanston, Ill.: Northwestern University Press, 1974.

Gutting, Gary. *French Philosophy in the Twentieth Century.* Cambridge: Cambridge University Press, 2001.

Haar, Michel. *Heidegger and the Essence of Man.* Translated by William McNeill. Albany: The State University of New York Press, 1993.

Han, Beatrice. *Foucault's Critical Project: Between the Transcendental and the Historical.* Translated by Edward Pile. Stanford, Calif.: Stanford University Press, 2002.

Hegel, G. W. F. *Phänomenologie des Geistes.* Hamburg: Meiner, 1952. English translation by A. V. Miller as *Phenomenology of Spirit.* Oxford: Oxford University Press, 1979.

Huffer, Lynn. *Mad for Foucault: Rethinking the Foundations of Queer Theory.* New York: Columbia University Press, 2010.

Hyppolite, Jean. *Logique et existence.* Paris: Presses Universitaires de France, 1952. English translation by Leonard Lawlor and Amit Sen as *Logic and Existence.* Albany: The State University of New York Press, 1997.

Jakobson, Roman, and Morris Halle. *Fundamentals of Language.* The Hague: Mouton, 1971.

Jankélévitch, Vladimir. *Henri Bergson.* Paris: Presses Universitaires de France, 1959.

Johnson, Galen. *The Retrieval of the Beautiful: Thinking Through Merleau-Ponty's Aesthetics.* Evanston, Ill: Northwestern University Press, 2010.

Johnston, Adrian. *Time Driven: Metapsychology and the Splitting of the Drive.* Evanston, Ill.: Northwestern University Press, 2005.

Juranville, Alain. *Lacan et la philosophie*. Paris: Presses Universitaires de France, 1984.

Kenny, Anthony. *A New History of Western Philosophy, Volume 4, Philosophy in the Modern World*. Oxford: Oxford University Press, 2007.

Kern, Iso. "The Three Ways to the Transcendental Reduction in the Philosophy of Edmund Husserl." In *Husserl: Expositions and Appraisals*, ed. Frederick A. Elliston and Peter McCormick, pp. 126–49. South Bend, Ind.: University of Notre Dame Press, 1977.

Kockelmans, Joseph J. *Edmund Husserl's Phenomenology*. West Lafayette, Ind.: Purdue University Press, 1994.

Lacan, Jacques. *Écrits*. Paris: Seuil, 1966. English translation by Bruce Fink as *Écrits: The First Complete Edition in English*. New York: Norton, 2006.

———. "L'instance de la letter dans l'inconscient ou la raison depuis Freud." In *Écrits*. English translation by Alan Sheridan as "The Instance of the Letter in the Unconscious." In *Écrits: The First Complete Edition in English*. New York: Norton, 2006.

———. *Les quatre concepts fondamentauz de la psychanalyse*. Paris: Seuil, 1973. English translation by Alan Sheridan as *The Four Fundamental Concepts of Psycho-analysis*. New York: Norton, 1981.

Lambert, J. H. "La Phénoménologie comme doctrine de l'apparence." First article of the fourth part of *Neues Organon. Alter* no. 5 (1997): pp. 223–39.

Laplanche, Jean. *Life and Death in Psychoanalysis*. Baltimore, Md.: The Johns Hopkins University Press, 1976.

———. *The Unconscious and the Id*. Translated by Luke Thurston with Lindsay Watson. London: Rebus Press, 1999.

Laplanche, J., and J.-B. Pontalis. *Vocabulaire de la psychanalyse*. Paris: Quadrige Presses Universitaires de France, 2009, p. 403, entry for "*rejetons.*" English translation by Donald Nicholson-Smith as *The Language of Psycho-Analysis*. New York: Norton, 1973.

Lawlor, Leonard. *The Challenge of Bergsonism*. London: Continuum, 2003.

———. *Derrida and Husserl: The Basic Problem of Phenomenology*. Bloomington: Indiana University Press, 2002.

———. *The Implications of Immanence: Toward a New Concept of Life*. New York: Fordham University Press, 2006.

———. "Phenomenology." In *Columbia Companion to Twentieth Century Philosophies*. New York: Columbia University Press, 2007, pp. 389–401.

———. *Thinking through French Philosophy: The Being of the Question*. Bloomington: Indiana University Press, 2003.

Lefort, Claude. "Préface." In Maurice Merleau-Ponty, *L'Œil et l'esprit*. Paris: Folio Essais Gallimard, 1964.

Levinas, Emmanuel. *Totalité et infini. Essai sur l'extériorité*. The Hague: Martinus Nijhoff Publishers, 1961. English translation by Alphonso Lingis as *Totality and Infinity: An Essay on Exteriority*. Pittsburgh, Pa.: Duquesne University Press, 1969.

Lotz, Christian. *From Affectivity to Subjectivity: Husserl's Phenomenology Revisited*. London: Palgrave MacMillan, 2007.

Löwith, Karl. *From Hegel to Nietzsche*. Translated by David E. Green. Garden City, N.Y.: Doubleday, 1967.

Madison, Gary. *The Phenomenology of Merleau-Ponty*. Athens: Ohio University Press, 1981.

Marion, Jean-Luc. *Reduction and Givenness*. Evanston, Ill.: Northwestern University Press, 1998.

Matthews, Eric. *Twentieth Century French Philosophy*. New York: Oxford University Press, 1996.

McGushin, Edward F. *Foucault's Askesis: An Introduction to the Philosophical Life*. Evanston, Ill.: Northwestern University Press, 2007.

Mullarkey, John. *Bergson and Philosophy*. Edinburgh: Edinburgh University Press, 1999.

Nancy, Jean-Luc, and Philippe Lacoue-Labarthe. *The Title of the Letter: A Reading of Lacan*. Translated by François Raffoul and David Pettigrew. Albany: The State University of New York Press, 1992.

Nietzsche, Friedrich. *Morgenröte, Idyllen aus Messina, Die fröhliche Wissenschaft, Kritische Studienausgabe, 3*. Munich: Deutscher Taschenbuch Verlag GmBH and Co. KG, 1988. English translation by Walter Kauffman as *The Gay Science*. New York: Vintage Books, 1974.

Oksala, Johanna. *Foucault on Freedom*. New York: Cambridge University Press, 2005.

Orth, Ernst Wolfgang. *Edmund Husserls "Krisis der europäischen Wissenschaften und die transzendentale Phänomenologie": Vernunft und Kultur*. Darmstadt: Wissenschaftliche Buchgesellschaft, 1999.

Pearson, Keith Ansell. *Philosophy and the Adventure of the Virtual*. London: Routledge, 2003.

Plato. *Collected Dialogues*. Edited by Edith Hamilton and Huntington Cairns. Princeton, N.J.: Princeton University Press, 1961.

Pöggeler, Otto. *Martin Heidegger's Path of Thinking*. Translated by Daniel Magurshak and Sigmund Barber. Atlantic Highlands, N.J.: Humanities Press, 1987.

Reed, Edward S. "The Separation of Psychology from Philosophy: Studies in the Sciences of Mind, 1815–1879." In *Routledge History of Philosophy, Volume VII: The Nineteenth Century*, ed. C. L. Ten, pp. 297–356. London: Routledge, 1994.

Reynolds, Jack. *Chronopathologies: Time and Politics in Deleuze, Derrida, Analytic Philosophy and Phenomenology*. Lanham, Md.: Lexington Books, 2011.

Ricœur, Paul. *De l'interprétation. Essai sur Freud*. Paris: Seuil, 1965. English translation by Denis Savage as *Freud and Philosophy: An Essay on Interpretation*. New Haven, Conn.: Yale University Press, 1970.

Riquier, Camille. *Archéologie de Bergson. Temps et métaphysique*. Paris: Presses Universitaires de France, 2009.

Russell, Bertrand. *Logic and Knowledge*. New York: Putnam, 1971.

Russell, Matheson. *Husserl: A Guide for the Perplexed*. London: Continuum, 2006.

Sallis, John. "The Question of Origin." In *Derrida's Interpretation of Husserl. Spindel Conference 1993, The Southern Journal of Philosophy* XXXII (1993 supplement): pp. 89–106.

Schmidt, Dennis J. *Germans and Other Greeks*. Bloomington: Indiana University Press, 2001.

Sheehan, Thomas, and Richard Palmer, eds. *Edmund Husserl: Psychological and Transcendental Phenomenology and the Confrontation with Heidegger (1927–1931)*. Dordrecht: Kluwer, 1997.

Simons, Jon. *Foucault and the Political London*. London: Routledge, 1995.

Steinbock, Anthony. *Home and Beyond: Generative Phenomenology after Husserl.* Evanston, Ill.: Northwestern University Press, 1995.

Ten, C. L., ed. *Routledge History of Philosophy, Volume VII: The Nineteenth Century.* London: Routledge, 1994.

Toadvine, Ted. *Merleau-Ponty's Philosophy of Nature.* Evanston, Ill.: Northwestern University Press, 2009.

Vieillard-Baron, Jean-Louis. *Bergson.* Paris: Presses Universitaires de France, 1991.

Waehlens, Alphonse de. "Les equivoques du Cogito." In *La philosophie et les experiences naturelles.* The Hague: Martinus Nijhoff, 1961, pp. 41–58.

———. *La philosophie et les experiences naturelles.* The Hague: Martinus Nijhoff, 1961.

———. *Schizophrenia.* Translated by W. Ver Eecke. Pittsburgh: Duquesne University Press, 1978.

Worms, Frédéric. *Annales bergsoniennes I. Bergson dans le siècle.* Paris: Presses Universitaires de France, 2002.

———. *Annales bergsoniennes II: Bergson, Deleuze, la phénoménologie.* Paris: Presses Universitaires de France, 2004.

———. "La conception bergsonienne du temps." In *Philosophie* 54 (1 juin 1997): pp. 73–91.

———. "Intuition." In *Le vocabulaire de Bergson.* Paris: Ellipses, 2000, pp. 37–39.

Zahavi, Dan. *Self-Awareness and Alterity: A Phenomenological Investigation.* Evanston, Ill.: Northwestern University Press, 1999.

# INDEX

**Leonard Lawlor** is Edwin Erle Sparks Professor of Philosophy at Penn State University. He has written several books, including *This Is Not Sufficient: An Essay on Animality and Human Nature in Derrida; The Implications of Immanence: Towards a New Concept of Life; Thinking through French Philosophy: The Being of the Question* (Indiana University Press, 2003); and *Derrida and Husserl: The Basic Problem of Phenomenology* (Indiana University Press, 2002). He is one of the editors of *Chiasmi International: Trilingual Studies Concerning the Thought of Merleau-Ponty.*